INVESTMENT,
INTEREST,
AND CAPITAL

INVESTMENT, INTEREST, AND CAPITAL

J. Hirshleifer

Professor of Economics,
University of California, Los Angeles

PRENTICE-HALL, INC.,

Englewood Cliffs, N.J.

© 1970 by
PRENTICE-HALL, INC.

*All rights reserved. No part of this book
may be reproduced in any form or by any means
without permission in writing from the publisher.*

13-502955-4
Library of Congress Catalogue Card No.: 73-100591
Current printing (last digit):
10 9 8 7 6 5 4 3 2 1

Printed in the United States of America

PRENTICE-HALL INTERNATIONAL, INC., *London*
PRENTICE-HALL OF CANADA, LTD., *Toronto*
PRENTICE-HALL OF AUSTRALIA, PTY. LTD., *Sydney*
PRENTICE-HALL OF JAPAN, INC., *Tokyo*
PRENTICE-HALL OF INDIA, PRIVATE LTD., *New Delhi*

PREFACE

The closely related topics of investment, interest, and capital are widely considered to be among the most difficult portions of economic theory. In some degree, this view is correct, for in the broadest interpretation these topics—which together constitute what we denote, for brevity, "capital theory"—represent an extension of economic analysis into the domain of *time* and consequently of *uncertainty* (the future being intrinsically uncertain). All of standard (certain, timeless) theory is thus incorporated as a special simplified case. Often, however, what has baffled the student has been obscurity of expression rather than expression of obscurity. As an ill-assorted melange of ideas, without a unifying conception, any analytical system would be difficult to understand. It is the aim of this work to set forth an analytical structure (the main lines of which are by no means original with the writer) that will make capital theory a meaningful whole.

The unifying conception has been alluded to already. Capital theory is a generalization of economic theory into the domain of time; in the analytical structure the fundamental economic concepts of resources and commodities, preferences and productive processes, and private and social decisions must all be generalized so as to involve time in an essential way. That is, we will deal with *dated* commodities, with *time*-preferences, and so on. The special terminology of capital theory is perhaps unfortunate in veiling the essential identity of the underlying concepts with those of standard price theory. Thus, to "invest" is to sacrifice goods of a current date for goods of a later date; "interest" is an element in the price ratio (exchange rate) between present and future goods; "capital" is the present embodiment of future-dated consumptive goods. When systematically constructed as a theory of allocation of resources over time, the core of capital theory loses most of its air of mystery (which is not to say, of course, that many advanced topics will not continue to present serious difficulties).

While capital theory is one of the more difficult branches of economics from the theorists' point of view, it is also a branch of intense immediate concern from the viewpoint of the practical man of affairs. Economists are only rarely called upon to employ the theory of demand or of cost or of production to assist a government or business administrator or a national planner. But the questions of criteria for efficient investments and optimum financial budgeting are of such urgent practical interest that a whole literature—possessing only tenuous connection with "mainstream" economic theory—has grown up in response. In fact, it would be more correct to say that three whole subliteratures have grown up: the first in the area of business economics (the problem of "capital budgeting"), the second in the sphere of government expenditure decisions, especially but not exclusively in relation to public resource investments ("cost-benefit analysis"), and the third in the crucial but ill-understood topic of national development ("growth strategies"). A secondary purpose of this book will be to indicate the bearing of capital theory—more specifically, of the economic theory of intertemporal resource allocation—upon some special problems in each of these fields.

This book is addressed to "the student," in the broad root sense of that honorable term. It is hoped that as a relatively brief and comprehensible, yet systematic, treatment of capital theory, it may earn a place on the general economist's bookshelf. The book may be useful to students (in the narrower sense) in graduate price-theory courses, where the weakness of the standard texts in the area of capital theory demands some supplementation; the earlier chapters may also be helpful to undergraduates. Finally, the book attempts to be of value for professionals in the crucial bridging roles between pure theory and practical affairs: business and government economists, systems analysts, and development planners.

The organization of the book is made reasonably clear by the Table of Contents, but a few remarks may be helpful here. The introductory chapter is a review and summary of price theory (i.e., of economic theory abstracted from the dimension of time); its essential role is to illustrate the logical structure of economic theories of choice. The main text following is in two parts. The first considers choice over time, but in the absence of risk and uncertainty. This restriction permits a relatively elementary theoretical development, and does not preclude the consideration of a number of topics possessing great theoretical and empirical interest. Part I is to a considerable degree within the accepted corpus of economic analysis, so that the discussion is largely expository. In Part II, where uncertainty is specifically incorporated into the analysis, a somewhat higher level of analytical difficulty is unavoidably encountered. Still, the central ideas are seen to be rather natural generalizations of those already developed, while the extension of the domain of the analysis permits attack on a number of problems that cannot be resolved under the artificial assumption of certainty. The approach throughout attempts to unify the analysis of private and social intertemporal allocation of resources, under both certainty and uncertainty, with the general economic theory of choice.

While the sequence of subjects covered follows a single consistent plan, the *method* of argument is eclectic. "Literary" reasoning, geometrical demonstration, and analytical and algebraic proofs are all employed—as called for by the nature of the topic, by the psychological need for variety in exposition, and by the author's desire to provide examples of all major types of economic argument. Furthermore, emphasis will be placed at times upon the parallels between different methods of argument applied to the same proposition or economic theorem.

This study has been so embarrassingly long in preparation that a complete list of acknowledgments has become infeasible. I must, however, express my thanks to the organizations and institutions that have provided me with fellowship support and/or clerical assistance at various stages: Guggenheim Foundation, Center for Advanced Study in the Behavioral Sciences, Ford Foundation (Faculty Research Fellowship), National Science Foundation (Senior Postdoctoral Fellowship), Center for Operations Research and Econometrics at the University of Louvain, and of course my home institution, University of California, Los Angeles. The series of dedicated typists over the years I can only thank collectively. I should like to acknowledge the suggestions and corrections offered by a number of my students, including Barbara Gardner, Julie Da Vanzo, Robert M. Gay, Michael McDowell, Patricia Richards, and Edward Gallick. Portions of the manuscript were read and criticized by colleagues at UCLA and elsewhere, including Armen Alchian, Axel Leijonhufvud, Harold Demsetz, Steven N. S. Cheung, Jan Mossin, and Gordon Pye. Thanks are especially due to Professor of Finance Frederick Amling of the University of Rhode Island and Professor Stewart C. Myers of M.I.T., who read the manuscript and offered valuable criticism and comments.

University of California, Los Angeles   J. Hirshleifer

CONTENTS

ix

PART II

INVESTMENT,
INTEREST,
AND CAPITAL

1 INTRODUCTION: REVIEW AND SUMMARY OF PRICE THEORY

A. THE STRUCTURE OF ECONOMIC THEORIES OF CHOICE

Theoretical structures within economics have a characteristic form. This form interweaves two levels of analysis—the lower, "individual" (sometimes called "private") level, and the higher, "social" level. More precisely, the former is the level of the *decision-making agent*, since the analysis applies not only to individuals proper but also to groupings of individuals such as households, firms, and government departments. The key assumption is that any such grouping can be treated as a unitary body making decisions analogous to those of a self-interested individual. (For some purposes, it is instructive to view the family, firm, or other collective agency as a miniature society with conflicts of interest among its component individuals, but this range of phenomena will not be considered here.)

On the level of the decision-making agent, the theory concerns choice among *desired objects* (commodities or goods). Each agent has a *preference function* ordering alternative combinations of the desired objects, and he also has an *opportunity set* indicating the range of combinations that are attainable for him. Sometimes this is expressed by specifying the upper limit or boundary of the opportunity set as the *constraint* on the agent's choice. The operative behavior principle for the agent (in standard theory) is maximization, or rather *optimization*: the achievement of a preferred combination of goods within the opportunities available.[1]

---

[1] Variations of standard theory can incorporate other behavior principles—such as irrational or random choice. See, for example, G. Becker, "Irrational Behavior and Economic Theory," *Journal of Political Economy*, **70** (Feb., 1962).

It is useful to distinguish three separate components of the opportunity set. The first is the agent's *endowment*, a combination of goods that provides a starting point for optimizing choice. A second consists of *exchange opportunities*—the range of alternative combinations opened up for the agent by the possibility of trading with other members of society. Obviously, exchange opportunities arise only in a social context; Robinson Crusoe, before Friday's arrival, had none. The third component consists of *productive opportunities*, representing the range of alternative combinations attainable by transforming or dealing with Nature rather than with other individuals (as when Crusoe fells a tree to build a canoe).

The higher, social level of analysis treats of the net resultant of interactions among decision-making agents through the process of exchange. The operative principle here is *equilibrium*. Exchange is assumed to take place through the mechanism of a *market*, which (under certain idealizing assumptions) determines unique *prices* or exchange ratios among the various commodities. At equilibrium each agent is satisfied that he cannot attain, within the opportunity set available to him, a combination of commodities superior to the one he has acquired through productive and exchange transformations of his endowment, taking account of the market prices established. If even one of the agents is not so satisfied, he will attempt to make further exchanges or productive transformations, thus creating imbalances between supply and demand for one or more commodities and leading to a corrective movement of prices.

Since the quantity supplied of any commodity must equal the quantity taken, the algebraic sum of supplies and demands in exchange must be zero for every commodity. We can say, then, that exchange "conserves" the social totals of commodities. Production, in contrast, involves the physical transformation of some commodities into others; in Robinson's case just mentioned, there is one less tree but one more canoe.

B. A SIMPLE CHOICE-PARADIGM: PURE EXCHANGE

Let us imagine a world with a large number (I) of individuals (who are the only economic agents), and with the convenient feature of having only two desired goods, A and B. The choices to be made will be "timeless"; it is as if the individuals expected to live only one time-period, or as if only a single decision could be made by each individual, which decision would determine his consumption in the form of flows of commodities as constants to infinity (or to the finite time-horizon envisaged). Furthermore, we will assume for this example a world of "pure exchange"—in which each individual starts with his own endowment, and can modify this only by trading with other individuals but *not* by productive transformations involving Nature.

Consider a particular individual i. Let the quantities of A and B that he may consume be denoted c_A^i and c_B^i—or, since the superscript will ordinarily be suppressed except as a point of emphasis or where some confusion might otherwise arise, simply as c_A and c_B. Figure 1-1 illustrates the preference

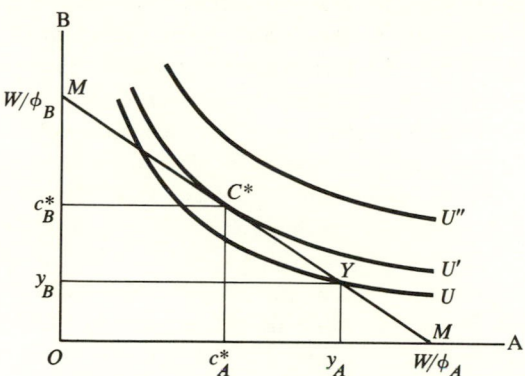

FIG. I–I. Individual endowment, preferences, and exchange opportunities

function of such an individual by the utility contours (indifference curves) U, U', U'', and so on that rank alternative consumptive combinations ("baskets") or vectors (c_A, c_B). The *endowment* combination Y consists of the individual's given initial basket (y_A, y_B). The market line MM represents the exchange opportunities (combinations of A and B he can acquire by selling some A from his endowment for more B, or vice versa); this construction implies that market prices for the commodities, ϕ_A and ϕ_B, have been established (by a process to be examined shortly). The entire opportunity set for this individual is the triangle OMM, but all baskets off the boundary or constraint MM can be dismissed as inferior.

If we imagine that there exists, in addition to the two desired commodities, a pure "money of account" (not a physical currency, but simply a scale for valuing commodities), then the value of the endowment when commodities are priced in the money of account is $\phi_A y_A + \phi_B y_B$, which value we may denote the individual's *wealth*, W. The B-intercept of MM, the amount of B that can be acquired if no A is taken, is W/ϕ_B; similarly, the A-intercept is W/ϕ_A. If, instead of a money of account, one of the two real commodities, say A, is the monetary unit or *numeraire*, then ϕ_A can be set equal to unity and the A-intercept becomes itself the monetary value of the endowment $(W/\phi_A = W)$. A slight departure from familiar usage may be noted here; in textbook presentations $\phi_A y_A + \phi_B y_B$ would ordinarily be called the "income" (or budget) rather than "wealth" constraint. The distinction (wealth is a stock, income a flow) is of no great significance here in dealing with timeless choice, but when we later come to choice over time the corresponding constraint (market value of the individual's endowment) will properly be *wealth* rather than income.

Turning back to Fig. 1-1, the endowment combination $Y = (y_A, y_B)$ is not an optimal position for the individual. He should move along the market line MM to arrive at the consumptive optimum C^*, representing the basket (c_A^*, c_B^*), where his highest possible indifference curve (here U') is attained. This movement will represent a process of market exchange, whereby the individual gives up $(y_A - c_A^*)$ of the commodity A in exchange for an increment $c_B^* - y_B$ of commodity B. The price ratio ϕ_A/ϕ_B (which is also the absolute value of the slope of the constraint MM) must be the reciprocal of the ratio of the quantities exchanged: $(c_B^* - y_B)/(y_A - c_A^*) = \phi_A/\phi_B$, or equivalently $\phi_A(y_A - c_A^*) = \phi_B(c_B^* - y_B)$. The latter formulation expresses the condition that, in a market exchange, the value of the commodity sold must equal the value of the commodity bought. With the commodity A as numeraire so that $\phi_A = 1$ (as will be assumed regularly henceforth), we get the simpler form $(y_A - c_A^*) = \phi_B(c_B^* - y_B)$—the amount of money given up equals price times the quantity of the (nonmonetary) commodity purchased.[2]

The individual portrayed in Fig. 1-1 is, at the price for B implicit in the slope $-1/\phi_B$ $(= -\phi_A/\phi_B)$ of the market line MM, a net demander of the commodity B. That is, he desires to hold c_B^*, a quantity of B greater than his endowed y_B. A higher price ϕ_B would be reflected in Fig. 1-1 by a flatter market line MM—still going through the point Y, however, as the endowment is fixed. There will be a *sustaining* price ϕ_B^+ just high enough to make the individual's net or *excess demand* for B zero—i.e., a price such that the individual desires to exactly hold his endowed quantity y_B. In the diagram, such a price would be represented by a market line MM exactly tangent to the indifference curve at the endowment point Y.

For still higher prices ϕ_B (flatter market lines), the individual would become a negative excess-demander, or an *excess-supplier*, of B. Note that, even where the individual's *excess* demand is zero or negative, he still will in general have a positive entire or *full* demand for the commodity B (in the sense that his consumptive optimum C^* still includes a positive quantity of B).

The information generated by considering the amount of B chosen at all different prices ϕ_B is summarized in two slightly different ways by the curves d_B' and d_B of Figs. 1-2(a) and 1-2(b), respectively. The first curve

---

[2] In the usual textbook formulation, the starting point for the individual (what is here called the endowment combination) is shown as the point M on the "money" (numeraire) axis where the consumer has only money A and none of commodity B. The formulation here (an endowment containing positive amounts of each commodity) is clearly more general.

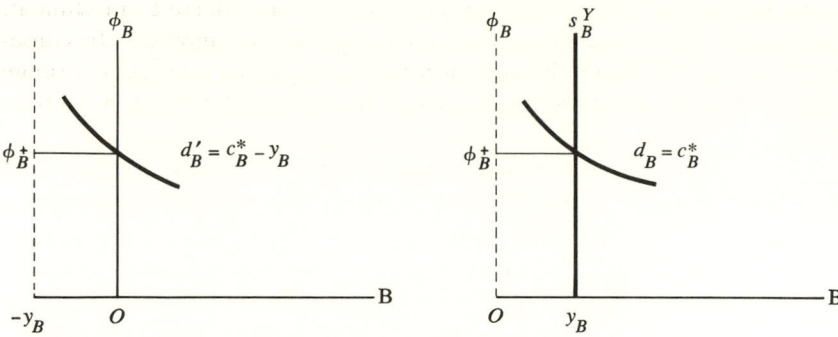

FIG. 1–2. (a) Individual excess-demand for B, (b) Individual full-demand for B

shows the *excess* demand $d'_B = c^*_B - y_B$ for B as a function of the price ϕ_B. The vertical (dashed) line at the left is a limit, which indicates that a negative net amount demanded (positive net amount supplied) can never exceed in magnitude the individual's endowed quantity y_B. The *full demand* $d_B = c^*_B$ in Fig. 1-2(b), on the other hand, is the demand for B inclusive of the endowed amount y_B. An *endowed-supply* curve, s^Y_B, vertical at the quantity y_B, can also be defined for this individual. Evidently, Figs. 2(a) and 2(b) are identical except for displacement of the horizontal axis by the amount y_B. The excess-demand and full-demand concepts are both useful,[3] but the discussion here will run primarily in terms of full demands—the quantities that enter into the utility function.

Throughout this volume it will be assumed that all the commodities or objects of choice dealt with are normal *superior* goods—i.e., goods for which the "marginal propensity to consume" as wealth rises is positive.[4] Then for prices lower than the sustaining price ϕ^+_B, the demand curves must be negatively sloped. In this region the individual is a net purchaser of B, so that a price increase represents an effective impoverishment for him. Hence the wealth effect reinforces the substitution effect in *reducing* the consumption of B as ϕ_B rises.[5] But in the region of prices above ϕ^+_B, the individual

---

[3] The excess-demand concept would be more convenient for the analysis of a tax on *transactions*, and the full-demand concept for a tax on *consumption*.

[4] That is, more of such goods are purchased when wealth increases, prices held constant.

[5] The total effect upon consumption of B of a change in price ϕ_B is traditionally divided into a "substitution effect" and a "wealth (or income) effect." The *substitution* effect shows how the individual would react if faced with a changed ϕ_B while being permitted to attain the same level of utility as in his original position. This amounts to comparing two different tangencies along the same indifference curve. Since indifference curves are convex to the origin, a smaller B will always be associated with a flatter tangency slope (higher ϕ_B) along the same indifference curve. The *wealth* effect represents the effective enrichment or impoverishment due to the price change (which depends upon whether the individual is a net seller or buyer of B) multiplied by the marginal propensity to consume B as wealth rises.

is a net seller of B. Here a rise in ϕ_B represents an effective enrichment, so the wealth effect and substitution effect oppose one another. In consequence, for prices above the sustaining price ϕ_B^+ there may exist a range within which the demand curve "bends backward" (takes on a positive slope).[6]

Let us now shift from the individual to the social level of analysis. The curve D_B^C in Fig. 1-3 shows the total of the I individual full consumptive

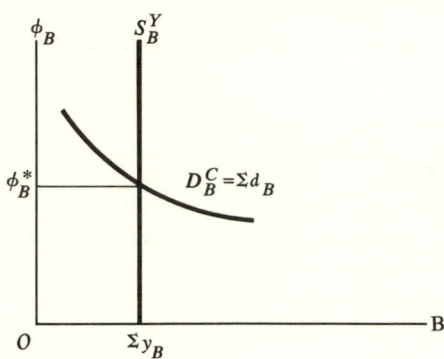

FIG. 1–3. Market demand, supply, and equilibrium for B

demands for B at each possible price ϕ_B. That is, the individual quantities of the various "d" curves of Fig. 1-2(b) are added horizontally $\left(D_B^C = \sum_{i=1}^{I} d_B^i\right)$ to find the sum demanded from the market at each price. The market endowed-supply curve is defined as the horizontal sum $S_B^Y = \sum_{i=1}^{I} s_B^Y$. Equality of supply and demand (the intersection of S_B^Y with D_B^C) determines the equilibrium price ϕ_B^*.[7] This fixes the slope of the constraint MM for each individual in the market. The entire analytical process leads to a joint determination of the price ϕ_B and the amounts c_A^i and c_B^i consumed by every individual.

It will be convenient now to formalize the choice-theoretic structure underlying the verbal and geometrical discussion by a set of equations that will cast additional light on the logical elements of the theory.

$$\left.\frac{dc_B}{dc_A}\right|_U = \Upsilon(c_A, c_B) \qquad \begin{array}{c}\text{Preference function}\\ (I \text{ equations})\end{array} \qquad (1)$$

---

[6] Textbooks usually recognize that individual *supply* curves may be "backward-bending." Positive net supply corresponds to negative *excess* demand, but positive *full* demand.

[7] The equilibrium price ϕ_B^* is, under pure exchange, a "sustaining price" for the community as a whole. That is, ϕ_B^* is such that individuals in the aggregate are just willing to hold the aggregate endowments. But of course it will not in general be true that every individual ends holding his original endowment.

Equation (1) says that the rate at which the individual is just willing to exchange an increment of one commodity for a decrement of the other (the slope of the indifference curve, denoted as the derivative $dc_B/dc_A |_U$ along the curve) is a function of the amounts of commodities A and B that he chooses to consume. There will be one such equation for each of the I individuals in the society. Equation (1) is the algebraic equivalent of the geometrical indifference map.

It would also be possible to express the absolute amount of utility in the form $U = U(c_A, c_B)$. This would serve to define the "cardinal" scale of the indifference curves. However, only the "ordinal" properties, and in particular the indifference-curve slopes, enter into the choice-theoretic system.

$$c_A + \phi_B c_B = y_A + \phi_B y_B \qquad \text{Wealth constraint, or exchange}$$

$$\text{opportunities}$$
$$(I \text{ equations}) \qquad (2)$$

Equation (2) specifies the opportunities for (or conversely, the constraints upon) each individual's exchanges: the market value of his consumption combination must equal the market value of his endowment combination (his wealth). Here A is the numeraire, so $\phi_A = 1$ and need not be explicitly introduced. Again, there is an equation of this form for each individual. Equation (2) is the algebraic expression of the "market line" MM.

$$\left. \frac{dc_B}{dc_A} \right|_U = \frac{-1}{\phi_B} \qquad \text{Individual optimum}$$
$$(I \text{ equations}) \qquad (3)$$

Equation (3) is obtained formally by maximizing utility subject to the constraint (2).[8] It says that at the individual's optimum the rate at

---

[8] The standard technique is to form the expression $\mathscr{L} = U(c_A, c_B) - \lambda(c_A + \phi_B c_B - y_A - \phi_B y_B)$, where λ is an undetermined "Lagrangian multiplier." Maximizing λ with respect to c_A and c_B, the first-order conditions obtained are

$$\frac{\partial \mathscr{L}}{\partial c_A} \equiv \frac{\partial U}{\partial c_A} - \lambda = 0$$

$$\frac{\partial \mathscr{L}}{\partial c_B} \equiv \frac{\partial U}{\partial c_B} - \lambda \phi_B = 0$$

Shifting the λ terms to the right-hand sides, and then dividing the first equation by the second, leads to

$$\frac{\partial U/\partial c_A}{\partial U/\partial c_B} = \frac{1}{\phi_B}$$

But along the utility isoquant

$$dU \equiv \frac{\partial U}{\partial c_A} dc_A + \frac{\partial U}{\partial c_B} dc_B = 0,$$

so that

$$\left. \frac{dc_B}{dc_A} \right|_U = - \frac{\partial U/\partial c_A}{\partial U/\partial c_B} = - \frac{1}{\phi_B}$$

which he is just willing to exchange the two commodities (slope of his indifference curve) must be equal to the rate at which the market will permit him to make exchanges (slope of the market line, or the price ratio). If this condition failed, the individual would want to make additional exchanges in one direction or the other. This equation corresponds geometrically to the tangency of the market line MM with an indifference curve that determines the consumptive vector C^*. Again, there is one equation for each individual.[9]

$$\sum_{i=1}^{I} c_A^i = \sum_{i=1}^{I} y_A^i$$

$$\sum_{i=1}^{I} c_B^i = \sum_{i=1}^{I} y_B^i$$

Conservation relations (two equations, of which one is independent) $\qquad(4)$

The two equations of (4) say that, summing over all individuals, the total of the individual consumptions of commodity A must equal the total of the endowments, and similarly for commodity B. Equivalently, we could say that the net algebraic sums of the individual exchanges, $\sum_i (y_A - c_A)$ for commodity A and $\sum_i (y_B - c_B)$ for commodity B, must each be zero.

In a logically consistent and complete analytical system, the number of independent equations must equal the number of unknowns. In the system as set down there are $3I + 2$ equations. The unknowns are the c_A^i, c_B^i, and $dc_B^i/dc_A^i \big|_U$ for each individual and the single price ϕ_B—$3I + 1$ in number. The disparity is explained by noting that the two conservation relations are not independent—if one is satisfied, the other must also be. This follows directly from adding I equations (2), so as to obtain $\sum c_A + \phi_B \sum c_B = \sum y_A + \phi_B \sum y_B$. Then if $\sum c_A = \sum y_A$, it must be the case that $\sum c_B = \sum y_B$. The redundant equation could be deleted, but retaining it preserves a helpful symmetry in the treatment of the commodities.

NUMERICAL EXAMPLE

Assume that all the individuals in the economy have the same utility function $U = c_A^{.8} c_B^{.2}$, so that the indifference-curve slopes are $dc_B/dc_A = -4c_B/c_A$. This corresponds to equation (1). Let there be equal numbers of individuals of types j and k, differing in their endowments as indicated in Table 1. The system can then be solved by finding the full-demand curves for a typical pair (one individual each of types j and k) and then equating aggregate demand for the pair to the aggregate endowed supply available to the two.

[9] The full-demand curve d_B in Fig. 1-2(b) is a plot of the c_B of equation (2) against the ϕ_B of equation (3), where ϕ_B is regarded as an autonomously varying parameter and c_B as the responding variable. (A variation in c_A may be implied as well, but is not explicitly shown.)

Table I*

INDIVIDUALS	ENDOWMENT		TRANSACTIONS		CONSUMPTIVE SOLUTION	
	(Y)		$(C^* - Y)$		(C^*)	
	A	B	A	B	A	B
j	40	45	+10	−20	50	25
k	60	5	−10	+20	50	25
Totals	100	50	0	0	100	50

* Conditions: $U = c_A{}^{.8}c_B{}^{.2}$ (j, k)
Solution: $\phi_B{}^* = \frac{1}{2}$

By equation (3), for each individual $4c_B/c_A = 1/\phi_B$. Solving for c_A and substituting in equation (2) leads to the individual demand equation:

$$c_B = \frac{1}{5}\left(y_B + \frac{y_A}{\phi_B}\right)$$

Thus

$$c_B^j = \frac{1}{5}\left(45 + \frac{40}{\phi_B}\right) \quad \text{and} \quad c_B^k = \frac{1}{5}\left(5 + \frac{60}{\phi_B}\right)$$

The aggregate demand is then

$$D_B^C = \Sigma\, c_B = \frac{1}{5}\left(50 + \frac{100}{\phi_B}\right) = 10 + \frac{20}{\phi_B}$$

Since the aggregate endowed supply $S_B^Y \equiv \Sigma\, y_B$ is just 50, the second equation of (4) has the solution $\phi_B^* = \frac{1}{2}$. Both classes of individuals turn out to have wealth of $62\frac{1}{2}$. The optimal consumptive vectors can then be found directly from equation (2); as indicated in Table 1, they are (50, 25) for both j and k individuals. The indifference-curve slopes are both -2, equal to the slope $-1/\phi_B$ of the market line.

C. GENERALIZATIONS AND EXTENSIONS

The elementary theoretical structure outlined above shows how, in the paradigm of choice consisting of a pure-exchange world of I individuals and two commodities, the individuals' endowments and preferences interact through the social mechanism of trade to determine the price ratio between the two commodities, and the quantities of each consumed by every individual. This was presented as a microcosmic illustration of the structure of ordinary price theory, excluding explicit consideration of time and uncertainty. Even granting this exclusion—the main purpose of later chapters being to bring time and uncertainty into the format of price theory—the illustration is drastically oversimplified. Among the elements omitted are (1) consideration of more than two goods; (2) problems of monopoly and imperfect markets; (3) agents of choice other than natural individuals (families, firms, governments); and (4) production as well as exchange relationships. Each of these will be the object of comment in the remainder of this chapter.

Extension to more than two consumptive commodities poses no difficulty for the algebraic system outlined in equations (1) through (4), although geometrical representation becomes excessively intricate or even impossible. The extended system for any number of goods A, B, . . . , G can be set down immediately:

$$\left.\frac{\partial c_B}{\partial c_A}\right|_U = \Upsilon_B(c_A, c_B, \ldots, c_G)$$

$$\left.\frac{\partial c_C}{\partial c_A}\right|_U = \Upsilon_C(c_A, c_B, \ldots, c_G)$$

$$\vdots$$

Preference function

$[I(G - 1)$ equations]   (1')

$$\left.\frac{\partial c_G}{\partial c_A}\right|_U = \Upsilon_G(c_A, c_B, \ldots, c_G)$$

Here the rate at which each individual is just willing to exchange any single good such as B against the numeraire A is a *partial* derivative of the utility function (geometrically, the partial derivative $\partial c_B/\partial c_A$ is the slope of the utility contour in a plane cutting the surface in such a way as to hold constant the consumptions of all commodities except A and B). This partial derivative will in general depend on all the $c_A, c_B, \ldots, c_G$.

$$c_A + \phi_B c_B + \phi_C c_C + \cdots + \phi_G c_G = y_A + \phi_B y_B + \phi_C y_C + \cdots + \phi_G y_G$$

Wealth constraint or
exchange opportunities   (2')
(I equations)

The constraint equation also runs in terms of the value of all G goods together. Note that A is still the monetary commodity or numeraire.

$$\left.\frac{\partial c_B}{\partial c_A}\right|_U = -\frac{1}{\phi_B}$$

$$\left.\frac{\partial c_C}{\partial c_A}\right|_U = -\frac{1}{\phi_C}$$

$$\vdots$$

Individual optimum
$[I(G - 1)$ equations]   (3')

$$\left.\frac{\partial c_G}{\partial c_A}\right|_U = -\frac{1}{\phi_G}$$

Where there are G commodities, the individual can exchange each of the others against the monetary commodity to find his over-all optimum.

$$\sum c_A = \sum y_A$$
$$\sum c_B = \sum y_B$$

$\qquad\qquad$ Conservation relations
$\qquad\qquad$ (G equations, of which $\qquad\qquad$ (4')
$\qquad\qquad$ $G - 1$ are independent)

$$\sum c_G = \sum y_G$$

Here the unknowns are the $c_A, c_B, \ldots, c_G, \partial c_B/\partial c_A|_U, \ldots, \partial c_G/\partial c_A|_U$, and ϕ_B through ϕ_G—in number $GI + (G-1)I + (G-1)$. The equations number $(G-1)I + I + I(G-1) + G$, one in excess of the unknowns. Again, one of the conservation relations can be shown to be implied by the others (taken together as a group), by summing the equations (2') over the I individuals.

The second omission mentioned above is the failure to consider, in the simple model, problems of monopoly and imperfect markets. As one excuse for slighting the traditional topic of monopoly, the key price determined by intertemporal choice—the interest rate—is governed by the pressure of suppliers and demanders for generalized purchasing-power claims of divergent dates (as will be explained in detail below). The distribution of such claims is so diverse that monopoly will not be an empirically significant problem. Imperfect markets cannot be dismissed so easily on empirical grounds. In fact, when we come to the topic of uncertainty, the question of perfection and completeness of markets will play a central role.

The next omission is the failure to include what might be called "quasi-individuals" (families, firms, governments)—agents of choice that are not natural individuals. Following the standard tradition of economic analysis, no attempt will be made throughout this work to distinguish between the individual and the family or household as a decision unit. And again following this tradition, government will be treated as an agency outside the social-exchange relationship, purportedly acting in the interests of society as a whole rather than in the interests of the particular social grouping who happen to constitute the government. This leaves only firms as requiring explicit consideration.

Just what a firm is, and why the firm as an institution exists, are topics on which economists in general are not at all clear. The excellent discussion by Coase[10] connects the existence of the firm-institution with the necessity

[10] R. H. Coase, "The Nature of the Firm," *Economica*, N.S., **4** (1937). Reprinted in American Economic Association, *Readings in Price Theory* (Homewood, Ill.: Richard D. Irwin, Inc., 1952).

or convenience or efficiency of *delegating* discretionary authority (through a generalized contract)—since otherwise economic cooperation would be limited to undertakings that could be carried out by specific-performance contracts among the owners of productive resources. (This view founds the existence of the firm ultimately upon uncertainty or ignorance as to the actual state or shape of the world, now or in the future.)

Without necessarily disagreeing with Coase's explanation, we shall find it convenient to adopt here a more formal conception of the firm, to wit: The firm is a grouping of one or more individuals specialized to productive activities (transformations of commodity-combinations effected through dealing with Nature rather than through exchange with other economic agents). Furthermore, when firms are introduced as decision-making agents, the assumption will be that *only* firms produce; then, firms will have opportunities to produce or exchange, but natural individuals can only exchange. On the other hand, firms cannot consume; only individuals can. This conception is not too far from commercial practice (even the single proprietor may keep his business and personal accounts separate), and the segregation of productive from consumptive decisions is conceptually advantageous.

We have already entered the discussion of the fourth omission from the simple system described above—production. A sharp distinction between consumption and production will be maintained in this analysis. The key to the distinction is on the social level: exchange conserves, while production transforms, the social totals of commodities. Or to put it another way, production is "exchange" with Nature, while exchange proper represents redistribution of the commodities already made available with the help of Nature.

D. A PARADIGM OF PRODUCTION AND EXCHANGE

We can now consider a second simplified illustration of timeless price theory. This will consist of a paradigm spanning production as well as exchange decisions. The special role of the *firm* can best be clarified by presenting the analysis in two forms—in this section without, and in the next section with, firms as agents in addition to natural individuals. As the extension to an arbitrary list of G goods has been seen to be trivial, nothing will be lost by returning to the simple assumption that there are only two commodities, A and B. Also, A remains the numeraire, with ϕ_A equal to unity.

Figure 1-4 is similar to Fig. 1-1, differing only in showing an individual's opportunity set as incorporating the possibilities of productive as well

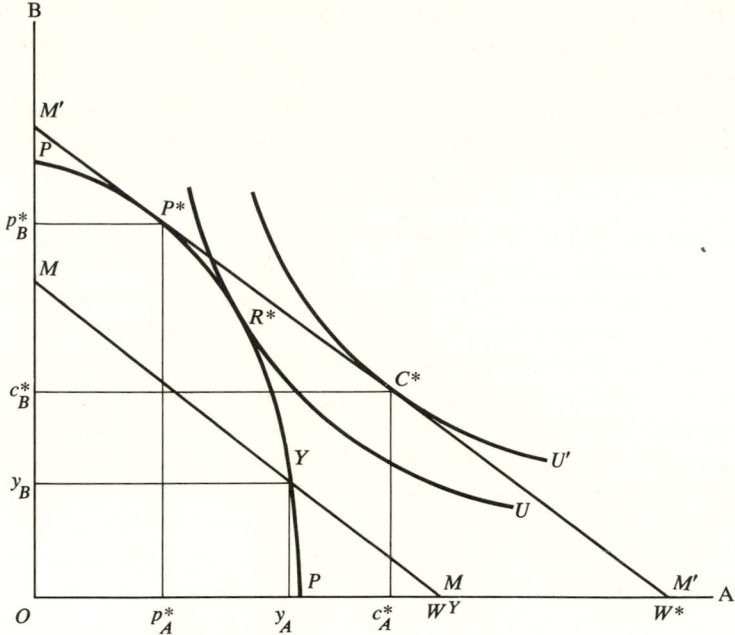

FIG. I-4. Individual productive optimum and consumptive optimum

as market transformations of his endowment Y. The curved locus PP, representing the constraint upon the individual's productive opportunities, is concave to the origin—indicating diminishing returns as the individual pushes toward its limit the conversion of A into B, or of B into A. (The absence of any "kink" in the curve at the endowment point Y indicates that the productive process is perfectly reversible; this is, of course, an idealizing assumption.) The curve PP may be expressed as the equation $P(p_A, p_B) = 0$, where p_A and p_B are elements of possible productive combinations or vectors. If there were no possibility of exchange, the productive opportunity set would represent all of the individual's attainable combinations. Thus, Robinson Crusoe would find his optimum at R^* by a direct tangency between PP at the boundary of the attainable region and his highest attainable indifference curve.

It is also convenient to define a q_A and q_B in terms of the input-output transformations between the elements of the productive and the endowment combinations:

$$q_A = p_A - y_A$$
$$q_B = p_B - y_B$$

The productive locus could thus equally well be written as $Q(q_A, q_B) = 0$. Then q_A and q_B must have opposite signs, assuming that the endowment Y

is an efficient point—i.e., is on the boundary or frontier PP rather than in the interior of the productive opportunity region OPP. More of one commodity output can be obtained only by sacrificing some of the other. The formulation in terms of the q-variables has the advantage of separating the productive transformation from the elements of the endowment combination—which is sometimes highly convenient for the analysis of the production process.

When there are *both* productive and exchange opportunities, the over-all opportunity set is extended to the entire triangular region $OM'M'$. Note that if there were only exchange opportunities, starting at Y, the opportunity set would consist only of the smaller triangular region OMM—and the individual would find his optimum along the market line MM (as in Fig. 1-1). All the combinations along MM, including the endowment combination Y, have market value $c_A + \phi_B c_B = W^Y$, which may be denoted *endowed wealth*. In general, there is a whole family of parallel market lines, characterized by differing levels of wealth—MM and $M'M'$ are two members of this family.

The crucial *Separation Theorem* asserts that the individual finds his over-all optimum C^* in Fig. 1-4 by a two-stage process. (a) First, he maximizes wealth (finds the highest market line $M'M'$) by moving along PP to the "productive optimum" P^* with coordinates (p_A^*, p_B^*). The maximized *attained wealth* is $W^* = p_A^* + \phi_B p_B^*$. (b) Second, he finds his consumptive optimum by moving along $M'M'$ to the indifference-curve tangency at C^*. Note that P^* and W^* are "objective," determined only by productive and market considerations and not by the individual's "subjective" utility function. As will be seen below, this is the key feature that permits the delegation of productive decisions to firms.[11]

We can now consider constructing the individual and market demand curves, analogous to those in Figs. 1-2 and 1-3 for pure exchange. The possibility of production creates some important differences, on both the supply and demand sides. The individual's full-supply function s_B in Fig. 1-5 now represents the horizontal sum of an endowed supply s_B^Y (as before, vertical at the endowed quantity y_B) and an upward-sloping produced supply s_B^Q. The latter shows the net produced *increment*, or productive excess supply $q_B^* = p_B^* - y_B$, as the productive optimum P^* varies in Fig. 1-4 in response to changes in price ϕ_B (changes in slope of the market line $M'M'$). That is, the quantities along s_B^Q in Fig. 1-5 are, for specified prices ϕ_B, the vertical differences between P^* and Y in Fig. 1-4. Similarly, the quantities along s_B are given by the B-coordinates of P^* as the latter varies in response to ϕ_B.

But the produced increment q_B can be positive or negative, so that s_B^Q has a negative region before becoming positive for sufficiently high prices

---

[11] It is here that the assumption of perfect markets turns out to be critical, as will be remarked in later chapters.

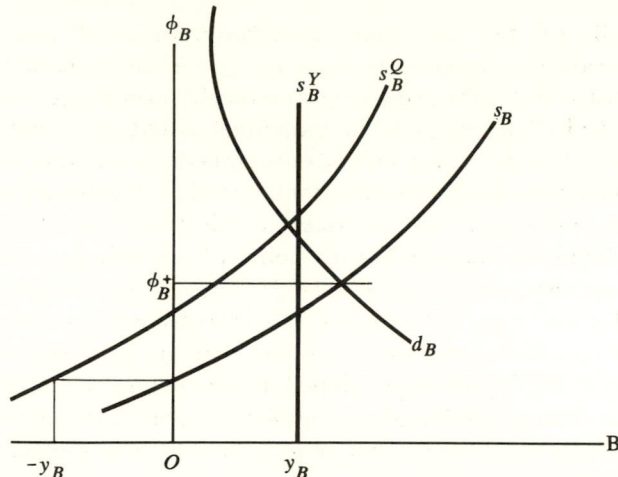

FIG. 1–5. Individual supply and demand functions

ϕ_B. (The produced supply will be zero at a price such that the market line $M'M'$ is tangent to PP at the endowment point Y.) The productive solution P^* need not be in the first quadrant of the diagram of Fig. 1-4.[12] Consequently, the produced-supply curve s_B^Q in Fig. 1-5 extends even to the left of $-y_B$, for sufficiently low prices ϕ_B. Since the full-supply curve s_B is simply a rightward displacement of s_B^Q by the endowed quantity y_B, it follows that s_B may similarly extend to the left of the origin.

Under pure exchange, the individual full-demand curve was determined by the movement of c_B^*, the B-coordinate of the consumptive optimum C^* in Fig. 1-1—as market lines MM of different slopes (representing different prices ϕ_B) were passed through the single endowment point Y. But in Fig. 1-4 the movement of c_B^* as ϕ_B changes is determined by passing market lines $M'M'$ of different slopes through corresponding tangencies at *differing* points along the productive locus PP. Consequently, the consumptive quantity demanded c_B^* does not represent preference considerations only but depends also upon the productive relationships.

As was the case under pure exchange, the full-demand curve d_B can be shown to be necessarily downward-sloping over *part* of its range, but not everywhere. Consider first a situation like that illustrated in Fig. 1-4. Here the price ϕ_B is such that, for a particular individual, C^* is southeast of P^*. Hence, in Fig. 1-5, at that price his full demand for B is less than his full supply $(d < s)$: the individual is thus on balance a supplier of B to the market. A rise in ϕ_B then effectively enriches[13] him, tending to increase his

---

[12] Productive solutions for *firms* are normally in the second or fourth quadrants, as we shall see shortly.

[13] In terms of the geometry of Fig. 1-4, a rise in ϕ_B (flatter market line) enlarges the set of attainable consumptive combinations to the *southeast* of P^* while contracting the set *northwest* of P^*. If and only if the individual's opportunities and preferences interact so that he wants to find his C^* southeast of P^*, he will have been made better off by the rise in ϕ_B.

demand for B. On the other hand, the substitution effect always tends to contract desired consumption of B as ϕ_B rises. So in such situations the slope of d_B is unclear. But if the price were in a much lower range, such that C^* lay northwest of P^* in Fig. 1-4, the individual would be on balance a demander of B. Then the wealth and substitution effects would be reinforcing, so that d_B would necessarily be smaller for higher ϕ_B. The boundary between the two price ranges is the specific price ϕ_B such that P^* and C^* coincide in Fig. 1-4—which must take place at the point R^*. At this price, the individual's s_B and d_B curves intersect in Fig. 1-5.[14] Thus, we see that the individual full-demand curve[15] d_B is necessarily downward-sloping below its intersection with s_B. It does not exactly follow that the *aggregate* consumptive demand curve D_B^C is negatively sloped below the intersection with S_B. But it will be certainly negatively sloped for a region of sufficiently low ϕ_B, and the boundary of the region can be presumed to be in the neighborhood of the intersection.

It might be remarked that despite the use here of the concept of endowed supply, the endowment *point* Y is not analytically essential; it is always the sum $p_B = y_B + q_B$ that is relevant. In effect, not the endowment point but the entire locus PP represents the relevant initial condition for the analysis. (The point Y would be of productive significance if the production process were not perfectly reversible.)

In Fig. 1-6 are shown the market summations of the individual supply and demand relations. The intersection of S_B and D_B, of course, determines the equilibrium price ϕ_B^*.

The equation system for the choice-theoretic structure can now be set down.

$$\left.\frac{dc_B}{dc_A}\right|_U = \Upsilon(c_A, c_B) \qquad \text{Preference function} \quad (I \text{ equations}) \qquad (1)$$

$$c_A + \phi_B c_B = (y_A + q_A) + \phi_B(y_B + q_B) \qquad \text{Wealth constraint} \quad (I \text{ equations}) \qquad (5)$$

$$\left.\frac{dc_B}{dc_A}\right|_U = -\frac{1}{\phi_B} \qquad \text{Consumptive optimum} \quad (I \text{ equations}) \qquad (3)$$

[14] This price does not sustain the *endowment* vector Y of Fig. 1-4, but does sustain the individual's position in the sense of placing the consumptive optimum C^* on his productive opportunity locus PP (at R^*); he has no incentive to trade. On the other hand, the price associated with a market line $M'M'$ tangent to PP at the endowment Y will lead to a produtive optimum at Y—but net trading to a consumptive optimum off PP will take place (unless $Y = R^*$).

[15] As before, if our main interest were in the volume of *market* transactions rather than aggregate consumption, it would be useful to employ a concept of excess demand. Defining the individual's excess-demand curve d_B' as the horizontal distance $d_B - s_B$ in Fig. 1-5, we see that the d_B' curve is necessarily downward-sloping for positive excess demand.

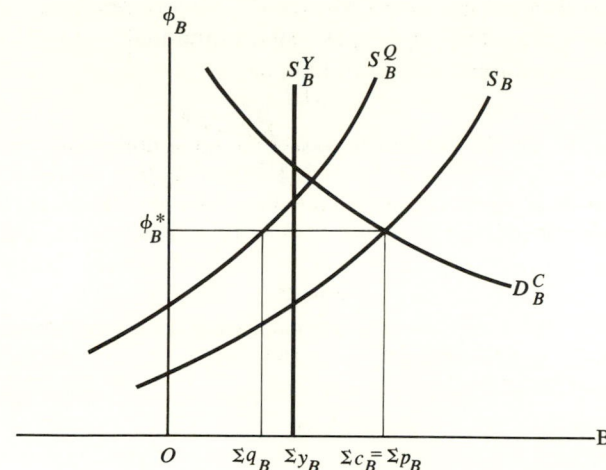

FIG. 1–6. Market supply and demand functions

Note that it is the attained wealth W^* (wealth value of the productive optimum P^*) that constrains the consumptive decision. Equation (5) could, of course, equally well have been formulated in terms of the produced quantities p_A and p_B rather than the input and output quantities (productive transformations) q_A and q_B.

$$Q(q_A, q_B) = 0$$

$$\frac{dq_B}{dq_A} = \omega(q_A, q_B)$$ Individual production function ($2I$ equations) (6)

$$\frac{dq_B}{dq_A} = -\frac{1}{\phi_B}$$ Productive optimum (I equations) (7)

Though expressed in terms of the q-variables, equations (6) represent the curve PP and the slope $dp_B/dp_A = dq_B/dq_A$. The slope is set equal to $-1/\phi_B$ in equation (7), which represents the productive optimum P^*. Finally, in the conservation equations it is the social totals of the produced quantities that set the limits upon exchange.

$$\sum_i c_A = \sum_i (y_A + q_A)$$ Conservation relations (two equations, of which (8)

$$\sum_i c_B = \sum_i (y_B + q_B)$$ one is independent)

As compared with the original pure-exchange equation system, we have here $3I$ additional equations (6) and (7)—corresponding to the additional variables q_A, q_B, and dq_B/dq_A for each individual. Thus the numbers of equations and variables remain in balance.

NUMERICAL EXAMPLE

As before, let all the individuals possess the same utility function—but now taking the symmetrical form $U = c_A^{.5} c_B^{.5}$. Then $dc_B/dc_A = -c_B/c_A$. Suppose again that there are two equally numerous classes of individuals j and k, with endowments as indicated in Table 2. We will assume that *only* type-j individ-

Table 2*

INDIVIDUALS	ENDOWMENT		PRODUCTIVE SOLUTION		CONSUMPTIVE SOLUTION	
	(Y)		(P^*)		(C^*)	
	A	B	A	B	A	B
j	40	20	20	80	30	60
k	40	40	40	40	30	60
Totals	80	60	60	120	60	120

* Conditions: $U = c_A^{.5} c_B^{.5}$ (j, k)

$$\frac{p_A^2}{20} + p_B = 100 \ (j)$$

Solution: $\phi_B^* = \frac{1}{2}$

uals possess productive opportunities, taking the form given by the equation $p_A^2/20 + p_B = 100$. This corresponds to $(q_A + 40)^2/20 + q_B = 80$, given the j-individuals' endowment.

We may solve the system by considering the interaction of a typical pair. The k-individual will provide a full supply of 40 of B at all prices. The j-individual will equate $dq_B/dq_A = dp_B^j/dp_A^j$ to $-1/\phi_B$ [equation (7)], so that the productive supply function can be expressed as $p_B^j = 100 - 5/\phi_B^2$. Then the market supply function for the pair will be $S_B \equiv \Sigma p_B = 140 - 5/\phi_B^2$. The demand functions can be derived from the condition $c_B/c_A = 1/\phi_B$. For the k-individual without productive opportunity, c_A may be eliminated from the equation by using the endowment constraint

$$c_A^k + \phi_B c_B^k = 40 + 40\phi_B$$

so that

$$c_B^k = \frac{1}{2}\left(40 + \frac{40}{\phi_B}\right) = 20 + \frac{20}{\phi_B}$$

But for the j-individual, the constraint runs in terms of the produced combination P^*:

$$c_A^j + \phi_B c_B^j = p_A^j + \phi_B p_B^j$$

After substitutions, this becomes

$$c_B^j = \frac{1}{2}\left(100 + \frac{5}{\phi_B^2}\right)$$

The aggregate demand for the pair is thus

$$D_B^C \equiv \frac{1}{2}\left(140 + \frac{40}{\phi_B} + \frac{5}{\phi_B^2}\right)$$

The market supply and demand curves intersect($S_B = D_B^C$) at the solution price $\phi_B^* = \frac{1}{2}$. The results in Table 2 can then be obtained by direct substitution in the various functions. The endowed wealth for the k-individual is 60, the same as the attained wealth of the j-individual—for whom the gain in wealth due to the productive opportunity is $60 - 50 = 10$.

E. PRODUCTION AND EXCHANGE WITH FIRMS

We can now consider how the paradigm of production and exchange is modified by the introduction of *firms* as specialized (and exclusive) productive agents. Here individuals will again possess only exchange opportunities; however, as we shall see, the constraints upon their consumptive choices will depend upon the productive decisions of the firms.

For a particular firm f, the productive opportunities are represented in Fig. 1-7(a) by the locus QQ. The shape of the locus reflects the following assumptions:

(1) The firm has null endowment (i.e., the only resources it can use must be made available to it from individuals). Geometrically, this means

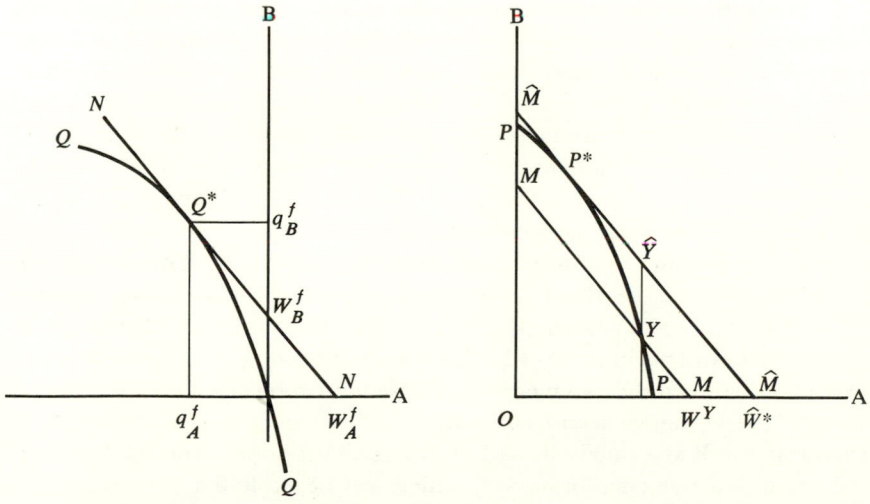

Fig. I–7. (a) Firm productive optimum, (b) Individual endowment as augmented by firm payout

that the endowment or starting point for the analysis of the firm's operations is the origin in Fig. 7(a). For this reason, the firm's productive decisions are naturally stated in terms of the input-output variables q_A^f and q_B^f (the superscript f will usually be added to avoid confusion with the individual variables q_A and q_B).

(2) Production is transformation of one commodity into another. Geometrically, this dictates the negative slope of the productive transformation locus QQ and, in combination with the above, restricts QQ to the second and (possibly) the fourth quadrant—corresponding to production of B with A as input, or of A with B as input, respectively. Thus, the produced quantities q_A^f and q_B^f must have opposite signs.

(3) Diminishing returns apply in production, throughout. This is represented by the concavity of QQ in the downward direction; as more of the output commodity is sought, Nature requires a larger and larger per-unit contribution of the input commodity.

The preferred production point for the firm is Q^*, where tangency with the highest "market line" NN (line of slope $-1/\phi_B$) is attained. At this point in the diagram, the firm has made an input of q_A^f to Nature ("produced" a negative amount q_A^f of commodity A) in return for which Nature has provided an increment q_B^f of B.

(4) The firm does not consume. This requires the firm to distribute its q_B^f output externally. We may regard it as doing so by exchanging B for A along NN (trading with other agents of the society) to end up somewhere in or on the boundary of the positive quadrant—and then distributing the resultant combination so obtained (the net income) to its owners.

It is perhaps most natural to assume that the firm pays out to owners the net "monetary" (numeraire) value of the output, which in Fig. 1-7(a) would be the distance between W_A^f and the origin on the A-axis. Here $W_A^f = q_A^f + \phi_B q_B^f$ is the firm's wealth increment or "profit." (The *gross* monetary value of the B produced, $\phi_B q_B^f$, is the distance between q_A^f and W_A^f, but of course the externally obtained input of q_A^f must be paid for in determining the *net* income to the owners.) Thus, the final situation is that the owners of the firm share an increment W_A^f to their A endowments. Alternatively, the payout might be in terms of the commodity B. Then the length $(q_B^f - W_B^f)$ would be the payment for the externally obtained input— $(q_B^f - W_B^f)\phi_B = -q_A^f$—and W_B^f would be the profit or increment to owners' endowments in units of B. This way of looking at it brings out the distinction between the two means available to firm-owners for converting A into B: the exchange transformation, which permits any holder of A to convert it into B at a rate indicated by the constant slope of the market lines, and the productive transformation, which will be exploited only so long as the slope along QQ remains more advantageous (steeper) than the slope of NN. In the equations below, payout is in terms of commodity B.

We shall need a relation showing the ownership of firms, and the corresponding distribution rule for the firms' net incomes. Let there be in all F firms, and as before I individuals, and let ϵ_f^i be the fraction of the fth firm owned by the ith individual. The ϵ_f^i are constants, and

$$\sum_{i=1}^{I} \epsilon_f^i = 1 \qquad \text{for } f = 1, 2, \ldots, F$$

We will use the simple distribution rule that the net income is paid out proportionately to owners (this may be regarded as defining the meaning of "ownership"). Thus, letting $\hat{Y} = (\hat{y}_A, \hat{y}_B)$ represent an individual's *endowment as augmented* by receipts from ownership rights, we have (assuming payout in the B commodity): $\hat{y}_B = y_B + \sum_{f=1}^{F} \epsilon_f W_B^f$, where W_B^f is the B-value of the profit of the fth firm. The owners' y_A is not reduced by the necessary A-input q_A^f, since this is purchased externally by the firm at market prices. (In this "timeless" treatment, we can ignore the fact that Nature ordinarily insists on receiving its input some time prior to yielding its output; the transaction with Nature is regarded as instantaneous, so that the firm obtains the necessary input by exchange against part of its own output yield.)

The firm-individual relationship can be conveniently pictured if we make the simplifying assumption that each individual is the sole owner of exactly one firm. Then we can regard Figs. 1-7(a) and 1-7(b) as a decomposition of the earlier Fig. 1-4 showing the individual's productive and consumptive optima. The QQ in Fig. 1-7(a), the firm's input-output relation in terms of the q^f-variables, represents the same data as the PP curve of Fig. 1-4 [repeated in Fig. 1-7(b)] in terms of the individual's p-variables. Note that the endowment point Y of Fig. 1-4 or Fig. 1-7(b) becomes the origin in Fig. 1-7(a); that is, when $p_A = y_A$ and $p_B = y_B$, $q_A^f = q_B^f = 0$. Similarly, the tangency point Q^* in Fig. 7(a) corresponds to the tangency P^* in Fig. 1-4 or 1-7(b). But where the productive relation is delegated to the firm, as assumed here, the individual does not attain P^*. Rather, the firm he owns attains Q^* and then pays out to the individual the proceeds of the productive transformations. If the proceeds are paid out in terms of B, the individual attains the illustrated augmented endowment $\hat{Y}$, which will serve as the constraint upon his consumptive optimization. Note that the difference between the original market line MM and the attained market line $\hat{M}\hat{M}$ in Fig. 1-7(b) is precisely measured by the height at the B-intercept of the line NN attained by productive transformations in Fig. 1-7(a); the vertical distance from W_B^f to the origin in Fig. 1-7(a) is precisely the B-difference between Y and $\hat{Y}$. Or, in terms of numeraire A, the horizontal distance from W_A^f to the origin (the firm's "profit," or wealth equivalent of Q^*) is the wealth increment $W^* - W^Y$ of the individual (difference between the wealth values of $\hat{Y}$ and Y). More generally, if the individual owns fractions of a number of firms, it remains true that the wealth value of his augmented endowment $\hat{Y}$ will reflect his proportionate shares in the wealth produced by his owned firms.

It is now hardly necessary to go over the development of the firm's supply curve or the individual's demand curve. For, in Fig. 1-5 we already have distinguished the productive supply s_B^Q (developed in terms of the individual's q-variables) from the endowed supply s_B^Y. Now, the firm's supply curve s^f will simply incorporate the same data in terms of the q^f variables. On the aggregate level, under the simplifying assumption that each individual is the sole owner of one firm, the market supply-demand relationships of Fig. 1-8 must be identical with those of Fig. 1-6 (except that S_B^Q has been

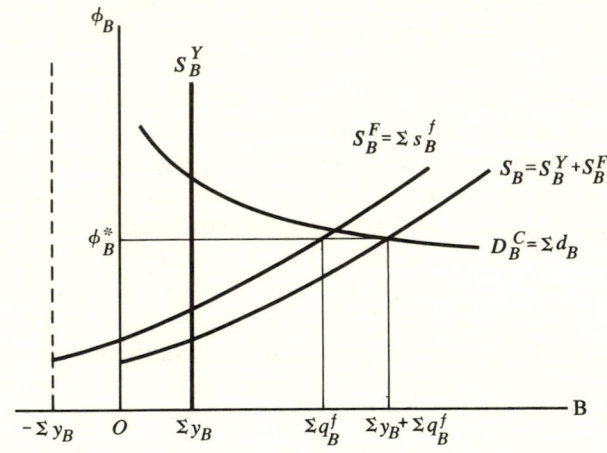

FIG. I–8. Supply-demand equilibrium, individuals and firms

relabelled S_B^F). In general, the s_B^f curves are aggregated over firms into an S_B^F curve, and the endowed-supply curves over individuals into an S_B^Y curve—the horizontal sum of the two being the market full-supply curve S_B. The development of the individual full-demand curves is the same as before. Again, the curve will reflect productive as well as preference considerations—for changes in price will affect the Q^* solutions of owned firms and the wealth increments paid out to owner individuals. Thus, we cannot be sure that the individual full-demand curves d_B^i or the aggregate full-demand curve D_B^C will be negatively sloped throughout. But, as indicated in the previous section, the individual and aggregate demand curves have negative slope for sufficiently low ϕ_B.

The choice-theoretic system incorporating production and exchange, with individuals and firms, can now be summarized.

$$\frac{dc_B}{dc_A}\bigg|_U = \Upsilon(c_A, c_B) \qquad \text{Preference function} \\ \qquad\qquad (I \text{ equations}) \qquad (1)$$

$$c_A + \phi_B c_B = y_A + \phi_B\left(y_B + \sum_{f=1}^{F} \epsilon_f W_B^f\right) \qquad \text{Wealth constraint} \\ \qquad\qquad (I \text{ equations}) \qquad (9)$$

$$\frac{dc_B}{dc_A}\bigg|_U = -\frac{1}{\phi_B} \qquad \text{Individual optimum} \\ \qquad\qquad (I \text{ equations}) \qquad (3)$$

Equations (1) and (3) are identical with the corresponding equations of the pure-exchange system. But equation (9) replaces equation (2); it constrains the individual's consumption expenditures to equal the value of his endowment *as augmented* by payout, assumed to be all in B-units, of profits (wealth increments) from owned firms.

$$Q^f(q_A^f, q_B^f) = 0 \qquad \text{Firm's productive opportunity} \\ \qquad\qquad (2F \text{ equations}) \qquad (10)$$

$$\frac{dq_B^f}{dq_A^f} = \omega(q_A^f, q_B^f)$$

The first equation corresponds to the QQ locus in Fig. 1-7(a) and the second gives the slope along the curve. These equations would be identical with (6), except that firm q^f variables have replaced the individual q^i variables.

$$\frac{dq_B^f}{dq_A^f} = -\frac{1}{\phi_B} \qquad \text{Productive optimum} \\ \qquad\qquad (F \text{ equations}) \qquad (11)$$

Equation (11) identifies the productive optimum point (Q^*) as the tangency of QQ with a market line of slope $-1/\phi_B$. It corresponds to (7), except for the change to *firm* variables.

$$\phi_B q_B^f = \phi_B W_B^f - q_A^f \qquad \text{Firm's financial distribution} \\ \qquad\qquad (F \text{ equations}) \qquad (12)$$

This states that the value of the firm's gross output is paid out partly to owners as profit in B-units (W_B^f) and partly to buy the required A-input (note that here q_A^f is a negative quantity, so the purchase payment is $-\phi_A q_A^f$, or just $-q_A^f$ since $\phi_A = 1$).

$$\sum_{i=1}^{I} c_A^i = \sum_{i=1}^{I} y_A^i + \sum_{f=1}^{F} q_A^f \qquad \text{Conservation relations} \\ \qquad\qquad (\text{two equations, of which} \qquad (13) \\ \sum_{i=1}^{I} c_B^i = \sum_{i=1}^{I} y_B^i + \sum_{f=1}^{F} q_B^f \qquad \text{one is independent})$$

Exchange here conserves not the original endowments, but the endowments as modified by the net effect of the productive transformations.

The augmented system has $3I + 4F + 2$ equations. The unknowns are the $dc_B/dc_A \mid_U$, c_A^i, c_B^i; dq_B^f/dq_A^f, q_A^f, q_B^f, W_B^f; and ϕ_B—again, one of the conservation relations is redundant.

NUMERICAL EXAMPLE

It will suffice here simply to reinterpret the numerical example associated with the data of Table 2 above. The type-j individuals may now be considered to be "entrepreneurs"—each being the owner of a firm having the same numerical transformation function $(q_A^f + 40)^2/20 + q_B^f = 80$ previously associated with the j-individuals themselves. Then at equilibrium the price ϕ_B equals $\frac{1}{2}$, and each firm produces 60 of B ($q_B^f = 60$) at the expense of 20 of A ($q_A^f = -20$). The firm's profit in A-units is $W_A^f = 10$, or in B-units is $W_B^f = 20$. The distribution of this profit to the owner of the firm gives the j-individual an augmented endowment whose wealth value is again 60, leading to the same consumptive solutions as in Table 2.

F. PARETO-OPTIMALITY

One other topic must be covered in a review and summary of price theory: the question of *social*, as opposed to private, optimality. In this area, only a rather limited criterion has gained wide acceptance among economists—the principle of Pareto-optimality. This criterion says, essentially, that one particular economic configuration (i.e., productive and consumptive arrangement over all individuals) is socially superior to another if, and only if, no person judges himself materially worse off (i.e., has a smaller or less-desired consumptive combination) and at least one person judges himself better off. In utility terms, a change lowering no one's utility and raising at least one person's is a movement in the direction of Pareto-optimality. It seems intuitively appealing that such changes "ought" to be approved by everyone. The Pareto-optimal *set* consists of all those configurations from which no further change satisfying the Pareto condition remains possible.

Extended discussion of the ethical judgments that might serve as basis for the principle of Pareto-optimality cannot be provided here. It should be mentioned, however, that such undoubted behavior-motivating phenomena as *benevolence* ("I am happier because you are better off") on the one hand, or on the other hand *envy* ("I am unhappier because you are better off"), are ruled out of court by the criterion. For, given such "utility interdependency effects," it will no longer be true that a change in the direction of Pareto-optimality in the material sense would in fact be preferred by everyone—nor that a change not satisfying the Pareto condition would *fail* to be preferred by everyone. On another level of argument, it has also been urged against the Pareto principle that it lends undue weight to, and in effect sanctifies, the *status quo*.

Nevertheless, Pareto-optimality does serve a useful logical function in economic systems. The attainment of some one of the Pareto-optimal set of configurations represents meeting a kind of economic efficiency test. In effect, a change in the direction of Pareto-optimality increases the aggregate size of society's "pie" while assuring that no one's absolute portion is reduced.

Analytically, the Pareto-optimal set is traditionally shown geometrically—for two individuals and two commodities, in pure exchange—as the locus of mutual indifference-curve tangencies in the "Edgeworth-box diagram." The student is assumed to be familiar with this construction. The corresponding algebraic proof is less familiar, but quite simple. It is based upon the idea of maximizing one individual's utility, holding constant the utility level of the other as a constraint. The generalization to any number of individuals and commodities is then obvious. The crucial condition for Pareto-optimality under pure exchange, in the two-commodity case, can be written as

$$\left.\frac{dc_B^i}{dc_A^i}\right|_{U^i} = \left.\frac{dc_B^j}{dc_A^j}\right|_{U^j}$$

for all individuals i and j.[16] That this equality of marginal rates of substitution

[16] The procedure is to maximize, say, $U^i(c_A^i, c_B^i)$ subject to the constraints that

$$U^j(c_A^j, c_B^j) = K \text{ (a constant)}$$

$$c_A^i + c_A^j = y_A^i + y_A^j = Y_A \text{ (a constant)}$$

$$c_B^i + c_B^j = y_B^i + y_B^j = Y_B \text{ (a constant)}$$

Introducing the Lagrangian multipliers λ, μ, and ν, $\mathscr{L}$ can be defined as

$$\mathscr{L} = U^i(c_A^i, c_B^i) - \lambda[U^j(c_A^j, c_B^j) - K] - \mu(c_A^i + c_A^j - Y_A) - \nu(c_B^i + c_B^j - Y_B).$$

Maximizing with respect to c_A^i, c_A^j, c_B^i, and c_B^j leads to

$$\frac{\partial U^i}{\partial c_A^i} - \mu = 0$$

$$\frac{\partial U^i}{\partial c_B^i} - \nu = 0$$

$$-\lambda \frac{\partial U^j}{\partial c_A^j} - \mu = 0$$

$$-\lambda \frac{\partial U^j}{\partial c_B^j} - \nu = 0$$

Since, for each individual,

$$\left.\frac{dc_B}{dc_A}\right|_U = -\frac{\partial U/\partial c_A}{\partial U/\partial c_B}$$

it follows that

$$\left.\frac{dc_B^i}{dc_A^i}\right|_{U^i} = \left.\frac{dc_B^j}{dc_B^j}\right|_{U^j}$$

in consumption is attained in competitive-market equilibrium is evident from equation (3) above, in which, for each individual, $-dc_B/dc_A\big|_U$ is set equal to $1/\phi_B$.

The incorporation of a range of productive transformation opportunities for individuals, in place of the fixed endowment constraint of pure exchange, is algebraically only a little more complicated. A threefold condition results:[17] (1) as before, equality among individuals of the marginal rates of substitution in consumption:

$$\frac{dc^i_B}{dc^i_A} = \frac{dc^j_B}{dc^j_A}$$

and now in addition, (2) equality among individuals of the marginal rates of substitution in productive transformations:

$$\frac{dq^i_B}{dq^i_A} = \frac{dq^j_B}{dq^j_A}$$

and (3) for each individual, equality of his consumptive and productive marginal rates of substitution:

$$\frac{dc^i_B}{dc^i_A} = \frac{dq^i_B}{dq^i_A}$$

All three conditions are met in competitive equilibrium; for, as indicated by equations (3) and (7) in the choice-theoretic structure shown above for

---

[17] Again, the procedure is to maximize one individual's utility, holding constant the utility of the other. If $U^i(c^i_A, c^i_B)$ is to be maximized, there are now five constraints in place of the three for the pure-exchange case:

$$U^j(c^j_A, c^j_B) = K \text{ (a constant)}$$

$$Q^i(q^i_A, q^i_B) = 0$$

$$Q^j(q^j_A, q^j_B) = 0$$

$$c^i_A + c^j_A - q^i_A - q^j_A = y^i_A + y^j_A = Y_A \text{ (a constant)}$$

$$c^i_B + c^j_B - q^i_B - q^j_B = y^i_B + y^j_B = Y_B \text{ (a constant)}$$

The second and third constraints represent the transformation opportunities, while the last two represent the condition that the sum of the consumptive and productive demands for each commodity must equal the endowed supply. Forming the Lagrangian expression $\mathscr{L}$ and maximizing in the usual way leads to the results in the text.

the paradigm of production and exchange,

$$\frac{dc_B}{dc_A} = \frac{dq_B}{dq_A} = -\frac{1}{\phi_B}$$

for each individual.[18]

G. REMARKS

This introductory chapter, "Review and Summary of Price Theory," represents only the barest of the bare bones of that branch of economic analysis. Where, the student may well ask, are such central concepts as factors of production, the cost function, and short-run versus long-run equilibrium? And what of newer analytical developments, most particularly the use of linear production models ("linear programming") enabling us to dispense with the assumption of continuous curved productive loci? Evidently, the attempt to provide adequate coverage of such topics would convert an introductory chapter into an introductory volume. What has been done here is to provide a minimal foundation that will permit us to treat at least the simpler aspects of the problem of intertemporal choice. As and when it is needed to cope with increasingly difficult problems, the necessary price-theoretic foundation will be extended in later chapters.

The absence of factors of production from the choice-theoretic systems developed above warrants some comment, however. Factors are *productive commodities*, while the models above treated only of *consumptive* commodities. The fact of production was not omitted. But the possibilities of production were summarized by an opportunity set—a range of alternative combinations of *consumptive* commodities attainable by physical transformations. Such an abstraction could be valid, even though in fact physical outputs of consumptive commodities are generated by processes involving factors of production, so long as the analyst is not interested in the productive process itself. The chief complication would be if there were preference relations involving the *productive* commodities. Thus, the abstraction from factors of production in a utility diagram like that of Fig. 1-4 represents a hidden assumption that variations in the individual's use of productive commodities do not affect utility. Consequently, it is implicit that the individual's factor-supply curves for productive uses are vertical (unaffected by factor prices). This assumption is most conspicuously violated in the case of labor. Formally speaking, the difficulty can be escaped by adding reservation (nonproductive) uses of the factors (e.g., leisure) to the list of consumptive commodities as objects of

[18] The equation systems of this chapter strictly apply only for "interior" solutions; each individual is supposed to consume positive quantities of all commodities. Otherwise, the consumptive optimum equations, starting with equation (3) above, would be replaced by *inequalities*. This is more than a mere technical nicety, but the topic cannot be pursued here.

choice. To begin with, however, in the interest of simplicity it will be convenient to deal with structures of choice that abstract from productive commodities.

In the chapters that follow we will consider structures of choice involving time (in Part I) and uncertainty (in Part II). The key to the successive steps of the argument is the specification of the nature of the objects of choice, or commodities. In dealing with riskless choice over time, generalized dated consumptive claims will serve as the commodities. Thus, instead of choosing between "timeless" apples and oranges, we choose between this year's apples-or-oranges and next year's apples-or-oranges. Note that this is both a generalization and a reduction. It is a generalization since disparate dates differentiate commodities. But it is a reduction in that we do not concern ourselves with the choice among contemporaneous consumptive commodities (or reservation uses of productive commodities), but only with generalized consumption claims ("dollars") for each date. In Part II the concept of commodity will be further extended, so as to refer to consumption at a specified date and under a specified "state of the world" or contingency—or, alternatively, to statistical parameters of probability distributions of consumption. Each such modification requires reconsideration of preference patterns, production possibilities, and exchange opportunities—all of which must be appropriately specified for the objects of choice. But underlying this diversity and increasing complexity will be the stable logical form of the economic theory of choice.

A comment is in order here on the relation between this presentation and the great work of Irving Fisher.[19] The logical structure illustrated in this chapter was devised in essentially this form by Fisher, and applied by him to the explanation of individual investment decisions as intertemporal choices among consumption opportunities (under certainty) and to the determination of interest rates as equilibrium prices clearing markets for generalized consumption claims of specified dates. The over-all treatment here follows Fisher in spirit and in form. The analysis goes beyond Fisher's treatment in three main respects: (1) in introducing the *firm* as a decision-making agent in addition to individuals, (2) in studying *capital* as a factor of production, and the process of *accumulation* over time, and (3) most important, in providing a rigorous treatment of intertemporal decision under *uncertainty*.

Hopefully, the present study may be regarded as, in some respects, perfecting and extending Fisher's work.

[19] Irving Fisher, *The Rate of Interest* (The Macmillan Company, 1907); *The Nature of Capital and Income* (The Macmillan Company, 1912); *The Theory of Interest* (The Macmillan Company, 1930; reprinted [Kelley] 1955).

PART **I**

2 INTERTEMPORAL CHOICE— BASIC CONCEPTS

A. OBJECTS OF CHOICE

Consumption will be postulated to be the sole end of economic activity. The word "consumption" will not here be verbally defined; it is a primitive term in the theory.[1] The postulate itself is not such a self-evident truth as might appear at first sight:

> There is the "work to live" school, in which wants are treated as ends, and the "live to work" school, in which activities are treated as ends. . . . One who (implicitly, perhaps) takes the former position, like Alvin Hansen, is likely to regard existing wants as primary and the consumer as the dominant economic entity. From this it is but a short step to the idea of a stable consumption function and from the stable consumption function to the idea of stagnation. On the other hand, one who takes the latter viewpoint, like Schumpeter, will conceive of activities as primary. The producer-innovator is the dominant economic entity; innovation is the prevailing theme, even though it may come in waves, and one arrives at a theory of economic development.[2]

This divergence of point of view has special significance in the theory of intertemporal choice, where one school of thought has it that saving or

---

[1] A fully formalized theoretical development, not attempted here, would require a set of primitive terms sufficient to permit the definition of all other theoretical terms needed. Such a primitive set might also include the words "individual," "commodity," "choice," and so on. In order to *apply* the theory the student must be able to associate undefined terms with real-world objects or processes, but this is apart from the logical structure of the theory.

[2] Milton Friedman, *Price Theory: A Provisional Text* (Aldine Publishing Co., 1962), p. 12.

accumulation is but deferred consumption ("save to live") while the other maintains that accumulation is an object of choice independent of consumption ("live to save"). The main theoretical development here accepts the consumption-oriented viewpoint, the traditional line of economic theory, though certainly all the complexities of human motivation are not fully represented thereby.

The ultimate objects of choice to be dealt with—the goods, or desired commodities—are dated consumption claims. These claims are to be interpreted as titles to real *generalized consumption* of a given date: we shall speak of these titles as "claims," "dollars," or "funds"[3] of time 0 (the "present"), of time 1, and so on. The analysis is thus simplified by factoring out the decision among classes of consumption claims of the same date (the choice between today's apples and today's oranges is ignored). The objective of the individual economic agent is to achieve a preferred time-pattern of consumption, an optimal balance among consumption claims of differing dates. Figure 2-1 illustrates a consumer's "time-preference" function

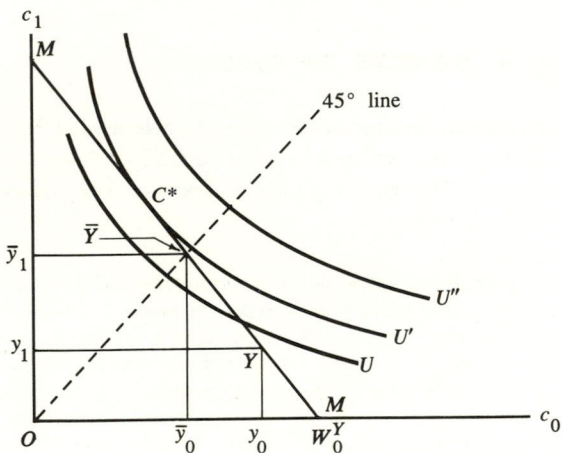

FIG. 2-1. Time-preference, time-endowment, market oportunities, and equalized incomes

(utility indifference curves U, U', U'') as among combinations of present funds (c_0) and funds dated one time unit from the present (c_1). In general, of course, the consumer would choose an optimal balance among consumption claims of more than two dates; the figure is an illustrative reduction, like the exactly corresponding Fig. 1-1 illustrating choice between just two contemporaneous commodities.

[3] These terms are intended to represent quantities of a generalized *real* consumptive commodity, though the terminology unavoidably suggests monetary quantities. Money as a specialized commodity will not be introduced until a later chapter.

B. OPPORTUNITY SET

The individual attempts to maximize utility within his opportunity set. Three different components of the opportunity set were distinguished in Chapter 1: endowment, market opportunities, and productive opportunities. Each of these concepts continues to apply when we deal with choices involving time. That is, we will be thinking in terms of time-distributed endowments, market opportunities for exchanges of funds of differing dates, and productive opportunities for physically transforming present consumption claims into future ones (or vice versa). Figure 2-1, like Fig. 1-1, shows the opportunity set for an individual—with market opportunities only—as the consumption combinations attainable by market exchanges starting from an endowment Y. Geometrically the opportunity set is the triangle bounded by the market-opportunity line MM through Y. The time-claim elements of the endowment vector will be denoted y_0 and y_1, paralleling the notation of the previous chapter.

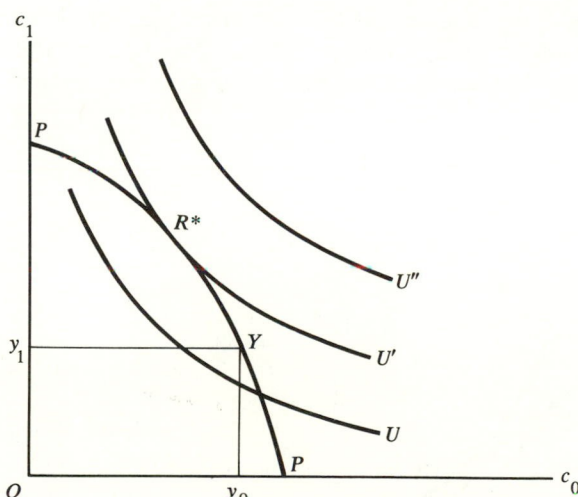

FIG. 2-2. Time-preference, time-endowment, and productive opportunities

Figure 2-2 shows the opportunity set where, like Robinson Crusoe, the individual cannot exchange but has only productive opportunities—i.e., all he can do is physically transform one commodity into another. Geometrically, the opportunity set is the area bounded by the concave curve PP through the endowment Y. PP, the productive opportunity locus, represents all the combinations (p_0, p_1) attainable by physical transformations of the individual's endowment vector. The symbol q_t will signify the transformation quantity in any period t, so that $p_0 = y_0 + q_0$ and $p_1 = y_1 + q_1$. With $q_0 < 0$, $q_1 > 0$ we have a real investment; in the reverse case, a disinvestment.

In Fig. 2-1 the value of any (c_0, c_1) combination, where prices are quoted in a "money of account," would be $\phi_0 c_0 + \phi_1 c_1$. Let us make the obvious choice of the commodity c_0 (claims to present consumption, or present dollars) as numeraire. Then ϕ_0 can be set equal to unity. The wealth, or c_0-value of any combination, is $W_0 = c_0 + \phi_1 c_1$. The market line MM represents all combinations of c_0 and c_1 having the same market value as the endowment Y—or, equivalently, all combinations that can be achieved from the starting point Y by trading c_0 for c_1 (or vice versa) at the market price ϕ_1. Thus, the slope of MM is $-1/\phi_1$, and the equation of the endowed market line is $c_0 + \phi_1 c_1 = y_0 + \phi_1 y_1 = W_0^Y$. The endowed wealth W_0^Y, the value of the endowment in c_0-units, corresponds to the intercept of MM on the c_0-axis in Fig. 2-1.

Figure 2-3, the analogue of Fig. 1-4, shows the enlarged opportunity set for an individual with *both* market and productive opportunities. The highest attainable market line $M'M'$ is characterized by a maximal level of attained wealth $W_0^* = p_0^* + \phi_1 p_1^*$—where p_0^* and p_1^* are the coordinates of the tangency P^* between the productive-opportunity set and $M'M'$.

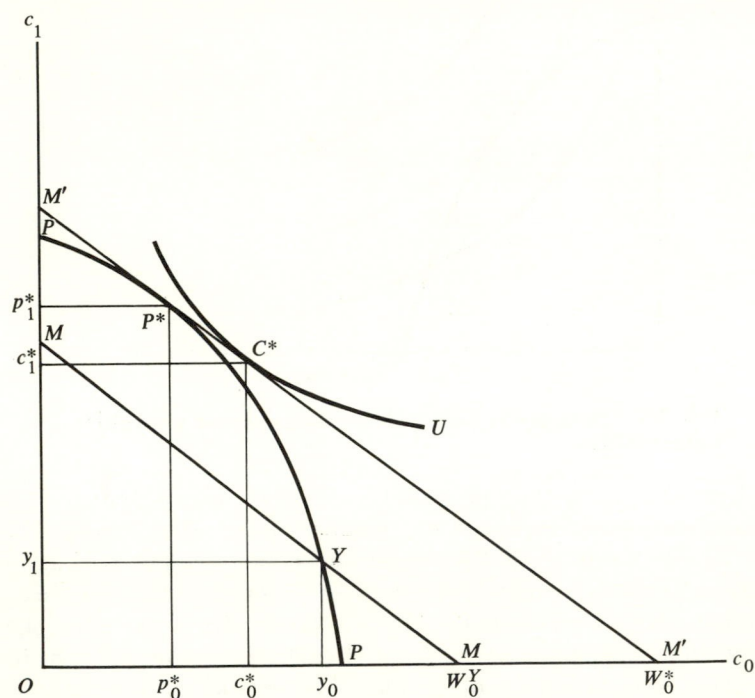

FIG. 2-3. Productive and exchange opportunities

C. THE RATE OF INTEREST

In the usual treatment of optimization over time, a departure is made from the ordinary price notation. Instead of quoting the value of a dollar receipt one time unit (say, one year) from the present, in terms of current dollars, as ϕ_1, we ordinarily say that a dollar today is worth (exchanges in the market for) the promise of $1 + r_1$ dollars a year hence. Here r_1 is the *annual rate of interest* (assuming no intermediate compounding). This states the price of a current dollar, in terms of one-year future dollars, as $1 + r_1$. Symbolizing by a subscript the commodity priced, and by a superscript the commodity in terms of which prices are quoted (the unit of account), we have $\phi_0^1 = 1 + r_1$. Then ϕ_1^0, the price of a one-year future dollar in terms of current dollars, or simply ϕ_1 (since the numeraire c_0 is presumed to be the unit of account in the absence of contrary indication) can be written:

$$\phi_1 = \frac{1}{1 + r_1}$$

With this revised notation wealth W_0 equals $c_0 + c_1/(1 + r_1)$, the *discounted* or *present value* of the combination (c_0, c_1). The equation of the endowed-market line—the endowed-wealth constraint—becomes

$$c_0 + \frac{c_1}{1 + r_1} = y_0 + \frac{y_1}{1 + r_1} = W_0^Y$$

This says that the individual's intertemporal allocation decision must be such that the discounted value of his consumption stream equals the discounted value of his endowment stream. The slope of the market line is $-(1 + r_1)$, so that a higher rate of interest r_1 corresponds geometrically to a steeper negative slope of MM in Fig. 2-1.

The rate of interest has thus been introduced as a way of expressing the price ratio between current and future claims, while the analysis is still in the realm of pure exchange with no productive transformations between present and future.[4] This is sometimes called the "agio" or "premium" concept of interest.[5]

[4] A point worth mentioning because some theorists have insisted that interest is "essentially" a productive phenomenon. Even in a pure-exchange world with fixed, immutable aggregate endowments of c_0 and c_1, the market would establish a price ratio ϕ_1 for c_1 in terms of c_0, thus implicitly fixing the interest rate r_1.

[5] The term "premium" suggests that current dollars trade for future dollars at better than one for one; since production has been excluded, some authors attribute the premium arising in exchange to subjective bias or preference for current consumption. This topic is to be analyzed in detail below. But it should be pointed out that, at least in a two-period model like this one, there is no logical reason to exclude the possibility of tastes and endowments so interacting that the market exchange price $\phi_1 > 1$. This in turn would imply $r_1 < 0$—a negative interest rate.

D. INCOME, SAVING, INVESTMENT

The terms already interpreted (endowment, commodity, price, and so on) in connection with the general theory of economic choice can now be utilized to explain the terminology conventionally employed in connection with the theory of saving and investment—intertemporal choice. In addition to the concepts of interest and wealth, already used above, we need the ideas of income, capital, saving, and investment. For the sake of clarity, these interpretations can run in terms of the simple two-period model: the not too difficult matter of multiperiod generalization can be left for later.

Income is a rather troublesome concept. Almost all writers agree in employing it to represent "potential consumption,"[6] in the sense of the amount that could be consumed in any time period without "trenching on" or impairing future consumption.[7] But, in the broadest sense, *any* present consumption trenches on future consumption—so long as there is an opportunity set permitting market or productive conversions between the two. One resolution of this difficulty is to denote as "income" the amount of consumption that can be taken as a *time-equalized flow* from the endowment. For example, in a two-period situation with market opportunities only, imagine that the endowment vector is $Y = (100, 50)$. That is, y_0, the present element of the endowment, equals 100 and y_1, the future element of the endowment, equals 50. Suppose also that the rate of interest, r_1, is 0 per cent (so that current dollars and future dollars exchange at par). Then the individual could choose to consume 75 in the present period, and exchange the remaining 25 units of his y_0 for a corresponding number of units of c_1 to add to his y_1, thus equalizing his consumption over time at the rate of 75 per period. His *equalized* or *net income* vector is then $\bar{Y} = (\bar{y}_0, \bar{y}_1) = (75, 75)$. In Fig. 2-1 the equalized incomes $\bar{y}_0 = \bar{y}_1$ derivable from a given endowment Y and market opportunities MM are determined by finding the intersection of MM with a line of 45° slope drawn through the origin. A similar construction could have been performed for Fig. 2-2 to find the equalized incomes derivable from Y and the productive opportunities PP.

A disadvantage of the equalized-income concept is that the amount is not independent of the rate of interest (or, more generally, of the rate of time conversion between claims of differing dates), since the equalizing process requires explicit or implicit exchanges over time. Thus, if in the example above the interest rate were 50 per cent instead of 0 per cent, it

---

[6] Fisher is an exception; he explicitly defined "real" income as *actual* consumption (*Theory of Interest*, pp. 11–12). But a term for the *potential*-consumption concept is still needed.

[7] Many writers say "without trenching on *capital*," but the term "capital" is better avoided for the moment.

would be possible to equalize the consumption flow from the same endowment at 80 (by exchanging 20 units of c_0 it would be possible to augment c_1 by 30 units).

One potential-consumption or income concept free of this difficulty is represented by the periodic *elements of the endowment itself*. Thus, pursuing the example above once more, 100 is the amount that can be consumed in the present without trenching on the *endowed* 50 units of future consumption. We will call this concept *endowed* or *gross income*. So, of the gross income of 100 units of c_0, at 0 per cent interest 25 units (at 50 per cent interest, 20 units) is the amount that must be deducted to arrive at net or equalized income. The usage here distinguishing gross and net income is consistent with ordinary accounting or business practice.[8]

Corresponding to the gross and net concepts of income are gross and net concepts of *saving*. The excess of current endowed income over actual consumption, $y_0 - c_0$, is current gross saving; the excess of net (equalized) income over actual consumption is current net saving, $\bar{y}_0 - c_0$. Note that while gross saving is an actual market magnitude (the difference between endowed income and actual consumption), net saving is not—it is a "fiction" in the literal (nonderogatory) sense of being a mental construct rather than an observation.

The use of the term *investment* is also often a source of confusion. In this study, the term will be limited to what is sometimes called "real" investment—the physical sacrifice of current consumption by *productive* transformations (as takes place when, for example, seed corn is planted rather than eaten). Thus, current gross investment $i_0 = -q_0 = y_0 - p_0$. Note that when investment is positive, the transformation q_0 will be negative—a mathematical convenience that warrants the verbal inconvenience. On these definitions, an individual's *saving* $y_0 - c_0$ will in general differ from his *investment* $y_0 - p_0$—the former is a "financial," the latter a "real" magnitude. But we will see that in market equilibrium it must be the case that, over all individuals, $\sum c_0 = \sum p_0$—so that saving equals investment.

E. GENERALIZATION OF CONCEPTS; TIME COMPOUNDING AND DISCOUNTING

It will be convenient to present here some algebraic material on compounding and discounting, while at the same time generalizing several of the basic concepts developed above to any number of time periods.

Let there be T distinct future time periods, and of course a present period as well. T will be called the "economic horizon," and may be infinity.

---

[8] Except that we have eschewed use of the word "capital" in expressions such as "maintaining capital intact" or "not dipping into capital."

The objects of choice—consumption claims in each time period—are $c_0, c_1, c_2, \ldots, c_T$. The endowment Y is the vector or stream $(y_0, y_1, y_2, \ldots, y_T)$, where y_t will also be called the "gross income" of period t. The combination attained by productive transformations (real investments and disinvestments) will be denoted $(p_0, p_1, \ldots, p_T)$. If c_t is actual consumption in the tth period, and p_t is the element of the productive combination attained, then "gross saving" for the period is $y_t - c_t$ while "gross investment" is $y_t - p_t = -q_t$.

In the two-period analysis above (where $T = 1$), the wealth W_0 associated with an arbitrary consumption combination (c_0, c_1) was defined by $W_0 = c_0 + c_1/(1 + r_1)$, where r_1 is the interest rate established by the market for exchanges between funds of time 0 and time 1. More generally there will be distinct market interest rates $r_1, r_2, \ldots, r_T$ for exchanges between each time t and the preceding period $t - 1$. The equation for wealth may then be written as

$$W_0 = c_0 + \frac{c_1}{1 + r_1} + \frac{c_2}{(1 + r_2)(1 + r_1)}$$
$$+ \cdots + \frac{c_T}{(1 + r_T) \cdots (1 + r_2)(1 + r_1)} \qquad (1)$$

In this formula the consumption element c_t for each time period has been carried back in time, to the present or 0th period, by successively discounting at the rates established by the market for conversion of dollars of each period into dollars of the next preceding period.[9] Thus c_1 is discounted by the factor $(1 + r_1)$, c_2 by the product of the successive factors $(1 + r_2)$ and $(1 + r_1)$, and so on. The endowed wealth W_0^Y and the equalized incomes $\bar{y}$ are then defined in

$$W_0^Y = y_0 + \frac{y_1}{1 + r_1} + \cdots + \frac{y_T}{(1 + r_T) \cdots (1 + r_2)(1 + r_1)} \qquad (1\mathrm{a})$$

$$W_0^Y = \bar{y}_0 + \frac{\bar{y}_1}{1 + r_1} + \cdots + \frac{\bar{y}_T}{(1 + r_T) \cdots (1 + r_2)(1 + r_1)} \qquad (1\mathrm{b})$$

It will also be useful to define the concept of attained wealth—the wealth associated with the attained-income vector $(p_0, p_1, \ldots, p_T)$, where $p_t = y_t + q_t$—as

$$W_0^P = p_0 + \frac{p_1}{1 + r_1} + \cdots + \frac{p_T}{(1 + r_T) \cdots (1 + r_2)(1 + r_1)} \qquad (1\mathrm{c})$$

---

[9] Only one-period (short-term) interest rates are used here. The relationship between short-term and long-term interest rates will be indicated shortly.

The symbol W_0^* used earlier represented the *maximized* value of attained wealth, that associated with the productive optimum $P^* = (p_0^*, p_1^*, \ldots, p_T^*)$. The term "attained wealth" will be used for both W_0^P as a variable and W_0^* as the maximized value of this variable.

Less frequently, we will be concerned with the *compounded* or *terminal* value W_T—wealth measured in units of c_T—as opposed to the discounted or present value W_0.

$$W_T = c_0[(1 + r_1)(1 + r_2) \cdots (1 + r_T)] + c_1[(1 + r_2) \cdots (1 + r_T)]$$

$$+ \cdots + c_{T-1}(1 + r_T) + c_T \quad (2)$$

Compounding is the inverse process to discounting.

All *wealth* measures summarize in value terms the over-all claim combinations (endowed, productive, or consumptive) representing actual or attainable income sequences of an economic agent—individual or firm. A more general value concept, symbolized as V_0, will be useful in dealing with claim sequences that are not necessarily over-all income streams for some economic agent—for example, a sequence of payments associated incrementally with purchase of a machine for productive purposes.

Denote an arbitrary sequence of dated dollar payments (positive or negative) as $s_0, s_1, s_2, \ldots, s_T$. Then the *present value* V_0 of this sequence is given by

$$V_0 = s_0 + \frac{s_1}{1 + r_1} + \frac{s_2}{(1 + r_2)(1 + r_1)}$$

$$+ \cdots + \frac{s_T}{(1 + r_T) \cdots (1 + r_2)(1 + r_1)} \quad (3)$$

(The terminal value V_T would be defined correspondingly.) Wealth is thus a particular present value, namely, the present value of a sequence of claims that constitute the over-all position of an economic agent.

It is sometimes of importance to deal with the special case where $r_1 = \cdots = r_T$—that is, where the interest rate is constant over time at some level, which will be denoted simply r. Then the discounting or valuation formula simplifies to

$$V_0 = s_0 + \frac{s_1}{1 + r} + \frac{s_2}{(1 + r)^2} + \cdots + \frac{s_T}{(1 + r)^T} \quad (4)$$

If, in addition, there is a level infinite sequence $(T = \infty)$ of payments beginning with time 1 (i.e., $s_0 = 0$, and $s_1 = s_2 = \cdots = s_t = \cdots = s$, a constant) we get the formula:

$$V_0 = \frac{s}{r} \quad (5)$$

For the same sequence beginning with time 0 (that is where s_0 also equals s) the formula is

$$V_0 = s + \frac{s}{r} = s\left(1 + \frac{1}{r}\right) = \frac{s(1 + r)}{r} \tag{5a}$$

The net or equalized income, $\bar{y}$, is determined implicitly, for finite T under the assumption of a constant interest rate r, in the wealth equation:

$$W_0^Y = y_0 + \frac{y_1}{1 + r} + \cdots + \frac{y_T}{(1+r)^T} = \bar{y}_0 + \frac{\bar{y}_1}{1 + r} + \cdots + \frac{\bar{y}_T}{(1+r)^T}$$
$$= \frac{\bar{y}(1 + r)^{T+1} - 1}{r(1 + r)^T} \tag{6}$$

If T is infinite, the expression on the right reduces to a simpler form:

$$W_0^Y = \bar{y}\frac{1 + r}{r} \tag{7}$$

F. CAPITAL

The word "capital" is used in economic writings in a number of grossly or subtly different senses, and is thus the source of enormous confusion. The various underlying concepts will be considered in detail in Chapter 6. At this point it will be necessary to mention only the two central ideas—"real capital" and "capital value." The purpose will be to indicate how it is that "capital" concepts can be avoided in our primary discussion of investment (optimization of consumption over time) in Chapter 3 and of interest (market equilibrium over time) in Chapters 4 and 5.

Real capital is an aggregate of physical capital goods—in the traditional phrase, of "produced means of production." Thus, real capital represents an "intermediate good": something not desired in and of itself, but only insofar as it contributes to the production of something else. Now the primary formulation here of the problem of intertemporal choice views production as a process of transformation among alternative combinations of dated end products or *final* goods (consumption baskets). The productive role of capital goods as well as of other factors appears implicitly, rather than explicitly, in the shape of the productive-opportunity set (locus of attainable combinations). We can thus, for the time being at least, interpret investment as sacrifice of current for future consumption rather than as an increment to the stock of capital goods leading only indirectly to increases in future consumption.

Capital value is not a real object like a capital good, but is rather the result of a process of calculation or market valuation. The term is often used simply as a synonym for "*present* value." V_0 in equation (3) could thus be interpreted as the capital value of a specified stream of payments over time, or W_0 in equation (1) as the capital value of an economic agent. Since we already have the term "present value," we will never need to employ "capital value" in this sense.

There is a slightly modified sense of "capital value" that will be useful later on, however. "Capital value" sometimes refers to the present value K_0 of a stream of *future* payments, thus standing in contrast against current income flow. Under this definition, for example, it is possible to divide endowed wealth in equation (1a) into endowed current income and endowed capital value:

$$W_0^Y = y_0 + K_0^Y \tag{8}$$

Here the process of saving (choosing $c_0 < y_0$) leads automatically to an increment to capital value ($K_0 > K_0^Y$).[10] This formulation is convenient, in that it collapses what might be a very complex pattern of future claims ($c_1, \ldots, c_T$) into a single scalar magnitude K_0. But in the next two chapters the main concern will be precisely to make explicit the implications of individual intertemporal optimization and market equilibrium for the pattern of intertemporal claims. Hence the abbreviation represented by the capital-value K_0 concept will not be needed until later chapters.

G. TIME—DISCRETE vs. CONTINUOUS

In the formal treatment so far, time has been represented as a succession of equidistant discrete points $t = 0, 1, 2, \ldots, T$. But a terminology has also been used (e.g., in referring to *periods* of time) suggestive of time continuity. The great advantage of dealing with time as discrete points, or as discretized periods,[11] is that it permits limiting attention to a denumerable set of objects of choice.[12] We ordinarily think of time as "really" continuous, of course,

[10] If only market transactions were engaged in, as when savings are invested in financial instruments such as bonds, wealth would be unaffected—so the increment to capital value must exactly equal value of saving. But this equality will not in general hold if the individual saves to make *productive* investments, since these can modify wealth W_0.

[11] A period is discretized by cumulating flows of income or of consumption within the period into a single total. Implicitly, the assertion is that the detailed intraperiod distribution of the flow is irrelevant, with respect either to consumptive preferences or to conversion (via financial or productive transactions) into other objects of choice. Such an assumption is not a true description of reality, but the discrepancy may be small if the unit period is short.

[12] A set is denumerable if its members can be arranged in one-to-one correspondence with the arithmetical integers. All sets with finite numbers of members can be so "numbered" and are therefore denumerable. And some infinite sets, like the set of integers itself, can also be numbered. The set of discrete time periods is obviously numbered by the time subscripts attached, even when we permit the horizon T to go to infinity.

but the continuity of time can be approximated by making the mesh of discrete points as fine as desired. Thus, instead of taking the year as the interval between points, one may take the month, day, or hour.

For certain purposes, however, especially in connection with physical growth—an essential element of many productive processes—it is more natural and mathematically convenient to employ a continuous-time concept. It will therefore be useful here to set down some crucial relations between continuous growth and its discrete analogue—compounding.

An interest rate r conventionally refers, implicitly or explicitly, to a time period or time interval of one year. Where this conventional period does not correspond to the relevant transaction or decision period for consumptive, productive, or exchange purposes, "intermediate compounding" will be involved. In such cases, n, the number of compoundings per year, must be indicated. The expression "an interest rate of 10 per cent compounded quarterly" really means, in terms of compounding-discounting formulas, a time period of a quarter-year, and with respect to that interval an interest rate of 10 per cent/4 or $2\frac{1}{2}$ per cent. Note that with intermediate compounding, as in this example, a dollar would compound to more than \$1.10 in a year—actually, to about \$1.104. In general, with r always quoted "per annum," the interest rate for actual use in the formulas is r/n, in association with a compounding time-interval of $1/n$ years. After the course of a year, a dollar would then compound to $(1 + r/n)^n$ dollars. After the course of t years it would have compounded to $(1 + r/n)^{nt}$ dollars.

We may now ask, what happens if we increase the frequency n, of compounding per year, until it approaches infinity? Mathematically, we seek the limit of $(1 + r/n)^{nt}$, as n goes to infinity. This limit is e^{rt}, where $e\ (= 2.718+)$ is the exponential limit or base of the natural logarithms.[13] As before, r is still nominally stated per annum, though it represents the rate of continuous growth. After the course of a year with r at 10 per cent "per annum" a dollar would compound to about \$1.105. It is worth noting that an n of only 4 (quarterly compounding) already accounts in this case for the bulk of the increase in terminal value in going from annual $(n = 1)$ to continuous $(n = \infty)$ compounding.

One other question sometimes asked is: What is the rate of interest, annually compounded, that yields the same terminal value as a given continuously compounded rate, or vice versa? To avoid possible confusion between the two rates, in answering this question we should write out the frequency of compounding explicitly in parentheses in each case:

$$1 + r(1) = e^{r(\infty)} \tag{9a}$$

[13] By definition, $e = \lim_{h \to \infty} (1 + 1/h)^h$. The result in the text follows by making the substitution $h = n/r$. With r constant, as n goes to infinity, h goes to infinity.

or equivalently:

$$\ln [1 + r(1)] = r(\infty) \tag{9b}$$

where ln indicates "natural logarithm of." For relatively low interest rates, it is possible to approximate the terminal value under continuous compounding by using the same r—i.e., ignoring the distinction between $r(1)$ and $r(\infty)$—in the compounding formulas. This can be written $1 + r \doteq e^r$, where the symbol $\doteq$ means "approximately equal to." If this approximation is not adopted, the equivalent rates can be found in interest tables. Henceforth, it will be understood that the interest rate will always be defined as appropriate for the actual compounding interval in use. Thus e^r indicates a continuously compounded value; unless otherwise specified, the r in such an expression will always be $r(\infty)$—that is, it will always be a number smaller than the single annual-compounding $r(1)$ that yields the same terminal value at the end of a year.

Under continuous compounding, with a continuous payments stream $s(t)$, terminal value V_T and present value V_0 are given as follows:

$$V_T = \int_0^T s(t) e^{rt} \, dt \tag{10}$$

$$V_0 = \int_0^T s(t) e^{-rt} \, dt \tag{11}$$

As in the discrete case, what are multiplicative factors for successive payment elements in compounding are dividing factors in discounting.[14] An individual's *wealth* W_0 would be the present value of his consumption stream $c(t)$, endowed wealth the present value of an endowment stream $y(t)$, and attained wealth the present value of an attained-income stream $p(t)$.

$$W_0 = \int_0^T c(t) e^{-rt} \, dt \tag{12a}$$

$$W_0^Y = \int_0^T y(t) e^{-rt} \, dt \tag{12b}$$

$$W_0^P = \int_0^T p(t) e^{-rt} \, dt \tag{12c}$$

Note, however, that the capital concept K_0 defined above—a present value

[14] Continuous compounding or discounting as a process of calculation does not necessarily require that the payments stream $s(t)$ be a continuous flow. Discrete or discontinuous payments can be continuously compounded or discounted.

of *future* payment elements alone—becomes difficult to interpret when the future is no longer separated by a discrete gap from the present.[15]

As before, simplifying assumptions lead to some special formulas. If r is constant, and $s(t)$ is a level flow s over time, we get for the present value of such a stream of payments:

$$V_0 = \frac{s}{r}(1 - e^{-rt}) \tag{13}$$

and if we let T go to infinity this simplifies to[16]

$$V_0 = \frac{s}{r} \tag{14}$$

Maintaining the assumptions of constant r and infinite T, we then determine the equalized or net income $\bar{y}$ that can be exchanged for an arbitrary endowment stream $y(t)$ as $\bar{y} = rW_0^Y$, where W_0^Y is defined as in (12) above, but with $T = \infty$. This corresponds to the dictum that (net) income is the yield of wealth.

H. ORDER OF TOPICS

The remaining chapters of Part I ascend a ladder of subjects of gradually increasing complexity. The primary discussion, the pure theory of intertemporal choice, occurs in the next two chapters. Chapter 3 is devoted to

[15] Formally speaking, it would be possible to define K_0 as an integral over the "semi-open" interval extending at the upper limit up to and including T but at the lower limit down to and *not* including 0. This K_0 would differ from V_0 if there were a discrete payment element at $t = 0$.

[16] One somewhat puzzling result is that, with a *continuous* level flow s extending from $t = 0$ to $t = \infty$, equation (14) tells us that $V_0 = s/r$. For a corresponding *discrete* level flow from $t = 0$ to $t = \infty$ we might have expected the same equation to hold. But according to equation (5a), for such a flow $V_0 = s(1 + r)/r$. Indeed, equation (5) tells us that the equation $V_0 = s/r$ holds for level discrete flows extending not from $t = 0$ but from $t = 1$ to $t = \infty$. Two separate elements are invovled in the seeming discrepancy. *First*, we must keep in mind the difference between annual and continuous compounding: the r implicit in equations (5) and (5a) is $r(1)$, while that implicit in (14) is $r(\infty)$. Consider now a level discrete flow starting at $t = 0$ with $s = 1$ and $r = 10$ per cent. Then the continuous equation (14) tells us that $V_0 = 1/.1 = 10$—while the discrete equation (5a) says $V_0 = 1(1.1)/.1 = 11$. If, however, we make the relations (5a) and (14) more precisely comparable by employing in (5a) the annual compounding rate $r(1) = 10.5$ per cent *equivalent* to the continuous compounding rate $r(\infty) = 10$ per cent employed in (14)—obtained by using relation (9a) and exponential tables—the result is $V_0 = 1(1.105)/.105 = 10.52$. Thus, about half the discrepancy is accounted for. *Second*, upon reflection it will appear that a discrete level sequence of payments at times $t = 0, 1, \ldots, \infty$ is better approximated by a level continuous flow to infinity beginning at $t = \frac{1}{2}-$ rather than at $t = 0$. Carrying out the integration gives us, for the continuous flow, a revised $V_0 = e^{r/2}(s/r) = 1.051(1/.1) = 10.51$—practically the same as that obtained for the discrete flow using the corrected 10.5 per cent annual discounting rate.

the theory of *investment*: intertemporal allocative decisions of individuals and firms, taking market opportunities as given. In Chapter 4 we will turn to the theory of *interest*, advancing from the level of the economic agent to the social level of analysis. That chapter will cover the determination of price ratios among objects of choice—dated consumption claims—through the market interaction of economic agents. These prices are, of course, determined jointly with the corresponding quantities (dated consumptions or, correspondingly, dated savings and returns on saving). Chapter 5 introduces a monetary commodity, so that the relations between monetary and real interest rates can be explored. Chapter 6 represents a reconsideration of the topics of the primary analysis, bringing in factors of production in the form of labor and, especially, real capital. Finally, Chapter 7 introduces the topic of imperfect or incomplete funds markets. All of these extensions of the standard theory are carried out within the maintained assumptions of a world of certainty. We will see that this raises a number of questions, pointing to the need for the analysis taking explicit account of *uncertainty* that gets under way in Part II.

BIBLIOGRAPHY

A treatment of capital theory rejecting the postulate that consumption is the sole end of economic activity:

DONALD DEWEY, *Modern Capital Theory* (Columbia Univ. Press, 1965).

Concepts of income, saving, investment, and capital:

IRVING FISHER, *The Nature of Capital and Income* (The Macmillan Company, 1906).

IRVING FISHER, *The Theory of Interest* (The Macmillan Company, 1930; reprinted [Kelley] 1955), Chap. 1.

J. R. HICKS, *Value and Capital*, 2nd ed. (Oxford University Press, 1946), Chap. 14.

PAUL A. SAMUELSON, "The Evaluation of 'Social Income': Capital Formation and Wealth," in F. A. Lutz and D. C. Hague (eds.), *The Theory of Capital* (The Macmillan Company, 1961).

Analysis of interest and capitalization formulas:

EUGENE L. GRANT and W. GRANT IRESON, *Principles of Engineering Economy*, 4th ed. (The Ronald Press, 1960).

3 OPTIMAL INVESTMENT DECISION

The theory of investment concerns the principles of intertemporal choice—the allocation of resources for consumptive and productive purposes over time. The optimization involved can be examined on the level of the individual or the firm, and also on the level of the community as a whole. Practical decision-makers—businessmen and government administrators—are also interested in principles of intertemporal choice. From their point of view, the questions involved are usually posed in the following forms: (1) What decision rule will correctly indicate which of the many possible projects or investment opportunities should be undertaken? (2) Given any particular set of chosen productive investments, what is the best method for "financing" those investments?

The first question asks what *productive* opportunities should be adopted. The second asks how the necessary investment inputs are to be obtained, taking account of the market opportunities. Ultimately, this reduces to the question of how the investor should rearrange intertemporal *consumption* plans on the basis of having chosen a given set of productive investments. We shall see, for example, that someone who tries to reap the benefit of investment mostly in the form of current consumption will have to borrow more heavily to "finance the investment" than someone more inclined to reap the benefit in the form of enhanced future consumption.

The problem of optimal investment decision will first be approached here from the point of view of the practical decision-maker. Several of the best-known "*investment decision rules*" proposed for the guidance of such administrators will first be explained. After that, the alternative rules will be evaluated in the light of solutions on the theoretical level—in which context choice-paradigms of gradually increasing complexity (e.g., two-period, then multiperiod, then continuous-time decision problems) will be considered. Throughout the chapter, the assumption will be maintained that markets for intertemporal claims ("capital markets") are complete and perfect.[1] That is, between any pair of successive time periods at dates s and t from the present, it will be assumed that there exist in the market a unique price ratio ϕ_t/ϕ_s and a corresponding discount factor $1/(1 + r_t)$ that cannot be significantly influenced by the decisions of single economic agents.

A. INVESTMENT DECISION RULES

Many difficulties face the practical decision-maker who must choose among productive investment opportunities (in the form of *projects*, or sets of projects) for his own account, or on behalf of other people or institutions for whom he is empowered to act. Surely the greatest difficulty is lack of certainty about the true costs and benefits attaching to each of the courses of action available, and in Part II of this volume we shall consider the problems posed for investment choice by elements of risk, ignorance, and uncertainty. But, even knowing the full consequences of each project or course of action, and assuming these can all be expressed as dollar costs and benefits,[2] the decision-maker might ask: What rule shall I use to choose among the opportunities available? Investment decision rules are formulas that purport to guide choices correctly under such circumstances.

Some writers have discussed rules for *ranking* investment alternatives, apart from the rules specifying the set that should actually be *adopted*. Such a distinction could be administratively useful; it might often be very convenient to take advantage of a division of labor, whereby one group of planners ranks all available projects, while another (presumably, of higher authority) then need only locate the lowest-ranking one worthy of adoption. Unfortunately, it is *not* in general true that investment opportunities can be uniquely ranked; the desirability of any one may be affected by the other project elements in any over-all package into which it enters. Thus, a correct ranking rule for individual projects is not generally possible. Furthermore, while such a rule would be convenient, it is never actually necessary; if the decision-maker knows the correct set of projects to be adopted, there is no need to rank them in order of desirability. We therefore need not consider ranking rules and can limit our attention to adoption rules.

[1] Choice in a context of incomplete or imperfect markets will be considered in Chapter 7.

[2] In many practical decision problems there are "intangibles" or "incommensurables" that cannot be reduced to dollar equivalents; in such cases an irreducible element of subjective judgment must enter into the actual decision.

It is important to distinguish between *rules* and *criteria*. A *criterion*, as the word is used herein, is some mathematical formula (e.g., present value) computed on the elements of a cost-benefit or payments stream. A *rule* indicates the acceptability of a project, by directing a comparison between the criterion computed and some other number or formula (e.g., "adopt if the present value is greater than zero"). The failure to distinguish between *rules* and *criteria* has been responsible for considerable confusion, since in some cases divergent rules can be proposed for the employment of the same criterion.

Present-Value Rules

The adoption criterion most often used by economic theorists (but not, it appears, by practical decision-makers) is known as *present value* (or *present worth*), defined as V_0 in equation (3) of Chapter 2 for a dated sequence of discrete payments, and in equation (11) for a corresponding continuous stream. There are several versions, all essentially equivalent, of rules employing present-value criteria. Let us consider situations where it is appropriate to deal with income or payment flows discretized over $T + 1$ yearly time periods (the current period, and T future dates). T here is the "horizon," and may be infinite. W_0, wealth, has already been interpreted in Chapter 2 as the present value of a stream of payments representing the over-all position of an economic agent. *Endowed* wealth W_0^Y is the present value of the endowment sequence $y_0, y_1, \ldots, y_T$. *Attained* wealth W_0^P is the present value of the sequence of potential-consumption flows $p_0, p_1, \ldots, p_T$—the attained income stream.

Let us also make the simplifying assumption (to be relaxed later) that the annual interest rate r is constant over time. Then the fundamental version of the present-value rule directs the adoption of the set of projects maximizing the present-value criterion represented by the attained wealth of the economic agent:

$$W_0^P = p_0 + \frac{p_1}{1 + r} + \frac{p_2}{(1 + r)^2} + \cdots + \frac{p_T}{(1 + r)^T} \qquad (1)$$

The maximized value of W_0^P will be symbolized as W_0^*, the present value of the productive optimum $P^* = (p_0^*, p_1^*, \ldots, p_T^*)$.

Alternatively, consider the sequence of "productive transformations" $q_t = p_t - y_t$ associated with the *ensemble of all productive projects* engaged in by the agent. Then a second criterion, the present value of the over-all productive transformation (project ensemble), is W_0^Q in

$$W_0^Q = q_0 + \frac{q_1}{1 + r} + \frac{q_2}{(1 + r)^2} + \cdots + \frac{q_T}{(1 + r)^T} \qquad (2)$$

The corresponding version of the present-value rule directs the adoption of that ensemble of projects whose over-all present value W_0^Q is greatest. It follows directly from the definitions that

$$W_0^P = W_0^Y + W_0^Q \tag{3}$$

That is, attained wealth is the sum of endowed wealth and the present value of the project ensemble adopted. The measure W_0^Q will therefore also be sometimes called the *wealth gain*. It is evident from the constancy of endowed wealth that maximizing the wealth gain is equivalent to maximizing attained wealth.

If the decision-making agent is the firm rather than the individual, the endowed wealth is assumed to be zero. Then, for the firm, the wealth gain or value of the project ensemble *is* the attained wealth. It will suffice therefore to use the single symbol W_0^f for present value of the firm—computed from the firm's productive-transformation sequence $q_0^f, q_1^f, \ldots, q_T^f$.

Consider now the present value V_0 of a *particular project* with payments sequence $s_0, s_1, \ldots, s_T$:

$$V_0 = s_0 + \frac{s_1}{1+r} + \frac{s_2}{(1+r)^2} + \cdots + \frac{s_T}{(1+r)^T} \tag{4}$$

If such a project is being evaluated as an addition to a project ensemble, the payments s_t can be regarded as increments Δq_t or (equivalently) Δp_t. Correspondingly, V_0 can be regarded as incremental present value ΔW_0^Q or ΔW_0^P. If the increments s_t are of infinitesimal scale, as may be the case if the productive-opportunity set has a continuous form, we may speak of a *marginal* project and a corresponding *marginal* present value. Note however, that only for a special class of projects—those we may call "independent"—will it be the case that the s_t (and, consequently, the V_0) are invariant with respect to the choice of partner projects within the adopted ensemble.

For a project considered as an increment to an adopted ensemble, the associated present-value rule is: Adopt if and only if $V_0 > 0$. One special case that frequently arises is choice among mutually exclusive projects:[3] here the rather obvious rule is to select the one for which V_0 is greatest.

The present-value rules may be summarized as in Table 1.

A simple metaphor may help to illustrate the three versions of the present-value rule. Imagine that in a certain landscape higher altitude (greater wealth) is preferred. Then the first version—maximize W_0^P—says to take whatever steps will get you to the top of the highest mountain

---

[3] Projects that are mutually exclusive may be regarded as displaying an extreme form of nonindependence.

Table I
PRESENT-VALUE RULES

Criterion	Computed on	Symbol	Rule
Present value of income stream (attained wealth)	$p_0, \ldots, p_T$	W_0^P	Maximize W_0^P
Present value of project ensemble (wealth gain)	$q_0, \ldots, q_T$	W_0^Q	Maximize W_0^Q
Present value of incremental project	$s_0, \ldots, s_T$	V_0	Adopt if $V_0 > 0$

(attained wealth) in the landscape. The second version—maximize W_0^Q—says to take that set of steps that maximizes the *improvement* in altitude (value of adopted project ensemble) over your starting position. The third version says always take *another* step so long as you can increase your altitude thereby. Note that if there are several mountains in the area the third version might bring you first to the top of an inferior hill; you must then be prepared to take a giant step across the valley to a higher position on another mountain.[4]

NUMERICAL EXAMPLE

Consider a two-period paradigm of intertemporal choice (horizon $T = 1$). The individual's endowment vector $Y \equiv (y_0, y_1)$ is (100, 60). The interest rate r is 50 per cent. Then the individual's endowed wealth W_0^Y equals $100 + 60/1.5 = 140$. Suppose the projects a, b, and c are available, with payments sequences as indicated in Table 2. (If the sequences can be so tabulated, it must be that the projects are independent—i.e., the returns on each are unaffected by the adoption or nonadoption of the others.) Note also that c is a bit unusual, being a *disinvestment* opportunity. The project present values V_0 are also shown, calculated using equation (4). (The last column may be ignored at this point.) Projects a and c have positive present worth of 4 and 1, respectively. The $a + c$ pair is the best ensemble with present value W_0^Q of 5.

Table 2

Project	s_0	s_1	V_0	ρ_x
a	−6	15	4	150%
b	−10	12	−2	20%
c	5	−6	1	20%

[4] This point explains why the third version of the present-value rule was stated in terms of possibly discrete *incremental* projects rather than *marginal* projects, the latter term being used herein only to refer to increments of infinitesimal scale. The rule, adopt all *marginal* projects for which present value is positive, may lead only to a local peak. This rule would be satisfactory only if (as explained below) certain "regularity conditions" hold for the productive-opportunity set—specifically, in our mountain metaphor, that the landscape be continuous and single-peaked.

This figure can be obtained either by summing the two (independent) project V_0 values or by considering the ensemble's transformation stream $(q_0, q_1) = (-6 + 5, 15 - 6) = (-1, 9)$, yielding a wealth gain of 5 via equation (2). The maximum attained wealth can similarly be found to be $W_0^Y + W_0^Q = 140 + 5 = 145$.

Internal-Rate Rules

An entirely different criterion is that variously called the rate of return, internal rate of return, or just *internal rate*[5]—the term we shall ordinarily use here. The internal rate ρ for an ensemble of projects can be defined as the discounting rate that makes the present worth of the productive transformations zero. Thus ρ is determined implicitly in the equation:[6]

$$0 = q_0 + \frac{q_1}{1+\rho} + \frac{q_2}{(1+\rho)^2} + \cdots + \frac{q_T}{(1+\rho)^T} \tag{5}$$

For a particular project x, an internal rate ρ_x can similarly be defined in terms of the project payments:

$$0 = s_0 + \frac{s_1}{1+\rho_x} + \frac{s_2}{(1+\rho_x)^2} + \cdots + \frac{s_T}{(1+\rho_x)^T} \tag{6}$$

It sometimes proves convenient to break up the element q_t or s_t into a benefit or receipt component b_t and an outlay or cost component o_t. Then the equations defining ρ for a set of projects (or similarly for a particular project) can be rewritten:

$$o_0 + \frac{o_1}{1+\rho} + \cdots + \frac{o_T}{(1+\rho)^T} = b_0 + \frac{b_1}{1+\rho} + \cdots + \frac{b_T}{(1+\rho)^T} \tag{7}$$

There is no direct correspondence between the previous altitude metaphor and the internal-rate concepts. A more convenient image for the internal rate is growth rate over time. If, for a particular project or set of projects, all the cost elements o_t were zero except for the initial outlay o_0 and all the benefit elements b_t were zero except for the final receipt b_T, the defining equation (7) for ρ would become $o_0(1+\rho)^T = b_T$. Then ρ would be

[5] Also rate of return over cost, and marginal efficiency of capital (or of investment).
[6] For the equation to have a solution, it is necessary that there be at least one sign reversal among the terms on the right-hand side. Since the endowment sequence $y_0, \ldots, y_T$ contains nonnegative elements only, it has no internal rate. The $p_0, \ldots, p_T$ sequence may also be nonnegative. But the transformation sequence $q_0, \ldots, q_T$ must have a sign reversal—for, if not, either the endowment vector Y or the attained vector P must have been inefficient.

interpreted as the rate of annually compounded growth that takes the initial input o_0 into the terminal output b_T. For a more general stream of benefits and outlays, ρ would be interpreted as some average rate of growth that takes the several o_t into the various b_t.

Proposed rules employing internal-rate criteria take two logically quite different forms, according to whether they direct (1) that an ensemble of projects be adopted so as in some sense to *maximize* ρ, or (2) that a set of projects, or a single incremental project, be adopted on the basis of a *comparison* between ρ and the market rate of interest, r.

ρ-*Maximization rules*

What might be called the simple ρ-maximization rule calls for the adoption of an ensemble of projects so that the aggregate-payments stream (over-all transformation stream) $q_0, q_1, \ldots, q_T$ displays a maximum calculated internal rate. This rule does not seem to be endorsed by any theorist, though careless formulations of the *conditional* ρ-maximization rule (see below) may take this form. The simple rule in some elementary cases leads to absurd results. For example, if two independent investment projects yielding 10 per cent and 8 per cent happened to be available, this rule would tell us to adopt only the first—because accepting the other must necessarily reduce the ρ calculated for the over-all adopted set.[7] But the 8 per cent project might nevertheless be a highly desirable opportunity that should also be adopted.

What will be called the *conditional ρ-maximization rule* has won a degree of support among economic theorists. This rule would select the project ensemble maximizing ρ, on the condition—argued by some to be a factually true or relevant assumption—that the aggregate current outlay o_0 (or, in some formulations, the firm's or the individual's aggregate "capital" available for investing) is fixed.[8] Then, the argument goes, for given current sacrifice (or given "capital") we certainly want to adopt that project ensemble maximizing the rate of growth of outlay into future benefit. This rule is evidently incomplete in failing to indicate the scale of investment to be adopted—the optimal balance between current consumption and current investment outlay. Furthermore, we will see below that even waiving this objection, the rule is not in general correct.

ρ, r *Comparison rules*

Rules based on a *comparison* between a calculated internal-rate criterion ρ and the market or "external" rate of interest r will be shown below to have a much wider range of validity than the ρ-maximization rules. The ρ, r comparison rules also appear in three forms, exactly parallel to the

---

[7] However, if one project is an investment and the other a *disinvestment*, the aggregate of the two may show an internal rate greater than either separately.

[8] For varying versions of this viewpoint see F. and V. Lutz, *The Theory of Investment of the Firm* (Princeton Univ. Press, 1951), pp. 17, 20, 42; T. Scitovsky, *Welfare and Competition* (Richard D. Irwin, Inc., 1951), pp. 208–209.

three versions of the present-value rule in Table 1. That is, the first runs in terms of the attained incomes p_t, the second in terms of the productive transformations q_t associated with the ensemble of projects adopted, and the third in terms of the payments s_t of a single project considered as an addition to an adopted ensemble (see Table 3). The criterion ρ calculated from the p_t, more particularly from the differences between two p_t streams, is known as "Fisher's rate of return over cost"[9]—a shorter name to be used here is "over-all ρ."

To employ a dramatic image, call "Defender" (D) the attained-income stream of the p_t^D associated with the project ensemble now currently planned, and "Challenger" (C) an alternative stream of the p_t^C associated with an alternative proposed ensemble. (Some individual projects that are elements of D may also be contained in C.) Then Fisher's rate of return over cost, or over-all ρ, is defined in

$$p_0^D + \frac{p_1^D}{1+\rho} + \cdots + \frac{p_T^D}{(1+\rho)^T} = p_0^C + \frac{p_1^C}{1+\rho} + \cdots + \frac{p_T^C}{(1+\rho)^T} \quad (8)$$

Note that since $p_t = y_t + q_t$, and the y_t's are the same on both sides of (8), the equation is equivalent to

$$q_0^D + \frac{q_1^D}{1+\rho} + \cdots + \frac{q_T^D}{(1+\rho)^T} = q_0^C + \frac{q_1^C}{1+\rho} + \cdots + \frac{q_T^C}{(1+\rho)^T} \quad (9)$$

Thus, we are led to exactly the same "over-all ρ," whether we compare the attained-income streams or the transformation streams of two alternative project ensembles.[10] The over-all ρ criterion is an internal rate, in the sense of equation (5), for the difference stream of the $(p_t^C - p_t^D) = (q_t^C - q_t^D)$.

The *over-all ρ, r comparison rule* can be expressed as follows: In comparing two alternative project ensembles, adopt the "later" (as defined below) if ρ calculated on the difference stream exceeds r—but adopt the "earlier" if $\rho < r$. Note that the calculated ρ in (8) or (9) remains the same when we interchange Challenger and Defender. This is why the identification of an "earlier" and "later" is necessary.

The Challenger would be unambiguously "later" than the Defender if the differences $p_t^C - p_t^D$ or $q_t^C - q_t^D$ were all negative up to a certain date, and thereafter all positive. Or, slightly more generally, were at first all nonpositive (with at least one negative element), and then all nonnegative

[9] Irving Fisher, *The Theory of Interest* (The Macmillan Company, 1930; reprinted [Kelley] 1955), p. 155.

[10] In Table 1, the first two versions of the present-value *rules* were equivalent, but the *criteria* W_0^P and W_0^Q were not identical. The corresponding *criteria* are themselves identical in the corresponding versions of the ρ, r comparison rules.

(with at least one positive element). If this condition holds, we can say that the Challenger is an *investment relative to* the Defender—since investment (as contrasted with disinvestment) entails early sacrifice for future benefit. Unfortunately, only in a limited class of simple cases will the differences be such that one set of projects is unambiguously "later" than the other.[11] For example, the sequence of dated differences between Challenger and Defender might be $(-100, +25, +300, -200)$, or might take on an even more complex pattern of mixed positive and negative terms. It is evident that this ambiguity severely impairs the operational usability of the over-all ρ criterion.

It is possible to show that, in those cases where one project ensemble is definitely later than the other so that the overall ρ, r comparison rule is meaningful, the rule is equivalent to the corresponding present-value rule. Thus, suppose that the Challenger is later than the Defender, and $\rho > r$, where ρ is defined in equation (8) or (9) above. Then it follows that $W_0^{Q(C)} > W_0^{Q(D)}$ or equivalently that the attained wealth $W_0^{P(C)}$ associated with the Challenger is greater than the attained wealth $W_0^{P(D)}$ associated with the Defender[12].

For a particular project x, ρ_x has been defined in equation (6) above as the internal rate computed on the payments stream $s_0, s_1, \ldots, s_T$. Suppose that such a project is proposed as an increment to an ensemble of projects already adopted (or considered for adoption). Then what will be called the *incremental ρ, r comparison rule* says to adopt such a project if ρ_x (or incremental ρ) as calculated above exceeds r.[13] The project payments s_t

---

[11] Most presentations fail to call attention to the difficulty, but Fisher was quite aware of it (*Theory of Interest*, p. 159n).

[12] Consider r to be a variable discounting rate in

$$W_0^{Q(C)} - W_0^{Q(D)} = (q_0^C - q_0^D) + \frac{q_1^C - q_1^D}{1+r} + \cdots + \frac{q_T^C - q_T^D}{(1+r)^T}$$

Descartes' rule of signs tells us that such an equation has at most as many roots in the range $r > -1$ as there are sign reversals in the sequence of terms on the right-hand side. Here, since C is "later," a sequence of negative (or nonpositive) terms is followed by a sequence of positive (or nonnegative) terms. Then there is only one sign reversal, and a single root (since we know that ρ is a root). If we imagine that r grows indefinitely large, $W_0^{Q(C)} - W_0^{Q(D)}$ must eventually become negative—since the (positive) terms involving high powers of $(1 + r)$ in the denominators on the right will go to zero faster than the (negative) terms involving low powers of $(1 + r)$. But if the present-value difference is negative for any values of r greater than the single root ρ, it must be positive for values of r less than ρ. Hence $W_0^{Q(C)} - W_0^{Q(D)}$, evaluated at the external interest rate r, is positive if and only if $\rho > r$, proving the assertion in the text above.

[13] In various versions this rule has been put forward by Fisher (who limited it to the case of productive opportunities with continuous gradations, calling the criterion "marginal rate of return over cost"), *Theory of Interest*, pp. 159–161; J. M. Keynes, who called the criterion "the marginal efficiency of capital," *The General Theory of Employment, Interest, and Money* (Harcourt, Brace & World, Inc., 1935), pp. 135–141; and Joel Dean, *Capital Budgeting* (Columbia Univ. Press, 1951), pp. 17–19. This rule is popular in business practice, at least among relatively sophisticated practitioners.

are here to be interpreted in the sense of Δq_t—increments to the payments of the project ensemble. Again, only if a project is "independent" will it be the case that the s_t are invariant with respect to the other members of the project ensemble adopted.

The analysis of this rule parallels that developed above for over-all ρ. The payments stream of the incremental project can be regarded as Challenger, while the zero on the left-hand side of (6) can be regarded as a "null stream" acting as Defender. Suppose we adopt the Challenger because $\rho_x > r$, and now someone proposes that we reverse the adoption. Then the payments stream for the "undoing" of Challenger will simply be the negative of that originally obtained for Challenger—calculation will reveal the same ρ_x for the undoing as for the original doing! Obviously, it is absurd to both do and undo, but was the original adoption correct? The answer depends, again, on whether the payments stream of the project is "later" than the null stream—that is, if the differences between Challenger and Defender (or, since the latter is null, we may speak directly of the elements of Challenger) are first nonpositive, then nonnegative.

Again, we obtain by analogy the result that if the Challenger payments stream for a project is later than the null sequence and $\rho_x > r$ (or earlier and $\rho_x < r$), then $V_0 > 0$—that is, the project represented by the Challenger stream will generate an increment of present value for the project set into which it enters.

On the other hand, if we have two mutually exclusive incremental projects a and b, both later than the null sequence, and if $\rho_a > \rho_b > r$, it does not follow that the present value of a is greater than that of b. This is immediately evident from the fact that the "sizes" of a and b may be very different: a may have a very high ρ, but be such a trivial project in size that b yields a greater increment of present value. We could then go on to calculate ρ on the *differences* between a and b as Challenger and Defender, but the comparison could be made only if one were clearly "later" than the other.

To sum up, only in certain special cases—where a project or set of projects is definitely "later" or "earlier" than an alternative—do the ρ, r comparison rules, whether over-all or incremental, provide clear guides. Where the rules are clear, they are equivalent to the corresponding versions of the present-value rule.

Hence it also follows that, provided they have clear meaning, the over-all and incremental ρ, r comparison rules are equivalent to each other. This is not surprising. If a particular project is being considered for adoption as an increment to a given ensemble, the ensemble as enhanced by that incremental project can be regarded as the Challenger relative to the original project set as Defender. Then, if the incremental project is "later" than the null project, the enhanced or Challenger ensemble must be "later" than the Defender. And if incremental ρ exceeds r for the project under consideration, the over-all ρ calculated on the differences between Challenger and Defender must obviously be exactly the same and so also be greater than r.

Leaving aside the defective rules involving *maximization* of an internal-rate criterion, the more useful internal-rate rules that run in terms of ρ, r comparisons are summarized in Table 3. The correspondences with the

Table 3

ρ, r **COMPARISON RULES**

Criterion	Computed on	Symbol	Rule*
Rate of return over cost (over-all ρ)	$\left\{\begin{array}{l} p_0^C - p_0^D, \ldots, p_T^C - p_T^D \\ q_0^C - q_0^D, \ldots, q_T^C - q_T^D \end{array}\right.$ $\left.\begin{array}{l}\rho \\ \rho \end{array}\right\}$		Choose "later" if $\rho > r$ and "earlier" if $\rho < r$
Project's internal rate (incremental ρ)	$s_0, \ldots, s_T$	ρ_x	Adopt project if $\rho_x > r$ and "later" than null project, or if $\rho_x < r$ and "earlier"

*Rules meaningful only if associated income streams can be unambiguously characterized as "earlier" and "later."

several present-value rules are evident, although, unlike the present-value rules, the internal-rate rules are meaningful only in a special class of cases.

NUMERICAL EXAMPLE

We can use again the projects a, b, and c described in Table 2. The last column shows the ρ_x calculated on the payments streams of the individual projects via equation (6). Since the projects are assumed independent, these sequences can be used in ρ, r comparisons with the null project—without regard to the other members of the adopted project ensembles. Note that both b and c have precisely the same incremental ρ (20 per cent), although b has negative and c has positive present value (at the market interest rate $r = 50$ per cent). But project b as Challenger is "later" than the null series as Defender, so the incremental comparison rule "adopt if $\rho_x > r$" is failed by b. Project c is "earlier," so the rule "adopt if $\rho_x < r$" is passed by c. Project a is "later," and it passes the relevant rule since its incremental ρ is 150 per cent. So a and c are adopted.

If we look at project sets, we can start with the null set as Defender and a alone as Challenger. Then a should clearly be adopted, and so becomes the Defender set for the next comparison. Now consider $a + b$ as Challenger against a alone. But the over-all comparison that runs in terms of the difference series between $a + b$ and a is clearly identical (again, given project independence) with the incremental comparison between b alone and the null series. The same applies to c. Consequently, we again end up with $a + c$ as the optimal set.

Other Proposed Criteria

We will here briefly review other criteria and associated rules occasionally encountered in the investment literature, but which will not be considered further in this volume.

Terminal value

The terminal value V_T for a given project is determined by compounding receipts and payments forward to some future date T rather than discounting them back to time 0:

$$V_T = s_0(1 + r)^T + s_1(1 + r)^{T-1} + \cdots + s_T \qquad (10)$$

Here T need not literally be the horizon, but can be any date after the last nonzero s_t of any of the projects considered. The corresponding rule is, of course, to adopt if $V_T > 0$. With obvious modifications, this rule could also be expressed in terms of an attained-wealth criterion W_T^P, or the wealth gain (value of the adopted project ensemble) W_T^Q. The parallel between discounted present value and compounded terminal value is complete, but it is more natural to deal with the current magnitudes represented by the former.

There can be differences between project evaluations in terms of V_0 and V_T, if the *reinvestment* rate r' at which "intermediate cash throwoffs" of a project can be compounded differs from the *discount* rate r employed in the present-value calculations.[14] Such cases cannot arise under the assumption of perfect funds markets. We will see in Chapter 7 that divergences between what are sometimes called the "borrowing rate" and "lending rate" can also be analyzed without introducing terminal-value concepts.

Reinvested rate of return

Some theorists have attempted to avoid the ambiguities of the internal-rate concept while still preserving a criterion in the form of a rate (percentage per unit of time) that can be compared with the rate of interest. One such proposal[15] is based on taking all the "intermediate cash throwoffs" of a multiperiod payment stream and reinvesting them at the external interest rate—or, for intermediate cash *inputs*, charging interest at the external interest rate—so as in effect to compound everything forward to the terminal time T. The result is that at time T, for every possible project a terminal measure will be obtained, which would be the V_T as defined above *except* for omitting the compounded current element s_0 (presumed to be an outlay or input o_0). The reinvested-rate criterion would then be defined for a particular

[14] See E. Solomon, "The Arithmetic of Capital-Budgeting Decisions," in E. Solomon (ed.), *The Management of Corporate Capital* (The Free Press of Glencoe, Inc., 1959), pp. 74–79.
[15] Solomon, *ibid.*

project as $\hat{\rho}$ in

$$\frac{s_1(1 + r)^{T-1} + s_2(1 + r)^{T-2} + \cdots + s_T}{o_0} = (1 + \hat{\rho})^T \qquad (11)$$

where o_0 is written in the denominator in place of $(-s_0)$. The reinvested-rate concept hews rather close to the idea of compounded growth of the original input o_0 into a terminal output. A parallel criterion can be constructed for an adopted ensemble of projects. The rules corresponding would direct a comparison of over-all or incremental $\hat{\rho}$ with r, adopting the investment project or set if $\hat{\rho} > r$. Note that the reinvested rate is not a pure "internal" rate, but mixes internal and external elements. It avoids the problem of defining "earlier" and "later" projects, since, if the initial s_0 is negative, the terminal measure *must* be positive (for the project to be worth consideration at all), so there is just one sign reversal. If the initial s_0 were positive, we would have a "disinvestment" project (assuming that the terminal measure will then be negative); the criterion for adoption would then become $\hat{\rho} < r$.

It is simple to show that the incremental reinvested-rate rule is equivalent to the incremental present-value rule. Thus, if we are dealing with an investment (as opposed to a disinvestment), and $\hat{\rho} > r$, then $V_0 > 0$.[16] A similar equivalence can be proved for the reinvested-rate and present-value rules both applied to project ensembles. Thus, the reinvested rate is a definite improvement upon the ordinary internal rate as investment criterion. However, the reinvested rate is really not a very handy concept. Whereas ρ is clearly an "internal" measure whose comparison with the "external" r has clear intuitive meaning, $\hat{\rho}$ already combines internal and external elements. We shall see later in the chapter that the ambiguities of the internal rate can be eliminated by a generalization that preserves the internal character of the criterion.

Payoff period

The criterion here is the length of time up to "payoff"—the date when the summed benefits (undiscounted, in the usual formulation) have recovered

---

[16] If $\hat{\rho} > r$, so that the incremental investment should be adopted, then

$$o_0(1 + \hat{\rho})^T > o_0(1 + r)^T$$

But the left-hand side of this inequality equals the numerator on the left in (11), interpreting the latter in an incremental sense. Now, subtracting $o_0(1 + r)^T$ from both sides of the inequality gives us

$$-o_0(1 + r)^T + s_1(1 + r)^{T-1} + \cdots + s_T > 0$$

But the left-hand side is just V_T (because $o_0 = -s_0$). The incremental present value is positive, since we saw above that $V_0 > 0$ if $V_T > 0$.

the summed costs—it being presumed that the flow of net benefits is consistently positive after an initial investment period. The rule, employed ordinarily only in an incremental version and for the choice between mutually exclusive projects, says to select that project with the shorter payoff period. It is obviously defective in ignoring possibly vast differences between projects accruing at dates later than payoff.

The survival of the rule in business practice may be due to the fact that it provides a way of allowing for uncertainty of the future. But it does so in the crudest of fashions, allowing full credit for receipts up to an arbitrary date, and no credit whatsoever afterward. We shall see in Part II that rules can be devised that allow for uncertainty in a correct, or at least a more defensible, manner.[17]

B. ELEMENTARY PARADIGMS OF INVESTMENT CHOICE

In this section theoretical solutions will be developed for two especially simple paradigms or frameworks for the analysis of intertemporal choice. The first paradigm, the two-period model, is the choice between c_0 and c_1—consumption this year and consumption next year—already introduced for illustrative purposes in Chapter 2. The second paradigm, the discrete-perpetuity model, epitomizes the investment decision problem in terms of choice between c_0 and c—consumption this year versus a level perpetual discrete sequence of annual consumptions, beginning next year (at time 1). These elementary choices can be regarded as "atoms of investment,"[18] building blocks for more complex investment decision patterns. The parallel between the intertemporal analysis here and the ordinary price-theory analysis reviewed in Chapter 1 will be quite evident.

Two-Period Model

Figures 3-1 and 3-2 represent (like Figs. 2-1 and 2-2) the two-period choices, first, of an individual with only market opportunities MM (a "rentier"), and second, of an individual with only productive opportunities PP (Robinson Crusoe). The productive opportunities are assumed to be *independent*, in the sense that adoption of any individual project does not

---

[17] A number of theorists have explored the very special conditions necessary in order for the payoff-period method to give answers consistent with the present-value or other rules. See, for example, H. Bierman, Jr. and S. Smidt, *The Capital Budgeting Decision* (The Macmillan Company, 1960), pp. 32–33; M. J. Gordon, "The Payoff Period and the Rate of Profit," in Solomon, *Management of Corporate Capital*, pp. 48–55.

[18] See A. P. Lerner, *The Economics of Control* (The Macmillan Company, 1944), Chap. 25.

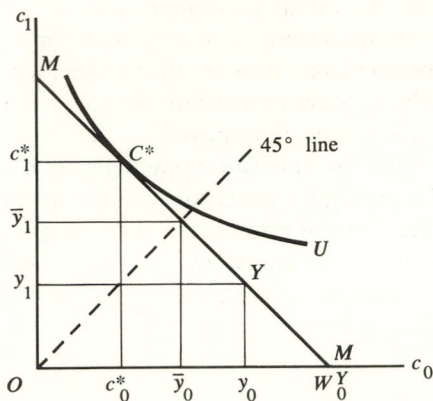

FIG. 3-1. Individual with market opportunities only

affect the net payments stream associated with any other. Such independence in the two-period analysis makes possible a unique ranking of projects in order of desirability (in terms of the ratio s_1/s_0 of payments associated with individual projects). Furthermore, it is assumed that projects are infinitesimal in scale, and that there is a smooth gradation of return per unit sacrifice; then s_1/s_0 can be regarded as the differential ratio or derivative dp_1/dp_0. These conditions define what will be called "regular" productive opportunities. They permit the PP curve in Fig. 3-2 to be shown as unique, continuous, and with smoothly flattening slope moving northwest (diminishing marginal returns as scale of investment increases). Each individual seeks his preferred

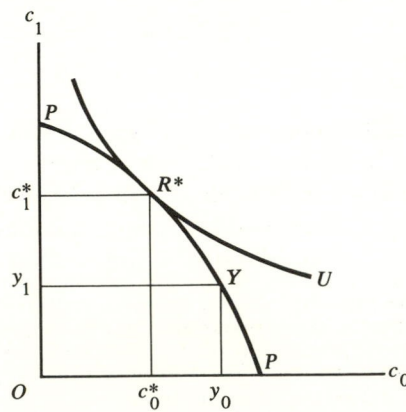

FIG. 3-2. Individual with productive opportunities only

position (attempts to attain the highest indifference curve possible). The respective tangency solutions are C^* in Fig. 3-1 and R^* in Fig. 3-2.

If we next assume that an individual has both the market opportunities of Fig. 3-1 *and* the productive opportunities of Fig. 3-2, his total opportunity set is represented in Fig. 3-3 as the area bounded by the market line $M'M'$

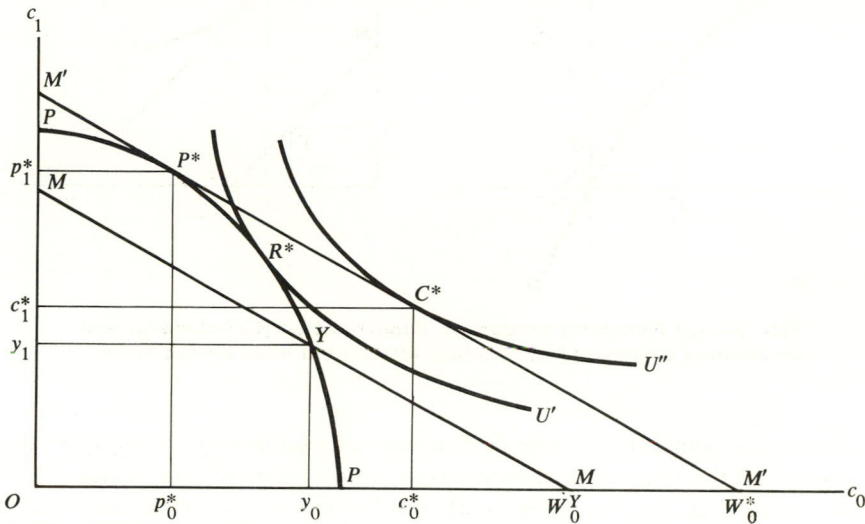

FIG. 3-3. Individual with productive and market opportunities combined

that just touches PP at P^*. As in Chapter 1, the optimizing process takes place in two stages. First, the individual undertakes physical investments to reach the "productive solution" P^* on the highest attainable market line. Second, he then borrows (gives up c_1 for c_0) to move along the market line to his preferred consumption position C^*. In this case physical investment was combined with market borrowing to "finance" the investment. More generally, physical investment or disinvestment would be possible, and either could be combined with market lending or borrowing—depending upon the shapes of the opportunity and preference functions. Note that the presence of market opportunities has shifted the productive solution away from the Robinson Crusoe position R^*, shown in Fig. 3-3 as the tangency of PP with U'. The market opportunities permit the individual to ignore—as Robinson Crusoe could not—his own time preferences in attaining the maximum-wealth position at P^*.

If we segregated the productive decision by adopting the concept of the firm as the agent of individuals specialized for production (as outlined in Chapter 1), the typical firm and typical individual would be represented by

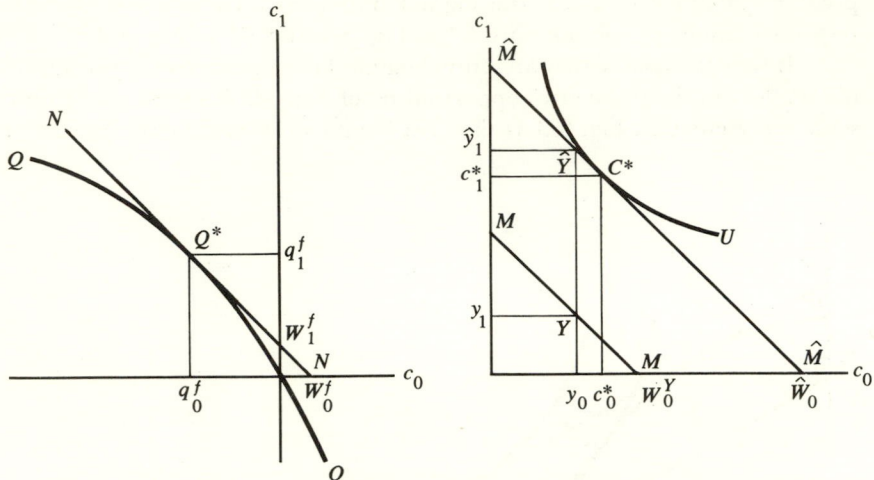

FIG. 3-4. (a) Firm with productive opportunities, (b) individual with endowment augmented by earnings distributed from owned firms

Figs. 3-4(a) and 3-4(b). The firm attains the solution Q^* along QQ. But note that if the firm invests it *must* borrow, since it has null endowment. The individual now has a simple market solution, but with an augmented endowment $\hat{Y}$. Assuming that the net incomes of firms are paid out entirely and in proportion to ownership, and that the payout is in c_1-units, the individual's augmented endowment $\hat{Y}$ is composed of elements $\hat{y}_0^i = y_0^i$, and $\hat{y}_1^i = y_1^i + \sum_{f=1}^{F} \epsilon_f^i W_1^f$. As in Chapter 1, ϵ_f^i is the fraction of the fth firm owned by the ith individual, and $W_1^f = q_1^f + q_0^f(1 + r_1)$ is the net income (after repayment of borrowing) of the fth firm in c_1-units.

For the situations illustrated by Figs. 3-1 and 3-2 we do not have either a decision-rule question or a financing problem: in Fig. 3-1 there are no productive investments to choose among, while in Fig. 3-2 there is no market for funds in which "financing" can take place. The problems of decision rules and financing arise where there are both market and productive opportunities—a situation represented in two different ways by Fig. 3-3 in the one case, and Figs. 3-4(a) and 3-4(b) together in the other.

The individual attaining the solution C^* in Fig. 3-3 must have *maximized present value* in the sense of attained wealth (W_0^*) in his productive decision. With the productive set PP available to him he has chosen the point P^*, on the highest market line he can attain $(M'M')$. But market lines, we know, are lines connecting combinations of equal present value, or alternatively we can say that wealth is the present-value measure of the combinations along the market line.[19] The highest attainable wealth W_0^P is that corresponding to the line $M'M'$. So the rule directing maximization of over-all present value is correct in this case—*subject to the qualification* mentioned above that the individual in productively attaining $P*$ will actually make the market transactions (in this case sell the titles to c_1, or equivalently borrow the c_0) necessary to consumptively attain $C*$.

This qualification takes on more significance when we turn to Figs. 3-4(a) and 3-4(b), representing a situation in which the productive decision is made by the firm, as agent possibly for a number of individuals. One might wonder whether the *firm* should maximize wealth in its productive decisions. Or should it instead try somehow to take account of the time preferences of its owners—which will, in general, not be mutually consistent? But, given perfect markets for the exchange of c_0 and c_1, there is no difficulty caused by this separation of productive and consumptive decisions. The firm maximizes over-all present value (wealth) at $Q*$, and then distributes the proceeds of the investment (after repaying the borrowings) to owners—whether in the form of W_0^f or W_1^f does not matter, though the illustration makes the distribution in c_1-units. Each individual is then free to attain his consumptive optimum as a rentier by moving, via market transactions only, from his enhanced endowment $\hat{Y}$ to his preferred consumptive combination.

The principle that, given perfect and complete markets, the *productive* decision is to be governed solely by the objective market criterion represented by attained wealth—without regard to the individuals' subjective preferences that enter into their *consumptive* decisions—will appear repeatedly throughout this study. We will call this principle the *Separation Theorem*. The precise conditions for its validity will be examined in detail in later chapters, when the perfect-markets assumption is relaxed.

It should be noted that in a world of certainty the individual need not personally "finance" the investment (actually provide the current c_0-input) from his own y_0-endowment—for he will be able to borrow the full productive input (plus any consumptive increment of c_0 over his endowed y_0 that he desires and can pay for in c_1-units) on the strength of the prospective future c_1-yield of his investment. In fact, the latter is the better way of thinking about the problem, because it permits an individual to undertake investments for which the current c_0-input required is larger than his endowed y_0 (i.e., investments for which $P*$ lies in the second quadrant, to the left of the origin). And similarly for the firm: it need not obtain the required c_0-input from its owners, because the entire amount can be borrowed on the market using the security of the prospective returns from investment. While this has been shown only for a highly special case, it is evident that the conclusion would apply under extended time-horizons, and for other generalizations

[19] The equation of any two-period market line is $c_0 + c_1/(1 + r_1) = W_0$, where the constant W_0 is the present value.

to be presented shortly. Given the postulated world of certainty, and with perfect funds markets, investments can be financed entirely by market borrowing (i.e., the owners of the investment opportunity need not put in any "equity" contribution).

We have seen that the present-value rule, in the version that calls for the adoption of the ensemble of projects maximizing attained wealth W_0^P of the decision-making agent, is correct in this case—i.e., it is a first step toward attainment of the best possible consumption combination C^*. We know from the preceding discussion that the other versions of the present-value rule are equivalent, so a brief comment will suffice. The second version of the present-value rule calls for adoption of the project ensemble of maximal present value. The present-value line associated in Fig. 3-3 with the endowment Y is MM, and the corresponding endowed-wealth measure is W_0^Y, or the length $\overline{OM}$ along the c_0-axis. The line $M'M'$ represents the highest present value W_0^P attainable, that associated with the productive solution P^*. This highest W_0^P is denoted W_0^*, or geometrically $\overline{OM}'$ along the c_0-axis. The present value of the ensemble of projects adopted is then $W_0^* - W_0^Y$ or $\overline{MM}'$, and of course this must be the project set of greatest present value. The third version of the present-value rule says to adopt any project for which incremental present value is positive. In Fig. 3-3 the increments are infinitesimal because of the continuity of the productive-opportunity locus PP. Since infinitesimal movements up and to the left along PP represent successive adoptions of marginal projects, we are directed to keep moving so long as PP keeps crossing higher lines of constant present value (wealth). We are thus led to the same solution at P^* on the highest attainable market line.

Turning to the internal-rate concept, the several rules using that criterion—in contrast with the versions of the present-value rules—are not all logically equivalent. The simple ρ-maximization rule (which unconditionally maximized the over-all internal rate), in this case as in general leads to an absurd result: it calls for adoption of the single project of greatest internal rate, implying only an infinitesimal movement in Fig. 3-3 along PP from Y. The conditional ρ-maximization rule requires the scale of investment to be arbitrarily given. It directs us here to choose the point on PP corresponding to some given $p_0 = y_0 + q_0$ on the horizontal axis—i.e., it tells us to choose a point on the upper boundary PP rather than any lower point in the interior of the set OPP. The rule is, in this case, trivial, in addition to its failure to specify how the correct p_0 is to be determined.

The rules directing a comparison of ρ and r (r_1 in the two-period model) are more interesting. The application of the over-all ρ, r comparison rule in this model can be seen in Fig. 3-5—which isolates three productive income-stream vectors from the opportunity set PP of Fig. 3-3. The vector P^* representing the productive optimum is to be compared with two others. P', to the southeast, is "earlier" than P^*; its p_0 is greater and p_1 smaller than the

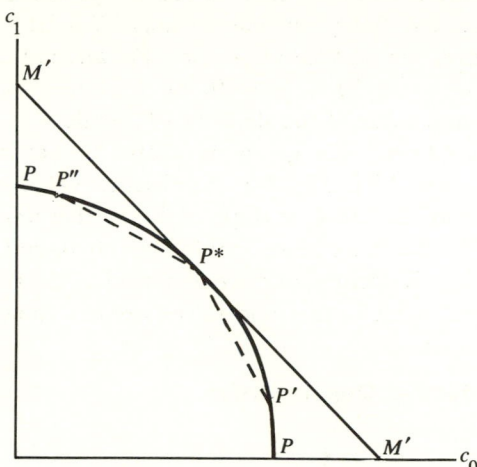

FIG. 3-5. ρ, r comparisons

corresponding elements of P^*. P'', to the northwest, is "later" than P^*. (Ambiguity as to later versus earlier cannot arise in the two-period model, since there can be but one sign reversal in the difference sequence between any pair of attained income streams.) The market line $M'M'$ through P^*, like all market lines, has the absolute slope $(1 + r_1)$.[20] The dashed lines between the pair P^* and P', and between the pair P^* and P'', have the absolute slopes $(1 + \rho)$, where ρ is in each case calculated on the difference sequence between each pair.[21]

Now, since P' regarded as Challenger is earlier than P^* as Defender, P' should be chosen if $\rho < r_1$—geometrically, if the dashed line between P' and P^* is flatter than the market lines. But the dashed line here is steeper, so $\rho > r_1$ and P' as Challenger is rejected. On the other hand, if the roles of Challenger and Defender were reversed, P^* as Challenger would be later than P'. Then, since $\rho < r_1$, the Challenger would be successful, and again P^* is shown to be superior. A corresponding analysis with P'' as Challenger against P^* would again leave P^* victorious—since P'' is later than P^* while $\rho < r_1$.

Thus, in the two-period model the over-all ρ, r comparison rule does get us to the correct productive solution P^* associated with the maximum attained wealth W_0^*. It is immediately apparent that the incremental ρ, r comparison rule will do the same, by a slightly different process. The

[20] Along any market line, $c_0 + c_1/(1 + r_1) = W_0$, so that $dc_1/dc_0 = -(1 + r_1)$.

[21] Between P^* and P', ρ is defined in $(p_0^* - p_0') + (p_1^* - p_1')/(1 + \rho) = 0$. Between P^* and P'', of course, the elements of P'' replace those of P' above. Note that for a given pair ρ remains the same, in whichever direction the comparison is made.

latter directs us to move incrementally (again the increments would be infinitesimal, by the assumption here of regular productive opportunities) northwest—i.e., toward "later" income streams—if ρ defined in terms of the increments exceeds r_1—or southeast if $\rho < r_1$. For an infinitesimal increment, ρ is defined in $dp_0 + dp_1/(1 + \rho) = 0$, or $1 + \rho = -dp_1/dp_0$. That is, $1 + \rho$ is the absolute value of the slope of PP, while $1 + r_1$ is the absolute slope of the market lines. The geometry shows us that moving northwest from Y along the curve PP in Fig. 3-3, the absolute value of the slope $1 + \rho$ is in fact greater than the absolute slope of the market lines $1 + r_1$ until we get to the point P^*. But if we move any further northwest, $\rho < r_1$. We are once again led to P^*. Evidently, in the two-period model the ρ, r comparison rules are equivalent to each other and to the present-value rules.

Nonregular Productive Opportunities

Now consider a situation just as before except that the productive opportunities are no longer "regular." Projects could be interdependent (the returns from one depend upon the other elements of the ensemble adopted),

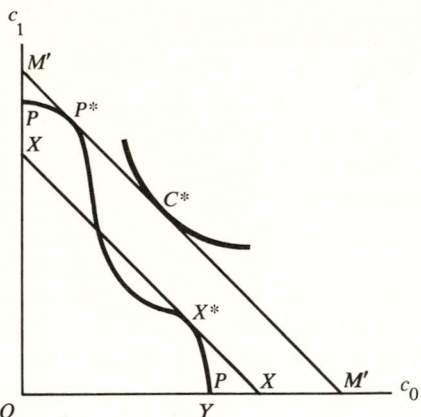

FIG. 3-6. Interdependent productive opportunities: poorer projects prerequisite to better ones

which implies that they cannot be simply ordered in terms of diminishing incremental productivity. Or productive opportunities could be *discrete*, so that investments of infinitesimal scale would not be always available. Figures 3-6 through 3-9 display different types of nonregularity.[22]

---

[22] In these diagrams the endowment point Y is placed along the horizontal axis: i.e., the endowment consists exclusively of current funds. This has been done solely to simplify the representation.

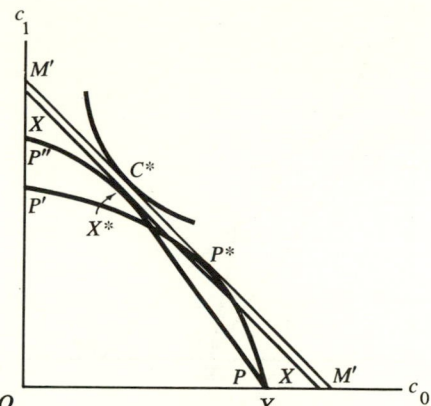

FIG. 3-7. Interdependent productive opportunities: alternative investment sets

Figure 3-6 illustrates *interdependence* such that it is at times necessary to adopt relatively unproductive investments as prerequisites for higher-yielding ones; the *PP* curve then has a region of increasing absolute slope. Here it is necessary to distinguish the true productive solution $P*$ from the "false solution" $X*$ along *PP*. $X*$ is a false solution, since it would make impossible the attainment of a consumption vector as desirable as $C*$; the individual adopting the set of productive projects implied by $X*$ would be constrained to market trading along *XX* rather than $M'M'$. In Fig. 3-7 we see a somewhat different interdependence pattern. Here the idea is that *PP'*

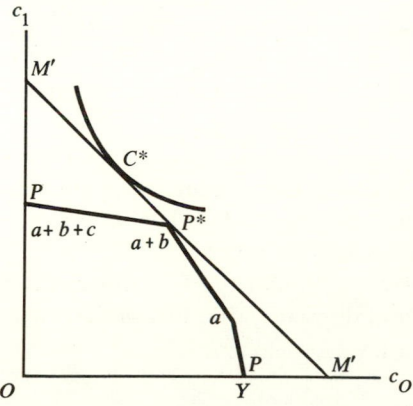

FIG. 3-8. Discrete but independent productive opportunities

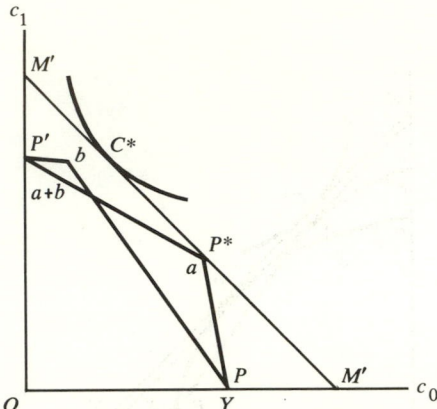

FIG. 3-9. Discrete and interdependent productive opportunities

and PP'' represent alternative (i.e., mutually exclusive) productive invest-ment sets. Thus, a company might be considering agricultural development of certain lands at varying scales or intensities, or alternatively industrial development of the lands—but it cannot do both. Here the set PP' is relatively more productive for smaller scales of development, but PP'' dominates for larger scales. Again, there is a correct solution $P*$ as well as a false solution $X*$.

In terms of the decision rules, we see by inspection that maximizing attained wealth, or choosing the set of projects of greatest over-all present value, leads always to the correct $P*$; wealth along $M'M'$ is greater than along XX. The incremental version of the present-value rule also leads to $P*$, but here to avoid error the investor *must* consider noninfinitesimal as well as infinitesimal increments. Thus, in Fig. 3-6 if he moved along PP by infinitesimal increments only he would be led to point $X*$—since from $X*$, all infinitesimal changes entail reductions in present value. He can get to $P*$ only if he considers finite jumps taking him from $X*$ to some point on PP lying above the line XX. A similar argument applies to the situation illus-trated in Fig. 3-7.

The analysis in terms of the ρ, r comparison rules is quite analogous. Moving incrementally along the productive-opportunity locus would lead the investor to the correct $P*$, provided that, where called for, jumps as well as infinitesimal movements were taken.

In Fig. 3-8 we see nonregularity of PP due not to interdependence but to the limited number of discrete individual projects available (a, b, and c).[23]

---

[23] The lines connecting the points a, $a + b$, and $a + b + c$ are merely to guide the eye. Only the named specific points (the vertices of the polygon) are supposed to be actually attainable by productive transformations.

The present-value rules take us correctly to P^*, as do the ρ, r comparison rules—provided that the incremental rules are interpreted so as to permit the necessary noninfinitesimal comparisons, of course. The conditional ρ-maximization rule, as always, directs us only to choose a point on PP (i.e., to go to the boundary rather than the interior of the productive-opportunity set). Figure 3-9 combines discreteness and interdependence for two projects a and b. Here a and b can be adopted either separately or jointly, but the adoption of a makes b less productive than it would otherwise be, and adoption of b makes a less productive. This does not absolutely preclude their joint adoption, but in the case illustrated the productive solution P^* entails adoption of a alone.

Discrete-Perpetuity Model

Especially in dealing with questions concerning "capital" (to be discussed in Chapter 6), some economists characteristically pose the problem of intertemporal decision as a choice between current consumption c_0 and perpetual or "permanent" future income flows. The discrete-perpetuity model interprets the latter as a level annual sequence of consumptions, symbolized here as c, beginning at time 1 (one year from the present) and extending to infinity.

Fortunately, the analytical solution to the simple discrete-perpetuity model need not be developed in detail, since everything moves quite in parallel with the two-period model. The reason is that the decisions still involve only two objects of choice—c_0 and c instead of c_0 and c_1. Hence, one or two illustrative comments will suffice to give the picture.

In Fig. 3-10 we see illustrated the endowment vector Y, the preference function, and the market line MM associated with the endowed wealth W_0^Y. The vertical axis here is c, the level discretized consumption sequence running from time 1 to infinity. In general, the endowment $Y = (y_0, y)$ will not have $y_0 = y$. The 45° line defines points where $c_0 = c$, and along the 45° line we can pick off the *equalized* (or "net") income vector $(\bar{y}_0, \bar{y})$, where $\bar{y}_0 = \bar{y}$. The equation of the market line MM is

$$W_0^Y = y_0 + \frac{y}{r} \tag{12}$$

employing the result obtained in the previous chapter that s/r is the present value of an infinite sequence of level payments s starting at time 1. The slope of the market line is $-r$. The wealth constraint may also be expressed as $W_0^Y = \phi_0 y_0 + \phi_\infty y$, where ϕ_0 is the price of a unit of c_0 and ϕ_∞ is the price

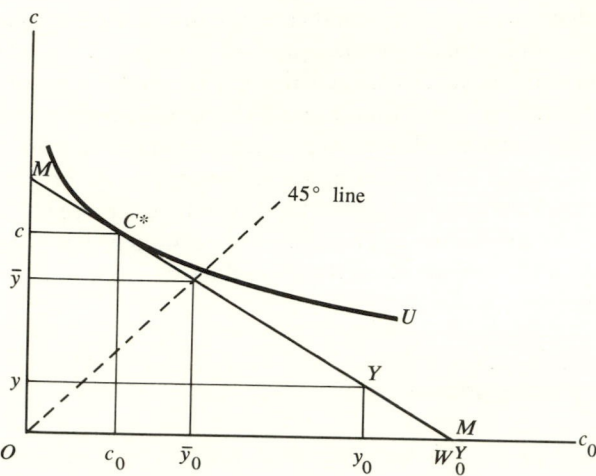

FIG. 3-10. Choice between current consumption and perpetuity (individual with market opportunities only)

of the unit perpetuity starting at time 1. With c_0 taken as numeraire, we then have $\phi_0 = 1$ and $\phi_\infty = 1/r$.

Figure 3-10 corresponds, except for the different "atom of investment," to Fig. 3-1 in representing an individual with market opportunities only. We could construct a whole set of diagrams corresponding to Figs. 3-2 through 3-5, merely by replacing the vertical axis c_1 of the earlier diagrams by the axis c, making the appropriate changes in the shapes of the curves. The entire group of revised diagrams would represent, successively, the choices of an individual with market and with productive opportunities, and with both together, and then the associated productive and consumptive choices of a firm and individual. Furthermore, by dropping the assumption of regular productive opportunities, we could then go on to construct diagrams corresponding to Figs. 3-6 through 3-9. In every case the geometrical solutions are perfectly analogous to those of the two-period model.

Algebraically, the correspondences are also quite direct. Maximum attained wealth in the perpetuity model is $W_0^* = p_0^* + p^*/r$, where (p_0^*, p^*) are the coordinates of the productive solution P^*. This solution is the attainable income stream of maximum present value. The analysis for the ρ, r comparison rules is also essentially the same. The main difference is that in the perpetuity case the slope along the market lines is $-r$, so that the absolute slope directly represents the rate of interest. The internal rate ρ, calculated on the differences between a Challenger and a Defender along PP, would be the absolute slope of the chord between the respective income vectors along the productive-opportunity locus (corresponding to the dashed lines shown in Fig. 3-5).[24] In terms of infinitesimal increments ρ would be the absolute slope along the locus itself.[25]

C. GENERAL DISCRETIZED MODEL: ARBITRARY HORIZON T

We can now leave the elementary solutions and turn to the general case in which time is treated as a sequence of discretized periods extending from $t = 0$ to an arbitrary horizon $t = T$, where T may be infinite. The objects of choice are $c_0, c_1, \ldots, c_T$; any basket or consumption combination can be represented by a point or vector in a $(T + 1)$-dimensional space. Figure 3-11 is a diagrammatic representation for $T = 2$. Here the endowment Y has the coordinates (y_0, y_1, y_2). The triangular construction is a section of the "market plane" $MM'M''$ (a three-dimensional generalization of the two-dimensional market *line*) through Y. The equation of the market plane can be written as

$$W_0^Y = \phi_0 y_0 + \phi_1 y_1 + \phi_2 y_2$$

Or, with c_0 as numeraire and using discounting notation,

$$W_0^Y = y_0 + \frac{y_1}{1 + r_1} + \frac{y_2}{(1 + r_2)(1 + r_1)} \tag{13}$$

For general T:

$$W_0^Y = y_0 + \frac{y_1}{1 + r_1} + \cdots + \frac{y_T}{(1 + r_T) \cdots (1 + r_2)(1 + r_1)} \tag{14}$$

Note that r is not taken as constant over time: there are different discounting rates r_1 between time 1 and time 0, r_2 between time 2 and time 1, and so on. In Fig. 3-11 endowed wealth W_0^Y is represented by the c_0-intercept of the $MM'M''$ plane. The slope of $MM'M''$ in the plane formed by the axes c_0 and c_1 is $-(1 + r_1)$; in the plane formed by c_1 and c_2 the slope

---

[24] Let P' and $P*$ be Challenger and Defender points along PP in the construction on (c_0, c) axes analogous to Fig. 3-5. Then ρ would be defined in

$$p_0' + \frac{p'}{\rho} = p_0^* + \frac{p^*}{\rho} \quad \text{so that} \quad \rho = -\frac{p' - p^*}{p_0' - p^*}$$

the absolute value of the slope between the points.

[25] Here, between any two infinitesimally separated points on PP, using the differential notation dp and dp_0 to indicate the vertical and horizontal differences or increments, $0 = dp_0 + dp/\rho$. Then $\rho = -dp/dp_0$—the absolute slope along the curve.

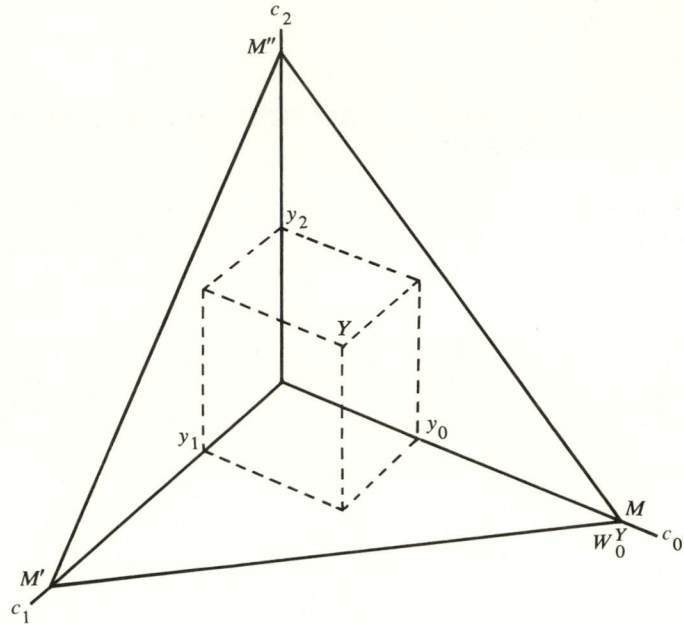

FIG. 3-11. Choice among consumptions of times 0, 1, and 2

is $-(1 + r_2)$; and in the plane formed by c_0 and c_2 the slope is $-(1 + r_2) \times (1 + r_1)$. The preference function is not graphed in Fig. 3-11; loci of indifference among alternative consumption baskets would be represented by three-dimensional shells convex to the origin, nested like the skins of an onion. Finally, there would be a productive-opportunity locus (also not displayed in Fig. 3-11) that, if "regular," would be a unique three-dimensional surface everywhere concave to the origin. An individual possessing productive opportunities can in general attain a wealth level W_0^P greater than that represented by the market value of his endowment (i.e., he can attain a market plane higher than the plane $MM'M''$ going through his endowment).

In order to deal with more than three dimensions ($T > 2$), it is necessary to turn to algebraic rather than diagrammatic representation. This is not the place to present the entire system of equations for choice over time, in parallel with those of Chapter 1 for timeless choice, since the analysis here covers only the optimizing decisions of the economic agent. However, it will be useful to present the algebra for the productive decision alone. "Regularity conditions" will be assumed. If the regularity conditions did not hold, the investor's optimum could not be determined simply by marginal equalities between slopes of the productive locus and the market hyperplane (i.e., as a tangency). It would have to be expressed in the form of rather complex inequalities, to allow for the multidimensional analogues of the various types of nonregularities illustrated for the two-dimensional case in Figs. 3-6 through 3-9.

Let the equation for the individual's productive opportunities (or constraint) be $P(p_0, p_1, \ldots, p_T) = 0$. Or, regarding the opportunities as transformations of an endowment sequence, they could be denoted as $Q(q_0, q_1, \ldots, q_T) = 0$. Subject to the constraint of this opportunity set, the agent attempts to maximize attained wealth W_0^P. The necessary conditions resulting are:[26]

$$\left.\frac{\partial p_1}{\partial p_0}\right|_P = -(1 + r_1)$$

$$\left.\frac{\partial p_2}{\partial p_1}\right|_P = -(1 + r_2)$$

$$\cdot$$
$$\cdot$$
$$\cdot$$
$$\tag{15}$$

$$\left.\frac{\partial p_T}{\partial p_{T-1}}\right|_P = -(1 + r_T)$$

[26] We use the usual method of Lagrangian multipliers for maximizing subject to a constraint. Let $\mathscr{L} = W_0^P - \lambda P(p_0, p_1, \ldots, p_T)$, where λ is the Lagrangian multiplier, $W_0^P = p_0 + p_1/(1 + r_1) + \cdots + p_T/[(1 + r_T) \cdots (1 + r_2)(1 + r_1)]$, and $P(p_0, p_1, \ldots, p_T) = 0$ is the productive-opportunity constraint. The necessary conditions for an optimum are

$$\frac{\partial \mathscr{L}}{\partial p_0} = 1 - \lambda \left(\frac{\partial P}{\partial p_0}\right) \qquad\qquad = 0$$

$$\frac{\partial \mathscr{L}}{\partial p_1} = \frac{1}{1 + r_1} - \lambda \left(\frac{\partial P}{\partial p_1}\right) \qquad\qquad = 0$$

$$\cdot$$
$$\cdot$$
$$\cdot$$

$$\frac{\partial \mathscr{L}}{\partial p_T} = \frac{1}{(1 + r_T) \cdots (1 + r_2)(1 + r_1)} - \lambda \left(\frac{\partial P}{\partial p_T}\right) = 0$$

Therefore

$$\left.\frac{\partial p_1}{\partial p_0}\right|_P = \frac{-\partial P/\partial p_0}{\partial P/\partial p_1} = \frac{-1/\lambda}{1/\lambda(1 + r_1)} \qquad\qquad = -(1 + r_1)$$

$$\left.\frac{\partial p_2}{\partial p_1}\right|_P = \frac{-\partial P/\partial p_1}{\partial P/\partial p_2} = \frac{-1/[\lambda(1 + r_1)]}{1/[\lambda(1 + r_2)(1 + r_1)]} \qquad = -(1 + r_2)$$

$$\cdot$$
$$\cdot$$
$$\cdot$$

$$\left.\frac{\partial p_T}{\partial p_{T-1}}\right|_P = \frac{-\partial P/\partial p_{T-1}}{\partial P/\partial p_T} = \frac{-1/[\lambda(1 + r_{T-1}) \cdots (1 + r_2)(1 + r_1)]}{1/[\lambda(1 + r_T) \cdots (1 + r_2)(1 + r_1)]} = -(1 + r_T)$$

The partial derivatives here represent the slopes of the productive-opportunity locus with respect to transformations between the p's of successive dates—e.g., between p_{t-1} and p_t. Of course, since $q_t = p_t - y_t$, $\partial p_t/\partial p_{t-1} \equiv \partial q_t/\partial q_{t-1}$, so that the same relations could be expressed in terms of the transformation derivatives $\partial q_t/\partial q_{t-1}$. And if the firm rather than the individual were making the production decisions, the partial derivatives would be $\partial q_t^f/\partial q_{t-1}^f$. Between each such pair the slope is set equal, in absolute value, to one plus the interest rate connecting the same pair of successive dates.

A different way of representing the same multidimensional solution would be in terms of opportunities between the pair of dates 0, t rather than between the typical pair of *successive* dates $t - 1$, t. In other words, instead of comparing each period with its predecessor, we can compare it with time 0. In either representation, with $T + 1$ objects of choice there are just T comparisons to be made. Now the reciprocal of $(1 + r_t) \cdots (1 + r_2)(1 + r_1)$ is the factor discounting dollars of time t into dollars of time 0. Or, we can say, $\phi_t = 1/[(1 + r_t) \cdots (1 + r_2)(1 + r_1)]$. The necessary conditions for the productive solution are[27]

$$\left.\frac{\partial p_1}{\partial p_0}\right|_P = -(1 + r_1) \qquad\qquad = -\frac{1}{\phi_1}$$

$$\left.\frac{\partial p_2}{\partial p_0}\right|_P = -(1 + r_2)(1 + r_1) \qquad = -\frac{1}{\phi_2}$$

$$\cdot$$
$$\cdot$$
$$\cdot$$

$$\left.\frac{\partial p_T}{\partial p_0}\right|_P = -(1 + r_T) \cdots (1 + r_2)(1 + r_1) = -\frac{1}{\phi_T}$$

$$(16)$$

That is, in each case the slope along the productive-opportunity locus is set equal to the slope of the corresponding market line for exchanges between c_t and c_0. This formulation is closer to the discussion in Chapter 1, in which commodities B, . . . , G were exchanged against the same numeraire A.

In considering decision rules for the general discretized case, it is evident that the various versions of the present-value rule all remain correct—since they lead the investor to the highest wealth level W_0^*, thus permitting attainment of the best consumption basket C^*. Furthermore, the present-value rules extend without difficulty to the case of changing interest rates over time $(r_1, r_2, \ldots, r_T$ not all equal), since the definition of W_0^P does not require r to be constant. And, given perfect markets for dated income claims, the

---

[27] We obtain these, using the method of Lagrangian multipliers as in the previous footnote. At the last step, however, we make the divisions appropriate for forming the derivatives $\partial p_t/\partial p_0$ rather than $\partial p_t/\partial p_{t-1}$.

present-value rules apply even if the productive opportunities are not regular, by direct analogy with our discussion earlier for the two-period case.

But for the ρ, r comparison rules, a number of interesting questions arise. In the two-period case $(T = 1)$, the ρ, r comparison rules, like the present-value rules to which they were then equivalent, gave correct results. The question is whether this holds also for general T. The seemingly obvious way to proceed is to use the multiperiod internal-rate criterion, as already defined in equation (5), for comparison with r. Since a number of theorists and practitioners have supported and used this multiperiod criterion and rule, a full discussion of how and why the rule fails will be presented here. In the course of the discussion, we shall see how the correct two-period ρ, r comparison rule *should* be generalized to continue to be correct in application to multiperiod investments.

Note, first of all, that the usual formulation directing a comparison of multiperiod ρ with *the* rate of interest r presumes that r will be constant over time—a condition that does not hold in the general case. The natural specification of the rule for nonconstant r is as follows: Adopt if multiperiod ρ is such that $(1 + \rho)^T > (1 + r_T) \cdots (1 + r_2)(1 + r_1)$. If ρ is interpreted as a growth rate, this specification suggests that a dollar invested in the process at time 0 grows faster to time T than a dollar compounded at market interest. But the failure of the proposed rule can be shown even granting the assumption of constant r.

Consider a particular three-period investment opportunity[28] that can be characterized as $(-1, 2, 1)$. This notation indicates an outlay of 1 dollar at time 0, a receipt of 2 at time 1 and further receipt of 1 dollar at time 2. Direct calculation shows the multiperiod ρ for this opportunity to equal $\sqrt{2}$, or 141.4 per cent.[29] And, in fact, if the rate of interest r (assumed constant over time) is less than $\sqrt{2}$, the investment can be shown to be desirable by

---

[28] This is a discrete opportunity, or project. However, there is nothing to preclude the interpretation that all the projects used here for illustrative purposes are of infinitesimal rather than discrete scale. Thus, the failure of multiperiod ρ is not due to abandoning of the "regularity conditions."

[29] Mathematically, ρ is the root of the formula for the present value of a productive opportunity. If we denote the annual elements s_0, s_1, and s_2—and let s_0 equal -1—the formula for the roots is

$$\rho = \frac{(s_1 - 2) \pm \sqrt{s_1^2 + 4s_2}}{2}$$

We can ignore the negative square root, in any case where s_1 and s_2 are both positive (in other words, where there is only one sign reversal of the payments sequence), since this root will be less than -1. (Only fractional negative values for ρ need be considered, because $\rho = -100$ per cent implies that the original outlay s_0 is totally lost with no return.)

These illustrations are chosen for convenient numerical values of ρ, which will typically be larger than one would ordinarily expect to encounter in practice (e.g., 141.4 per cent, 200 per cent, and so on). The principles involved are, of course, unaffected.

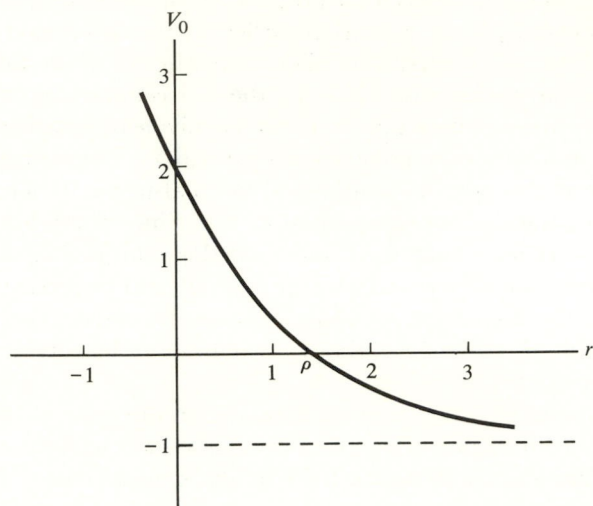

FIG. 3-12.   Present value and internal rate of option $(-1, 2, 1)$

the present-value rule. Figure 3-12 plots the present value V_0 of this opportunity as a function of the discounting rate r. As may be seen, the present
value is declining as r increases throughout the relevant[30] range (from
$r = -1$ to $r = +\infty$). The internal rate ρ is that r for which the present
value is zero. Evidently, for any $r < \rho$ the present value V_0 is positive, so
that the project should then be adopted—the reverse holding if $r > \rho$.

However, the fact that the comparison of ρ and r leads to the correct
decision in a particular case or class of cases does not mean that it is correct
in principle. And in fact, the defects of the rule under consideration were
first discovered by its failure in certain special cases. One example is the
choice between two investment opportunities that are mutually exclusive
alternatives. Then the one with the higher ρ is not in general the correct one
to adopt, even if we eliminate the size factor[31] so as to make the initial outlay
the same in each case. In fact, the decision as between the two projects
cannot be correctly made, in general, without knowledge of the appropriate
external discounting rate. This is illustrated in Fig. 3-13, which portrays two
such alternative opportunities.   Opportunity a is $(-1, 2, 1)$ as before.

---

[30] As indicated in the previous footnote, the function is mathematically defined and
has another root in the nonrelevant range to the left of $r = -1$. It has an infinite discontinuity
at $r = -1$, jumping from $+\infty$ to $-\infty$. This is due to the division by $(1 + r)$ in the discounting formula.

[31] As indicated earlier, internal-rate rules fail to deal properly with scale problems
for nonindependent projects. It would obviously be foolish to choose a high-ρ project of
trivial scale if it precluded adopting a very large project with slightly lower ρ.

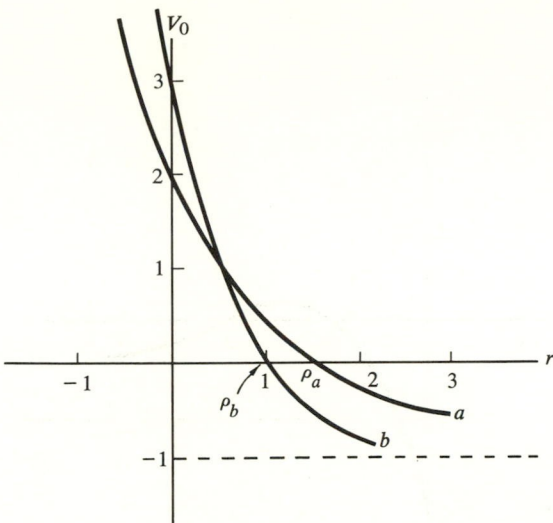

FIG. 3-13. Comparison of options $a = (-1, 2, 1)$ and $b = (-1, 0, 4)$

Opportunity b is $(-1, 0, 4)$. Evidently, b is superior in present value at low rates of interest, while a is superior at high rates of interest. The internal rate for a is higher (141.4 per cent as compared with 100 per cent for b), but that does not conclusively make a preferable to b. At a rate of interest such as 10 per cent, for example, adoption of b permits attaining a higher wealth level W_0^P.

An even more fundamental difficulty was revealed when investigators discovered that ρ may not be unique—there may be more than one seeming solution or root of the defining equation within the relevant range. Consider, for example, the investment opportunity $(-1, 5, -6)$, plotted in Fig. 3-14. Calculation and geometry both reveal roots at 100 per cent and 200 per cent. Inspection of the diagram reveals that the opportunity has positive present value when r ranges between 100 per cent and 200 per cent, but has negative present worth otherwise. In other words, the opportunity is worthy of adoption *only* when the interest rate is between 100 and 200 per cent. Still more complex cases can arise when more time periods are admitted. For example, the opportunity $(-1, 6, -11, 6)$ plotted in Fig. 3-15 has three roots in the relevant range. Again, inspection of the present values in the diagram tells us immediately that the project is worthy of adoption if r is negative, *or* if r lies between 100 and 200 per cent—but not otherwise.

The alternation of signs in the receipt stream determines the possibility of multiple ρ's. Descartes' rule of signs tells us that the number of solutions in the allowable range (the number of points where present value equals zero, for $r > -1$) is at most equal to the number of reversals of sign in the

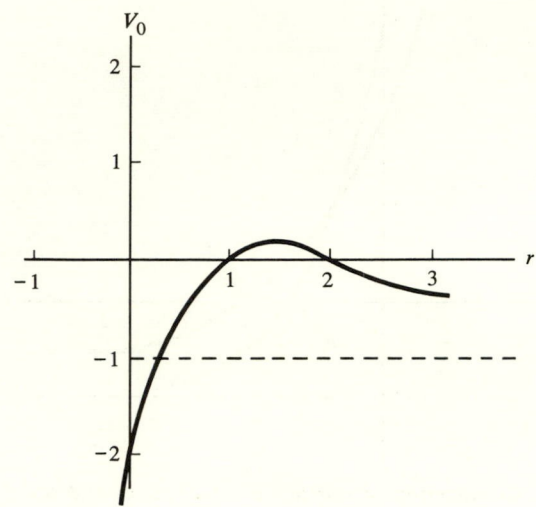

FIG. 3-14.   Sketch of option (−1, 5, −6)

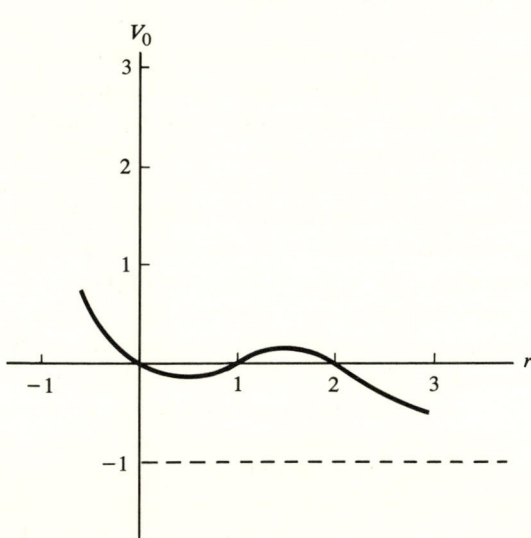

FIG. 3-15.   Sketch of option (−1, 6, −11, 6)

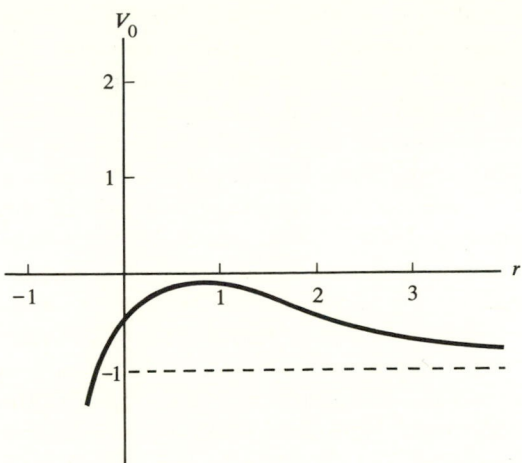

FIG. 3-16. Sketch of option $(-1, 3, -2\frac{1}{2})$

receipts sequence. Therefore, a two-period investment has at most a single ρ, a three-period sequence at most a dual ρ, and so on.

In fact, investment opportunities may have *no* internal rates (when the present-value equation has only imaginary roots). An example is the opportunity $(-1, 3, -2\frac{1}{2})$. Figure 3-16 shows that its present value is always negative in the relevant range. This is, nevertheless, a perfectly respectable opportunity: there exist interest-rate patterns for which the project *would* be desirable—though it is never desirable for any single constant rate of interest. It may be verified that for this project, if $r_1 = 100$ per cent and $r_2 = 200$ per cent, the present value would be $+\frac{1}{12}$.

These examples may serve to remind us of the difficulty about "earlier" and "later" discussed above. It was pointed out that ρ, r comparison rules give no clear indication unless one alternative is clearly "later" than the other—i.e., unless there is only one sign reversal in the stream of income differences or payments $s_0, s_1, \ldots, s_T$. Thus the multiple-root problem arises precisely in the case where the ρ, r comparison rule was seen earlier to be ambiguous. The project $(-1, 5, -6)$, for example, is *not* clearly "later" than the null alternative, and so we had no reason to assume that it was an *investment* project (for which the rule would be: adopt if $\rho > r$) rather than a *disinvestment* project (for which the rule would be: adopt if $\rho < r$). Those espousing the multiperiod ρ rule have been content, it would appear, to infer from the negative sign of the very first element (current outlay) that the project is an investment. But, as we shall see, where there is more than one sign reversal the project is really a combination of an investment and a disinvestment.

The multiperiod ρ criterion and the corresponding rule are thus quite thoroughly discredited as guides to multiperiod investment decision—although the simple two-period ρ, r comparison rule *was* valid for two-period investments. But, one may ask, is there perhaps a somewhat different generalization of the two-period ρ, r comparison rule that does lead to correct multiperiod decisions? And actually there is. The correct generalization for infinitesimal investments is indicated by the optimum conditions of equations (15). These equate, between *every pair* of successive periods $t-1$ and t, the marginal rate of productive substitution between p_{t-1} and p_t with $1+r_t$. This is equivalent to equating the marginal "partial" ρ calculated in terms of the two-period differences or payments p_{t-1} and p_t alone, which we will denote here ρ_t, with r_t, the market rate for discounting funds of period t into funds of period $t-1$. Thus for each successive pair of periods the marginal *partial* internal rate is set equal to the corresponding market rate of discount. Note that what we have is not one $(T+1)$-dimensional comparison, but T separate two-dimensional comparisons.[32] An analogous formulation could be made in terms of equations (16), invoking T separate comparisons between time 0 and each time t.

The optimum conditions of equations (15) can be translated into a decision rule that runs in terms of inequalities and so is not limited to infinitesimal projects. Consider any multiperiod project complicated by more than one sign reversal—for example, the opportunity $(-1, 5, -6)$ portrayed in Fig. 3-14. Suppose in the example that the market two-period interest rates, which we will not assume to be equal, are in fact $r_1 = 100$ per cent and $r_2 = 200$ per cent. Then a multiperiod project is desirable if it is possible to break it up into T separate two-period productive transformations—such that in each transformation that represents an *investment* the partial $\rho_t > r_t$, while for each transformation that is a disinvestment the partial $\rho_t < r_t$.[33] In our example $(-1, 5, -6)$ can be broken into $(1, 2\frac{1}{2}, \_\_)$ and $(\_\_, 2\frac{1}{2}, -6)$. Calculation shows that the partial $\rho_1 = 150$ per cent and the partial $\rho_2 = 140$ per cent. Then $\rho_1 > r_1$, while $\rho_2 < r_2$. But the first transformation is an investment (early sacrifice for later benefit), while the second is a

---

[32] Curiously, Fisher is responsible for both the correct and the incorrect generalizations of the valid two-period internal-rate criterion! In *The Theory of Interest*, his algebraic solution (appendix to Chap. 13) is quite explicitly in terms of T pairs of two-period comparisons. But his text is equally explicit and consistent in referring always to comparisons between what was here called "multiperiod ρ" (a single discount rate reducing the multiperiod differences to zero present worth) and an assumed constant interest rate r. Oddly enough, Fisher was elsewhere quite insistent in emphasizing that the interest rate is *not* in general constant over time. There is one place where Fisher indirectly suggests his awareness of the difficulties discussed here: in *The Rate of Interest* (p. 155) he advises using the present-value method rather than ρ, r comparisons wherever more than a single sign alteration takes place in the payments sequence.

[33] This procedure was first described in Martin J. Bailey, "Formal Criteria for Investment Decisions," *Journal of Political Economy*, **67** (1959).

disinvestment. Hence the project as a whole is desirable—has positive present value, and thereby provides an enhancement of attained wealth.[34]

We may conclude with a practical comment. The discovery of a correct version of the multiperiod ρ, r comparison rule provides a certain sense of intellectual satisfaction. But it is evident that, in dealing with a project involving more than three periods, the analyst is much better advised to apply the present-value criterion directly rather than attempt the very tedious task of breaking up the payments stream so as to be able to make T different two-period comparisons.

D. CONTINUOUS TIME: PROBLEMS OF DURATION AND REPLACEMENT

Up to this point, time has been represented as a sequence of separated points—or, we have usually said in recognition of the underlying continuity, of "discretized" periods. In actual affairs, discretized approximations of continuous time are always employed. In the capital markets, funds are

---

[34] A general demonstration that present value V_0 is positive, if and only if it is possible to break up the payments stream in the manner described in the text, is rather tedious. The following for the three-period case suggests the general line of proof. In the three-period comparison with an initial outlay, the only situation of any complexity (more than one sign reversal) has $s_0 < 0$, $s_1 > 0$, $s_2 < 0$. Suppose the positive s_1 can be broken into two positive elements s_1^* and s_1^{**} such that the the partial ρ_1 (calculated in terms of s_0 and s_1^*) exceeds r_1, while the partial ρ_2 (calculated in terms of s_1^{**} and s_2) is less than r_2. The ρ_t are defined by

$$s_{t-1} + \frac{s_t}{1 + \rho_t} = 0$$

In general, for any two-period calculation in terms of payments s_{t-1} and s_t, the discounted value as of time $t - 1$ can be expressed as

$$V_{t-1} = s_{t-1} + \frac{s_t}{1 + r_t} = -s_{t-1}\left(\frac{1 + \rho_t}{1 + r_t} - 1\right)$$

Then V_0 can be expressed in two different ways:

(a)
$$V_0 = \left(s_0 + \frac{s_1^*}{1 + r_1}\right) + \left[\frac{s_1^{**}}{1 + r_1} + \frac{s_2}{(1 + r_2)(1 + r_1)}\right]$$

(b)
$$V_0 = -s_0\left(\frac{1 + \rho_1}{1 + r_1} - 1\right) - \frac{s_1^{**}}{1 + r_1}\left(\frac{1 + \rho_2}{1 + r_2} - 1\right)$$

Since $s_0 < 0$ and $\rho_1 > r_1$, the first term of (b) is positive. Since $s_1^{**} > 0$ and $\rho_2 < r_2$, the second term is positive. Hence $V_0 > 0$. Conversely, if V_0 is positive and $s_0 < 0$, $s_1 > 0$, $s_2 < 0$, it is possible to break up V_0 into two arbitrary positive summands V_0^+ and V_0^{++} equal to the two large enclosed expressions in (a). The s_1^* and s_1^{**} thus determined must be such that $\rho_1 > r_1$ and $\rho_2 < r_2$.

distinguished by the day but not by the hour or minute.[35] Analytically, the advantage of the discrete formulation is the ready analogy between ordinary commodities of price theory and the dated consumption claims (c_0, c_1, and so on) that constitute the objects of choice in the discrete model. Furthermore, the approximation is innocuous in that the model can be extended in the direction of perfect continuity to any degree desired—by taking the unit period as the year, month, day, hour, or minute as required by the problem at hand.

However, certain questions are more simply or conveniently analyzed in terms of a continuous model of time. The class of stock-flow problems falls into this category. But as these tie in closely with the concept of "capital," the issues involved had better be postponed until the latter concept is taken up in Chapter 6. A continuous representation of time will be used in this section to analyze some interesting though special problems of *duration* and *replacement*. In the next section a more general class of problems will be considered involving the choice of optimal time paths of production and consumption.

Choice of Optimal Duration

In simplest form, duration problems—when to cut a growing tree, when to bottle an aging wine—involve only an initial current outlay and a terminating receipt. Any such process is called point-input, point-output. The theoretical question is: What is the *optimal interval* θ between input and output? As the problem has traditionally been formulated, the initial outlay q_0 (a negative quantity) is a given constant.[36] The problem is thus converted into a form representing a variation on one of the elementary discrete paradigms, the two-period model. As in the two-period model, there are here just two choice-objects: current claims and future claims. In the two-period model the variables for the productive solution are the produced quantities p_0 and p_1—or, equivalently, the transformations q_0 and q_1—with the time interval, of course, held fixed at one year. For the problem of simple duration, the input q_0 is fixed; the variables are the optimal interval θ and the associated output q_θ. In the two-period model, the problem was to select the optimal scale of investment, the duration of the investment being constant; here the problem is to select the optimal duration, the scale being constant.

---

[35] The degree of discretizing is itself presumably a response to the relative weight of transaction costs on the one hand, and losses due to imperfect time approximations on the other. If interest rates were typically of the order of 100 per cent rather than 5 or 10 per cent, funds of different hours on the same day might be treated as distinct commodities. Something of this kind has in fact been observed in hyperinflations.

[36] The notation here implies that the single "project" envisaged is the entire productive-opportunity set for the economic agent. This assumption is inessential; the same principles would apply even if this were only one project of many available to an individual or a firm.

The former choice is sometimes called "capital widening," the latter "capital deepening."

Although this parallelism is instructive, there is a great danger in the deepening problem: the analyst is tempted to forget that investment is ultimately a process for redistributing *consumption* over time. This cannot be forgotten in the widening problem; even for the productive decision, the "widening" variables represent (at least potentially) "consumption now" and "consumption deferred." But the deepening choice *presumes* the sacrifice of "consumption now"; the question of degree of deferment may not present itself forcefully as a prelude to an ultimate *consumption* choice. Some analysts have thus been led here to forget about consumption opportunities entirely, and to argue as if the investor's aim is to achieve some merely technical objective of maximal or optimal "rate of growth" of the given initial outlay into a terminating receipt.

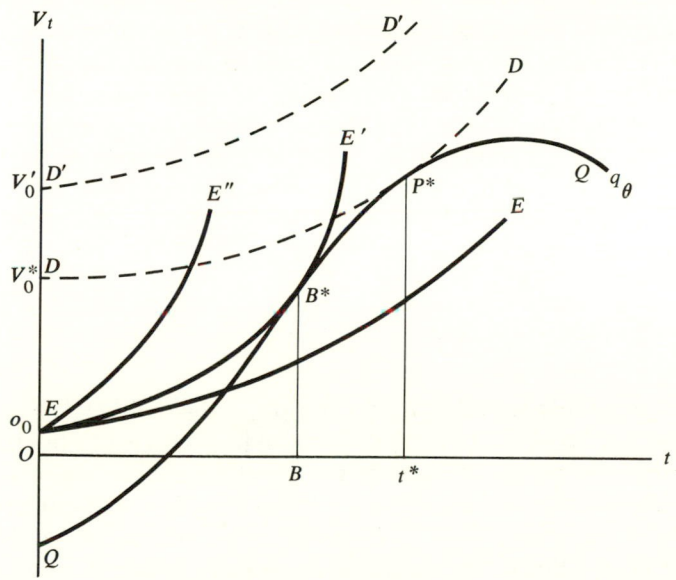

FIG. 3-17. Problem of simple duration, with maximum present-value and maximum growth-rate solutions

Consider the familiar (but still controversial!) problem of when to cut a growing tree. Figure 3-17 shows an initial outlay o_0 ($= -q_0$), and a production-possibility or "growth curve" QQ showing the possible output q_θ as a function of time; q_θ (the stumpage or timber value as of time $t = \theta$, defined only for $\theta > 0$) is net of harvesting costs, and so may take on negative values over a certain range. (Since the input is a negative quantity, the negative region for q_θ can never be relevant for the solution.) Diminishing returns with respect to time are represented by the declining slope (after a certain point) of the curve QQ.

The diagram also shows two "discount curves" DD and $D'D'$. These curves are members of a family, with general equation:

$$Vt = V_0 e^{rt} \qquad \text{or equivalently} \qquad V_0 = Vte^{-rt} \qquad (17)$$

Here V_t is the value as of time t, obtained by continuous compounding of an arbitrary present value V_0 (the intercept of the curve on the vertical axis). Similarly, V_0 is the present value[37] corresponding to the future value V_t. For simplicity, the interest rate r is assumed constant throughout. The only future values V_t involved here are the terminal receipts q_θ. Then the discount curves correspond to the "market lines" of the earlier analysis in being loci of constant present value; i.e., a (t, V_t) point can be transformed by market exchanges into any other point $(t', V_{t'})$ on the same discount curve.

The growth curve QQ similarly represents the productive-opportunity set. The productive solution, under the rule of maximizing present value, is at P^* in Fig. 3-17—the associated cutting date or duration being denoted θ^*. For the opportunity to be desirable at all, naturally, it must be the case that V_0^*—the present value of the receipt q_θ at the most favorable θ^*— exceeds o_0. If that condition holds, the wealth increment associated with the solution P^* is measured by $V_0^* - o_0$ (or $V_0^* + q_0$). The condition defining the solution may be written in the form

$$r = \frac{\dot{q}_\theta}{q_\theta} \qquad (18)$$

where q_θ is the stumpage value at time θ and $\dot{q}_\theta$ is the time rate of change of q_θ (the derivative $dq_\theta/d\theta$). This condition requires setting the interest rate r equal to the *proportionate* time rate of growth of the productive receipts.[38]

An alternative solution has, however, been put forward for this problem: to select the duration $\theta = B$ that *maximizes the internal rate ρ* defined in $q_0 + q_\theta e^{-\rho\theta} = 0$. Since the outlay q_0 is constant, this is a conditional ρ-maximization rule in terms of the classification earlier in this chapter. The

[37] V_0 here does not have the same connotation as in equation (4) above. There it represented the present value of the sequence of current and future payments associated with some project. Here it represents the value of the future output alone, before deducting o_0.

[38] The condition is derived by maximizing the present value $V_0 = q_\theta e^{-r\theta}$ along the growth curve. Then

$$\frac{dV_0}{d\theta} = \left(-rq_\theta + \frac{dq_\theta}{d\theta}\right)e^{-r\theta} = 0$$

Cancelling the factor $e^{-r\theta}$ leads to the equation (18).

choice of duration B is supported by the plausible argument that, the original outlay being fixed, the investor should surely seek to maximize its rate of growth into some terminal receipt. For the two-period model (the widening choice, with constant duration) we found that the conditional ρ-maximization rule led to trivial and incomplete results—trivial in directing that for given investment the solution should be on the boundary of the opportunity set rather than at an interior point, and incomplete in giving no indication of how to determine the scale of investment q_0. Where q_0 is held fixed but the duration is variable, the rule leads to results that are actually wrong—despite plausible arguments that can be adduced in its favor.[39] It will, therefore, be of some importance to explain the pretended solution and to show where the error lies.

In Fig. 3-17, it is possible to draw another family of discount curves (EE, EE', EE''), possessing the property that each member of the family connects the initial outlay o_0 with some point on the production-possibility function or q_θ curve. This family has the general equation $q_\theta = o_0 e^{\rho\theta}$, where ρ represents the continuous compounding rate that takes o_0 into the specified point $q(\theta)$ on QQ, or alternatively the discounting rate that makes the present value of the point $q(\theta)$ just equal to o_0. In Fig. 3-17 the crucial member of this family is the curve EE' just tangent to QQ at the point B^*. Evidently, this is the member of the family with the largest possible ρ ($= \rho^*$). Thus, given the productive opportunities, ρ is maximized by cutting the tree when $\theta = B$ rather than waiting until $\theta = \theta^*$ when its present value will be somewhat higher.

The argument for the superiority of the solution B^* over P^* is sometimes based upon the premise that the productive opportunity QQ can be *replicated with proportionate expansion of scale* whenever we decide to cut the tree. This point is somewhat easier to illustrate if the arithmetic vertical scale of Fig. 3-17 is transformed into a logarithmic scale as in Fig. 3-18. Note that (for constant r) the discount curves are now represented by a family of parallel straight lines (D_1D_1, D_2D_2, D_3D_3) of slope r.[40] Then, the argument goes on, consider the initial growth curve denoted $Q^{(1)}$—the logarithmic version of QQ in Fig. 3-17. If we cut at $t = B$, we can *simultaneously replant* the current net value of the timber $q_B^{(1)}$ to set up a second growth cycle. The second-cycle growth curve $Q^{(2)}$ will be a proportionate expansion of $Q^{(1)}$, so that if we cut $Q^{(2)}$ when $t = 2B$, the then-current timber value $q_{2B}^{(2)}$ will stand in the same ratio to $q_B^{(1)}$ as the latter did to o_0. The ratio is evidently $e^{\rho^* t}$, where $t = B$. On a logarithmic vertical scale, then, the points B_1^*, B_2^*, and so on all lie on a straight line of slope ρ^* through the intercept $\ln o_0$

[39] The rule of maximizing the internal rate for this case has been endorsed by a number of economists, and especially by K. E. Boulding in his influential text, *Economic Analysis*, 4th ed. (Harper & Row, Publishers, 1966), **1** "Microeconomics," Chap. 30.

[40] The equation $V_t = V_0 e^{rt}$ becomes, in logarithmic form, $\ln V_t = \ln V_0 + rt$, which is linear in t.

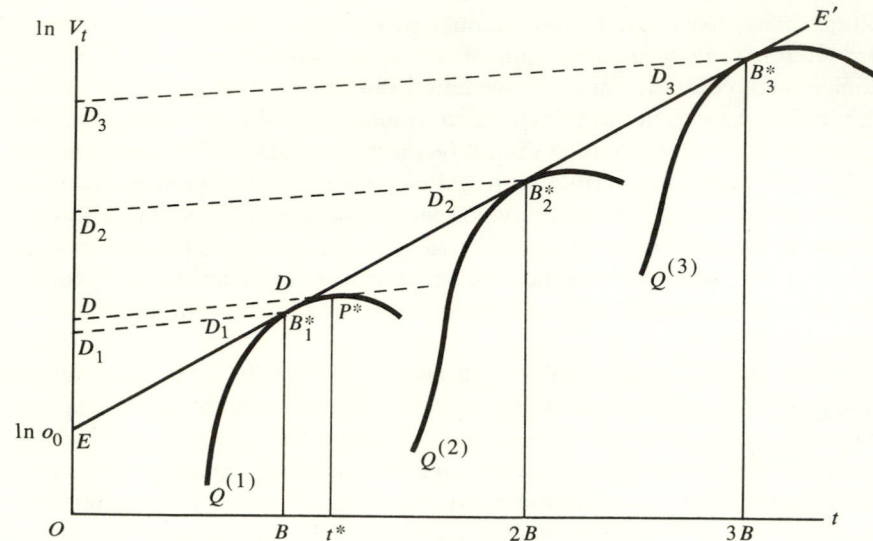

FIG. 3-18. Problem of infinite rotation, replication with proportionate expansion

on the vertical axis. This straight line EE' in Fig. 3-18 represents a continuously compounded growth rate of ρ^*. On the original Fig. 3-17, the corresponding points $B_1^*, B_2^*, \ldots$ would also all lie along the extended EE' curve of that diagram; on an arithmetic scale, the upward curvature shows continuous exponential growth.

It does appear, then, that in the multicycle situation described in Fig. 3-18 it is indeed better to cut at B rather than θ^* for the first cycle, and correspondingly thereafter. By cutting and replanting successively at B, $2B$, $3B$, ..., the investor can attain an average rate of proportionate growth equal to ρ^*—whereas if he holds the tree in the first cycle beyond B, the slope or marginal proportionate growth rate along $Q^{(1)}$ is less than the slope that can be attained along EE'.

Was the present-value rule, as applied to the example of Fig. 3-17, then incorrect? No, because the rule must evidently be interpreted as referring to the maximization of present value along the *relevant* productive-opportunity locus. By the definition of the problem represented by Fig. 3-17, this locus was the single curve QQ, without possibility of replication. If replication is to be admitted as a productive possibility, QQ must be modified accordingly. In fact, the result is like that represented in Fig. 3-18, showing essentially that a *series* of points along EE' are attainable. Thus the rule, for problems of *simple* duration, to maximize present value (the wealth, or wealth increment of the decision-making agent)—leading geometrically to the solution P^* at time θ^* in Fig. 3-17—is not disproved by showing that a different solution would be correct if the problem were different. (Problems admitting the possibility of productive replication fall into the class of *rotation* or replacement problems, to be taken up shortly.)

The correct solution P^* in Fig. 3-17 is also yielded, it may be noted, by the ρ, r comparison rule. This conclusion is based upon the interpretation of the proportionate rate of growth $\dot{q}_\theta/q_\theta$ as ρ_θ—the *marginal* internal rate with respect to extensions of duration.[41] It is evident that so long as $\rho_\theta > r$ along $Q^{(1)}$, funds held in the productive process grow in value faster than funds at the market rate of exchange, and so yield a wealth increment. So, the ρ, r comparison rule is here equivalent to the present-value rule.

NUMERICAL EXAMPLE

Let the growth curve QQ, consequent upon an initial input $q_0 = -1$, be given by the equation $q_\theta = \ln \theta$. Let the market interest rate $r = 5$ per cent. The condition (18) for maximizing present value is $r = \dot{q}_\theta/q_\theta$ ($= \rho_\theta$, the *marginal* internal rate). Since $\dot{q}_\theta = 1/\theta$, the condition here takes the form $\theta \ln \theta = 20$. From log tables, the optimal duration is $\theta^* \doteq 9.1$ years. At this point $q_{\theta*} = 2.21$, so that the value of the project (wealth gain) is $q_0 + q_\theta e^{-r\theta} \doteq -1 + 2.21(.635) \doteq .40$.

The incorrect $\theta = B$, obtained by maximizing the internal rate ρ, can be calculated for comparison. Since ρ is defined in $q_0 + q_\theta e^{-\rho\theta} = 0$, we obtain $\rho = (\ln q_\theta)/\theta$. Maximizing ρ leads to the condition $\ln (\ln \theta) = 1/(\ln \theta)$. Tables yield the numerical solution $\theta = B \doteq 5.9$ years—which, as expected, is shorter than θ^*. With this shorter duration, the wealth increment of the *single cycle* opportunity is $-1 + 1.775(.745) \doteq .32$, less than for $\theta = \theta^*$. The internal rate itself is $\rho = (\ln q_\theta)/\theta = 1.775/5.9 = 30.1$ per cent. Note that at $\theta = B$ the marginal internal rate $\rho_\theta = \dot{q}_\theta/q_\theta \doteq 9.5$ per cent—so that the ρ, r comparison rule correctly suggests a further "deepening" of the investment.

[41] Geometrically, this proportionate growth rate is simply the slope along the logarithmic growth curves of Fig. 3-18. The marginal rate ρ_θ with respect to extensions of duration is defined in

$$-q_\theta + q_{\theta+\Delta\theta}e^{-\rho_\theta\Delta\theta} = 0$$

Then

$$e^{\rho_\theta\Delta\theta} = \frac{q_{\theta+\Delta\theta}}{q_\theta} = \frac{q_\theta + \dot{q}_\theta\Delta\theta}{q_\theta} = 1 + \frac{\dot{q}_\theta}{q_\theta}\Delta\theta$$

Now $e^{\rho_\theta\Delta\theta}$ can be expressed as the infinite series

$$e^{\rho_\theta\Delta\theta} = 1 + \rho_\theta\,\Delta\theta + \frac{(\rho_\theta\,\Delta\theta)^2}{2!} + \frac{(\rho_\theta\,\Delta\theta)^3}{3!} + \cdots$$

Then

$$\frac{\dot{q}_\theta}{q_\theta}\,\Delta\theta = e^{\rho_\theta\Delta\theta} - 1 = \rho_\theta\,\Delta\theta + \frac{(\rho_\theta\,\Delta\theta)^2}{2!} + \frac{(\rho_\theta\,\Delta\theta)^3}{3!} + \cdots$$

Dividing by $\Delta\theta$, and then letting $\Delta\theta$ approach zero as a limit, all terms on the right-hand side after the first drop out, so that

$$\frac{\dot{q}_\theta}{q_\theta} = \rho_\theta$$

The Rotation Problem

We may now ask whether the rule just described to maximize the internal rate (geometrically, to cut and replant at $t = B, 2B, 3B, \ldots$) is really correct for *rotation* problems. And if so, does it conflict with the present-value rule as applied to the same situation? Accepting the condition of replication by proportionate expansion shown in Fig. 3-18, take the line EE' as representing the productive opportunities.[42] The conditional ρ-maximization rule tells us to cut and replant so as to get on the line EE'. But the cuttings and replantings cancel out, so that after the outlay q_0, *the attained income stream is actually null except for an infinite element at $t = \infty$ along EE'*. When we consider the present-value rule in such a situation, the first thing to notice is that as t increases along EE', the present value rises without limit. Since EE' is steeper than the common slope r of the discount curves (DD, $D_1 D_1$, $\ldots$), it must eventually exceed any prespecified level of present value. In short, an investor who had productive opportunities like those summarized in the line EE' *would have infinite wealth!* Given the situation, of course the present-value rule would also dictate attaining the maximum (infinite) wealth position, so the two rules would coincide here in recommending the productive solution at infinity along EE'.

But is this a possible situation? We obviously do not observe individuals or firms possessing infinite wealth in the real world. Yet there was nothing that seemed absurd as such in the description of the productive-opportunity locus of Fig. 3-18—an opportunity for replication with proportionate expansion at the rate ρ^*, where ρ^* happens to exceed the market interest rate r. The answer is that we cannot rule out such a locus on *a priori* grounds; but if such an opportunity were to come into existence (as by a new invention or discovery), it would necessarily set in motion forces that would adjust the rate of interest r upward so as to make the agent's attainable wealth finite again.[43] But, remarkably and ironically, under the conditions of this problem the wealth increment can become less than infinite only if it is zero! The present value attainable along EE' remains infinite so long as EE' is steeper than the discount curves ($\rho^* > r$). But when r is driven up until it is equal to ρ^*, the line EE' itself becomes a discount curve (line of constant present value). Thus the receipt q_θ (for any $\theta > 0$) just equals in present value the outlay $-q_0$. In these circumstances, the solutions P^* and B^* coalesce. In

---

[42] Actually, only the particular points B_1^*, B_2^*, B_3^*, $\ldots$ along EE' are attainable, but this is not essential.

[43] We have to anticipate developments in the next chapter to analyze the implications for the market rate of interest. Briefly, an individual possessing the opportunity EE' of Fig. 3-18 could, at existing market prices, buy up all of society's (finite) current income flow. (And *still* have infinite wealth left!) His attempt to exchange, for consumptive purposes, enormous *future* flows for large fractions of society's *current* income would drive up the price of the latter relative to the former—raise the rate of interest r. The process can only stop when r rises high enough to make his wealth finite.

short, under the conditions as given, the wealth increment is either infinite or at most zero. Under either condition the rule to maximize present value tells us the "correct" action to take—to attain the infinite wealth if it were possible to do so, or the zero wealth increment as the best attainable otherwise. It is also true that the rule to maximize the internal rate equally well tells us the "correct" actions for these cases. But the main conclusion we must draw is that the situation of infinite replication by proportionate expansion of scale must either be absurd (infinite wealth increment) or trivial (zero wealth increment).

We now turn to a more interesting model of rotation, which permits infinite replication but in the form of *constant-scale repetition* rather than proportionate expansion of scale. This situation corresponds to productive opportunities in the form of forest growth on a given acreage of land, where conditions of growth and market relationships are expected to hold constant over time.[44] The solution is inconvenient to represent geometrically, but algebraically may readily be derived by maximizing present value with respect to the rotation time θ. The equation for the present value of the infinite sequence is

$$W_0^Q = q_0 + (q_\theta + q_0)e^{-r\theta} + (q_\theta + q_0)e^{-2r\theta} + \cdots$$

$$= \frac{q_\theta + q_0 e^{r\theta}}{e^{r\theta} - 1} \tag{19}$$

When this expression is maximized with respect to θ, the resulting condition determining the optimal rotation period θ^{**} is

$$\dot{q}_\theta = \frac{r(q_\theta + q_0)}{1 - e^{-r\theta}} \tag{20}$$

where again $\dot{q}_\theta$ represents the derivative $dq_\theta/d\theta$. This is known as the Faustmann solution. We may contrast it with the condition $\dot{q}_\theta = rq_\theta$ determining the optimal period θ^* in simple duration problems. The main point to appreciate is that both θ^* and θ^{**} are present-value solutions, differing only because of the different specification of the productive opportunities. There is, therefore, no conflict between them.[45] Also, notice that even though we

---

[44] By way of contrast, the assumption of infinite proportionate expansion seems to imply the ability to extend cultivation at constant costs into additional land, where the pace of expansion is limited only because the harvest of each cycle serves (as seed, perhaps) for the periodic replanting.

[45] The Faustmann solution, published in 1849, was rediscovered and brilliantly analyzed in M. Mason Gaffney, "Concepts of Financial Maturity of Timber and Other Assets," A. E. Information Series No. 62, Dept. of Agricultural Economics, North Carolina State College (Raleigh, N.C., Sept. 1957). Gaffney seems to go astray, however, in arguing as if there were a conflict between the Fisher solution and the Faustmann solution.

are dealing here with an infinite sequence of replications, the present value of the opportunity is finite.

It is possible to show that the Faustmann interval θ^{**} will, assuming normal (concave downward) curvature of the $q(\theta)$ function in the relevant range, always lie between θ^* and B. The formal proof is rather cumbersome, and only an intuitive argument will be presented here. Under the conditions for which the Fisher solution θ^* is optimal (only a single-cycle productive opportunity is available), the alternative to holding the growing tree is investment at the external market rate r. Hence the tree is not cut until the proportionate growth rate $\dot{q}_\theta/q_\theta$ falls into equality with r at time θ^*. Given the replication, it is possible on the next cycle to obtain an average growth rate greater than r, but only on the amount o_0 required as input for the replication. (The growth rate must be greater than r for there to be positive present value for the opportunity.) The balance of funds at the time of cutting, $q_\theta^* - o_0$, can only earn the external rate r. But ability to earn at a rate greater than r, even on only a fraction of the funds freed, dictates cutting earlier than θ^* to liberate the site for a new rotation. On the other hand, cutting as early as $\theta = B$ would be optimal only if it were possible to earn the maximum growth rate ρ^* on *all* funds freed by cutting. Since this cannot be done, it pays to let the tree grow until $\dot{q}_\theta/q_\theta$ falls somewhat below ρ^*.

NUMERICAL EXAMPLE

The same data as for the previous example of simple duration can now be applied to the rotation problem. If replication by proportionate expansion were actually possible, the rotation $\theta = B \doteq 5.9$ years would be optimal. But then the original investment would grow without limit at the rate $\rho^* \doteq 30.1$ per cent, greater than the market rate $r = 5$ per cent. Wealth would be infinite—an impossible result. If the productive opportunity permits only replication by constant-scale repetition, the Faustmann condition (20) applies. With $q_\theta = \ln \theta$ and $r = 5$ per cent, this takes the form

$$\frac{1}{\theta} = \frac{.05(q_\theta - 1)}{1 - e^{-.05\theta}}$$

Tables show the Faustmann solution to be approximately $\theta^{**} \doteq 6.5$ years—as expected, lying between the θ^* and B obtained above. The value of this production opportunity, using equation (19), is found to be $W_0^Q \doteq 1.27$.

Duration and Rotation with Variable Scale of Investment

The productive solutions above, the Fisher interval θ^* for the simple duration problem and the Faustmann interval θ^{**} for the rotation problem, both represent present-value maxima under the hypothesized conditions. The maximized wealth will then permit the attainment of the individual's preferred distribution of consumption over time, again subject to the assumed conditions. But one of these conditions, to wit, the fixed investment quota o_0, is unacceptable! Only under very special and extreme conditions can the productive-opportunity set take the form of "deepening" choices only, with absolutely no freedom to "widen" the scale of investment. (The elementary paradigms above—the two-period model and discrete-perpetuity model—represented equally extreme pure "widening" choices, but these models were introduced only as first steps toward understanding more generalized intertemporal models.)

A generalization of optimal-duration models, so as to permit simultaneous choice of interval of investment and scale of investment (amount of current sacrifice), is actually not very difficult. Under the assumption of perfect markets for intertemporal claims, Fisher's Separation Theorem continues to apply. Then by maximizing wealth, the investor makes possible the attainment of his consumptive optimum.

In the conditions of this problem, the wealth gain associated with the productive opportunity is given by

$$W_0^Q = q_0 + q_\theta e^{-r\theta} \tag{21}$$

where q_0, q_θ, and θ are all variable. The production function shows the output q_θ as determined by input q_0 and time θ:

$$q_\theta = \Omega(q_0, \theta) \tag{22}$$

The maximization of W_0^Q with respect to the decision variables q_0 and θ leads to the results

$$\frac{\partial q_\theta}{\partial \theta} = r q_\theta$$

$$\frac{\partial q_\theta}{\partial q_0} = -e^{r\theta} \tag{23}$$

The first of these is the original Fisher condition (18). The variability of the scale of investment does not affect the result that the investment should be held until its rate of proportionate time growth just equals the rate of interest. The second condition is also readily comprehensible. It says that the scale of investment should be expanded until, on the margin, the output per unit of input just equals what could have been earned at compound interest on the external market.

It is also possible to verify that the conclusions for the Faustmann rotation problem are analogous. That is, the Faustmann condition continues to hold for the decision as to time interval, and the scale of investment is governed by the condition of the second equation above.

Consider the specific production function $q_\theta = A \ln (-q_0) + B \ln \theta - C$. The conditions for the productive optimum are $\partial q_\theta / \partial \theta = B/\theta = r q_\theta$, and $\partial q_\theta / \partial q_0 = A/q_0 = -e^{r\theta}$. With the numerical parameters $A = B = C = 10$ and the interest rate $r = 10$ per cent, it may be verified that the solution is, approximately, $\theta = 4.3$ years, $q_0 = -6.5$, and $q_\theta = 23.3$. The wealth gain is approximately $-6.5 + 15.2 = 8.7$.

E. CONTINUOUS TIME: OPTIMAL PATHS OF PRODUCTION AND CONSUMPTION

In the previous section, time was treated as continuous. However, the productive choices were among vectors of discrete (lump-sum) incomes: (q_0, q_t) for simple duration problems, $(q_0, q_t, q_{2t}, \ldots)$ for rotation problems. The problem of dealing with income as a *flow* over time—which could hardly have been evaded if attention were turned to consumptive choices—was passed over by limiting the discussion to the productive solution only. Here that problem will be faced. But in the interests of simplicity, the assumption in this section will be that productive consumptive incomes appear only in the form of continuous flows over time. Thus no attempt will be made to deal with mixed discrete-continuous sequences.[46]

In a model of continuous income flow over time, the discrete endowment sequence $(y_0, y_1, \ldots, y_T)$ is replaced by a continuous endowment stream or time path $y(t)$ as in Fig. 3-19, with time ranging as before from $t = 0$ to a horizon $t = T$. This endowed-income curve can be productively transformed into any one of a number of attained-income streams, such as the level $p(t)$ curve shown in the diagram. The transformation stream $q(t) = p(t) - y(t)$ is also shown; in general, the $q(t)$ curve will have negative sections representing *investment* periods as well as positive sections representing disinvestment periods. And, of course, there will ultimately be a consumption stream $c(t)$, not shown in the diagram.

Consider first the productive solution. Evidently, with a given endowment curve $y(t)$ there would in general be a number of alternative attainable $p(t)$ paths. The range of possibilities would be limited by some kind of productive constraint. By direct analogy with the discrete analysis, it is evident that the best attainable $p(t)$ stream and corresponding $q(t)$ stream

---

[46] Actually, it would not be inordinately difficult to cope with such systems. The individual might, for example, have an endowment partly in the form of discrete payments at specified dates, partly in the form of a continuous flow of income. The productive opportunities might require both lump-sum and continuous inputs, and might yield outputs in both forms. In any case, the individual will first maximize wealth subject to his productive constraint, and then distribute consumption over time so as to maximize a utility function within the wealth constraint. The production, wealth, and utility functions might have as arguments both continuous flows and lump-sum discrete payments.

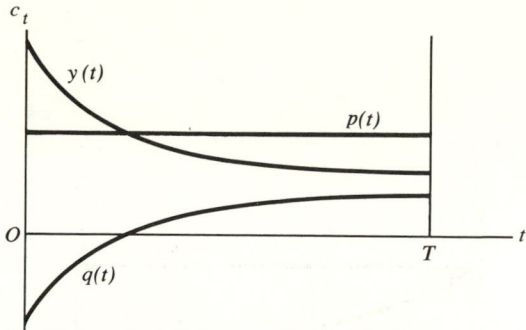

FIG. 3-19. Endowed-income and attained-income streams (continuous time)

are those that maximize attained wealth W_0^P and the wealth gain W_0^Q, respectively (where, as before, $W_0^Q = W_0^P - W_0^Y$, the difference between the attained wealth and the endowed wealth). All the wealth measures are, of course, based upon the continuous discounting equation developed in Chapter 2 for determining the present value V_0 of a stream of payments $s(t)$:

$$V_0 = \int_0^T s(t)e^{-rt}\, dt \tag{24}$$

It will be a little more convenient to work with the attained-income stream $p(t)$ rather than the transformation stream $q(t)$ for describing the productive opportunities. The problem is to choose a stream that will maximize attained wealth W_0^P in

$$W_0^P = \int_0^T p(t)e^{-rt}\, dt \tag{25}$$

The level $p(t)$ curve is shown again in Fig. 3-20, together with the corresponding curve of the (continuously) discounted quantities $p(t)e^{-rt}$. The increasing gap between the two curves is, of course, due to the fact that incomes at more distant future dates are discounted more heavily. The maximand W_0^P is the shaded area under the latter curve. The *constraint* or intertemporal production function would typically also be expressed as an integral holding constant some other function γ of the $p(t)$.[47]

$$\int_0^T \gamma[\, p(t)]\, dt = G \quad \text{(a constant)} \tag{26}$$

[47] Only a very special class of the conceivable intertemporal production functions can be put into this form. Aside from the continuity assumptions, another special feature is that the integrand is a function solely of t and $p(t)$—and does not at all depend, for example, upon the rate of change $dp(t)/dt$.

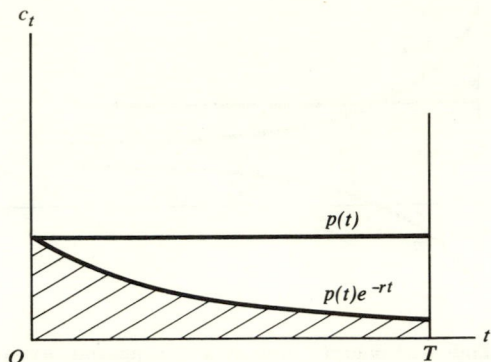

FIG. 3-20. Attained-income and discounted attained-income streams

Mathematically, the choice of a maximizing function or curve subject to a constraint is a problem in the calculus of variations. The solution for this problem can be written as

$$e^{-rt} = \lambda \frac{d\gamma}{dp} \tag{27}$$

where λ is a constant whose value can be determined from the constraint conditions.[48]

NUMERICAL EXAMPLE

Let the horizon $T = \infty$, and the constraint equation take the form

$$\int_0^\infty p^2(t)\, dt = G$$

[48] The procedure is to use λ as a Lagrangian multiplier in forming a new maximand

$$\mathscr{L} = \int_0^T \{p(t)e^{-rt} - \lambda\gamma[p(t)]\}\, dt = \int_0^T f(t)\, dt$$

Textbooks give the solution in the form of Euler's equation:

$$\frac{\partial f}{\partial p} = \frac{\partial}{\partial t}\left(\frac{\partial f}{\partial p'}\right) \qquad \text{where} \quad p' = \frac{dp}{dt}$$

But since p' does not enter into f here, Euler's equation reduces to

$$\frac{\partial f}{\partial p} = 0$$

The indicated differentiation leads directly to the equation in the text.

The solution is $e^{-rt} = \lambda(2p)$. Then $p = e^{-rt}/2\lambda$. Substituting for p in the constraint equation and carrying out the integration yields the result $\lambda = (1/8Gr)^{1/2}$. So $p(t) = (2Gr)^{1/2}e^{-rt}$. The attainable-income stream of maximal present worth starts with $p(0) = (2Gr)^{1/2}$ at time 0 and thereafter diminishes but at a decreasing rate so as to always remain positive up to infinity. The wealth attained is found by carrying out the integration in (25), and in this case is $W_0^* = (G/2r)^{1/2}$. Specifically, if $G = 125$ and $r = 10$ per cent, the wealth attained is 25, with $p(t) = 5e^{-rt}$ so that $p(0) = 5$.

Proceeding from the productive to the consumptive solution—that is, choosing an optimal $c(t)$ path given the wealth maximization associated with the $p(t)$ path—involves a very similar mathematical procedure. Utility as the maximand is now to be regarded as a function of the path $c(t)$, while all the allowable $c(t)$ paths must satisfy the wealth constraint. The utility function might be expressed[49] in the form:

$$u = F(U) \qquad \text{where} \quad \frac{dF}{dU} > 0 \quad \text{and} \quad U = \int_0^T e^{-\eta t}v[c(t)]\,dt \qquad (28)$$

The specification $u = F(U)$ is intended to indicate that any positive monotonic function of U is also a satisfactory utility function; a maximum of U will then be a maximum of any u. This is the well-known "ordinal" property of utility. And $v[c(t)]$ is a preference-scaling function for income at any given date—i.e., an a-temporal utility-of-income function. The parameter η plays an important role as indicator of "time-preference bias" in this special function. The constraint is, of course, attained wealth W_0^*, regarded here as a constant:

$$W_0^* = \int_0^T e^{-rt}c(t)\,dt \qquad (29)$$

The general solution is

$$e^{-\eta t}\frac{dv}{dc} = \lambda e^{-rt} \qquad (30)$$

where, as before, λ is a constant whose value can be determined from the constraint condition.[50]

NUMERICAL EXAMPLE

Let the horizon $T = \infty$, and let $v[c(t)] = \ln c(t)$. Then, the solution equation (30) becomes $e^{-\eta t}/c = \lambda e^{-rt}$, or $c = e^{-(\eta-r)t}/\lambda$. Substituting for c in the constraint equation and carrying out the integration yields $\lambda = 1/\eta W_0^*$. The

---

[49] As in the case of the production constraint, only a special class of intertemporal utility functions can be expressed as an integral of this form.

[50] The mathematical development again uses the Lagrangian multiplier technique, and the solution stems directly from the Euler equation $\partial f/\partial c = 0$, where $f(t) = e^{-\eta t}v[c(t)]' - \lambda e^{-t}c(t')$.

time path is then $c(t) = W_0^* \eta e^{-(\eta-r)t}$. This path is a level one if $\eta = r$, a declining one if $\eta > r$ (since the time bias favoring early consumption is greater than the interest factor favoring deferral of consumption), and a rising one if $\eta < r$.

Note that the solution in the example above collapses if there is *no* time bias $(\eta = 0)$; in effect, all consumption would be deferred to infinity! The difficulty is due to the fact that the utility integral in (28) does not converge if $\eta = 0$. We thus have a significant result: if a finite level flow of income into perpetuity is possible, a degree of time bias is necessary to make utility finite.

For a given transformation stream $q(t)$, an internal rate ρ can be defined as that rate of continuous discount making the associated present value zero in the equation

$$\int_0^T e^{-\rho t} q(t) \, dt = 0 \tag{31}$$

A $q(t)$ curve and the corresponding discounted curve $q(t)e^{-rt}$ are shown in Fig. 21. A value for r that makes the net sum of the positive and negative

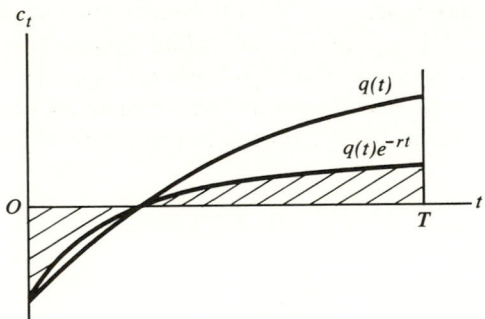

FIG. 3-21. Transformation stream and discounted-transformation stream

shaded areas under the discounted curve equal to zero will be an internal rate ρ. It will be geometrically evident that ρ will be unique if there is only a single sign reversal of the $q(t)$ stream. Then, furthermore, there must be a positive wealth increment W_0^Q if and only if $\rho > r$—assuming, of course, that the negative segment of $q(t)$ precedes the positive segment, so that the Challenger stream incorporating the $q(t)$ transformation is "later." If the Challenger is "earlier," the condition for positive wealth increment is $\rho < r$. But in general there will be multiple sign reversals, so that the difficulties with the ρ, r comparison rule remain just as in the multiperiod discrete paradigm of choice.

F. CONCLUDING REMARKS

This chapter has been concerned solely with decisions on the "private" level of analysis. Market conditions were taken as given. Furthermore, the more specific assumption of perfect and complete markets for all objects of choice (for temporal claims of every date) was maintained throughout. The main purpose of the chapter was to reveal the essential principles of intertemporal choice, through a consideration of how alternative investment decision rules work in a number of alternative frameworks or paradigms of choice over time.

Subject to these assumptions, we found that the three main versions of the present-value rule (running in terms of attained wealth W_0^P, wealth gain W_0^Q, and project value V_0, respectively) are all equivalent and correct, but in a restricted sense. They all lead to a maximum-wealth productive solution, which is the best attainable *provided* that the individual is then going to make market exchanges (lending or borrowing) to attain a time-consumptive optimum. But otherwise, the productive solution attained by following the present-value rules will not in general be correct. Presumably, the force preventing a consumptive optimization could be analytically set up as an additional constraint, which would then affect the productive solution as well. But in this volume the only constraints to be considered are those expressed by the limits on productive and market opportunities.[51]

A number of different frameworks of intertemporal choice were introduced here. The variety of models is embarrassing. But one of the great difficulties in this branch of economic thought is that different authors have seized upon particular paradigms as representative of the essence of intertemporal choice. It is only by comparison with more general models that the limitations of proposed solutions for special cases can be appreciated. Thus, the ρ, r comparison rules are perfectly correct in the elementary two-period model—difficulties do not become evident except in passing to a multiperiod paradigm of choice.

The solutions obtained, it should be re-emphasized, did not follow from the a priori adoption of some more or less plausible formula, but from carrying out the optimization directed by the established pattern of choice-theoretic systems. In the investment-decision literature—more particularly in the business literature, but to some extent even in theoretical works—there has been a certain tendency to place formulas prior to economic analysis. We have seen that the optimum is always determined by the relation between the opportunity set (the endowment plus the productive and exchange opportunities) on the one hand and the preference function on the other.

---

[51] An example of another sort of constraint, not considered here, would be limited computational ability of an investor.

This permitted a determination of the range of correctness of all the usual formulas. The present-value criteria, or rather the associated rules, were indeed shown to be correct—subject to the proviso noted about the consequent consumptive choices being made—under the conditions of this chapter. It is the assumption of perfect and complete funds markets, permitting the application of Fisher's separation principle, that leads to this result. As we shall see in Chapter 7, under conditions of imperfect markets for intertemporal claims even the present-value rule is no longer an absolute guide.

BIBLIOGRAPHY

Readings on investment decision criteria:

     IRVING FISHER, *The Rate of Interest* (The Macmillan Company, 1907), Chaps. 8–9.

     IRVING FISHER, *The Theory of Interest* (The Macmillan Company, 1930), Chaps. 10–13.

     J. HIRSHLEIFER, "The Investment Decision," *International Enclyclopedia of the Social Sciences* (The Macmillan Company and The Free Press of Glencoe, Inc., 1958).

     P. A. SAMUELSON, "Some Aspects of the Pure Theory of Capital," *Quarterly Journal of Economics*, **51** (May 1937).

     M. BAILEY, "Formal Criteria for Investment Decisions," *Journal of Political Economy*, **67** (Oct. 1959).

     M. M. GAFFNEY, "Concepts of Financial Maturity of Timber and Other Assets," Agricultural Economics Information Series, No. 62, North Carolina State College (Raleigh, N.C., Sept. 1957).

Readings on intertemporal consumption paths:

     F. P. RAMSEY, "A Mathematical Theory of Saving," *Economic Journal*, **38** (Dec. 1928).

     E. MALINVAUD, "Capital Accumulation and Efficient Allocation of Resources," *Econometrica*, **21** (April 1953).

4 MARKET EQUILIBRIUM: INTEREST RATES AND AGGREGATE INVESTMENT

Chapter 3 surveyed the principles of optimal *private* choice underlying the intertemporal productive and consumptive decisions of economic agents. Such private optimizing is subject to the constraint of given market conditions (i.e., the pattern of interest rates) that specify the terms according to which the agents can exchange funds of different dates. In this chapter we will see how private decisions interact on the *social* level of analysis to form the supplies and demands for funds that determine the market interest rates themselves. The equilibrium between supplies and demands that sets the pattern of market rates of interest will also simultaneously establish the aggregate levels of dated consumptions for the community as a whole—just as, in ordinary price theory, the equilibrium of supply and demand that fixes prices also determines the corresponding quantities produced and exchanged.

It is convenient to describe the market equilibrium as determining aggregate *investment*, just as the individual optimizing process was described as the process of *investment* decision. But it should not be forgotten that investment is only an instrumental variable, marking a transfer of consumption over time. In principle, what the interacting private choices determine are not "the" level of current investment and "the" rate of interest, but rather the entire timed sequence of individual and aggregate dated consumptions (and the correspondingly timed investment pattern necessary to achieve this sequence), together with the time structure of interest rates $r_1, r_2, \ldots, r_T$.

In this chapter we will find that for the two elementary paradigms— the two-period model and the discrete-perpetuity model—it *is* true that the solution determines a single rate of interest and a one-time level of invest-ment. This no longer holds when we turn to more generalized discrete paradigms of choice. Later in the chapter the solution for the continuous-time "deepening" model will also be outlined. The results obtained will be applied to some controversial theoretical and empirical issues.

A. TWO-PERIOD MODEL

Pure Exchange

To begin with, it will be helpful to deal with the world of pure ex-change, in which no productive opportunities exist for physically transform-ing consumption of time 0 into consumption of time 1, or vice versa. Each individual will then have market opportunities only, as in Fig. 3-1. An individual facing only market opportunities might have his endowment entirely in the present ($y_1 = 0$), so as to be necessarily a lender; or his endowment might be entirely in the future ($y_0 = 0$), making him necessarily a borrower. For mixed endowments the individual could be either borrower or lender, depending upon the price ratio of c_0 and c_1. (And, if the individual has literally *no* endowment, he has no wherewithal for either transacting or consuming.)

In constructing market supply and demand curves for current and future funds or consumption claims from the individual data of Fig. 3-1, analogy with the general model of choice outlined in Chapter 1 would suggest dealing with c_1 as the commodity demanded and supplied. Its price ϕ_1 would, of course, be quoted in terms of the numeraire commodity c_0, as indicated by the more explicit notation ϕ_1^0. As we saw in Chapter 2, $\phi_1^0 = 1/(1 + r_1)$, where r_1 is the interest rate for exchanges of funds between time 0 and time 1.

Figure 4-1(a) shows the market excess-demand curve D_1' for future funds as a function of the price ϕ_1^0. Thus, D_1' is the horizontal summation of I individual excess-demand curves $d_1' = c_1^* - y_1$. Similarly, Fig. 4-1(b) shows the market *full*-demand curve D_1, the horizontal summation of the individual full-demand curves $d_1 = c_1^*$. These curves are in every way analogous to the corresponding demand curves derived under pure exchange in Chapter 1 [Figs. 1-2(a), (b), and 1-3] for arbitrary commodities A and B. Since c_1 is assumed to be a "superior good," for *positive* excess demand ($c_1^* > y_1$) the individual demand curves underlying Figs. 4-1(a) and 4-1(b) must have negative slope. To the left of the endowment y_1 (i.e., where the individual is an excess supplier) the substitution and income effects oppose one another—so that the curves may curl back to the right.[1]

---

[1] See the discussion in Chapter 1, Section B.

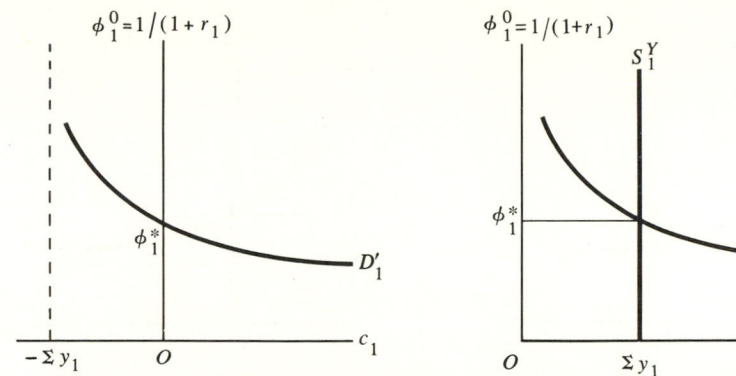

FIG. 4-1. (a) Excess-demand curve for c_1 and equilibrium ϕ_1^0 under pure exchange, (b) Full-demand for c_1 and equilibrium ϕ_1^0 under pure exchange

The market conditions shown in Fig. 4-1(a) determine the equilibrium price ϕ_1^* at the intersection of D_1' with the vertical axis—i.e., where market excess demand is zero, as it must be under pure exchange. The corresponding equilibrium in Fig. 4-1(b) is where the market full-demand curve intersects the endowed-supply curve S_1^Y—a vertical line representing the sum $\sum_i y_1$. This equilibrium establishes the aggregate consumption of "future funds" $\sum c_1$ as equal to the aggregate endowment $\sum y_1$, by finding the market-clearing price ϕ_1^* (thus implicitly determining r_1).

It is more familiar, however, in intertemporal analysis to deal with "current funds" c_0 rather than "future funds" c_1 as the commodity demanded and supplied. We can only do this, of course, by pricing c_0 in terms of something else—in this model, in terms of c_1. Figures 4-2(a) and 4-2(b) display the excess-demand and full-demand curves for current claims c_0 as a function of the price $\phi_0^1 = 1 + r_1$—that is, of the price of c_0 expressed as the number of units of c_1 that a unit of c_0 commands. (Where no confusion is likely to arise, we can again omit the superscript.) Obviously, $\phi_1^0 = 1/\phi_0^1$. Figures 4-2(a) and (b) are also derived from the individual data represented in Fig. 3-1; each ϕ_0^1 is represented by a differently sloped market line, with corresponding c_0^* at the indifference-curve tangency C^*.

Of course, the diagrams of Figs. 4-1 and 4-2 do not show independent solutions for c_0 and c_1, but rather are different representations of a single c_0, c_1 equilibrium. For example, for some low price ϕ_1^0 such that the excess demand for c_1 is positive, the price ϕ_0^1 must be so high that the excess demand for c_0 is negative. Positive excess demand for one commodity implies excess supply (negative excess demand) for the other.

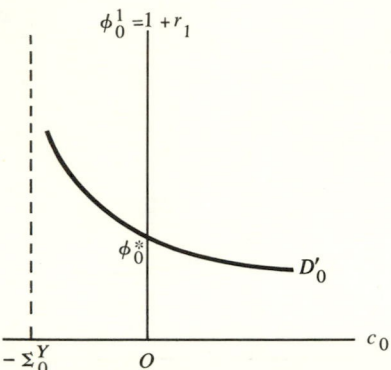

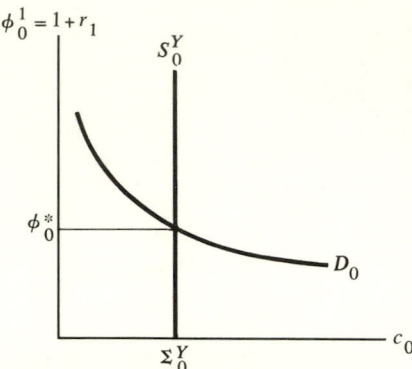

FIG. 4-2. (a) Excess-demand curve for c_0 and equilibrium ϕ_0^1 under pure exchange, (b) Full-demand for c_0 and equilibrium ϕ_0^1 under pure exchange

The representation in terms of c_0 in Fig. 4-2 can be interpreted as showing the disposition of present endowment between current consumption and current saving or investment. *Saving* for an individual would be defined in this model as $y_0 - c_0$; *investment* would be indicated by the difference $y_0 - p_0 = -q_0$. But under pure exchange there are no investment opportunities, so we are here concerned only with saving. At prices below ϕ_0^*, individuals in the aggregate would like to currently consume a quantity greater than the total of endowments; they are attempting to "dis-save." But while *some* individuals can dis-save in pure exchange, in the aggregate the total of consumptions must equal the total of endowments. The community as a whole has no way of transforming present consumption claims c_0 into future ones c_1. So savers (lenders) must balance dis-savers (borrowers).[2]

The equation system (1)–(4) of Chapter 1 is directly applicable to this pure-exchange equilibrium upon substitution of c_0 and c_1 for c_A and c_B.

NUMERICAL EXAMPLE

We can use exactly the same data as for the numerical example of pure exchange in Chapter 1, Section B—simply renaming commodity A as c_0 and commodity B as c_1. Table 1 here then shows the endowments, transactions, and consumptive solutions for the two types of individuals, j and k. Since $\phi_1 = 1/(1 + r_1)$, and the solution price is $\phi_0^* = \frac{1}{2}$, the interest rate is $r_1 = 1 = 100$ per cent. This relatively high premium on current funds, despite the fact that the endowments are in the aggregate weighted more heavily toward c_0, is due

---

[2] The statements about saving here run in terms of the "gross" concept: saving equals current endowment minus current consumption. *Net* saving will not equal gross saving unless the current gross income (endowment) element y_0 equals the future element y_1. In particular, if $y_0 > y_1$, zero gross saving implies negative net saving. The description of pure exchange thus takes a simpler form when the gross concept is used.

Table I*

INDIVIDUALS	ENDOWMENT		TRANSACTIONS		CONSUMPTIVE SOLUTION	
	(Y)		$(C^* - Y)$		(C^*)	
	c_0	c_1	c_0	c_1	c_0	c_1
j	40	45	$+10$	-20	50	25
k	60	5	-10	$+20$	50	25
Totals	100	50	0	0	100	50

* Conditions: $U = c_0^{.8} c_1^{.2}$ (j, k)

Solution: $\phi_1^* = \frac{1}{2}$ (or, $r_1 = 1$)

to the high time preference reflected in the exponents of the utility function. Note that despite the high r_1, individual j with a relatively balanced time endowment seeks to dis-save; individual k, with an endowment very heavily weighted in present funds, is willing to save the corresponding amount.

By referring back to the diagrams and numerical example, it will also be possible to interpret the implications of autonomous changes in the given data of the problem—the endowments and utility functions. An uncompensated increase in the current-endowment elements y_0 will tend to push the supply curve S_0^Y of Fig. 4-2(b) to the right,[3] lowering ϕ_0^1 and thus reducing the interest rate r_1—the premium on current funds (and discount on future funds). A relative increase in future endowments will evidently have the opposite effect. Shifts in the utility functions can be described in terms of changes in the marginal rate of substitution dc_1/dc_0 at the previous equilibrium positions. In the numerical example, an increase in the exponent of c_0 would tend to steepen indifference curve slopes;[4] this makes individuals desirous of consuming more c_0 and thus tends to increase the interest rate. An increase in the relative weight of c_1 in the expression for dc_1/dc_0 would, of course, have the opposite effect.

Note that a redistribution of given totals of endowments that leaves unchanged the endowed wealths (calculated at the original prices) will *not* affect the solution. Therefore, if the redistribution is such as to increase the endowed "specializations" of individuals in particular commodities, the only effect will be to enlarge the volume of market transactions. On the

---

[3] The demand curve D_0 also moves to the right (the wealth effect), but by a smaller amount; individuals will desire to employ some of their increased wealth in purchasing c_1.

[4] If $U = c_0^\alpha c_1^{1-\alpha}$, then

$$\left. \frac{dc_1}{dc_0} \right|_U = -\frac{\alpha c_1}{(1 - \alpha)c_0}$$

An increase in α will increase the absolute value of the slope.

other hand, if endowed wealths are changed by a redistribution, even though endowment totals remain unchanged, the price ratio and individual quantities will in general be affected.[5]

Production and Exchange

Where individuals may have both productive and market opportunities, the development in terms of arbitrary commodities A and B in Chapter 1, Section D, can again be reformulated in terms of present and future consumptions c_0 and c_1. Figure 4-3 thus parallels the earlier Fig. 1-6. The

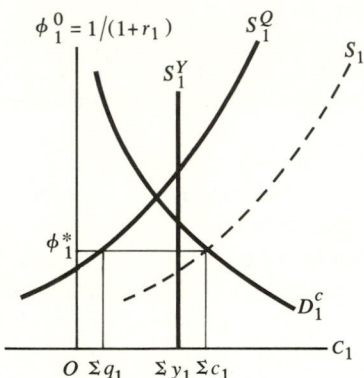

FIG. 4-3.   Consumptive demand and endowed and productive supplies, for c_1

endowed-supply curve S_1^Y is added horizontally to the produced-supply S_1^Q to determine the total supply S_1; the intersection with the consumptive full-demand curve D_1^C determines the equilibrium price $\phi_1^* = 1/(1 + r_1)$. And, as indicated in Chapter 1, Section E, aside from minor changes in notation the same diagram remains applicable if the productive opportunities are assumed to belong to *firms*—see Fig. 1-8.

Shifting attention from c_1 to c_0 leads to the reformulation indicated in Fig. 4-4. The solution in Fig. 4-3 has the price $\phi_1^* = 1/(1 + r_1)$ sufficiently high that the produced supply S_1^Q of c_1 is positive—there is positive gross investment. It follows, then, that the same solution represented in Fig. 4-4 must have price $\phi_0^* = 1 + r_1$ so low that the produced supply S_0^Q of c_0 must

---

[5] In one important special case, that of homothetic utility functions, individual quantities change in proportion to the wealth changes but the price ratio does remain the same when the social totals of endowments are unchanged. For such functions, dc_1/dc_0 evaluated at the point (mc_0, mc_1) is the same as at the point (c_0, c_1). Consequently, holdings change proportionately as wealth varies, but the previous price remains the equilibrium solution. The function in the numerical example is of this homothetic form.

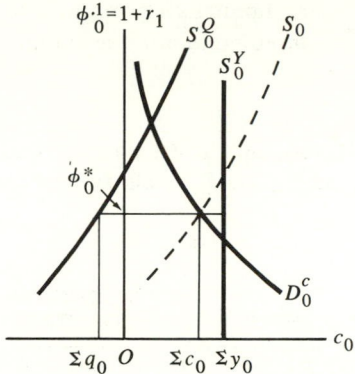

FIG. 4-4. Consumptive demand and endowed and productive supplies, for c_0

be negative—i.e., a productive sacrifice of c_0 is taking place. Of course, for high enough ϕ_0 (and r_1) the produced supply of c_0 would be positive—disinvestment would occur.

But it is more familiar, in concentrating upon c_0, to speak of a normally *positive productive demand* rather than a normally *negative productive supply*. This reinterpretation leads to Fig. 4-5, in which the productive demand D_0^Q is simply the negative of S_0^Q in the previous diagram. The equilibrium condition, determining the same ϕ_0^*, is $S_0^Y = D_0^C + D_0^Q \ (= D_0)$, instead of $D_0^C = S_0^Y + S_0^Q \ (= S_0)$. That is, the aggregate endowed supply of current funds $\sum y_0$ is distributed between the consumptive demand $\sum c_0$ and the productive or investment demand $\sum i_0 = \sum (-q_0)$.

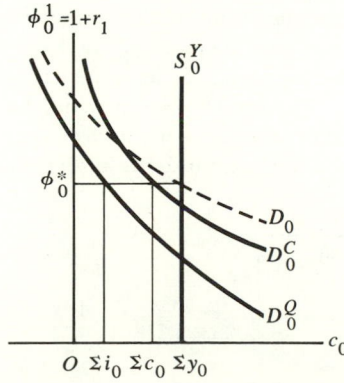

FIG. 4-5. Consumptive and productive demands, endowed supply for c_0

The systems of equations in Section D of Chapter 1 (without firms) and Section E (with firms) are immediately applicable to the corresponding problems of *intertemporal* production and exchange—upon substitution of c_0 for c_A and c_1 for c_B.

NUMERICAL EXAMPLE

We can use here the example of Chapter 1, Section D—modified only by translating c_A into c_0 and c_B into c_1. Table 2 reproduces the data and the results.

Table 2*

INDIVIDUALS	ENDOWMENT		PRODUCTIVE SOLUTION		CONSUMPTIVE SOLUTION	
	(Y)		(P^*)		(C^*)	
	c_0	c_1	c_0	c_1	c_0	c_1
j	40	20	20	80	30	60
k	40	40	40	40	30	60
Totals	80	60	60	120	60	120

* Conditions: $U = c_0^{.5} c_1^{.5}$ (j, k)

$\dfrac{p_0^2}{20} + p_1 = 100$ (j)

Solution: $\phi_0^* = 2$ (or, $r_1 = 1$)

In Chapter 1 the solution was worked out for a typical j, k pair in terms of the relation $D_B^C = S_B^Y + S_B^Q$, leading to the price $\phi_B^* = \frac{1}{2}$. Rewriting c_B as c_1 gives us immediately the corresponding $\phi_1^* = \frac{1}{2}$, implying $r_1 = 1$. It may be helpful, however, to see how the system can be solved in terms of c_0, and in particular using the equation $S_0^Y = D_0^Q + D_0^C$. This corresponds to the relations as pictured in Fig. 4-5, where the earlier solution corresponded to Fig. 4-3.

The endowed supply for the j, k pair is simply $S_0^Y = \sum y_0 = 80$. The productive demand $D_0^Q = \sum -q_0$ applies to the j-individual, the only one possessing a productive opportunity. The productive locus $p_0^2/20 + p_1 = 100$ becomes, in terms of the q-variables, $(q_0 + 40)^2/20 + q_1 = 80$. Setting $dq_1/dq_0 = -1/\phi_1 = -\phi_0$ leads to the productive-demand equation $D_0^Q = -q_0^j = 10(4 - \phi_0)$. The consumptive demand for the k-individual without productive opportunity can be derived from the consumptive optimality condition and budget constraint in terms of the endowment. Thus

$$\frac{-dc_1}{dc_0} = \frac{c_1}{c_0} = \phi_0 \quad \text{and} \quad c_0 + \frac{c_1}{\phi_0} = y_0 + \frac{y_1}{\phi_0}$$

so that

$$c_0^k = \frac{1}{2}\left(40 + \frac{40}{\phi_0}\right)$$

For the j-individual, the consumptive demand is interrelated with the productive solution. Thus, $c_1/c_0 = \phi_0$, and $c_0^j = \frac{1}{2}(p_0 + p_1/\phi_0)$; after substitutions, the consumptive demand can be expressed as $c_0^j = \frac{1}{2}(5\phi_0 + 100/\phi_0)$.[6] The equality of supply and demand is then given by

$$80 = 10(4 - \phi_0) + \frac{1}{2}\left(40 + \frac{40}{\phi_0}\right) + \frac{1}{2}\left(5\phi_0 + \frac{100}{\phi_0}\right)$$

the solution being $\phi_0^* = 2$. At this price the k-individual's consumptive demand is 30; for the j-individual, productive demand (investment) is 20, and consumptive demand again 30. The j-individual's wealth gain is $60 - 50 = 10$.

Figure 4-6 illustrates a technique that will be used often from now on: the *representative-individual* device. If one makes the assumption that all

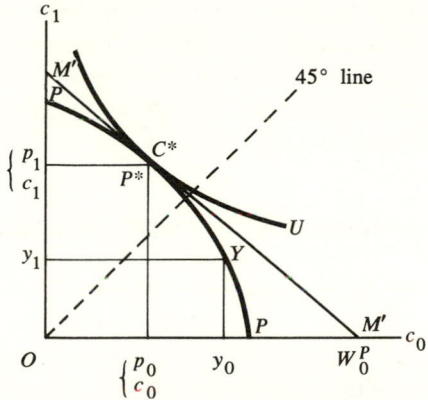

FIG. 4-6. Productive and consumptive optimum for representative individual

individuals have identical tastes and are identically situated with respect to endowments and productive opportunities, it follows that the individual optimum must be a microcosm of the social equilibrium. In this model the productive and consumptive solutions coincide, as in the Robinson Crusoe case. Nevertheless, market opportunities exist, as indicated by the market line $M'M'$ through the tangency point $P^* = C^*$. But the price reflected in the slope of $M'M'$ is a sustaining price, such that each individual prefers to hold the combination attained by productive transformations rather than engage in market transactions. The representative-individual device is helpful in suggesting how the equilibrium will respond to changes in exogenous data—the proviso being that such changes do not modify the distribution of wealth among individuals.

[6] Note that this demand curve "bends backward" (takes on a positive slope) for ϕ_0 greater than $(20)^{1/2}$.

A final remark will be in order here on the market implications of the *nonregular* productive opportunities studied in some detail for private investment decisions in Chapter 3. Nonregularity means that the productive-opportunity set PP for an individual (or QQ for a firm) is not everywhere continuous with smoothly diminishing absolute slope (diminishing marginal returns to investment) moving northwest. There may be ranges of constant or increasing returns (Fig. 3-6) or kinks in the locus (Fig. 3-7) or the productive-opportunity set may consist of discrete points rather than a continuous curve (Fig. 3-8)—and, finally, there may be combinations of all of these. In terms of the analysis of this chapter, these complications have their impact upon the productive supply or demand of c_0 and c_1. For concreteness, let us speak of the productive demand for current funds reflected in the D_0^Q curve of Fig. 4-5. Nonregularities may make the individual's productive-demand curve d_0^Q a step function of ϕ_0; that is, there may be ranges of ϕ_0 over which q_0 remains unchanged, and vice versa. But nonregularities will not affect the negative slope *in the large* of the curve.[7] When a great many firms or individuals are aggregated to obtain the market productive-demand curve D_0^Q, these steps tend to be ironed out.

B. DISCRETE-PERPETUITY MODEL

As in Chapter 3, the relatively full discussion of the alternative elementary paradigm—the two-period model—makes it unnecessary to go through the entire analysis for the discrete-perpetuity model. In all essential respects, the treatment of the "atom of investment" consisting of the exchange between c_0 and the level discrete perpetuity (beginning at time 1) c parallels the other "atom of choice," the exchange between c_0 and c_1. An illustration and a few remarks will therefore suffice. The price of the discrete perpetuity, measured in terms of c_0, can be expressed in terms of an interest rate in the form $\phi_\infty^0 = 1/r$, as seen in Chapter 3. Correspondingly, of course, $\phi_0^\infty = r$.

Figure 4-7, the illustration provided for the discrete-perpetuity model, is in a form that corresponds to Fig. 4-5 for the two-period model. That is, the aggregate endowed supply of current funds c_0 is balanced against the productive and consumptive demands. The general relationships are entirely parallel. In particular, a single interest rate r and a single level of aggregate productive investment $\sum i_0$ are determined.

---

[7] It might be thought that nonregularities that destroy the convex shape of OPP (e.g., ranges of increasing returns) would entail corresponding ranges of D_0^Q with positive slope. But this is not correct. In Fig. 3-6, for example, as the market lines shift from flatter to steeper slopes (that is, as the price $\phi_0 = 1 + r_1$ rises) the productive optimum will not follow the indentation of PP. Rather, there will be a market line just tangent to both humps along PP. At this price the productive optimum will jump over to the other hump, but the shift is always eastward as ϕ_0 rises.

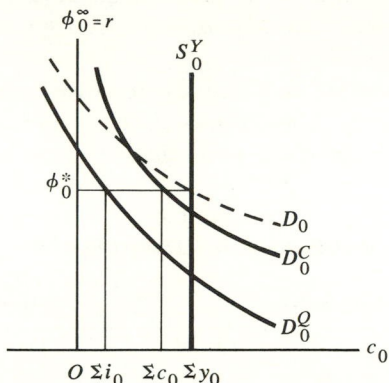

FIG. 4-7. Consumptive and productive demands, endowed supply for c_0 in terms of level perpetuity c

The supply-demand relationships of Fig. 4-7 are expressed in terms of the interest rate r as price, since $\phi_0^\infty = r$. Thinking in terms of the earlier two-period model led naturally to the "agio" concept of interest, as a premium on the value of current claims in comparison with claims of specified future dates. Thinking in terms of the discrete-perpetuity model leads to what has been called the *price concept* of interest—as the price of current funds measured in terms of the equivalent level perpetuity. The agio concept tends to emphasize the time structure of preferences and productivity. The price concept concentrates attention more upon the relation between stocks and flows, with the result that the time element is somewhat deemphasized. As we will see later, the perpetuity model and price concept of interest will be a convenient framework for the analysis of the productive role of "capital." There is no conflict between the concepts, when each is properly interpreted as associated with a special elementary paradigm of intertemporal choice. In this volume, the approach has been primarily from the agio point of view. It is not necessary to argue that the agio concept is in any ultimate sense superior. But it does provide a natural base for more general intertemporal solutions, as in the following section.

C. GENERALIZED DISCRETE EQUILIBRIUM OVER TIME

In the general model of discrete intertemporal choice, with arbitrary horizon T, individual agents utilize their productive and exchange opportunities to locate optimal time patterns of consumption $c_0, c_1, \ldots, c_T$. The market solution for general equilibrium over time establishes T price ratios that equate the productive and consumptive demands and supplies for funds of *every* period. The analytical system is a direct generalization of the elementary two-period model.

In this generalization, it is natural to price funds of each period in terms of the numeraire c_0. These prices are commonly expressed in terms of interest rates in two main ways, as indicated in the accompanying table.

Table 3

ALGEBRAIC EQUIVALENCES

Short-term Rates	Long-term Rates
$\phi_0 = 1$	$= 1$
$\phi_1 = 1/(1 + r_1)$	$= 1/(1 + R_1)$
$\phi_2 = 1/[(1 + r_2)(1 + r_1)]$	$= 1/(1 + R_2)^2$

$$\phi_T = 1/[(1 + r_T) \cdots (1 + r_2)(1 + r_1)] = 1/(1 + R_T)^T$$

Here the r_t, as before, are the discount rates that convert funds of any date t into funds of the preceding date (year) $t - 1$. The R_t are an average of the $r_1, r_2, \ldots, r_t$; repeated compounding at the "long-term" rate R_t transforms funds of time 0 into the same amount of funds of date t as would compounding at the successive "short-term" rates $r_1, r_2, \ldots, r_t$. In terms of the approach pursued here, the r_t are what are established in the funds market, the R_t being then implicitly determined—but one could equally well take the R_t as primary and then derive the r_t as implicit in the structure of the R_t.

On the pattern of the equation system for G commodities in Chapter 1, Section C, the set of equations for the $T + 1$ objects of choice $c_0, c_1, \ldots, c_T$ could be at once written down. But to avoid mere repetition, what will be presented here are the equations for the variant form in which all production lies in the domain of *firms*, as in Section E of Chapter 1.

$$\left.\frac{\partial c_1}{\partial c_0}\right|_U = \Upsilon_1(c_0, c_1, \ldots, c_T)$$

$$\left.\frac{\partial c_2}{\partial c_1}\right|_U = \Upsilon_2(c_0, c_1, \ldots, c_T)$$

$$\vdots$$

$$\left.\frac{\partial c_T}{\partial c_{T-1}}\right|_U = \Upsilon_T(c_0, c_1, \ldots, c_T)$$

Time-preference function
(*TI* equations)   (I)

These equations determine the partial slopes of the indifference loci of each individual—the marginal rates of substitution in consumption between funds of each date t and funds of the preceding date $t - 1$—as a function of the amount consumed at each and every date.

$$c_0 + \phi_1 c_1 + \cdots + \phi_T c_T = y_0 + \sum_{f=1}^{F} \epsilon_f W_0^f + \phi_1 y_1 + \cdots + \phi_T y_T$$

Wealth constraint
(I equations)   (2)

For each individual, the wealth constraint is expressed as the value of the endowment augmented by distribution of the present value of earnings of owned firms. Firm earnings could in principle be paid out in any mixture of present and future claims having value W_0^f, but it will here be convenient to assume that earnings are paid out exclusively in current funds c_0—i.e., that the firm immediately disburses to owners the present-value excess of its receipts over its outlays.

$$\left. \frac{\partial c_1}{\partial c_0} \right|_U = -\frac{1}{\phi_1}$$

$$\left. \frac{\partial c_2}{\partial c_1} \right|_U = -\frac{\phi_1}{\phi_2}$$

$$\cdot$$
$$\cdot$$
$$\cdot$$

Individual consumptive optimum
(TI equations)   (3)

$$\left. \frac{\partial c_T}{\partial c_{T-1}} \right|_U = -\frac{\phi_{T-1}}{\phi_T}$$

The necessary condition for the individual to be at a consumptive optimum is that his marginal rate of substitution in consumption, between funds of any pair of successive dates, be equal to the reciprocal of the price ratio of funds of those dates.

$$Q(q_0, q_1, \ldots, q_T) = 0$$

$$\left. \frac{\partial q_1}{\partial q_0} \right|_Q = \omega_1(q_0, q_1, \ldots, q_T)$$

$$\left. \frac{\partial q_2}{\partial q_1} \right|_Q = \omega_2(q_0, q_1, \ldots, q_t)$$

$$\cdot$$
$$\cdot$$
$$\cdot$$

Firm's productive opportunity
$[F(T + 1)$ equations]   (4)

$$\left. \frac{\partial q_T}{\partial q_{T-1}} \right|_Q = \omega_T(q_0, q_1, \ldots, q_T)$$

These equations determine the partial slopes along the productive-opportunity locus for each firm—the marginal rates of substitution in production between funds of successive pairs of dates—as a function of the productive input and output amounts of each and every date. The various q_t may be positive or negative, but of course at least one must have opposite sign from the others. The form of the equations is slightly different from the consumptive set (1) above, because in the productive-opportunity locus not all the variables $q_0, q_1, \ldots, q_T$ are independent—one follows from the rest of the set.

$$\left.\frac{\partial q_1}{\partial q_0}\right|_Q = -\frac{1}{\phi_1}$$

$$\left.\frac{\partial q_2}{\partial q_1}\right|_Q = -\frac{\phi_1}{\phi_2}$$

$$\cdot$$
$$\cdot$$
$$\cdot$$

$$\left.\frac{\partial q_T}{\partial q_{T-1}}\right|_Q = -\frac{\phi_{T-1}}{\phi_T}$$

Firm's productive optimum (TF equations) (5)

The condition for the productive optimum is that the marginal rates of substitution in production equal the reciprocals of the respective price ratios. This is a necessary condition for wealth maximization.[8]

$$\phi_1 q_1 + \phi_2 q_2 + \cdots + \phi_T q_T = -q_0 + W_0^f$$

Firm's financial distributions (F equations) (6)

This expresses the condition that the present value of the future elements of the firm's productive plan or solution—$q_1, q_2, \ldots, q_T$—is either paid out to purchase the needed input q_0 (assuming that the production plan requires a current input), or else is distributed immediately to owners.

$$\sum_{i=1}^{I} c_0 = \sum_{i=1}^{I} y_0 + \sum_{f=1}^{F} q_0$$

$$\sum_{i=1}^{I} c_1 = \sum_{i=1}^{I} y_1 + \sum_{f=1}^{F} q_1$$

$$\cdot$$
$$\cdot$$

$$\sum_{i=1}^{I} c_T = \sum_{i=1}^{I} y_T + \sum_{f=1}^{F} q_T$$

Conservation relations (T independent equations) (7)

[8] The special form of equations (5) is applicable only when the productive opportunities are "regular."

These express the condition that the total consumption of each date must equal the endowed supply plus the productive supply. In the complete system one of the conservation relations is redundant, since if the markets are cleared for T commodities they must also be cleared for the one remaining.

Thus, there are $2TI + 2TF + I + 2F + T$ independent equations to determine as unknowns the c_t^i, q_t^f, $\partial c_t^i/\partial c_{t-1}^i$, $\partial q_t^f/\partial q_{t-1}^f$, W_0^i, and ϕ_1 through ϕ_T—the equations being the same in number as the unknowns. Finally, the "short-term" interest rates are expressed in terms of the price ratios.

$$1 + r_1 = \frac{1}{\phi_1}$$

$$1 + r_2 = \frac{\phi_1}{\phi_2}$$

$$\cdot$$
$$\cdot$$
$$\cdot$$

$$1 + r_T = \frac{\phi_{T-1}}{\phi_T}$$

Price ratios and interest rates (8)

Of course, the last set of equations could equally well have been shown as determining the R_t by the conditions $(1 + R_t)^t = 1/\phi_t$.

The paradigm of choice over $T + 1$ discrete time periods, with given endowments and preferences for each of the I individuals, and with productive opportunities attaching to individuals and/or firms, can be regarded as the completion of the "real" (nonmonetary) theory of interest in the Fisherian tradition. The role of money cannot be permanently ignored, however. In the next chapter, a monetary commodity will be introduced, having the special character of being a source of "liquidity." The remainder of this chapter will be devoted to an exploration of a number of aspects of the "real" theory of interest that have been for many years the object of discussion and debate in economic literature.

D. THE DETERMINANTS OF INTEREST AND INVESTMENT

The determinants of interest and investment—more precisely, of the entire sequence of intertemporal price ratios $\phi_t/\phi_{t-1} = 1/(1 + r_t)$ and the corresponding sequence of the intertemporal productive transformations $q_t = p_t - y_t$—are traditionally classified under the headings of *time preference* and *time productivity*. The working of these forces is seen most simply in the two-period model, employing the analytical technique of the representative individual (see Fig. 4-6).

The effect of differences in marginal time preferences—of slopes dc_1/dc_0 along indifference curves—has already been explored in the discussion of pure exchange. Evidently, the effect will be very similar in a world of production and exchange. A general change in the slopes of all the indifference curves, or only a local change in the neighborhood of the initial equilibrium point, would modify the optimum $P^* = C^*$. The slope $dc_1/dc_0 \big|_U$ equals in equilibrium $-1/\phi_1$ or $-(1 + r_1)$. Hence a general or local steepening (a rise in marginal time preference) of the indifference curves *raises* the rate of interest, in the course of shifting the equilibrium point around to the southeast along PP. The rise in the interest rate is associated with a decrease in the amount invested, $-q_0 = y_0 - p_0$.

This example of two-period choice can easily be generalized to $T + 1$ periods, so that we can say that a shift of marginal time preferences for earlier over later consumption, generally, will tend to raise the whole structure of interest rates. Dropping the assumption of identical individuals, a shift in wealth distribution in favor of individuals with relatively strong marginal time preferences will also tend to increase interest rates. Diagrammatically, the consumptive demand curve D_0^C for current funds in Fig. 4-5 would be shifted to the right by such a redistribution. The wealth redistribution could be due either to a changed distribution of endowments or to a changed distribution of productive opportunities among the individuals.

Two kinds of differences in time-productivity relationships are illustrated in Figs. 4-8(a) and (b). In the first diagram, the steeper (dashed) productive opportunity locus $P'P'$ implies that, at each level of current sacrifice, the marginal productivity of c_0 in generating c_1 is greater than for the original locus PP. Thus, one society might possess more favorable

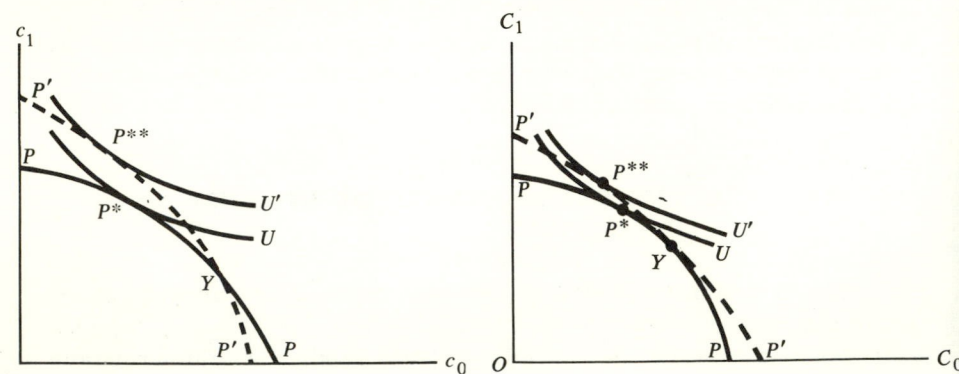

FIG. 4-8. (a) Increase in marginal productivity of c_0, (b) expansion of productive opportunity set

opportunities than another for physical conversion of c_0 into c_1. Note, however, that regarded as a technological change, the shift from PP to $P'P'$ would not be an unambiguous improvement—to the southeast of the endowment point Y, the opportunity set has contracted. Fig. 4-8(b) shows an unambiguous technological improvement: the new locus $P'P'$ is less subject to diminishing returns as transformations either of c_0 into c_1 (investment) or of c_1 into c_0 (disinvestment) take place.

If we consider only regions where investment is positive, in either diagram, the absolute slopes along the new locus $P'P'$ are greater than the slopes at corresponding (vertically aligned) points along the old locus PP. The new equilibrium at P^{**} must, it is geometrically evident, lie to the north of P^*, so that more c_1 is obtained for future consumption. However, P^{**} could be either east or west of P^*—i.e., there could either be less or more c_0. Thus, the amount invested (sacrificed) might either increase or decrease, but the returns from investment must increase. The slope at P^{**} must also be greater than at P^*.[9] Hence an improvement in investment opportunities, in the senses illustrated in Figs. 4-8(a) and (b), must raise the rate of interest.[10]

Finally, it should not be forgotten that the *endowment* itself plays an important role as a determinant. This has already been indicated in the discussion of pure exchange; in a world of production and exchange, the

[9] This conclusion depends upon the assumption that, at all price ratios or interest rates in the relevant range, both of the commodities c_0 and c_1 are "superior goods"—i.e., a rise in wealth with prices held constant would lead the consumer to purchase more units of each commodity. If this is the case, at the point on indifference curve U' directly north of the original equilibrium P^* on U, the absolute slope along U' must be greater than that along U at P^*. (This is necessary to assure that, if $M'M'$ were shifted upward without change of slope to represent a wealth increase with prices held constant, the new tangency would lie to the northeast of P^*—as required by the condition that more of *both* c_0 and c_1 be consumed.) Now if P^{**} is *northwest* of P^*, as in Fig. 4-8, the absolute slope along U' at P^{**} must be greater than that along U' directly north of P^*, and so a fortiori must be greater than the slope along U at P^*. If, on the other hand, P^{**} lies to the *northeast* of P^*, by the condition defining the improvement in productive opportunities the slope along the new productivity locus $P'P'$ just north of P^* must be greater than the slope along PP at P^*—hence, a fortiori, the slope at P^{**} along $P'P'$ northeast of P^* must be greater than the slope of the tangency of U with PP at P^*.

[10] We can, of course, imagine still other kinds of changes or differences in the productive opportunity locus. In Figs. 4-8(a) and (b) above, the old and the new loci both contained the original endowment point Y; thus, the changes considered were in the possibilities for transformation of a *given* intertemporal endowment. We might instead contemplate changes (for example, in the productivity of one or more factors) shifting the entire PP locus, including the endowment point, outward. (This could be regarded as the result of an a-temporal technological improvement.) Or, the changes illustrated in Figs. 4-8(a) and (b) might be modified so that, to the northwest of Y, the new *locus* remains everywhere above the old without the new *slope* being everywhere greater than the old. Such a change would represent an improvement in the average productivity of investment at all levels of current sacrifice, but not an increase in the marginal productivity at all levels. In contrast with the changes discussed in the text above, those considered here would not necessarily lead to an increase in the rate of interest.

result is essentially the same. An increase in the current element y_0 of endowments will tend to decrease the rate of interest—the premium on current funds. And, of course, an increase in the future element y_1 will tend to raise the rate of interest.

In one of the most famous discussions in the economic literature, Bohm-Bawerk ascribed the existence of (positive) interest to three "grounds": (1) perspective underestimation of the future, (2) the relative inadequacy of provision for present as against future wants, and (3) the "technical superiority" of present over future goods.[11] Without attempting to specify precisely what Bohm-Bawerk meant by each of these categories, we can see that they do roughly correspond to the three determinants mentioned above: time preference, time endowment, and time productivity.

E. EMPIRICAL IMPLICATIONS

Although the theory of real interest and investment was developed under a number of rather abstract and artificial assumptions (perfect certainty, a single consumption commodity at each date, perfect markets for funds, and so on), it is by no means empty. A number of implications of the theory will be listed briefly here. No attempt will be made to demonstrate that the implications are valid descriptions of actual behavior, but the reader will very likely gain the impression that the theory does have substantial predictive power.

1. An heir with "great expectations" will tend to be a borrower. His endowment being predominantly in the future, he will attempt to realize more of it in the form of current consumption.

2. A community struck by sudden catastrophe will tend to experience high rates of interest. The reason is that such a disaster, if not too severe, usually damages goods relatively close to consumption (e.g., growing crops) more drastically than the basic productive powers of the community (e.g., the site value and fertility of the land, the skill and energy of the laborers). Thus the members of the community in the aftermath of disaster are somewhat in the position of "heirs with great expectations"; their attempts to borrow one from another on the strength of their future productive powers drive up the price of current relative to future funds, so as to raise the rate of interest.

3. Social groups characterized by individual forethought and strong family affections tend, if isolated, to display low rates of interest; as part of a larger community, they will tend to become lenders. Examples traditionally

---

[11] E. V. Bohm-Bawerk, *The Positive Theory of Capital*, tr. William Smart (G. E. Stechert & Co., 1891), Book 5.

cited are the Scotch and the Jews. These groups may be said to possess relatively low time preference. The declining years of the Roman Empire were characterized by attenuation of the normal ties of family affection, and interest rates were high.

4. If one community possesses better productive opportunities than another, interest rates in the former will tend to be higher. Even though the respective funds markets are by no means insulated one from another, interest rates have consistently been higher in America than in England, and higher in California than in Massachusetts.

5. Widening of access to funds markets tends to stabilize rates of interest. In the examples given above, the disparity of interest rates between the more productive and less productive areas would be far greater if it were not possible for individuals in England to invest in America, or for individuals in Massachusetts to invest in California.

6. Where the productive opportunities are similar but one group has access to lower-interest finance than another, the former group will find it optimal to adopt productive techniques involving lower marginal time productivity—a higher degree of current sacrifice relative to output. Accordingly, it is observed in Malaya that peasant small-holders tap rubber trees of smaller girth than the operators of European plantations.

7. "Stagnant economies" may be divided into two groups, according to whether the reason for lack of growth is strong time preference or poor productive opportunities. In the former case interest rates will tend to be high, in the latter case low—though in both situations the rate of investment will be low. In the former situation opening of access to the world "capital markets" will tend to lead to an inflow of funds, in the latter case to an outflow of funds.

F. THE "NECESSITY" OF INTEREST; THE STATIONARY STATE

An earlier generation of economists was inclined to debate the question of whether the "existence" of interest was necessary in economic systems. In more modern terms, we need only ask: What are the conditions for the rate of interest to be positive?

In part, the debate illustrates the danger of thinking too exclusively in terms of the metaphor represented by a single elementary paradigm of intertemporal choice. For the discrete-perpetuity model, with the associated "price concept" of interest, a positive rate r is indeed almost a logical necessity. For r is by definition ϕ_0^∞—the price of current funds in terms of a future level perpetuity. Then r will be positive so long as the demand for current funds is not satiated, a condition that can be presumed always to hold.

The two-period elementary model and the associated "agio concept" of interest suggest a quite different answer. Here the rate of interest r_1 is defined in $\phi_1^0 = 1/(1 + r_1)$, or $\phi_0^1 = 1 + r_1$. Then the nonsatiation condition, that ϕ_0^1 be positive, implies only that r_1 be greater than -100 per cent. Fisher employs a famous example, the "figs" illustration.[12] Imagine a group of sailors stranded on a desert island, whose only resource is a given fixed stock of figs. The figs remain palatable indefinitely, but there is no way of preventing rats from getting one-fourth of the stores during the year. Then for every four pounds saved this year, only three pounds will be available next year. Using the representative-individual device, the situation would be illustrated in Fig. 4-6 by a productive-opportunity locus PP in the form of a straight line of slope $-\frac{3}{4}$. The market line $M'M'$, which must evidently then coincide with PP, has slope $-(1 + r_1)$. These conditions determine the interest rate as -25 per cent. Generalizing from the two-period model to any number of periods, there is no reason to exclude the possibility that any or all of the discount rates r_t might be negative.

One other famous debate concerns the existence of interest in a "stationary state"—a state of affairs in which production and consumption remain constant over time. In terms of the two-period model and the representative-individual device, the equilibrium must then be along the 45° line of Fig. 4-6—so that c_0 and c_1 are equal. (It is evident that an analogous illustration could be made for the discrete-perpetuity model; in terms of a generalized discrete model, we can imagine a 45° line in a $(T + 1)$-dimensional space of dated consumptions.) The contention in question is that a stationary-state solution must be associated with zero interest.[13]

The two-period illustration in Fig. 4-6 suggests the answer that, while a stationary-state solution *may* involve a zero interest rate, this would be a more or less accidental result. For, the stationary-state solution requires only that the tangency point $C^* = P^*$ fall along the 45° line; this condition can be satisfied by a common tangency slope of U and PP steeper than -1 (positive r_1) or flatter (negative r_1). Again, the conclusion generalizes without difficulty to a $(T + 1)$-period model. Two qualifications may be noted. First, if we insist upon using the elementary discrete-perpetuity model, the stationary state is still possible but *must* involve a positive interest rate r—for the reasons already indicated. Second, it may be that more or less compelling reasons may be given for the existence of particular shapes of the utility function and/or the productive-opportunity locus that will dictate zero interest at stationarity, but nothing in the logic of choice requires this. In Fig. 4-6, one of the necessary conditions for zero interest at stationarity is a 135° slope of the indifference curve U, where the latter cuts the 45° line.

---

[12] *Theory of Interest*, p. 191.

[13] J. A. Schumpeter, *The Theory of Economic Development* (Harvard Univ. Press, 1934), Chap. 1.

This can be interpreted as the absence of a "time bias" between time 0 and time 1. A more general condition can analogously be stated in terms of the $T + 1$ dates $0, 1, \ldots, T$.

Given the olympian impartiality of the theory as between positive and negative interest rates, the question arises as to why positive real[14] rates of interest are in fact almost always observed. This question brings us back to the determinants mentioned above: time preference, time productivity, and time endowment. Since the last of these can itself be regarded as an aspect of the productive-opportunity set, we need ultimately inquire only as to time preference and time productivity. The brute fact of time productivity on the margin (a net future return on current sacrifice, over and beyond what is attainable by mere "storage" transfer through time) may itself be explained by a number of considerations: a relatively vast number of profitable opportunities for investment, slowness of the pace at which the opportunities are exhausted (owing to the painful current sacrifice required), but probably most importantly the continual creation of new opportunities as a result of improvement of knowledge. These factors combine to assure positive interest *and* positive net investment (i.e., in Fig. 4-6 solutions northwest of the 45° line) except in highly abnormal times. The working of time preference as a brake upon investment has already been indicated. Even if there is no "time bias" (that is, if the utility function is symmetrical across the 45° line), solutions northwest of that line will be associated with positive marginal time preference. However, that a degree of time bias exists does seem plausible, surely so if we consider sacrifices for the very far-off future.

G. SAVING-INVESTMENT EQUILIBRIUM; EFFECTS OF INTEREST AND INCOME CHANGES

Especially in current "macroeconomic" studies, there has been much discussion of the nature of the saving-investment equilibrium, and the roles played therein by changes in interest rates and aggregate income. To some extent, the discussion is inextricably intertwined with monetary issues that cannot be considered here. But some of the questions can be clarified within intertemporal barter models.

First, refer back to Fig. 4-5, which shows for the two-period model (the issues involved would be identical for the discrete-perpetuity model) the determination of real interest and the scale of investment. Note that it is the supply and demand of current funds, for *productive and consumptive purposes combined*, that determines these magnitudes. It is possible to illustrate this

---

[14] We will see in the next chapter that the almost costless storability of money practically rules out negative monetary interest.

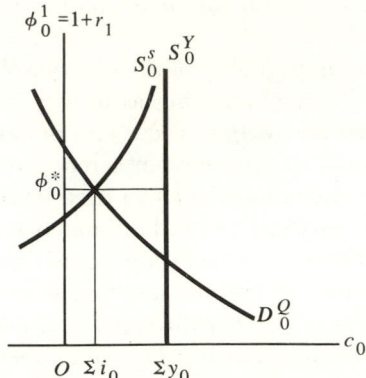

FIG. 4-9. Demand for investment and supply of savings, perpetuity model

same solution in a way (Fig. 4-9) that shows the rate of interest as determined by magnitudes that might reasonably be called "demand for investment" and "supply of saving (or of finance)." The *demand for investment* is the same D_0^Q curve as before, the demand for current funds to be used productively (as real current sacrifice, inputs to Nature). It is the aggregate over individuals (or firms) $\sum i_0 = \sum -q_0$. The *supply of saving*, labelled S_0^s, is a new curve derivable from the relations previously defined. Individual saving is the difference between endowment and consumption; in the aggregate, $S_0^s = \sum y_0 - \sum c_0$. Diagrammatically, S_0^s in Fig. 4-9 is the horizontal difference between S_0^Y and D_0^C in Fig. 4-5. The presentation of the equilibrium in Fig. 4-9 is thus perfectly legitimate, although the role of the *consumptive* demand that constitutes the tie with the time-preference diagram (as in Fig. 3-3) is somewhat obscured.[15]

The macroeconomic issues that lead to concern with these functions turn upon the following ideas. (1) The current level of national income, which may be associated with what has been called here the aggregate current endowment $\sum y_0$, is *not* a constant as assumed above—but, rather, a variable determined by macroeconomic forces. In particular, these forces may reach an underemployment equilibrium, so that the social endowment is not an efficient point but is in the interior of the aggregate productive-opportunity set.[16] (2) It is possible for the government, by monetary techniques (considered in the next chapter), to make effective in private calculations a rate

[15] Note the multiplicity of representations of the same equilibrium in Figs. 4-3, 4-4, 4-5, and 4-9!

[16] This statement is to be interpreted on the social level of analysis. For any individual, it remains true that his endowment Y is outside his control, on the frontier of his private opportunity set.

of interest that diverges from the equilibrium rate described above and illustrated in Fig. 4-9. In particular, if that rate is lower than the intersection of the demand-for-investment D_0^Q and supply-of-saving S_0^s curves, the excess of (planned) investment over (planned) saving will set in motion forces that tend to raise national income $\sum y_0$. The rise in income will in turn shift the two functions, the process continuing until the intersection of the D_0^Q and S_0^s functions becomes consistent with the interest rate imposed. (3) Alternatively, the government can by fiscal techniques affect income directly without acting through the intermediary of interest rates. Again, the functions in Fig. 4-9 will shift until a new equilibrium is reached, possibly with a changed interest rate.

The concern here will not be with these macroeconomic forces, but only with the nature of the D_0^Q and S_0^s functions: in particular, their response to imposed changes in interest rates (movement along the curves of Fig. 4-9) and to changes in incomes (shifts of the curves of Fig. 4-9).

Consider first the D_0^Q curve as a function of the interest rate. In the elementary paradigms of choice (two-period model and discrete-perpetuity model), we have seen that the demand for current funds for investment purposes must have a negative slope in the large. Nonregular productive opportunities may introduce steps into some individual d_0^Q curves, but these tend to be smoothed out in aggregating over individuals. One school of macrotheorists has argued that the D_0^Q curve is quite *inelastic* with respect to the interest rate. In consequence, lowering r need not create a substantial enough gap between the curves of Fig. 4-9 to bring about the restoration of full employment. The degree of elasticity is evidently an empirical question, which cannot be explored here. One further logical complication, however, is introduced when we turn to more general paradigms of choice. In particular, consider the possibility of productive opportunities with "multiple internal rates" (as sketched, for example, in Figs. 3-14 and 3-15). As we saw in Chapter 3, such "projects" can have positive present values within certain ranges of interest rates but negative present values at lower rates. If opportunities of this nature happened to be predominant in a community, as the rate of interest r declines the productive demand for current funds might *decrease* within certain ranges. The issue involved is somewhat clarified when we recollect that a "multiple-root" project can be resolved into a combination of one or more investments between given dates and disinvestments between other dates. A fall in the rate of interest (or, more generally, in the schedule of interest rates) makes the investment components more attractive but the disinvestment components less attractive. On balance, therefore, the result for a particular such project could go either way. But the existence of such indissoluble tie-ins between investment and disinvestment opportunities can be regarded as rather a special case.[17] Consequently, the negatively

---

[17] In addition, there is reason to believe that profitable *disinvestment* projects are very rare.

sloped D_0^Q curve still appears highly plausible even for general models of intertemporal choice.

Turning to the supply-of-savings curve S_0^s, we know that in the two-period model the market consumptive-demand curve D_o^C (see Fig. 4-5) may "bend backward" (shift to a positive slope) for sufficiently high price $\phi_0^1 = 1 + r_1$. Since $S_0^s = S_0^Y - D_0^C$, with the endowed supply S_0^Y simply a vertical line, it follows that the curve S_0^s will correspondingly "bend backward" (shift to a negative slope) for the same range of price and interest rate. This conclusion carries over to more general models of choice. However, we can go a little beyond because we are considering relatively low r, below the intersection of Fig. 4-9. The "bending backward" occurs when substitution and wealth effects work in opposite directions. Now, a fall in the interest rate reduces the premium on current funds—hence, the substitution effect will always dictate more current consumption and less current saving as r falls. As for the wealth effect, that depends upon whether individuals are net suppliers or demanders of c_0 in the market.[18] At the intersection of Fig. 4-9, individuals in the aggregate are just in balance. Below the intersection, in the aggregate individuals are demanders. Hence, a fall in the interest rate enriches them, thus reinforcing the substitution effect in inducing more consumption (less saving) of current funds.[19] In consequence, a strong presumption is justified that imposition of a below-equilibrium r will set up a positive gap between planned investment and planned saving.

We can now consider the effects of direct changes in income, as opposed to the effects just described that work through the interest rate (the distinction corresponding, roughly, to that between fiscal and monetary policy). One ambiguity is whether the hypothesized "fiscal" effects on income operate exclusively upon $\sum y_0$, or spill over to expectations of future endowments as well. For simplicity, the former assumption will be made here. With higher current endowments, individuals will in general want to consume more c_0 and *also* to save more (in order to consume more in the future as well). Hence, in Fig. 4-9 the supply-of-savings curve S_0^s will tend to shift to the right. Since the productive-transformation possibilities are not directly affected by the change in endowments, the D_0^Q curve is unaffected. The consequence is more investment at a new, somewhat lower equilibrium rate of interest.

So far as the analysis here indicates, there is a parallelism between monetary and fiscal policies to counter unemployment. The former imposes a low disequilibrium level of r, setting in motion an income-augmenting process (not itself analyzed here) that can in principle go on until the S_0^s

---

[18] See the discussion in Chapter 1, Section D.

[19] In a full-employment equilibrium, such beliefs or expectations about enrichment consequent upon a reduction of interest could not actually be realized. It is the fact of underemployment that makes the increased enrichment possible. For a somewhat parallel discussion in macroeconomic terms, see Axel Leijonhufvud, *On Keynesian Economics and the Economics of Keynes* (Oxford Univ. Press, 1968), Chap. 4.

curve shifts sufficiently to the right to make the imposed interest rate an equilibrium one. Fiscal policy does not act directly upon r, but works on income itself. However, the consequence is to bring about a new lower equilibrium for the interest rate. It is beyond the realm of the present investigation to assess the comparative desirabilities of the two policies (or, for that matter, to explain how an underemployment equilibrium can come into existence).

H. THEORY OF THE FIRM

The firm has been introduced into our analysis as an agency for physical conversion of some commodities (dated consumption claims) into others. But we have not made use of the familiar form of the theory of the firm, and in particular of the two propositions that specify, respectively, the traditional "short-run" and "long-run" competitive solutions: first, that production will be carried to where marginal cost equals price, and second, that competition will assure that average cost equals price, so that zero profits are

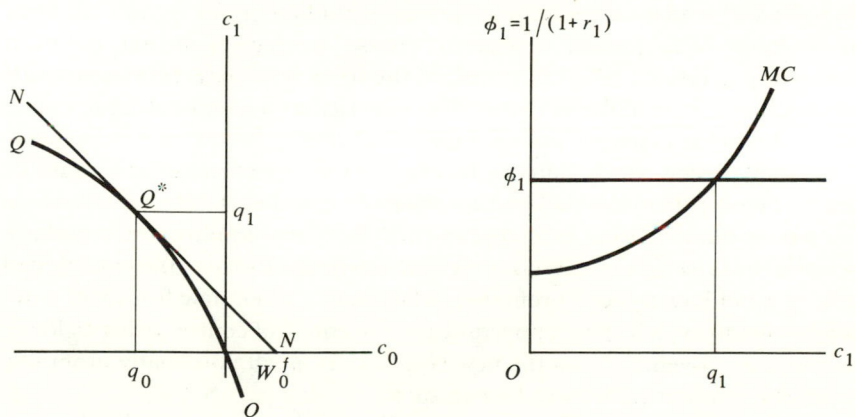

FIG. 4-10. (a) Productive equilibrium for the firm (short run), (b) Traditional short-run equilibrium

earned. The usual formulation of these theorems interprets "cost" in terms of payment for the employment of "factors of production." In the elementary two-period model, we can think of the firm as ordinarily a producer of c_1 (for positive gross investment), so c_0 can be regarded as playing the role of "factor of production."[20]

The maximum-wealth solution for the firm illustrated in Fig. 4-10(a) can readily be translated into the first "short-run equilibrium" proposition.

---

[20] In Chapter 6, explicit factors of production—i.e., productive commodities not themselves objects of consumptive choice—will be introduced.

The slope dq_1/dq_0 along the firm's productive-opportunity locus QQ shows the marginal rate at which c_0 can be converted into c_1. The reciprocal of the absolute slope, then, is the marginal cost in c_0-units of producing c_1. The maximum-wealth condition specifying the equality of the slope of QQ and $-1/\phi_1$ can then be directly restated as the equality of marginal cost MC and ϕ_1, illustrated in Fig. 4-10(b). The extension to other paradigms of choice (e.g., the choice between current funds c_0 and perpetual future flows c) follows immediately. Note, however, that in the general discrete case the firm will be producing (adding to the social endowment of) a number of different "products" c_t and using up (decreasing the social endowment of) a number of different "factors" c_s. Thus the distinction between product and factor is a merely relative one. A particular commodity c_t may be a factor for some firms and a product for others; furthermore, the direction of net social transformation may be reversed by a change in price ratios.

The "long-run equilibrium" proposition can also be expressed in terms of this analysis. The key idea in the usual formulation is that in the long run the entry or potential entry of new entrepreneurs into a previously profitable industry will tend to increase production and thus decrease product prices, and also will tend to increase factor prices (including "rents"), until all firms are earning "zero profits." Here, of course, we have only one industry, converting c_0 into c_1. We can translate the term zero *profits* into zero *wealth increment*: i.e., in equilibrium every firm experiences a zero wealth increment when all relevant charges are paid for.

The process works out as follows. First, there may be profitable productive opportunities such as those portrayed in Fig. 4-10(a), available to the society but not being exploited in the "short-run equilibrium" (perhaps because the price ϕ_1 has just suddenly and unexpectedly risen, the unexploited processes not having been profitable previously). Then new firms will enter production to exploit these opportunities, the effect, of course, being to lower the price ϕ_1. Eventually, at the new equilibrium ϕ_1 all potentially profitable production opportunities will be exploited.

We do not yet have the "zero-profit" condition, however. While there may be a marginal firm providing a zero (i.e., infinitesimal) wealth increment, inframarginal firms will still be yielding positive profit. If the productive-opportunity loci QQ for all firms have regular concave curvature, the "zero-profit" firm must be producing zero output. Conversely, firms with positive output will be providing a positive wealth increment. These profits, in the "long run," will be competed away by entrepreneurs bidding for the right to use the productive opportunities—or we may say bidding for ownership of the firms.

The price for the fth firm—or, equivalently, for the productive opportunity that characterizes the firm—must obviously be equal to W_0^f, the present value of the maximum-wealth solution for the firm. In long-run competitive equilibrium, the value of each of the fixed number of profitable productive opportunities is bid up by an assumed indefinitely large army of entrepreneurs willing to exploit the opportunity. Since the successful bidder must pay out W_0^f in order to gain the right to exploit the fth opportunity, *his* wealth increment will be zero. The "zero-profit" (zero wealth-increment) solution is obtained because the operator of the firm has actually bought the opportunity at its full wealth-increment value—or, in any case, he charges against the operation of the firm the value W_0^f that could be obtained immediately (at time 0) by selling the opportunity rather than producing. The amount W_0^f is sometimes said in these circumstances to be "imputed as economic rent" to the original owners of the productive opportunity. In Fig. 4-11(a), this charge to the firm is represented by a shift of the

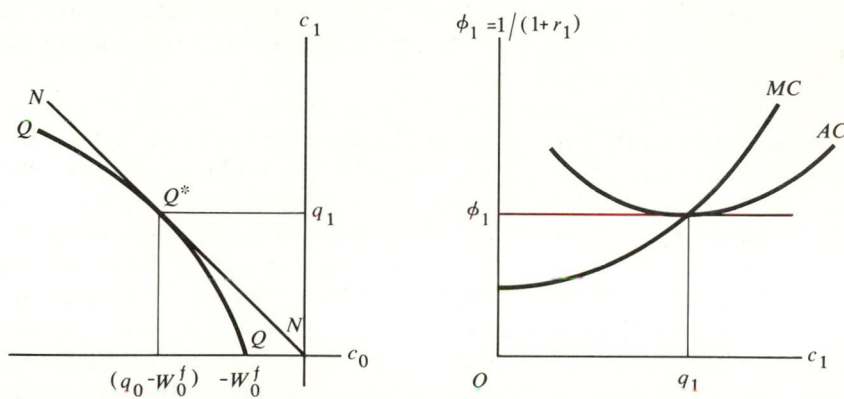

FIG. 4-11. (a) Productive equilibrium for the firm (long run), (b) Traditional long-run equilibrium

productive-opportunity locus QQ to the left by the amount W_0^f. The optimal solution Q^* now suffices only to attain a final zero-wealth level for the firm. For the traditional formulation as portrayed in Fig. 4-11(b), the marginal cost MC as before equals the reciprocal of the absolute value of the slope dq_1/dq_0 along QQ. The average cost AC at the equilibrium point equals $(-q_0 + W_0^f)/q_1$, on the assumption that the "rent" W_0^f is paid out as a lump sum to the owners or previous owners of the productive opportunity.

NUMERICAL EXAMPLE

We can employ the data of Table 2 in Section A, merely interpreting the productive opportunity as belonging to the firm owned by individual-j rather than to him in person. The firm's productive-opportunity function would then be $(q_0^f + 40)^2/20 + q_1^f = 80$. Thinking of c_1 as the commodity produced, we know that the equilibrium price $\phi_1 = \frac{1}{2}$, output $q_1^f = 60$, and input $q_0^f = -20$. Marginal cost is $-dq_0^f/dq_1^f = 10/(q_0^f + 40)$, so that $MC = \frac{1}{2}$, as expected. Average cost $AC = -q_0/q_1$ is $\frac{1}{3}$. Hence the firm's wealth gain W_0^f is $(\frac{1}{2} - \frac{1}{3})60 = 10$, the same as that obtained by the individual in the earlier example.

In long-run equilibrium, the value of W_0^f would have to be charged against the operations of the firm (as the individual could sell the firm to anyone for that amount). Consequently, the zero-profit condition obtains.

I. EQUILIBRIUM IN A CONTINUOUS-TIME MODEL

It will now be possible to indicate the nature of the market equilibrium attained in a paradigm of choice over continuous time. In full generality the problem poses a number of mathematical difficulties, excessive attention to which would be unprofitable here. Consequently, a solution will be presented only for a highly special (though still instructive) case, employing the representative-individual device.

In particular, the choice problem considered will be of the simple-duration type (e.g., the aging of wine) already analyzed on the level of the optimizing individual in Chapter 3, Section D. It will be recalled that the individual's decision involved the choice of the optimal level of current sacrifice q_0 and the optimal duration θ. As a radical simplification, it will be assumed here that a *stationary state* has been attained, so that there is a level steady flow of input and output. This condition can be reconciled with the point-input point-output nature of the simple-duration productive process. At each instant of time the individual lays down an input, setting under way a new productive interval of length θ, while simultaneously drawing the matured output of a terminated interval commenced θ time units earlier.[21]

The equation system can be suggestively indicated as follows. First, the production function and productive optimum conditions can be set down directly from the analysis in Chapter 3, Section D:

$$Q(q_\theta, q_0, \theta) = 0$$

$$\frac{\partial q_\theta}{\partial q_0} = \omega_0(q_\theta, q_0, \theta) \qquad \begin{array}{l}\text{Production function} \\ \text{(three equations)}\end{array} \qquad (9)$$

$$\frac{\partial q_\theta}{\partial \theta} = \omega_\theta(q_\theta, q_0, \theta)$$

[21] Despite the repetitive nature of the production, this is not a *rotation* situation. The distinguishing mark of the latter is the tie-in between the commencement of one productive cycle and the termination of an earlier one—as, for example, when land must be "liberated" from carrying a stand of mature trees before a new planting can be undertaken. Here the assumption is that the new opportunities come into existence autonomously at every date; the producer can make the choice of how long to carry mature older investments without directly affecting the new opportunities. In the terminology of Chapter 3, the "projects" of different dates are *independent*.

$$-\frac{\partial q_\theta}{\partial q_0} = e^{r\theta}$$

Productive optimum
(two equations) $\qquad$ (10)

$$\frac{\partial q_\theta}{\partial \theta} = rq_\theta$$

The consumptive side can now be developed on the basis of the continuous-time utility function introduced in Chapter 3, Section E:

$$U = \int_0^\infty e^{-\eta t} v(c_t) \, dt$$

Here η is the "time-bias parameter," while the "utility-of-income" function $v(c_t)$ provides a utility valuation as of time t for consumption of that date. Thus the parameter η can also be regarded as a "discount factor for future utilities." Then:

$$-\frac{\partial c_\theta}{\partial c_0} = \frac{v_0' e^{\eta \theta}}{v_\theta'}$$

Preference function
(one equation) $\qquad$ (11)

$$-\frac{\partial c_\theta}{\partial c_0} = e^{r\theta}$$

Consumptive optimum
(one equation) $\qquad$ (12)

Here v_0' is contracted notation for $dv(c_0)/dc_0$ and v_θ' for $dv(c_\theta)/dc_\theta$. $e^{r\theta}$ can be interpreted as $1/\phi_\theta$, as in the usual consumptive-optimum condition. Note that the indifference-curve slope in (11) is a function only of c_0 and c_θ. This feature permits the suggestive solution in terms of variables at $t = 0$ and $t = \theta$ only.

If the representative-individual device were not being used, it would be necessary to have a wealth constraint in the form

$$c_0 + \phi_\theta c_\theta = (y_0 + q_0) + \phi_\theta(y_\theta + q_\theta)$$

But for the representative individual, the market constraint is analytically redundant, being implied by the conservation conditions:

$$c_0 = y_0 + q_0$$

Conservation conditions

$$c_\theta = y_\theta + q_\theta$$

(one independent equation) $\qquad$ (13)

The redundancy of the second conservation equation follows here directly from the fact that the marginal rates of substitution in production and consumption are both set equal to $e^{r\theta}$.

Finally, we have the stationarity condition:

$$c_0 = c_\theta \qquad \text{Stationarity condition} \atop \text{(one equation)} \qquad (14)$$

There are thus nine independent equations to determine the variables: $\partial q_\theta / \partial q_0$, $\partial q_\theta / \partial \theta$, q_0, q_θ, θ; $\partial c_\theta / \partial c_0$, c_0, c_θ; and r.

Given the stationarity, it is intuitively evident that the solution can be generalized from the two dates $t = 0$ and $t = \theta$ to an infinity of dates—that is, to every pair consisting of time t and time $t + \theta$. One other point worthy of remark is that in this system the market interest rate r equals the time-bias parameter η. This we may see directly by comparing equations (11) and (12) under the stationarity assumption, so that $v_0' = v_\theta'$.[22]

NUMERICAL EXAMPLE

In the last numerical example of Chapter 3, Section D, an individual possessed a productive opportunity expressed by the equation $q_\theta = A \ln(-q_0) + B \ln \theta - C$, with $A = B = C = 10$. With a market interest rate of 10 per cent, the present value of the opportunity (wealth gain of the individual) was maximized at the (approximate) solution values $\theta = 4.3$ years, $q_0 = -6.5$, and $q_\theta = 23.3$. These solution values will remain valid on the social level of analysis under the assumed stationarity condition, if the utility function is consistent with the $r = 10$ per cent assumed in the earlier example. This can be achieved by setting the time-bias parameter $\eta = .1$, while $v(c_t)$ might take a form such as $\ln c_t$. Thus, the 10 per cent interest rate will hold at stationarity.

To assure that stationarity holds, it is necessary for the individual to possess an endowment stream $y(t)$ such that an investment of 6.5 at each time t and return on investment of 23.3 at each time $t + \theta$ lead to a constant attained flow $p(t) = c(t)$. If it is assumed that at the date $t = 0$ there exists an already-ongoing stationary process (so that productive investments at the rate of 6.5 have been made at all past dates at least back to $t = -\theta$), then it is evident that *any* level endowment stream will meet the desired condition. For, if $y_t = y$, a constant for all t, the level attained-income (and consumption) stream $y + 23.3 - 6.5 = y + 16.8$ can be maintained at all dates from $t = 0$ on. In particular, it would be possible to have $y = 0$ (though one might then ask where the original inputs came from, to start the process at some "prehistoric" date).

If it is assumed, on the other hand, that the process is started up at $t = 0$ with no ongoing production "in the works," the missing flow of 23.3 over the interval from $t = 0$ to $t = \theta$ would have to be provided by a correspondingly larger endowment for those dates.

---

[22] This result is only a special case. However, for any homothetic utility function it will be true that the interest rate at stationarity (along the 45° line) is necessarily determined by the constant slope of the indifference curves crossing that ray.

J. THE TERM STRUCTURE OF INTEREST RATES

One traditional question that has been extensively investigated, by both theorists and empiricists, is the following: Is there a normal pattern or *term structure* of the "long-term" interest rates $R_1, R_2, \ldots, R_T$ defined in Table 3 above? Do the average rates that discount future maturities to present values typically increase, or decrease, with term to maturity? Or do they follow some more complex law?

Lack of space precludes an adequate theoretical discussion of this issue here. And indeed, there is reason to believe that the question cannot be fully resolved without explicit consideration of the role of uncertainty. However, within the certainty model the major force at work is the anticipation today of changes over time in the *relative* provision (endowment as modified by productive transformations) of present and future goods. If we anticipate now that 1980 will be better-endowed relative to 1981 than 1970 relative to 1971, we are implicitly expecting a fall over time of the short-term (annual) interest rate r_1. This anticipation would express itself today in a declining term structure of the long-term rates R_t.

What are the determinants of the *relative* provisions of present and future incomes, at future dates? Assuming that there is no reason to expect any systematic changes in patterns of time-preference, the governing consideration must be what happens to time-productivity over time. Suppose first that there exists only a permanently fixed set of opportunities for productive conversion of present into future claims—as in the case of a mine, where only leaner and leaner strata remain to be exploited as the richer ones are exhausted. Then in the future, any given sacrifice of then-current consumption will lead to a lesser next-year return than is the case today. The downward course over time of average and marginal time-productivities will dictate a corresponding downward trend over time in the short-term interest rate—reflected today in a declining structure of long-term rates.

On the other hand, suppose that transformation opportunities between present and future claims are replenished over time. This might be due to some recurrent natural force, e.g., the regular inundation of the Nile that restores the fertility of its delta. More importantly in the modern world, of course, is the continuous improvement in technological knowledge that re-generates new opportunities as the old ones are exhausted. The forces tending to maintain or even increase marginal time-productivities over time lead to an anticipation of higher future short-term rates—whose reflection today will be a rising term structure of long-term rates of interest. At any moment of time, therefore, the term structure of (real) interest rates reflects the balance of these pessimistic and optimistic views today as to the course of time-productivity in the future.

K. SUMMARY AND PROSPECT

The central theme of this work, originally set forth in Chapters 1 and 2, is that the theory of investment and interest must not be regarded as following laws different from those of "mainstream" price theory. Rather, the theory of investment and interest *is* price theory applied to choice-objects of dated consumption claims. Under a number of simplifying assumptions, to be relaxed in later chapters—a world of certainty, perfect and complete markets for dated consumption claims, no demand for liquidity and so no money, and a single consumptive commodity distinguished only by date—the analysis here followed the standard format of price theory. (1) On the private level of decision (Chapter 3), individuals seek optimal consumptive combinations in terms of their intertemporal preference patterns (indifference maps), given the productive and market opportunities for converting their endowed baskets into alternative consumptive combinations. (2) On the social level of analysis (Chapter 4), prices and aggregate quantities produced and consumed, of each of the choice-objects, are determined by an over-all market supply-demand equilibrium.

Approached in this way, interest and investment are seen to be derivative rather than fundamental magnitudes in the theory of intertemporal choice. The fundamental magnitudes are the quantities and prices of the objects of choice—dated consumptions. Investment is not a choice-object but is the process of conversion (or the amount converted) of current funds or consumption potential into future consumption. Market equilibrium can, as we have seen, be regarded as determined by the supply of saving and the demand for investment. But this is a somewhat artificial way of looking at the equilibrium of supply and demand, for investment and consumption purposes *combined*, in the market for the choice-object of current funds.

Interest is also a magnitude derived from what the markets actually determine: the price relationships among funds of different dates. Thus, the equilibrium ϕ_1^0 in the elementary two-period model, the price of a future dollar or unit consumption claim in current dollars, is by definition equal to $1/(1 + r_1)$, where r_1 is the interest rate in the sense of the "agio" or premium on this year's as against next year's funds. Or, in terms of the discrete-perpetuity model, the market determines ϕ_∞^0—the price of a level perpetual future income flow—and this by definition equals $1/r$, where r is the interest rate in the sense of the annual perpetual yield on a principal sum. Much of the mystery of investment and interest theory is resolved by cutting through these derivative concepts so as to formulate the analysis directly in terms of prices and quantities of the desired objects—dated consumption claims.

Another source of confusion has been the use, by different authors, of one or another of the various models or paradigms of intertemporal choice. Each of these models is a reduction of the complex problem of choice over the entire continuum of present and future time into a format more convenient for our limited intuitions and analytical powers. Once it is appreciated that all of these paradigms are artifacts to guide the mind, and none is reality itself, each can be understood in its proper role as emphasizing one or another aspect of intertemporal choice.

The key substantive results of the analysis to this point can be briefly stated. On the private level of decision, given perfect and complete funds markets, the individual or firm is enabled to attain the best possible consumption combination by maximizing wealth—i.e., by choosing among the productive opportunities available so as to generate a time distribution of dated consumption claims whose present value is maximal. On the social level, the fundamental determinants of interest and investment—or ultimately of the prices and quantities of dated consumptions—are time preference and time productivity. The former represents the terms on which individuals are *willing* to exchange consumption claims of different dates; the latter represents the terms on which the physical opportunities provided by Nature *enable* individuals or firms to transform potential consumptions of different dates one into another.

Up to this point in the study, we have been concerned only with *real* interest theory: the relations between prices of dated funds that would hold in a world of barter. There is a view, not only widely held by the man in the street but also supported by prominent economists as well, that interest is "essentially" a monetary phenomenon. That this view cannot be true has been amply illustrated above; under quite a wide range of disparate paradigms of intertemporal choice, a perfectly clear meaning can be attached to the intertemporal price ratios that are related definitionally to interest rates. Further, these interest rates are determined by the real forces of time preference and time productivity, and in turn serve as market constraints upon individual consumption and investment decisions.

Nevertheless, it remains true that in the modern world money exists—and at least presumptively has important effects. The next chapter is devoted to an assessment, on the private and social levels of analysis, of the role of money as a determinant of the system of intertemporal price ratios and of consumption and investment.

BIBLIOGRAPHY

For the theory of investment and interest placed in the context of intertemporal choice and equilibrium, there is no substitute for a close study of Fisher's basic work cited below. The other references represent a variety of interesting modern developments.

IRVING FISHER, *The Theory of Interest* (The Macmillan Company, 1930; reprinted [Kelley] 1955).

ABBA P. LERNER, *The Economics of Control* (The Macmillan Company, 1944), Chaps. 20, 25.

ROBERT M. SOLOW, *Capital Theory and the Rate of Return* (Rand McNally & Company, 1964), Chap. 1.

AXEL LEIJONHUFVUD, *On Keynesian Economics and the Economics of Keynes* (Oxford University Press, 1968), Chap. 4.

GARY S. BECKER, *Human Capital* (National Bureau of Economic Research, 1964), Chap. 2.

PAUL A. SAMUELSON, "An Exact Consumption-Loan Model of Interest with or Without the Social Contrivance of Money," *Journal of Political Economy*, **66** (Dec., 1958).

5 MONEY, INTEREST, AND THE PRICE LEVEL

This chapter provides an introduction to the functioning of *money* as a peculiar commodity, distinct from the dated consumptive goods that have heretofore entered the analysis. The role of money cannot be fully comprehended under the assumption of a world of certainty. Nevertheless, an initial approach can be attempted, in which the "real" interest and prices of earlier chapters (denumerated in terms of a nonmonetary consumptive commodity as numeraire) are related to the money interest and prices observable in the world.

A. MONEY AS A COMMODITY

What is money? No verbal definition will be offered here, but only an ostensive one: moneys are the special commodities that we observe mediating the great bulk of transactions (except in the most primitive economies). The shoemaker does not exchange shoes for bread with the baker, but instead sells shoes for and buys bread with money. It will be convenient to characterize money, the medium of exchange, by a number of somewhat unrealistic, idealized properties: (1) Money is a mere counter, and does not consist of objects themselves desirable or useful for nonmonetary (productive or consumptive) purposes.[1] (2) Individuals and other private economic agents do

[1] Money historically *originated* in the form of useful commodities, and metallic coins may retain significant commodity value in comparison with their stated denominations. But paper moneys have only trivial commodity value, while demand deposits (not being physical objects) have none at all.

not produce or create money.[2] (3) Money can be stored costlessly over time. (4) Money does not bear interest—i.e., it does not yield any increment over time to its holder.[3]

Given these properties, why is money desired? Why is money ever *held*, rather than spent immediately for current consumables or lent at interest (in effect spent on the purchase of future consumables)? In terms of the choice-theoretic framework of this study, there are two main ways of answering this question. *First*, we might say that money-holding enters directly into preference functions, that people derive satisfaction from indulging their "taste" for holding money. This need not be miserly pleasure in mere hoarding, but rather can refer to the avoidance of certain (as yet unexplained) discomforts associated with being "short" of money as a particular form of wealth. Note that this line of answer seems to conflict with the basic postulate of this work that utility attaches only to consumption, not to the mere holding of assets.

Second, an ultimately more satisfactory explanation, consistent with the basic postulate, relates money-holding not to the subjective preference function but to the objective opportunity set. The contention would be that the use of money enlarges productive and consumptive opportunities by reducing "transaction costs," imperfections of the exchange process, from what they would be under barter. This means that in the absence of money, the market lines such as MM in Fig. 1-1 (representing exchange opportunities between two contemporaneous commodities A and B) and in Fig. 2-1 (representing exchange opportunities between dated consumptive claims c_0 and c_1) would actually *not* be straight lines through the respective endowment points. The financial-opportunity sets would not be the simple triangles OMM shown in the diagrams; transaction costs would make some combinations within the triangles impossible of attainment. Money-holding, while costly to private agents in terms of foregone production or consumption, would have the potentiality of enlarging the opportunity set (over at least a part of its range) by reducing or eliminating these transaction costs.

As an admittedly imperfect approximation, the first approach (actually, the standard one in the literature of monetary theory) will be adopted here: It is postulated that money is a peculiar commodity, such that people derive utility merely from holding it. The property of money that yields this benefit

[2] Historically, and even to this date, private agencies (banks) have been able to produce money in the form of notes or demand deposits. Recent work in monetary theory has emphasized the distinction between the "inside money" produced by private agencies in response to normal profit incentives, and the "outside money" generated by policy-making authorities. See J. G. Gurley and E. S. Shaw, *Money in a Theory of Finance* (The Brookings Institution, 1960), chap. 3.

[3] Interest-bearing currencies are not unknown, and at times interest has been paid on demand deposits. Also, some economists would include time deposits, and possibly other interest-bearing "liquid" assets, in the monetary category. As such assets do not ordinarily serve to mediate transactions, they are not here considered to be money.

is called *liquidity*, the measure of which is the "real value" of the money held—
its command over nonmonetary commodities. If there is a single monetary
commodity m and a homogeneous nonmonetary commodity or "good" c,
then at time t real cash-holding or liquidity is measured by m_t/ϕ_t^{mt}. Here ϕ_t^{mt}
is the price of c_t in terms of m_t—i.e., the *price level* at time t.

B. APPRECIATION AND INTEREST

This section relates the real and the monetary rates of interest to
movements of the price level over time. Following the definition above, the
current price level will be denoted ϕ_0^{mo}—the price of the current homogeneous
consumptive commodity c_0 in terms of current money m_0. This price is the
ratio $\Delta m_0/\Delta c_0$ at which exchanges at time 0 of money for commodities are
taking place. Similarly, ϕ_1^{m1} represents the price level at $t = 1$. We can
also symbolize by $\phi_{m_1}^{mo}$ the price of next year's money in terms of this year's
money—i.e., the market ratio $\Delta m_0/\Delta m_1$ effective in time 0 trading.

Within the two-period paradigm of choice, the *monetary rate of interest* r_1^m
is then defined in

$$\phi_{m_1}^{mo} = \frac{1}{1 + r_1^m} \tag{1}$$

That is, the money rate of interest is the rate of discount on future money
units (future dollars) m_1 as against current dollars m_0. Or, in terms of the
market ratio $\Delta m_1/\Delta m_0$, we can say that r_1^m is the "premium" on current
dollars—in the sense that $1 + r_1^m$ of future dollars m_1 equal in market value 1
dollar of m_0.

The corresponding *real* rate of interest (what was called in previous
chapters "the" rate of interest) was defined in

$$\phi_1^0 = \frac{1}{1 + r_1} \tag{2}$$

Thus, the real rate of interest is the rate of discount on future real claims c_1
in terms of current real claims c_0, or the "premium" on current real claims in
terms of future ones.

The exchange ratio between future dollars and current dollars,
$\Delta m_1/\Delta m_0 = 1 + r_1^m$, can then be expressed in terms of the real rate of
interest and the price levels at $t = 0$ and $t = 1$:

$$1 + r_1^m = \frac{\phi_1^{m1}(1 + r_1)}{\phi_0^{mo}} \tag{3}$$

This equation says, in effect, that the market ratio effective today between future and current monetary units must equal the market ratio between future and current real claims when each class of claims is multiplied by its respective price level. This is a condition that holds, in equilibrium, when the future price level is known. Or more precisely, equation (3) may be regarded as holding in terms of the currently observable real and monetary rates of interest, and the future price level as *anticipated* today.

The ratio $\phi_1^{m_1}/\phi_0^{m_0}$ can also be written as $1 + a$, where a is the proportionate anticipated price *appreciation* of the consumptive commodity in terms of money, or the anticipated rate of price inflation. Then

$$1 + r_1^m = (1 + a)(1 + r_1) \qquad (4)$$

or

$$r_1^m = a + r_1 + ar_1 \qquad (5)$$

Thus, the monetary rate of interest equals the real rate of interest plus the rate of anticipated inflation, plus the cross product of the latter two rates. When a and r_1 remain in their usual range of percentage points, the last term on the right in equation (5) can, to a good approximation, be ignored. The shorter the compounding period, the more correct is the approximation.[4] For continuous compounding, the relation $r_1^m = a + r_1$ is exact.

In terms of *realized* rather than *anticipated* changes, the equations above continue to hold if a is taken to refer to the actual proportionate price-level increase as observed at $t = 1$, and r_1 to the realized or *commodity rate* of interest earned on money loans made at $t = 0$. The commodity rate r_1 earned on money loans yielding nominally at the rate r_1^m is

$$r_1 = \frac{(1 + r_1^m)/\phi_1^{m_1}}{1/\phi_0^{m_0}} - 1$$

This is the proportionate real premium, the excess over par of real c_1-claims actually received per real c_0-claim sacrificed, by lending at interest at the monetary rate r_1^m. Thus $1 + r_1$ equals $(1 + r_1^m)/(1 + a)$, which leads again to equation (4). So the money rate is (approximately) equal to the sum of the actual *historical* price-level change and the realized *commodity* rate of interest, as well as to the sum of the *anticipated* price-level change and the *real* rate of interest. If anticipations are correct, of course, the commodity rate as realized at $t = 1$ will equal the real rate effective in the market at $t = 0$.

[4] With quarterly compounding, but defining r_1, a, and r_1^m as annual rates, equation (4) becomes

$$1 + \frac{r_1^m}{4} = \left(1 + \frac{a}{4}\right)\left(1 + \frac{r_1}{4}\right)$$

Then

$$r_1^m = a + r_1 + \frac{ar_1}{4}$$

C. IMPLICATIONS AND APPLICATIONS

The relations above have a number of direct implications—for example, that under circumstances of *anticipated* inflation (positive a) the monetary rate of interest r_1^m will tend to be relatively high [equation (5)]. This conclusion is based upon the premise that the real rate of interest, r_1, would not be greatly affected by the inflationary process. Monetary interest rates have indeed been observed to reach high levels when inflationary expectations have become established: e.g., during hyperinflations and the long-continuing inflationary developments of a number of Latin American countries.

Under more "normal" conditions, anticipations of price-level changes are not held so confidently. Nevertheless, a positive historical association of money rates and actual price-level changes has been found.[5] At the same time, the imperfect forecasting ability of investors shows itself in a realized commodity rate of interest that moves *inversely* to the price-level change. That is, the evidence indicates that instead of the money rate's adapting itself perfectly to the price-level change so that the commodity rate remain constant (equal to the presumably constant real rate), the money rate adapts only partially. For example, at the beginning of a particular year the anticipated price-level increase might have been 5 per cent, whereas the actual price-level increase later turned out to be 10 per cent. If the real rate was 4 per cent, the money rate determined at the beginning of the year would have been approximately 9 per cent—whereas 14 per cent would have been the correct (fully adjusted) rate. Thus, in terms of anticipations, equation (5) would have taken the (approximate) form $9\% = 5\% + 4\%$, but in terms of realizations $9\% = 10\% + (-1\%)$. The realized commodity rate r_1 thus tends to be low, and sometimes actually negative, to the extent that an actual price-level *increase* is not adequately anticipated; if it is an actual price-level *decrease* that is less than fully anticipated, the realized commodity rate will be high.

In conditions of inflation, there are often complaints about the high money rate brought about by the anticipated price-level change, as indicated in equation (5). In response to these complaints, the government might try to hold r_1^m down by attempting to issue enough additional currency to "meet the needs" of borrowers at a "reasonable" money rate. We will see below that, under certain conditions, an *unanticipated* increase in current money supply can lower r_1^m. But equation (5) suggests that unless anticipations are seriously mistaken, a lower equilibrium for r_1^m could never be obtained by this

[5] Irving Fisher, *The Rate of Interest* (The Macmillan Company, 1907), pp. 270–280. In his later *The Theory of Interest* (The Macmillan Company, 1930) Fisher obtained very high correlations by constructing an index of anticipated price-level changes based on a "distributed-lag" expectations model. That is, he assumed that anticipations were determined as a weighted average of past experience, higher weights being given to more recent years.

process—because r_1^m tends to be determined by the given a and r_1. Indeed, the increased issue of currency is likely to lead to a rise in the anticipated rate of price-level change a, and thus raise the money rate further. (It is true, however, that the inflationary process may eventually interfere with the productive economy so as to reduce the real rate r_1—this will not be a desired consequence, but it would have some counterbalancing effect on r_1^m.)

An interesting implication of equation (5) is that if the money rate of interest were zero, under conditions of fully anticipated changes the price level would have to be falling (assuming a normally positive real rate r_1). From this point of view, a positive monetary rate of interest can be regarded as a social invention designed to avoid inconveniences associated with a steadily falling price level.[6]

The assumed costless storability of money also sets a limit on the possible rate of fully anticipated price-level change. If money can be costlessly stored, $\phi_{m_1}^{mo}$, the discounted price of future money today, cannot be greater than unity—hence [from equation (1)] the monetary rate of interest r_1^m cannot be negative. Neglecting the product term ar_1, from equation (5) we can infer that the consumptive commodity cannot depreciate relative to money (the price level cannot fall, or a be negative) in a proportion greater than the real rate of interest. Thus, a real rate of interest of 5 per cent and a price-level fall of 10 per cent would be impossible as fully anticipated changes.

D. DEMAND FOR LIQUIDITY VS. DEMAND FOR GOODS[7]

Money and the Price-Level: "Timeless" Model

In constructing a choice-theoretic system involving the artificial commodity "liquidity," it will be helpful first to employ a "timeless" or one-period model like that introduced in Chapter 1. More specifically, in this section a world of pure exchange will be assumed in which the only desired commodities are consumption goods c and real liquidity m/ϕ; c corresponds to an even flow of a homogeneous consumptive commodity over the decision period, while m/ϕ represents a holding of monetary units divided by the price level.[8]

---

[6] A. P. Lerner, *The Economics of Control* (The Macmillan Company, 1944), chap. 20.

[7] The analysis of this section is a development of concepts expounded in D. Patinkin, *Money, Interest, and Prices*, 2nd ed. (Harper & Row, Publishers, 1965).

[8] In this section only, dealing with a timeless or single-period model, the time subscript will be dropped. If we imagine that the single decision period is the current one, then c here would be denoted c_0 in our standard notation, while m/ϕ corresponds to m_0/ϕ_0^{mo}.

The equation system for this problem takes on a familiar form, with m/ϕ now becoming one of the objects of choice.

$$\left.\frac{d(m/\phi)}{dc}\right|_U = \Upsilon\left(c, \frac{m}{\phi}\right) \qquad \text{Liquidity-preference function} \qquad \text{(I equations)} \qquad (6)$$

Equation (6) says that the marginal rate of substitution (m.r.s.) between real consumption and real liquidity (the slope along the indifference curve between the two objects of choice in Fig. 5-1) is a function of their respective

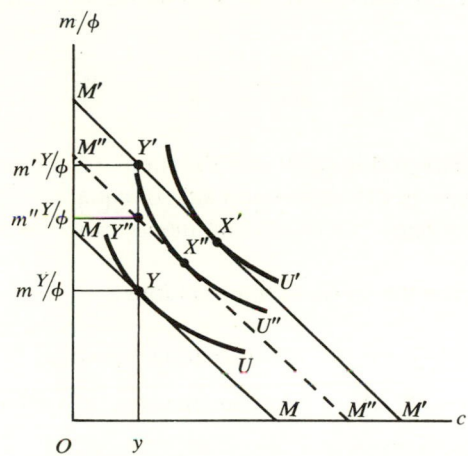

FIG. 5-1   Effect of change in all money-endowments

amounts. The formulation of the preference function in terms of *real* liquidity rather than nominal monetary quantities is called, in the literature of monetary theory, "absence of money illusion."

$$\phi c + m = \phi y + m^Y \qquad \text{Wealth constraint} \qquad \text{(I equations)} \qquad (7)$$

The wealth constraint here says that the value of consumption (i.e., the value of consumption goods endowed plus the increment purchased) plus monetary balances retained must equal the value of the goods-plus-money endowment. The same relation can also be expressed as

$$\phi(c - y) = m^Y - m \qquad (7')$$

This says that the value of the individual's excess demand for goods must equal his excess supply for money.

Maximizing utility subject to the wealth constraint leads directly to the individual's optimum condition:[9]

$$\frac{d(m/\phi)}{dc}\bigg|_U = -1 \qquad \begin{array}{l} \text{Consumptive optimum} \\ (I \text{ equations}) \end{array} \tag{8}$$

That is, the optimum balance between consumption and real liquidity is attained where the m.r.s. between the two is unity. This is obvious in that the "price" of *real* liquidity is simply a unit of consumption. Equation (8) can equivalently be expressed in terms of nominal monetary units as

$$\frac{dc}{dm} = -\frac{1}{\phi} \tag{8'}$$

The relationship between this result and the standard consumptive optimum is clarified if we think of the right-hand side of equation (8') as the ratio of the money price of money (unity) to the money price of the consumption good (ϕ).

Finally there are the conservation relations:

$$\sum c = \sum y \qquad \text{Conservation equations}$$
$$\sum m = \sum m^Y \qquad \text{(one independent equation)} \tag{9}$$

As usual, one of the conservation relations is redundant. The fact that the clearing of the market for goods implies the clearing of the market for money is known as *Walras' law*.

In the entire system of equations, then, there are $3I + 1$ independent equations to determine, for each of the I individuals, the variables $d(m/\phi)/dc$, c, and m—together with the unique market price ϕ.

This equation system leads directly to the simple relation between money and prices known as the *quantity theory*: that under certain standard

---

[9] The Lagrangian $\mathscr{L} = U(c, m/\phi) - \lambda(\phi[y - c] + [m^Y - m])$ is maximized with respect to the variables c and m/ϕ, leading to

$$\frac{\partial\mathscr{L}}{\partial c} = \frac{\partial U}{\partial c} + \lambda\phi = 0$$

$$\frac{\partial\mathscr{L}}{\partial(m/\phi)} = \frac{\partial U}{\partial(m/\phi)} + \lambda\phi = 0$$

Hence

$$\frac{d(m/\phi)}{dc} = -\frac{\partial U/\partial c}{\partial U/\partial(m/\phi)} = -1$$

conditions a given proportionate change in the quantity of money will lead to the same proportionate change in the price level. The conditions determining this result can be illustrated in the indifference map of Fig. 5-1, under the simplifying "representative-individual" assumption.[10] In Fig. 5-1 the initial situation is at $Y = (y, m^Y/\phi)$—y being the goods endowment, and m^Y the endowment of nominal and m^Y/ϕ the endowment of real cash balances. The point Y is an equilibrium situation given the initial conditions, as evidenced by the tangency with the indifference curve U for our representative individual. The wealth constraint MM in terms of c and real cash balances m/ϕ has a slope of -1—since a unit of consumption trades at par, by definition, against a unit of real liquidity. [This explains the condition of equation (8) specifying that the individual optimum occurs where the indifference curve attains a slope of unity.]

Now let us suppose that the nominal cash endowment for the representative individual unexpectedly doubles, so that $m'^Y = 2m^Y$. In Fig. 5-1 the individual now finds himself momentarily at Y', with a new wealth constraint $M'M'$ (having the same unitary slope as the old, of course). If the individuals of the society were willing, at their new wealth levels, to hold the baskets represented by Y', then the doubling of nominal money balances would lead to a doubling of real balances with no change in the price level. But, under the standard assumption that c is a *superior good*, each individual will attempt to employ part of the increment of his wealth for the enhancement of real consumption—i.e., he will seek to attain some point like X' on U', by exchanging cash for goods.[11]

But X' is not simultaneously attainable for all the members of the community—the actual amount of consumption goods available *per capita* remains only y. The attempt to exchange money holdings for goods will raise the price level to, say, ϕ', thus reducing the real-money endowment m^Y/ϕ. Let us consider, as a typical possibility, the revised endowment position Y'' in Fig. 5-1—where the momentary real-money endowment is m'^Y/ϕ'. Here again the superior-good condition leads to an attempt to move southeast from Y'' toward X'', the impossibility of which leads to a further rise in ϕ. Evidently, the only possible equilibrium is where the price level has risen enough to leave the real-money endowment unchanged from what it was before the increase in money endowment—i.e., to restore the equilibrium at Y. Thus, a proportionate increase in all money endowments, other things equal, will generate an equal proportionate change in the price level—as asserted by the "quantity theory."

---

[10] That is, a community of identical individuals is postulated, each with the same preferences, endowments, and opportunities.

[11] This "real-balance effect" (also known in the business-cycle literature as the "Pigou-effect") in the demand for commodities is, of course, only a special case of the "income (wealth) effect" of standard price theory. See Patinkin, *Money, Interest, and Prices*, p. 20.

NUMERICAL EXAMPLE

Let the utility function for the representative individual be $U = c^{.8}(m/\phi)^{.2}$, with the endowed quantities $y = 10$ and $m^Y = 100$, and let the price level $\phi = 40$. With these numbers the derivative $d(m/\phi)/dc = -4(m/\phi)/c$ has the value -1, so the endowed position is one of equilibrium. Let m^Y be suddenly increased in any given proportion, and (since c necessarily remains equal to y) ϕ must rise in the same proportion to maintain the equality with -1. This result is dictated by the "no money illusion" assumption, under which it is m/ϕ and never just m that enters into the utility function.

The exact quantity-theory relation between money and prices does not follow from the model, however, when the increased money supply no longer takes the form of a proportionate increase in *everyone's* money endowment. Figure 5-2 illustrates a case in which all individuals in the community have identical preference functions between consumption and real liquidity, and initially identical endowments at an equilibrium position Y. Now, however, assume that the money endowment doubles for *half* of the individuals (putting them, momentarily, at Y') but remains unchanged for the rest of the community (leaving them at Y). There has been a 50 per cent increase in the money supply, in the aggregate, but in addition the distribution has been shifted. As before, the individuals at Y' seek to move southeast toward X'; since the individuals at Y are in equilibrium, at the initial price level ϕ there will now be an excess demand for goods (excess supply of money). Consequently, the price level must again rise. But it need not rise in exactly the proportion 50 per cent to restore equilibrium. As the price level rises, the real endowments of both classes of individuals—those now at Y' and those still at Y—will fall vertically. The diagram illustrates a hypothetical case in which a 20 per cent rise in the price level has taken place; hence the height of Y'' is 80 per cent of the height of Y', and the height of $\overline{Y}''$ is 80 per cent of the

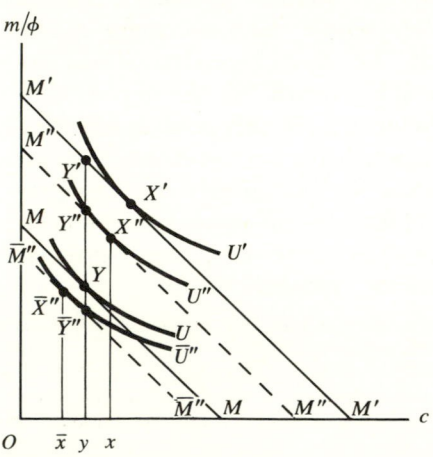

FIG. 5-2 Effect of change in half of money-endowments

height of Y. By construction, this has been made an equilibrium position; the individuals at the $\bar{X}''$ tangency have each given up the quantity $(y - \bar{x})$ of the consumption good, while those at the tangency X'' have each gained an equal amount $(x - y)$.

In the illustration above, the equilibrium rise in the price level was *less* than proportionate to the rise in the money supply. The wealth effect was so constructed that with increased real wealth an increment of real liquidity was mainly desired, while for decreased real wealth the contraction took place mainly in goods consumption. That is, real liquidity was assumed to be *relatively* (not absolutely) inferior for positions of the wealth line below MM, but relatively superior above MM. The necessity for assuming a peculiar shape for the indifference map could have been avoided by abandoning the representative-individual assumption. Suppose there are two types of individuals: one type for whom real liquidity is always relatively superior, another for whom the reverse is true. Then, if the increment in money endowment goes to the type of individual for whom real liquidity is relatively superior, the rise in the price level will tend to be *less* than proportionate to the aggregate increase in the money supply.

Despite the qualifying remarks of the last two paragraphs, it should be evident that the quantity relation between money and prices tends to hold, as a more or less precise approximation, within this "timeless" model.

Money, Interest, and Prices: Two-Period Model

In order to proceed to the more interesting problem of money supply in relation to *interest* as well as to *prices*, it is necessary to envisage a multiperiod decision situation. Even the simplest such situation—the two-period paradigm of choice under pure exchange—involves some difficulty for intuitive analysis when decisions must involve both goods and money at each date. But application of the standard format of our choice-theoretic structure will lead directly to a number of clear results.

We now consider *four* objects of choice: real consumption and real liquidity in each of two periods. Then there are *three* ratios of exchange to consider.[12]

$$\frac{\partial c_1}{\partial c_0}\bigg|_U = \Upsilon_1\left(c_0, c_1, \frac{m_0}{\phi_0}, \frac{m_1}{\phi_1}\right)$$

$$\frac{\partial (m_0/\phi_0)}{\partial c_0}\bigg|_U = \Upsilon_2\left(c_0, c_1, \frac{m_0}{\phi_0}, \frac{m_1}{\phi_1}\right) \qquad \begin{array}{l}\text{Time-and-liquidity} \\ \text{preference function} \\ (3I \text{ equations})\end{array} \qquad (10)$$

$$\frac{\partial (m_1/\phi_1)}{\partial c_1}\bigg|_U = \Upsilon_3\left(c_0, c_1, \frac{m_0}{\phi_0}, \frac{m_1}{\phi_1}\right)$$

[12] In this section, the simplified notation ϕ_0 will be used in place of $\phi_0^{m_0}$ for the current price level, and ϕ_1 in place of $\phi_1^{m_1}$ for the future price level. Thus, ϕ_1 here is *not* the same as $\phi_1^0 = 1/(1 + r_1)$, which has sometimes been written simply as ϕ_1 elsewhere in this work.

These equations express the three marginal rates of substitution in consumption or preference as functions of the amounts of the several objects of choice: the first m.r.s. is that between dated consumptions (pure time preference); the second is between consumption and real liquidity at $t = 0$; the third is between consumption and real liquidity at $t = 1$. (Still other marginal rates of substitution can be defined, e.g., between current and future real liquidity, but they will be implicitly determined by the three given above.)

The wealth constraint takes on a somewhat different form when we permit the *holding* as well as the *lending* of money. Specifically, we will assume that lending can only take place via money; lending can be regarded as the current-period purchase of bonds b_0, the future-period payoff on bonds being $b_1 = b_0(1 + r_1^m)$. Then, in the current period,

$$\phi_0 c_0 + m_0 + b_0 = \phi_0 y_0 + m_0^Y \qquad \text{(11a)}$$

That is, the value represented by current-period elements of the individual's wealth endowment can be distributed over consumption, money-holding, and bond purchases. We can also allow b_0 to be negative, representing the possibility of adding to current-period consumption (or money-holding) by drawing upon future-period elements of the wealth endowment. Such drawing is bound by the future-period constraint:

$$\phi_1 c_1 + m_1 - b_0(1 + r_1^m) = \phi_1 y_1 + m_0 + \Delta_1^m \qquad \text{(11b)}$$

Here the last term on the left-hand side represents the amount by which the value of time 1 consumption plus money-holding can exceed (if time 0 lending b_0 was positive) or fall short of (if b_0 was negative) the future-period endowment elements.[13] Of the last two terms on the right-hand side, m_0 represents the time 0 money-holding carried over to time 1, and Δ_1^m stands for any *anticipated* exogenous increment to money endowment between $t = 0$ and $t = 1$.

The two timed expenditure constraints (11a) and (11b) can now be combined into an over-all wealth constraint (11); note that bond-holding b_0 drops out of the equation:

$$\phi_0 c_0 + \frac{\phi_1 c_1}{1 + r_1^m} + \frac{r_1^m m_0 + m_1}{1 + r_1^m} = \phi_0 y_0 + \frac{\phi_1 y_1}{1 + r_1^m} + m_0^Y$$

$$+ \frac{\Delta_1^m}{1 + r_1^m} \qquad \begin{array}{l} \text{Wealth constraint} \\ (I \text{ equations}) \end{array} \qquad \text{(11)}$$

[13] In this formulation we do not say that an individual has an *endowment* of bonds; that is, we take the endowment situation as prior to any lending-borrowing decisions. This avoids some possible confusions, since the seeming analogy between bond endowment and money or godos endowment is a spurious one. In particular, the social total of bond endowments is necessarily zero; i.e., there would have to be for some individuals negative endowed bond quantities to balance any positive bond endowments. In contrast the goods endowments c_0 and c_1 and money endowments m_0 and m_1 are all necessarily nonnegative magnitudes for every individual.

Here the right-hand side can be regarded as the *sources* of wealth, and the left-hand side as the *uses* of wealth.[14]

The conditions for an individual optimum, obtained by the usual maximizing procedure, are given in equations (12).

$$\left.\frac{\partial c_1}{\partial c_0}\right|_U = -\frac{\phi_0}{\phi_1}(1 + r_1^m)$$

$$\left.\frac{\partial(m_0/\phi_0)}{\partial c_0}\right|_U = -\frac{1 + r_1^m}{r_1^m} \tag{12}$$

$$\left.\frac{\partial(m_1/\phi_1)}{\partial c_1}\right|_U = -1$$

As shown in equation (3), the expression on the right-hand side of the first equation above is also equal to $-(1 + r_1)$, where r_1 is the *real* rate of interest (under conditions of correctly anticipated price changes). This is, of course, the same result as that obtained earlier, in Chapter 4, for "moneyless" models. It would be wrong to infer, however, that the introduction of money-holding leaves unchanged the time-preference decision as among dated real consumptions, since the m.r.s. $\partial c_1/\partial c_0|_U$ will in general have been affected by the amount of real cash balances held as well as of c_0 and c_1 consumed [see equation (10)].

An asymmetry between the optimality condition governing present and future money-holding stands out clearly in the last two equations of (12). The third equation is in exactly the same form as equation (8) above for the "timeless" model. Since real money-holding at time 1, m_1/ϕ_1, represents sacrifice of an equal amount of real consumption c_1, the individual optimum must be where the marginal rate of substitution between the two real commodities is unity. But while real money-holding at time 0, m_0/ϕ_0, involves proximately a corresponding sacrifice of c_0, there are additional effects to consider. The time 0 money-holding is carried over to $t = 1$, making possible increased consumption (or money-holding) at the latter date; when this effect is taken into account at the initial $t = 0$ decision, the individual realizes that he need not sacrifice consumption c_0 unit-for-unit to hold liquidity m_0/ϕ_0. The equivalent c_0 sacrifice per unit of real liquidity is in fact $r_1^m/(1 + r_1^m)$—which can be interpreted as the c_1 consumption implicit in the *interest foregone*, $\phi_0 r_1^m/\phi_1$, discounted by the real rate of interest (m.r.s. between c_0 and c_1) on the right-hand side of the first equation of (12).

The asymmetry is a consequence of the two-period model, being due to the horizon assumption $T = 1$. It can be shown that, with a larger horizon,

---

[14] It may be noted that there is an asymmetry between the coefficients of m_0 and m_1, as compared with those of c_0 and c_1, on the left-hand side of (11). This asymmetry will be discussed below.

all but the last of the liquidity-versus-goods optima have the form of the middle rather than the last equation in (12).[15] Thus, the "timeless" liquidity-versus-goods equation (8) is fundamentally misleading. Setting the m.r.s equal to unity is optimal only if real liquidity represents a unit-for-unit sacrifice of consumption; when time is taken into account, this condition is true only in *terminal* periods (the "timeless" model really has a single period, which is therefore a terminal one).

The two-period model is completed by the conservation relations:

$$\sum c_0 = \sum y_0$$
$$\sum c_1 = \sum y_1$$
$$\sum m_0 = \sum m^Y \qquad \text{Conservation relations} \qquad (13)$$
$$\sum m_1 = \sum m_0 + \sum \Delta_1^m \qquad \text{(three independent equations)}$$

The last conservation equation diverges slightly from the usual form because of the autonomous increment Δ_1^m. As usual, one of the convervation equations is redundant.

We thus have, in the system of equations (10) through (13)—not counting (11a) and (11b), which were introduced only to lead up to the wealth constraint (11)—a total of $7I + 3$ independent equations. These determine, for each of the I individuals, the marginal rates of substitution $\partial c_1/\partial c_0$, $\partial(m_0/\phi_0)/\partial c_0$, and $\partial(m_1/\phi_1)/\partial c_1$, and the quantities c_0, c_1, m_0, and m_1—together with the market variables ϕ_0, ϕ_1, and r_1^m.

We can now turn to one of the central controversies of recent monetary theory and policy: Will an exogenous change in money supply act (exclusively or mainly) so as to raise the price level—as the quantity theory says?

---

[15] Consider a three-period model. Here c_2 and m_2/ϕ_2 also become objects of choice. We must now distinguish the two successive short-term rates r_1^m and r_2^m. The wealth constraint has the form

$$\phi_0 c_0 + \frac{\phi_1 c_1 + r_1 m_0}{1 + r_1^m} + \frac{\phi_2 c_2 + r_2 m_1 + m_2}{(1 + r_2^m)(1 + r_1^m)} = \phi_0 y_0 + m^Y + \frac{\phi_1 y_1 + \Delta_1^m}{1 + r_1^m} + \frac{\phi_2 y_2 + \Delta_2^m}{(1 + r_2^m)(1 + r_1^m)}$$

After the usual maximizing procedure, the optimum conditions (there are five in all) include

$$\left.\frac{\partial c_1}{\partial c_0}\right|_U = -\frac{\phi_0}{\phi_1}(1 + r_1^m)$$

$$\left.\frac{\partial(m_0/\phi_0)}{\partial c_0}\right|_U = -\frac{1 + r_1^m}{r_1^m}$$

$$\left.\frac{\partial(m_0/\phi_0)}{\partial c_0}\right|_U = -\frac{1 + r_2^m}{r_2^m}$$

Thus, the optimality conditions involving liquidity-versus-consumption at time 0 and time 1 both have the form of the middle equation of (12)—if time 1 is not the terminal period.

Or will its only or main effect be to reduce the monetary rate of interest—as the "Keynesian" theory has it? In the timeless model considered in the section above, a given proportionate change in money supply led to approximately the same proportionate change in the price level, in the manner dictated by the quantity theory (the effect being *precisely* in the same proportion when the augmentation of money supply took the form of a proportionate change in *all* individuals' money endowments). However, in the timeless model the interest rate does not even enter. Hence, only in a multiperiod model is it even possible to examine the alternative "Keynesian" hypothesis.

Of course, these hypotheses are being examined within the context of our model, some of the limitations or special features of which should be kept in mind. Among them are the general assumptions that only equilibrium states need be studied, and that there is full information (certainty) about future as well as present endowments, prices, and so on. Violation of one or both of these conditions may lead to behavior in the world inexplicable within the model. In Part II the assumption of certainty will be relaxed, but disequilibrium processes (which may be at the heart of much of the observed monetary phenomena) will not be considered in this work. Some of the specific assumptions bearing upon liquidity preference may also be recalled here: there is no money illusion, and consumption and real-liquidity are both superior goods.

Without further apology, we may now consider the effect of a change in money endowments upon the equilibrium of the system described in equations (10) through (13). The key question that arises is: What is meant by "a change in money endowments"? One example of such a change would be an increase in aggregate current money endowments $\sum m^Y$ (thus dictating a corresponding rise in current money holdings $\sum m_0$) such that *the monetary increment is carried over to the following period* (so as to similarly affect future money holdings $\sum m_1$). Alternatively, an augmentation of aggregate current money holdings $\sum m_0$ *relative to* the future aggregate $\sum m_1$ might be postulated. The implications of these two types of changes in money endowments will be quite different!

Starting with the first of these cases, assume to begin with that $\sum \Delta_1^m$—the aggregate autonomous increase in money endowments expected to occur in the interval between $t = 0$ and $t = 1$—is zero. Then, any aggregate proportionate change in $\sum m^Y$ necessarily leads to the *same* proportionate change in current and future money holdings, $\sum m_0$ and $\sum m_1$. Since monetary interest (in a two-period model) essentially measures the premium on current money relative to future money, intuition suggests that such an equiproportionate augmentation should tend to leave the money interest rate unchanged. This is strictly correct, within the model, if once again the aggregate change takes the form of the same proportionate increase in *every* individual's money endowment. We can think again in terms of a representative individual. An unexpected increase in nominal cash holdings m_0 and m_1, with prices (and interest) held constant, increases wealth—leading to the desire for augmenting the dated consumptions c_0 and c_1 at the expense of the now-excessive cash holdings. But the fixity of the social totals of goods endowments, $\sum y_0$ and $\sum y_1$, makes the satisfaction of this desire impossible—the effect being only to raise the price levels ϕ_0 and ϕ_1. Ultimately, the previous real equilibrium will be restored by increases in both ϕ_0 and ϕ_1 in the same proportion as the equiproportionate increments to $\sum m_0$ and $\sum m_1$.[16] From equations (12) it is evident that the monetary rate of interest r_1^m (and, also, the real rate r_1) remains unchanged.

NUMERICAL EXAMPLE

Let the utility function, for a representative individual, be

$$U = c_0^{.4}\left(\frac{m_0}{\phi}\right)^{.1} c_1^{.4}\left(\frac{m_1}{\phi_1}\right)^{.1}$$

Then equations (12) take on the forms:

$$\frac{c_1}{c_0} = \frac{\phi_0}{\phi_1}(1 + r_1^m)$$

$$4\,\frac{m_0/\phi_0}{c_0} = \frac{1 + r_1^m}{r_1^m}$$

$$4\,\frac{m_1/\phi_1}{c_1} = 1$$

Under the representative-individual condition $c_0 = y_0$, $c_1 = y_1$, $m_0 = m^Y$, and $m_1 = m^Y + \Delta_1^m$. Then, writing the initial-endowment vector in the form $(y_0, y_1;\ m^Y, m^Y + \Delta_1^m)$, the quantities involved will be specified as (10, 20; 100, 100). It may be verified that the implied initial equilibrium has $\phi_0 = 20$, $\phi_1 = 20$, and $r_1^m = 1$ (or 100 per cent). It may be verified also, from equation (3), that the real rate of interest r_1 also is 100 per cent.

Now, if m^Y is unexpectedly doubled, with the anticipated future money increment Δ_1^m held at zero, the revised endowment vector equals (10, 20; 200, 200). The market equilibrium becomes $\phi_0 = 40$, $\phi_1 = 40$, and $r_1^m = 1$. Thus, as predicted by the quantity theory, a given change in money supply affects price levels in the same proportion but leaves monetary interest unaffected. [The real rate of interest, being determined only by the ratio of c_1 to c_0 in the top equation of (12), remains the same under all of the manipulations of money endowments here considered.]

[16] The statement in the text would be strictly correct if the original equilibrium were unique—i.e., if the utility functions were such that only a single constellation of prices and interest cleared all markets. If this were not the case, the imposed endowment change and consequent adjustment process might conceivably lead to one of the other multiple equilibria instead of the original one.

So far, then, the results within this model support the "quantity" as against the "Keynesian" view: the impact of the money change is upon price levels, not rates of interest. (As before, if the change in monetary aggregates does not take the form of an equiproportionate change in *every* individual's endowment, the conclusion is true only in an approximate rather than exact sense.) What, then, of the familiar and intuitively appealing argument: Interest being the premium on money, if money becomes more plentiful, must not interest rates fall? The answer is that interest (monetary interest, that is) is the premium on *present* money as against *future* money; if both of these become equally more plentiful, there is no clear tendency for monetary rates of interest to fall.

This consideration suggests, however, that increased quantities of money would tend to reduce interest rates *if* the effect were to enlarge the aggregate of current relative to future money. There are a number of conceivable "changes in money endowments" having this effect. First, suppose that the aggregate expected increment in money supply $\sum \Delta_1^m$, taken into account in the private calculations underlying the initial equilibrium situation, were *positive* rather than zero. Then, since $\sum m_1$ is larger than $\sum m_0$, an unanticipated increase in current total money endowments $\sum m^Y$ would lead to a smaller *proportionate* change in later as against earlier money holdings. Under these conditions the change in $\sum m^Y$ *would* increase current money relative to future money, and thus tend to reduce the interest premium on current money. If the originally anticipated increment $\sum \Delta_1^m$ were of the order of 2 or 3 per cent per annum, this would be a minor effect. But with large anticipated money increments, an *unexpected* augmentation of current money may substantially reduce interest rates.

The effect just described would be strongly reinforced if the increments to current money endowments were not carried over at all to $t = 1$—i.e., were such as to leave the future total $\sum m_1$ unchanged. Such a situation involves *offsetting* changes in $\sum m^Y$ and $\sum \Delta_1^m$. Imagine a financial "panic." Current money is very scarce relative to future money—no one expects the panic to last more than a few months—and so monetary interest rates are very high. The monetary authorities might then provide an increment to $\sum m^Y$ while announcing that an equal aggregate amount of money would be retired at some date thereafter. Such a change, making current money relatively more plentiful (or less scarce) than before in comparison with future money, would clearly tend to reduce the monetary rate of interest.

NUMERICAL EXAMPLE

Table 1 (p. 150) illustrates the effects—upon current and future price levels, and upon the monetary interest rate—of a number of different senses of the expression "change in the quantity of money." A representative-individual

Table I*

EFFECTS OF THREE DIFFERENT "CHANGES IN QUANTITY OF MONEY"

		REAL ENDOWMENTS		MONEY ENDOWMENTS		PRICE LEVELS		INTEREST RATES	
		y_0	y_1	m^Y	$m^Y + \Delta_1^m$	ϕ_0	ϕ_1	r_1^m	r_1
I	*Before:*	10	20	100	100	20	20	100%	100%
	After:	10	20	200	200	40	40	100%	100%
II	*Before:*	10	20	100	200	$26\frac{2}{3}$	40	200%	100%
	After:	10	20	200	300	48	60	150%	100%
III	*Before:*	10	20	100	200	$26\frac{2}{3}$	40	200%	100%
	After:	10	20	200	200	40	40	100%	100%

* Conditions: $U = c_0^{.4}(m_0/\phi_0^m)^{.1}c_1^{.4}(m^1/\phi_1^m)^{.1}$

situation is assumed. Each pair of rows indicates a *before* and *after* set of equilibrium values, under the assumption that the changes take place at $t = 0$ in time to affect the market equilibrium.

The first pair of rows (comparison *I*) summarizes the previous numerical example, in which an unanticipated doubling of (equal) current and future money endowments leads simply to doubled current and future price levels, with no effect upon the monetary interest rate.

In the second pair of rows, the "before" situation is one in which a substantial increment in money supply Δ_1^m, between periods 0 and 1, is anticipated: the future money endowment is 200, where the current money endowment is 100. This consideration leads to a high money rate of interest (premium on current money) in the initial equilibrium. But then a given *unanticipated* increase of 100 in current *and* future money endowments represents a smaller proportionate increase for the latter. Consequently, we see that the future price level ϕ_1 rises by a smaller percentage than the current price level ϕ_0 —and the monetary interest rate (premium on current money) therefore declines.

In the third pair of rows, the "before" situation is again that in which a monetary increment $\Delta_1^m = 100$ is anticipated. But here the phrase "increase in the quantity of money" is taken to mean an increase in current money endowment that does *not* carry over to future money endowment. Hence the increase causes the monetary interest rate to fall sharply, while the current price level rises relative to the future price level.

The simple two-period model of choice between dated consumptive goods and dated real liquidities has been shown to be sufficiently comprehensive as to display *both* the quantity theorists' and the Keynesian theorists' predicted results consequent upon "changes in money supply." The seeming contradiction is resolved by noting that one result or the other follows, or possibly some mixture of the two, depending upon the precise meaning of the phrase "changes in the quantity of money." More exactly, the result follows from the assumption made about changes in the *time-distributed* endowments of money and consumptive goods.

E. CONCLUDING REMARK

In the modern literature of monetary theory, a "transactions motive" and an "asset motive" for holding cash are commonly distinguished. Indeed, in some models there are assumed to be two distinct *quantities* of money: transaction balances and asset balances. This classification is not ultimately satisfactory. When cash is held rather than expended in current transactions, its services are being reserved for *future* transactions. It is the potential dated transaction services of money that underlie the asset motive for holding cash.

This consideration points the way to a reconciliation of the demand for cash-holding with the postulate in this work that only consumption enters into preference functions. The seeming asset-demand for cash does not represent something desired for itself; rather, it is the current reflection of a future transaction-demand. And the transaction-demand is, as suggested earlier, a consequence of the functioning of money as a kind of *intermediate good* entering into the technology of exchange.[17] The "productivity" of money in exchange can make available preferred intertemporal consumption baskets, despite the sacrifice represented by real interest foregone on cash balances.[18] So an individual will hold cash not because of a "taste for liquidity," but only insofar as doing so is profitable in terms of the combination attained of his ultimate objects of choice—dated consumptions.

BIBLIOGRAPHY

Readings on real and money interest and the price level:

I. FISHER, *The Theory of Interest* (The Macmillan Company, 1930, reprinted [Kelley] 1955), Chaps. 2 and 19 (with appendix).

A. P. LERNER, *The Economics of Control* (The Macmillan Company, 1944), Chaps. 20 and 21.

R. A. KESSEL and A. A. ALCHIAN, "Effects of Inflation," *Journal of Political Economy*, **70** (Dec. 1962).

[17] The precise nature of this functioning, however, has not been explicated.

[18] It is a key theme of monetary theory that this private sacrifice is not a social sacrifice. For the community as a whole, there is no loss of real resources in holding the idealized money assumed in this chapter. (For a commodity money such as gold, of course, the conclusion is different.) The consequences of this divergence between the social and private costs of money cannot be explored here.

Readings on the demand for money and the quantity theory

M. FRIEDMAN, "The Quantity Theory of Money," *International Encyclopedia of the Social Sciences* (The Macmillan Company and The Free Press of Glencoe, Inc., 1968).

D. PATINKIN, *Money, Interest, and Prices*, 2nd ed. (Harper & Row, Publishers, 1965), Pt. 1.

M. BAILEY, "The Welfare Cost of Inflationary Finance," *Journal of Political Economy*, **64** (April 1956).

6 CAPITAL AND ACCUMULATION

The chapter preceding, designed to explain the interrelationships between monetary and real interest, represented a digression from the mainstream of this study. In the present chapter the analysis of *real* intertemporal choice and equilibrium, as developed in Chapters 3 and 4, will be coordinated with a more explicit theory of intertemporal production that takes account of the roles of labor and "capital" as *productive* commodities. In particular, it will now be admitted that the individual does not begin with an endowment of consumptive commodities, but rather an endowment of productive commodities—capital and labor—that must be converted via a productive process into objects of choice. In this development, the investment decision can be regarded as a choice between current consumption and formation of capital, while the rate of interest can be associated with the magnitude and rate of growth of the stock of capital. This chapter will touch on the nature of capital, its role in the productive process, and the considerations determining its magnitude over time (the topic of "accumulation").

A. THREE MEANINGS OF "CAPITAL"

The word "capital" is a source of enormous confusion because it is used by different authors—sometimes by single authors—in differing, inconsistent, and yet logically related senses. At least three distinguishable meanings are common in the literature; they may be denoted (1) *real capital*, (2) *capital value*, and (3) *liquid capital*.[1]

[1] The first two of these were mentioned in Chapter 2.

The distinction between real capital (sometimes called physical capital) and capital value is a familiar one, but one that must be formulated carefully. Real capital is a collection of *capital goods*. A capital good is a physical object existing in the present, but constituting the source of incomes or consumption opportunities in the future—as an apple tree is a source of future apples, corn seed a source of next year's corn, and a house a source of future shelter. The individual's choice between this year's corn and next year's corn, for example, could also be expressed as a choice between this year's corn and *this year's seed*. Capital goods are intermediate *productive* commodities, valuable not for their own sakes but only insofar as they represent the potentiality of generating the consumption goods that are the fundamental objects of choice. Real capital is thus coordinate with *labor*, the other main class of productive commodity.

Capital *value* may be thought of as the present market equivalent of the future income sequence or payments stream associated with some particular capital good. But it is useful to hold to the more abstract definition of Chapter 2, which does not necessarily require us to think in terms of explicit capital goods: Capital value is the *present* valuation of any sequence of *future* incomes or payments. (If we were to make it "any sequence of present or future incomes," capital value would be defined in the same way as wealth, but it is sometimes convenient to preserve a distinction between the two terms.) Thus, on this definition, endowed wealth can be divided into endowed current income and endowed capital value: $W_0^Y = y_0 + K_0^Y$.

These definitions of capital goods and capital values are *forward*-looking, not *backward*-looking. While it may be true that a capital good somehow "embodies" productive services of previous dates, the origin of a good representing a source of future productive services is not economically relevant. Thus for our purposes "natural resources" or "land"—whether or not these may be assumed to be in origin the gift of Nature or produced by man—are capital goods. And correspondingly, capital value does not derive from the historic values of previous inputs, or past outlay elements of an income stream; rather, capital value derives solely from the worth today of the future payments represented in the stream in question. The orchard yields the apples, but it is the value of the apples that determines the value of the orchard. Economic value is always prospective, never retrospective—"bygones are bygones."

Whereas confusion between real capital and capital value is rather infrequent, confusion between *capital value* and *liquid capital* is all too common. Liquid capital may be defined as a quantum of current funds c_0 available or intended for investment—sometimes called "free" capital. This is the sense of the word "capital" implicit in such phrases as "borrowing capital," "maximizing return on capital," "international capital flows," and so on. Capital value and liquid capital are both measured in units of current funds;

but the latter *is* a sum of current funds while the former is only a present valuation of future elements. Confusion often arises between the (possible) borrowing of liquid capital and the (impossible) borrowing of capital value. That is, one can borrow current investible funds on the strength of possession of an endowed or attainable future income stream—but an impoverished person cannot "borrow" an income stream or its equivalent capital value.[2]

In this study henceforth we will *never* find it necessary to speak of liquid capital. Avoiding the term reduces the possibility of confusion; we already have the perfectly satisfactory expression *investible funds* for this very concept.

B. CAPITAL VALUE

It is possible to reformulate, in terms of capital value, some of the results obtained above concerning investment decisions on the private level and market equilibrium on the social level of analysis. This can be done without explicit introduction of capital goods.

In Chapter 3 it was shown that, in a world of certainty and given the perfection of funds markets, maximization of wealth under the present-value rule is a correct principle for private investment decision. More specifically, the investor is advised to reach the productive solution P^* such that produced wealth W_0^P is a maximum, where

$$W_0^P = p_0 + \frac{p_1}{1 + r_1} + \cdots + \frac{p_T}{(1 + r_T) \cdots (1 + r_2)(1 + r_1)}$$

In this chapter, it will usually be convenient to employ the discrete-perpetuity model—choice between current consumption c_0 and a perpetual annual level sequence c (beginning at time 1). Then the productive solution P^* can be said to maximize attained wealth $W_0^P = p_0 + K_0^P$, where the attained capital value K_0^P equals p/r, the present value of the future level flow. The *amount* of current investment or current consumption sacrificed (which is also the *value* of current consumption sacrificed if c_0 is the numeraire commodity) is $i_0 = y_0 - p_0$; the return on investment is the future level flow $p - y$; and the present value of the return on investment is $(p - y)/r$. The present value of the return on investment is also the capital value "formed," $K_0^P - K_0^Y$. The present-value rule can then be restated: Adopt that set of projects maximizing the excess of capital value formed

---

[2] This is the point of such witticisms as: "A banker is someone who will lend money to good credit risks—when it is only bad credit risks who really need the money." A good credit risk is a person who is already endowed with or can attain (with the help of the loan) the future incomes necessary for repayment. Someone who does not have or cannot attain such an income stream (in the judgment of the lender) simply cannot borrow—he has nothing to offer in exchange for the current funds.

$(K_0^P - K_0^Y)$ over the value of current sacrifice $(y_0 - p_0)$. In the incremental version, the present-value rule says to adopt any project as an increment so long as $\Delta W_0^P > 0$, or equivalently so long as $\Delta K_0^P > \Delta i_0$. On the margin, the value of capital formed by an incremental investment will just equal the value of consumption sacrificed.

Turning now to the social level of analysis, it would be possible to express the determination of the interest rate r and aggregate level of investment $\sum i_0 = \sum y_0 - \sum p_0$ by a supply-demand equilibrium involving capital values. Thus one could construct, by analogy with Fig. 4-1, supply and demand curves for current funds c_0 in terms of the amount of capital value $K_0 = c/r$ given or received in exchange—or supply and demand curves for capital values K_0 in terms of c_0 paid in exchange. But this is liable to mislead, since the true objects of choice for the perpetuity paradigm are current consumption c_0 and future consumption sequence c—not c_0 and capital value K_0. K_0 is not in actuality a commodity, but is already a value—it is a quantity of the commodity c divided by the interest rate r, or equivalently multiplied by its price $\phi_\infty^0 = 1/r$. (Since K_0 is already a present value, *its* equilibrium "price" is necessarily unity in terms of c_0 as numeraire.) Therefore, no attempt will be made here to show how the market equilibrium of interest and investment could be derived in terms of demand and supply for capital values priced in terms of current funds (or demand and supply for current funds priced in terms of capital values) offered or received in exchange.[3]

C. CHOICE-THEORETIC STRUCTURE WITH PRODUCTIVE COMMODITIES

Real capital was defined above as a mass or collection of *productive* commodities. For simplicity, assume that there is a single homogeneous productive or capital-good commodity, possibly distinct from the consumptive commodity. The quantity of the capital good at time t will be denoted H_t. The productive decision problem no longer is one of simple transformations among consumptive time claims—e.g., between c_0 and c_t. Rather, the problem must now in general involve: (1) the production of capital goods, and (2) the utilization of capital goods in the production of consumptive goods. Furthermore, all the "factors" or productive commodities—specifically here, both labor and real capital—will in general be involved in production of both capital goods and consumption goods.

The choices to be described thus represent a considerable degree of complexity. Ultimately, the solution must be expressed in terms of time

---

[3] Such a formulation is provided in M. Friedman, *Price Theory* (Aldine Publishing Co., 1962), pp. 257–261.

patterns of consumption and the corresponding price ratios ϕ_1/ϕ_0, ϕ_2/ϕ_0, ...,
ϕ_T/ϕ_0. (These price ratios between dated consumption claims, of course,
determine the interest rates for correspondingly dated exchanges.) The
preference function as among dated consumptions continues to play essentially the same role as before in the choice-theoretic structure. However, if
labor as a productive-commodity is a choice-variable (i.e., if leisure is an object of choice), preference considerations will also enter the solution determining the $T + 1$ dated employments of labor $L_0, L_1, ..., L_T$ and the dated
wage rates $w_0, w_1, ..., w_T$. The process of solution will fix the course over
time of the capital-stock quantity $H_0, H_1, ..., H_T$ and of its price ϕ_H^0,
$\phi_H^1, ..., \phi_H^T$ (denominating this price, at each date, in terms of units of the
contemporaneous consumptive commodity c_t).

The introduction of productive commodities requires a reformulation
of the *opportunity set* of earlier chapters, so as to clarify the concepts of *endowment, production,* and *income.* There was, previously, an element of artificiality
in postulating a time-distributed endowment consisting of consumption
claims $y_0, y_1, y_2, ..., y_T$ imagined as somehow autonomously becoming
available now and in the future. In the formulation of this chapter, the
endowment consists exclusively of *present* objects—endowed quantities of the
productive commodities H_0 and L_0. In most general form, the current-period
decision problem is to transform the factor endowment vector (H_0, L_0) into
actual current consumption c_0 and the next period's endowment (H_1, L_1).
This would be a consumption-investment decision, where next year's labor
quantum as well as next year's real capital can in principle be regarded as
products of current-period decisions rather than as exogenous magnitudes.
Thus, a worker can invest either by buying a tool so as to acquire more H
or by improving his personal capacities so as to (in effect) acquire more L.[4]
Throughout this analysis, however, the problem will be simplified by treating
the labor supply over time as a given constant. Then the investment decision
will relate only to real capital H.

In Chapter 2, *income* was defined solely in terms of dated consumption
flows. The term "gross income" (or "endowed income") as of time t
referred to the element y_t of the endowment sequence of the consumptive
commodity. "Net income" (or "equalized income") $\bar{y}_t$ referred to the time-t
element of the highest equalized consumptive sequence attainable via
productive and market transformations of the consumptive endowment
vector. The symbols y_t and $\bar{y}_t$ in this chapter will represent, as before, *gross*
and *net incomes* (of the consumptive commodity), respectively, at time t.
However, we will be taking explicit account of the productive process that
generates consumptive income from *factor* endowments. It is necessary to
distinguish, first, between endowed capital H_t^Y and attained capital H_t^P:
the former is the stock of real capital before the consumption-investment

[4] See Gary S. Becker, *Human Capital* (Columbia Univ. Press, 1964).

decisions at time t, and the latter the capital stock after those decisions. Investment will increase, while depreciation will decrease, H_t^P relative to H_t^Y. But the identity $H_t^Y = H_{t-1}^P$ holds; the capital stock attained as a result of the productive and consumptive decisions at time $t-1$ becomes the endowed capital stock at time t. It is sometimes more convenient to think of income y_t as generated by H_{t-1}^P (thus emphasizing that it is the sacrifice at time $t-1$ that contributes to product at time t). But at other times it is easier to think of production as contemporaneous, with y_t generated by H_t^P (thus treating current real capital as a factor coordinate with current labor). The identity of H_{t-1}^P and H_t^Y makes either mode of presentation permissible.

In terms of current-period quantities, the factor-endowment vector (H_0^Y, L_0) may be regarded as generating a product vector (p_0, H_0^P)—i.e., as producing the quantum p_0 of current consumptive claims and H_0^P of real capital. In general, a range of alternative combinations of p_0 and H_0^P will be attainable from a given factor endowment. Assume, for simplicity, that depreciation takes place at a certain constant percentage rate δ, independent of age of capital goods or rate of current production. Then current *net income* $\bar{y}_0$ will be defined as the largest quantity p_0 that could be produced, consistent with $H_0^P = H_0^Y$—i.e., with real capital "maintained intact." This corresponds to the *equalized*-income concept of previous chapters (provided that labor supply is constant over time); for, maintaining real capital intact makes it possible to exactly replicate the decision process in each following period. This will result in consumptive income in each period equal to the $\bar{y}_0$ of the original period. Current *gross income* y_0 will be defined as the largest quantity p_0 that could be produced when $H_0^P = H_0^Y(1 - \delta)$—i.e., when no provision is made for replacement of the depreciating fraction of endowed capital. As in Chapter 2, *gross investment* would be defined as $i_0 = y_0 - p_0$—where p_0 is actual current-goods production at $t = 0$—and *net investment* as $\bar{i}_0 = \bar{y}_0 - p_0$. Gross and net *saving* can be defined correspondingly as $y_0 - c_0$ and $\bar{y}_0 - c_0$: the differences between gross and net income, respectively, and actual consumption c_0. Throughout the chapter, however, in the interests of simplicity it will be assumed that $\delta = 0$ (capital is "perpetual"). Then the distinction between $\bar{y}_0$ and y_0 and between $\bar{i}_0$ and i_0 can be ignored.

D. REAL CAPITAL AND THE PRODUCTIVE PROCESS

There are a number of conflicting "traditions" in capital theory; disagreements among their proponents have been ventilated in famous and lengthy controversies, detailed review of which will not be attempted here. But it is possible to learn something from each of the several schools, and to gain some insight into the points in dispute. Each tradition cuts into the complexity of the general problem of choice as among dated productive and consumptive commodities, by constructing a particular simplified picture of real capital and its role in the productive process.

Knight: Real Capital as a Growing Consumable Mass

The role of real capital in the time-productive process has been epitomized by Frank Knight in his instructive image of the "Crusonia plant."[5] We may think of this as an undifferentiated mass of consumables (a vast, edible fungus, perhaps) that physically grows, continuously and autonomously, at some over-all proportionate rate ρ over time—except as portions are excised for current consumption. Here real capital H_0 is a present stock of consumables and thus is measured in the same units as c_0.[6] The productive powers of the Crusonia plant do not weaken with age; i.e., the capital good does not depreciate. The rate of productive growth ρ will in general be a function of the existing mass H_0, but it is *not* affected by the dating of inputs entering into the accumulation of H_0. With this image of real capital, a "stationary state" would be achieved if the rate of consumption just offset the rate of productive growth. Alternatively, proportionate growth at a steady rate would be achieved, if ρ is a constant[7] independent of H, when consumption c_t is a constant fraction of H_t.

The Crusonia-plant image can be regarded as an *inventory* concept of capital—i.e., real capital as a stock of finished (consumable) goods.

Bohm-Bawerk: Real Capital as a Phased Collection of Maturing Consumables

The famous archetype of real capital associated with the name of Bohm-Bawerk also is a biological image of a growing consumable commodity.[8] But here the *timing* of inputs is an essential element; we must think of a time-phased collection of growing units rather than a simple homogeneous growing mass. A convenient example is a stand of trees whose ages are staggered over

[5] F. H. Knight, "Diminishing Returns from Investment," *Journal of Political Economy*, **52** (March 1944).

[6] However, c_0 is a flow, a rate of consumption per unit time, while H_0 is a stock. The implications of this distinction will be considered later.

[7] Models leading to constant proportionate growth with positive consumption generally require that the labor endowments $L_0, L_1, \ldots, L_T$ (or else the level of technology) be increasing over time. Labor does not explicitly appear in the Crusonia model of the productive process, but may be regarded as implicitly affecting the magnitude of ρ. Hence, as H grows relative to a *constant* labor supply L, it is reasonable to expect ρ to decline. But if the capital stock H and the labor supply are growing in the *same* proportion, under the traditional assumption of constant returns to scale ρ remains constant.

[8] E. v. Bohm-Bawerk, *The Positive Theory of Capital*, tr. William Smart (G. E. Stechert & Co., 1891).

time. Then a stationary state can be defined as a situation in which the age structure of the stand remains statistically unchanged as mature trees are cut each year for timber, the space made available being replanted in new trees. Since each individual tree has some growth curve like that illustrated in Fig. 3-17, the average and marginal rates of growth will vary as a function of the age to which trees are allowed to grow before cutting—the "period of production" θ. The stationary-state solution in terms of θ determines the over-all productive rate of growth and therefore the time rate of consumption achieved.

Under this construct there may exist at each moment of time a quantity of real capital in terms of an inventory of consumables. Thus, a stand of trees at any moment represents a definite mass of lumber. But this mass is only what might be called a "liquidation quantity"; the productive rate of growth, and therefore the potential flow of future consumption, depend not only on the mass but also on the time distribution of inputs summarized in the magnitude of θ. One stand of trees distributed over a 20-year span may contain the same amount of lumber as another stand distributed over a 10-year span, but the over-all timber-growth rates and stationary-state consumptive yields will in general be quite different.

Bohm-Bawerk's construct can be regarded as a *goods-in-process* concept of real capital, where the time structure of degrees of completion of the various physical units is essential to the description of the capital stock.

Real Capital as a Distinct Productive Commodity

Finally, perhaps the most common image of real capital is as a capital good H quite distinct from consumption goods—i.e., not itself consumable but yielding an output of consumables through some productive process (generally requiring also labor). As a biological example we can think of trees grown for fruit. Other examples are machines for producing shoes, or nets for catching fish. Here we may want to take account of two different productive processes: one in the "capital-goods industry" and the other in the "consumer-goods industry."

This image can be regarded as a *durable-goods* concept of real capital.

E. REAL CAPITAL, INVESTMENT, AND INTEREST: THE "CRUSONIA-PLANT" CONSTRUCT

The individual solution for optimal intertemporal choice, and the market equilibrium for investment and interest, take on relatively simple forms under the "Crusonia-plant" or "inventory" metaphor of real capital as a homogeneous mass of consumables. This image is implicitly employed in all those theoretical and empirical studies in which the ratio of capital-goods prices to consumption-goods prices is held constant—as is the case when "capital" is measured as an integrated total of saving over time.

Single-Period Equilibrium

In this chapter it is analytically convenient to think in terms of the discrete-perpetuity model, choice between current consumption c_0 and a perpetual level annual sequence c (beginning at $t = 1$). Expressing the decision involved in terms of real capital, the current-period choice to be made is between consumption c_0 and augmentation of the productive stock H_0. We continue to assume that the capital good is valued only as a source or representative of future consumption; thus, preference for H_0 is exactly the same as preference for the perpetual yield c that can be derived from H_0. (A more complete system would also examine choices between consumption and leisure, but the labor supply is here taken as a given constant.)

For simplicity, the verbal and diagrammatic analyses here employ the "representative-individual" device. Figure 6-1(b) portrays, for such an

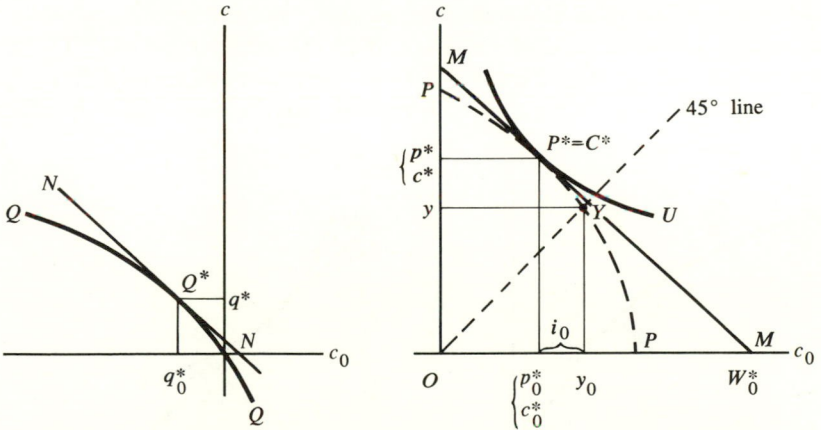

FIG. 6-1. (a) Productive opportunity locus for transformations between c_0 and c, with productive optimum, (b) Optimum and equilibrium conditions for current-period decision, perpetuity paradigm, representative individual

individual, a set of time preferences, productive opportunities, endowment, and so on between c_0 and c. The diagram is in a familiar format, as real capital H has not yet been introduced. The endowment point Y has been located on the 45° line, where $y_0 = y$; this is justified below. In Fig. 6-1(a) the productive opportunities possessed by the individual [the curve PP of Fig. 6-1(b)] appear in isolation as the curve QQ. As before, QQ in Fig. 6-1(a) represents the possibilities for productive *transformations* of the individual's endowment vector: $(q_0, q) = (p_0, p) - (y_0, y)$. Thus, the origin in Fig. 6-1(a) corresponds to the endowment point Y in Fig. 6-1(b).

If we like, we may think of each individual as the sole owner of a firm that exploits his own personal productive opportunities, so that Figs. 6-1(a) and (b) (interpreted as "firm" and "individual" diagrams, respectively) parallel Figs. 3-4(a) and (b). Then $-q_0$ in Fig. 6-1(a), interpreted as "firm" investment $-q_0^f$, must equal the representative individual's "personal" investment $i_0 = y_0 - p_0$ (endowed current income less the current-income element of the productive solution) and saving $y_0 - c_0$ in Fig. 6-1(b), while the gross return from investment q^f equals $p - y$.[9]

Given the representative-individual device, the productive solution $P^* = (p_0^*, p^*)$ must coincide with the consumptive solution $C^* = (c_0^*, c^*)$, as shown in Fig. 6-1(b). The tangency of PP and an indifference curve determine the market rate of interest $r = 1/\phi_\infty^0$ as the absolute slope of MM in Fig. 6-1(b) or of NN in Fig. 6-1(a); of course, since Q^* on QQ really represents the same point on the productive locus as P^* on PP, the slope at Q^* is the same as at P^*.

In Figs. 6-2(a) and (b) this familiar current-period solution is re-interpreted in terms of Crusonia real capital. We distinguish, as already mentioned, between *endowed* real capital of the current period, H_0^Y, and *attained* real capital H_0^P. Figure 6-2(b) is essentially unchanged from Fig. 6-1(b). But in Fig. 6-2(a), the horizontal axis in the second quadrant

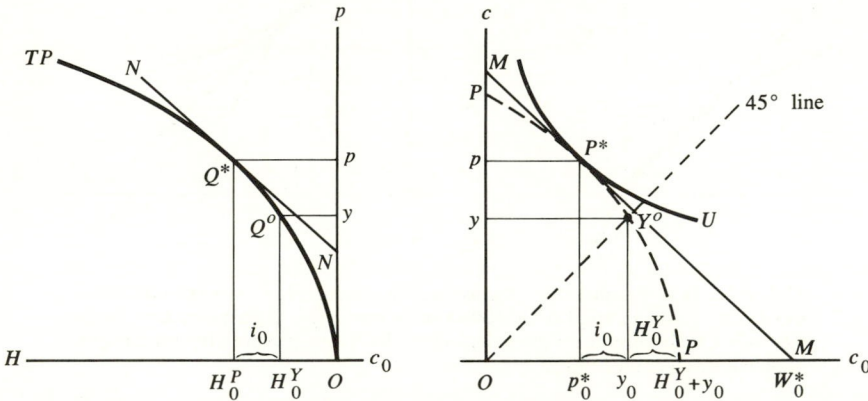

FIG. 6-2. (a) Total-product curve for Crusonia real-capital H, with current-period productive optimum, (b) Optimum and equilibrium conditions for current-period decision, perpetuity paradigm with Crusonia real-capital, representative individual

[9] If the assumption of identical individuals were not made, it still would remain true that $\Sigma(-q_0^f)$, summing over all firms, would have to equal the sums Σi_0 and $\Sigma(y_0 - c_0)$ over all individuals.

(measuring positive quantities to the *left*) represents quantities H of real capital used in production. Under the Crusonia-plant construct, real capital H_0 is in the same c_0-units as investment i_0 in the current period (investment also being a stock magnitude, since the current period is of discrete length); hence, Fig. 6-2(a) has the same dimensionality as Fig. 6-1(a). However, the origin has been shifted: where the origin of Fig. 6-1(a) corresponded to the endowment point Y in the right-hand diagram, the origin of Fig. 6-2(a) corresponds to the horizontal intercept of the productive-opportunity locus PP. Thus, the horizontal distance to the left of the origin in Fig. 6-2(a) represents the *entire quantity of real capital* rather than only the current investment. Similarly, the vertical axis in Fig. 6-2(a) represents the entire future income p associated with the level of real capital attained—rather than only the return on investment q.

The productive-opportunity set can also be regarded in a somewhat different light as a "total future-product" curve TP, showing the perpetual future sequence capable of being generated (with a constant labor supply L) by any productive real-capital stock H^P. The TP curve may be expressed as $p = \rho H^P$, where in general the proportionate growth rate ρ is not a constant but is a declining function of H^P. The level annual sequence p is, of course, the *equalized* or *net* income for future periods generated by the investment decisions determining H^P. The proportionate growth rate ρ is also the *average* future-product (p/H^P) of the capital good. It is measured geometrically by the slope of a line from the origin to the respective point on TP. The *marginal* future-product of the capital good, $p' = dp/dH^P$, is less than ρ, given the concavity (diminishing-returns) property of TP.

At $t = 0$, the representative individual is endowed with a stock of real capital H_0^Y and also with a corresponding net current income y_0. These are the result of the consumption-investment decision of the previous period $(t = -1)$ that formed the capital stock $H_{-1}^P = H_0^Y$. Since this capital stock determined a level-flow net income for all future periods (that is, future relative to the absolute time $t = -1$),[10] y_0 and y are numerically equal as elements of the level perpetual p-sequence associated with H_{-1}^P. This explains why the dated-consumption endowment points are placed on the 45° line in Figs. 6-1(b) and 6-2(b).

In Fig. 6-2(b) the productive-opportunity set PP is identical with the total future-product curve TP in Fig. 6-2(a), except for the difference of origin. The endowment point Y^o on the 45° line corresponds to Q^o in Fig. 6-2(a). The point in Fig. 6-2(b) where PP intersects the horizontal axis (the absolute maximum of current-period consumption possible) is at the

---

[10] In this chapter it will occasionally be necessary to distinguish between *absolute* and *relative* time. Absolute time refers to dating (e.g., time 0, the year 1492, or 1965); relative time refers to distance from "the present" as of any date. In the symbolism here, the time-subscript will refer to absolute time unless indicated otherwise.

c_0-quantity $y_0 + H_0^Y$; if this point were selected for the current-period choice, H_0^P would become zero. If the preferred solution were at the endowment point ($P^* = Y^o$), the actual current-period consumption p_0 would equal y_0, and future-period consumption p would equal y. Or, as this would usually be formulated, H_0^P would equal H_0^Y; real capital would be "maintained intact" by consumption of an amount equal to current income. In the solution illustrated, however, a positive amount of investment $i_0 = y_0 - p_0$ takes place. Since $H_1^Y \equiv H_0^P \equiv H_0^Y + i_0$, and $i_0 > 0$, the endowment presented to the future is greater than that inherited from the past.

The current-period solution can be characterized, in terms of dated production-consumption flows, by (p_0, p); in terms of current consumption versus investment, by (p_0, i_0); and in terms of consumption and attained real-capital stock, by (p_0, H_0^P). The interest rate $r = 1/\phi_\infty^0$ is determined by the absolute slope at the equilibrium point P^* (or Q^*). It is equal to $p' \equiv dp/dH^P$ at Q^* in Fig. 6-2(a)—the marginal future-product of the capital good—which in turn equals $-dp/di_0$ at P^* in Fig. 6-2(b).[11] The price ϕ_H^0 of the capital good is necessarily unity, since a unit of H_0 is physically identical with a unit of c_0—the numeraire commodity. (In general, the interest rate r is less than the over-all capital-growth rate ρ, the *average* future-product of H^P; r and ρ would be equal in equilibrium only if ρ were a constant, in which case the TP curve would be a straight line through the origin.) The attained wealth can be expressed as $W_0^P = p_0 + p/r = p_0 + (\rho/r)H_0^P$.

It will be helpful to formalize these results in a set of equations that comprises a system generally paralleling equations (1) through (8) of Chapter 4. At this point, firms will not be explicitly introduced. The algebraic formulation permits dropping the "representative-individual" assumption employed in the verbal and diagrammatical exposition.

$$\left. \frac{dc}{dc_0} \right|_U = \Upsilon(c_0, c) \qquad \text{Time-preference function}$$
$$\qquad\qquad\qquad\qquad (I \text{ equations}) \qquad\qquad (1)$$

$$c_0 + \phi_\infty c = p_0 + \phi_\infty p \qquad \text{Wealth constraint}$$
$$\qquad\qquad\qquad\qquad (I \text{ equations}) \qquad\qquad (2)$$

$$\left. \frac{dc}{dc_0} \right|_U = -1/\phi_\infty \qquad \text{Consumptive optimum}$$
$$\qquad\qquad\qquad\qquad (I \text{ equations}) \qquad\qquad (3)$$

The consumptive equations are in familiar form. The wealth constraint upon the consumptive choices depends upon the (p_0, p) combination achieved

---

[11] We will see below that while, in the perpetuity paradigm, the interest rate always equals the absolute value of dp/dp_0 at the equilibrium point, it is not dimensionally commensurate with the marginal product of the capital good dp/dH_0 *except* under the Crusonia-plant construct.

by the consumption-investment (capital-formation) decision.

$$y_0 = \rho(H_0^Y) \qquad \text{Current-income production function}$$

Current-income production function
(I equations) (4)

$$p = \rho(H_0^P) \qquad \text{Future-income production function}$$

Future-income production function
(I equations) (5)

$$p' = \omega(H_0^P) \qquad \text{Marginal product of capital}$$

Marginal product of capital
(I equations) (6)

$$p' = \frac{1}{\phi_\infty} \qquad \text{Productive optimum}$$

Productive optimum
(I equations) (7)

The productive equations take on somewhat different shape, but the only significant change is the addition of an equation *determining* "current income" y_0—which was always interpreted in earlier chapters as an exogenously given consumptive endowment. Here ρ and ω are to be understood as known functions of H.

$$H_0^P - H_0^Y = y_0 - p_0 \qquad \text{Capital-formation and investment}$$

Capital-formation and investment
(I equations) (8)

This equation defines the productive or real capital formation of the individual (his physical investment) rather than his saving (refraining from consumption). An individual with very good productive opportunities will be in a position to make his productive real capital H_0^P very large relative to his p_0; he would buy units of c_0 on the market, offering in exchange some of the p he is then enabled to generate by productive use of real capital formed from the endowed or purchased c_0-units available to him. Of course, the equality of the social totals of individual saving $\sum (y_0 - c_0)$ and individual investment $\sum (y_0 - p_0)$ is assured by the conservation equations.

$$\begin{aligned} \sum c_0 &= \sum p_0 \\ \sum c &= \sum p \end{aligned} \qquad \begin{aligned} &\text{Conservation equations} \\ &\text{(one independent equation)} \end{aligned} \qquad (9)$$

As usual, one of the conservation equations is redundant. Then, since there are I equations each of types (1) through (8) (one set for each of the I individuals), the total number of independent relations is $8I + 1$. This matches the number of the variables: I each of $c_0, c, p_0, p, y_0, H_0^P, dc/dc_0|_U$, and p', plus the unique price ϕ_∞.

The productive-optimum equation (7) can be regarded as an instance of the factor-employment equation of price theory—the value of the marginal product of real capital (here $p'\phi_\infty$) is set equal to factor price (ϕ_H^0, which is necessarily unity).

Finally, we can add the definition of the rate of interest:

$$r = \frac{1}{\phi_\infty} \tag{10}$$

This permits interpreting (7) as the *equality of the marginal product of capital with the rate of interest.*

NUMERICAL EXAMPLE

Table I*

		TIME 0		TIME I
		Endowment Position	Optimum Position	Endowment Position
Capital	H	100	133.3	133.3
Income	y_t	100	—	115.5
Investment	i_t	—	33.3	—
Consumption	c_t	—	66.7	—
Future income flow	p	100	115.5	115.5
Marginal rate of time preference	$-dc/dc_0\,\vert_U$	.25	.433	.25
Marginal future-product of capital	p'	.5	.433	.433
Interest rate	r	—	.433	—
Price of future flow	ϕ^0_∞	—	2.31	—
Wage rate	w	.5	.5775	.5775
Rental	h	.5	.433	.433

* Conditions: $U = c_0^{\cdot 2} c^{\cdot 8}$
$p = 10(H^P)^{1/2}$ [or, with $L = 100$, $p = (H^P)^{1/2}L^{1/2}$]
$H^Y_0 = 100$

Let the utility function for a representative individual be $U = c_0^{\cdot 2} c^{\cdot 8}$. Then the marginal rate of substitution in consumption, $dc/dc_0\,\vert_U = -\tfrac{1}{4}c/c_0$. [This corresponds to equation (1) above.] Let the production function be $p = 10(H^P)^{1/2}$ [equation (5)]; then $p' = 5/(H^P)^{1/2}$ [equation (6)]. Let the initial $H^Y_0 = 100$, so that current endowed income $y_0 = 10(100)^{1/2} = 100$ [equation (4)], endowed future income y being at the same numerical level. Under the representative-individual assumption, the conditions $c_0 = p_0$ and $c = p$ replace the conservation equations (9) and the wealth constraint (2). Then the equality of the absolute consumptive and productive marginal rates of substitution [equations (3) and (7)] can be expressed directly as

$$-\frac{dc}{dc_0}\bigg|_U = p' \quad \text{or} \quad \frac{1}{4}\frac{p}{p_0} = \frac{5}{(H^P_0)^{1/2}}$$

Substituting for $p = 10(H^P_0)^{1/2}$ and for $p_0 = H^Y_0 + y_0 - H^P_0$ [equation (8)] yields the solution $H^P_0 = 133.3$.

Thus, of the original 100 of endowed current income y_0, 66.7 has been consumed and 33.3 added to real capital. The new marginal future-product of capital p' equals approximately .433 (whereas before the investment decision it was .5); .433 is also the marginal rate of substitution in consumption and the rate of interest determined at $t = 0$, and is the reciprocal of the price of the future flow, $\phi_\infty^0 = 2.31$ [equation (7)]. The future flow p will be at the level of 115.5 per annum instead of the original 100. (The remainder of Table 1 will be explained later.)

Real Capital and Labor as Coordinate Factors of Production

So far, we have dealt with a formulation of the productive process that made explicit the role of real capital but left implicit the role of other factors. In order to bring out certain relationships among factors, and between factors and products, it will be desirable to employ a formulation with a fully explicit production function in terms of the factors of production. For one thing, it was noted above that with the production function as specified in the TP curve of Fig. 6-2(a), the marginal future-product of capital p' is less than the average product ρ. Since at the productive optimum capital as a factor is paid the value of its *marginal* product, not all the value of product is thus accounted for. The difference could be attributed to profits and to rents retained by factors specific to individual firms. However, if there are two or more factors whose quantities are variable to the firm, it is possible to have a zero-profit equilibrium without calling on such rents—if the production function displays constant returns to scale. We will accept that assumption here, and for simplicity we postulate the existence of only one other factor—labor, L, assumed to be in fixed supply to the whole economy.

The problem now becomes necessarily more complex: there are two productive commodities as well as the consumptive commodity. Let us proceed directly to the equation system for the single-period solution. Factors of production having been explicitly introduced, it is now convenient to conceive of *firms* as the agents of production (employers of the factors owned by individuals). On the consumptive side, we have for the various individuals:

$$\frac{dc}{dc_0}\bigg|_U = \Upsilon(c_0, c) \qquad \text{Time-preference function} \qquad (1')$$
$$\text{(I equations)}$$

$$\frac{dc}{dc_0}\bigg|_U = -\frac{1}{\phi_\infty} \qquad \text{Consumptive optimum} \qquad (2')$$
$$\text{(I equations)}$$

$$y_0 = L_0 w_0 + H_0^Y h_0 \qquad \text{Consumption claims and}$$
$$\qquad\qquad\qquad\qquad\qquad \text{factor incomes} \qquad\qquad (3')$$
$$c = Lw + H_0^P h \qquad \text{($2I$ equations)}$$

$$H_0^P = H_0^Y + (y_0 - c_0) \qquad \text{Capital and saving} \qquad (4')$$
$$\text{(I equations)}$$

The consumptive equations (1') and (2') are familiar, but (3') and (4') have a rather novel form. Equations (3') now play the role of the wealth constraint in defining the incomes limiting individuals' consumption expenditures. The firms, rather than the individuals, possess the productive opportunities—so the constraint on individual consumption is no longer the production vector (p_0, p) as in equation (2) above, but rather the earnings from owned factors. L_0 and H_0^Y are the amounts of labor and real capital owned by the individual and made available to the employing firms at $t = 0$; w_0 is the current-period wage rate, and h_0 the rental on capital goods. Since the rental is paid in c_0-units, and since under the Crusonia-plant metaphor the capital goods are measured in the same units, h_0 has the dimensions of a percentage. (As we shall see, h_0 must have been the rate of interest determined by the productive decisions at $t = -1$.) L and H_0^P are the factor quantities available for productive employment in future years, with w and h the corresponding wage and rental. (And we shall see that under the Crusonia-plant model, h must equal the current equilibrium interest rate r.) Assuming that the labor-supply curve is vertical (leisure is not an object of choice), current income y_0 will be given to the individual by his factor endowment and the ruling market prices. But his future consumption level c depends upon his attained capital H_0^P, and that quantity depends upon his saving as shown in (4')—the saving decision being made so as to achieve the consumptive optimum condition (2').[12]

Turning now to the productive side, we can symbolize by L_0^f and H_0^f the quantities of current labor and current real capital *employed* by the fth firm for current production.

$$p_0^f = \Omega(L_0^f, H_0^f)$$
$$p_{0L}' = \omega_L(L_0^f, H_0^f)$$
$$p_{0H}' = \omega_H(L_0^f, H_0^f)$$

Current-income production function (3F equations) (5')

These equations define the total current product and marginal current products of labor and capital as functions of the quantities employed of the two factors. Here p_0^f represents the quantity *produced* by a firm, in contrast with y_0 in (3'), which represents a quantity *earned* by an individual.

$$p^f = \Omega(L^f, H^f)$$
$$p_L' = \omega_L(L^f, H^f)$$
$$p_H' = \omega_H(L^f, H^f)$$

Future-income production function (3F equations) (6')

[12] It may be noted that, in the simpler system above, equation (8) showed the relation between H_0^P and real *investment* $(y_0 - p_0)$, whereas here (4') relates H_0^P to *saving* $(y_0 - c_0)$. The reason for the difference is that in the previous system individuals engaged in production, whereas here all production takes place through the firms.

The equations of (6') refer to the firm's future production. The corresponding quantities are denoted L^f and H^f for the future factor employments, and p^f for the future level flow of output.

$$p'_{0L} = w_0 \qquad \text{Current-income productive optimum}$$
$$p'_{0H} = h_0 \qquad \text{(2F equations)} \tag{7'}$$

$$p'_L = w \qquad \text{Future-income productive optimum}$$
$$p'_H = h \qquad \text{(2F equations)} \tag{8'}$$

Equations (7') and (8') express the productive-optimum conditions by equating, for each factor, the value of the marginal product to factor price—the corresponding wage or rental.

Definitional relations among the rental h, the price ϕ^0_∞ for the future flow of output, and the interest rate r are indicated by equations (9').

$$\phi_\infty h = 1 \qquad \text{Relations among } h, r, \text{ and } \phi_\infty$$
$$r = \frac{1}{\phi_\infty} \qquad \text{(two equations)} \tag{9'}$$

The first equation of (9') states the present value of the capital good—the incremental output flow times the latter's current price ϕ^0_∞—as unity. This, of course, must be the case, since the capital good H_0 is simply a unit of c_0. The second equation is familiar. It then obviously follows that $r = h$; the rate of interest is equal to the future rental, which in turn equals the marginal future-product of the capital good. The validity of this equality is limited to the Crusonia-plant image of capital. Also, the current rental h_0 can be regarded as having been determined by the capital-formation decision at $t = -1$ and thus to be equal to the equilibrium interest rate as of that date.

Given constant returns to scale, it is shown in standard texts on mathematical economics that "Euler's equation" holds:

$$p^f_0 = p'_{0L} L^f_0 + p'_{0H} H^f_0$$
$$p^f = p'_L L^f + p'_H H^f$$

Substituting from the productive-optimum conditions (7') and (8'), we see that the total current product and total future product are "exhausted" by the corresponding factor payments. The consequent absence of profits or rents justifies the formulation of (3') above. Otherwise, some consumption claims would have to be attributed to individuals in a position to receive profits or rents.

$$\sum L_0 = \sum L_0^f$$
$$\sum H_0^Y = \sum H_0^f$$
$$\sum L = \sum L^f \qquad \text{Conservation relations}$$
$$\sum H_0^P = \sum H^f \qquad \text{(four independent equations)} \qquad (10')$$
$$\sum y_0 = \sum p_0^f$$
$$\sum c = \sum p^f$$

In the conservation equations, the summations on the left are over the I individuals, and those on the right are over the F firms. There are six conservation relations, but it is easy to see that the last two follow from the previous four. Consequently, these plus the definitions in equation $(9')$ suffice to determine the prices: w_0, w, h_0, h, r, and ϕ_∞. The remainder of the system consists of $5I + 10F$ equations, there being I each of the "individual variables" (c, c_0, dc/dc_0, y_0, and H_0^P) and F each of the "firm variables" L_0^f, H_0^f, L^f, H^f, p_0^f, p_{0H}', p_{0L}', p^f, p_H', p_L'.

NUMERICAL EXAMPLE (see Table 1)

> The earlier numerical example can be extended easily, holding to the assumption of the "representative individual" and assuming an equal number of identical "representative firms." As a specific production function explicitly incorporating labor we may use $p = (H^P)^{1/2}L^{1/2}$. Then, assuming the labor supply is constant at $L = 100$, this becomes consistent with the earlier numerical data. Assume that the representative individual originally owns 100 units of L and 100 units of H_0^Y, while the representative firm correspondingly employs these to generate $p_0^f = 100$. The wage rate is $w_0 = .5$ and the rental or marginal product of endowed capital is $h_0 = .5$ (these follow from the current-period productive-optimum conditions). The saving-investment solution is the same as before; although the individuals now save with the intention of renting their augmented owned capital to firms rather than with the intention of producing themselves, the effect on their income flows is the same. Thus, the attained real capital H_0^P becomes 133.3, the future productive-consumptive flow $p = 115.5$, and the marginal future-product of capital $p_H' = .433$, which also equals the interest rate r and is the reciprocal of the price of the future level flow ϕ_∞. Using the future-income productive-optimum conditions, the wage rate $w = p_L'$ becomes .5775. The current-period accumulation, therefore, lowers interest and raises wages. However, the proportionate shares of labor and capital to the produced income each remain one-half (equal to the respective exponents of H and L in the specific production function assumed above)— a well-known characteristic of production functions of this "Cobb-Douglas" type.

The equilibrium solution of Chapter 4 showed the determination of the level of investment (more generally, of the entire intertemporal pattern of consumption) and of the real rate of interest (more generally, of the price ratios among intertemporal consumption claims). The level of investment was such as to bring into equality marginal time preference and marginal time productivity—the latter being the marginal net future return on current sacrifice. In the models of Chapter 4, the determinants of interest were thus summarized under the headings of time preference and time productivity.

In this chapter, the formulation on the time-preference side remains the same. But the productive transformation between current and future incomes takes place in two steps: (1) formation of capital by saving, and (2) employment of capital in production. The second step leads to the traditional proposition that *the rate of interest is equal to the marginal (future) product of capital.*[13]

The expression of intertemporal productive transformations in terms of an intermediating capital is certainly much more complicated than the Fisherian models of Chapter 4 that ran directly in terms of alternative combinations of dated consumptive claims. And the formulations involving capital become still more complicated when the Crusonia-plant metaphor is set aside. In return for this disadvantage, we are led to certain new results and insights. Dealing now with an explicit production function with inputs and outputs, the role of productive commodities like labor can be thrown into focus. The "endowment," a somewhat artificial concept viewed as an intertemporal *consumptive* combination, is more naturally understood as an initial holding of productive commodities. And the course of development over time can now be conveniently traced in terms of "accumulation" of capital. This forms the topic of the next section.

F. ACCUMULATION AND STOCK-FLOW ANALYSIS: "CRUSONIA-PLANT" CONSTRUCT

Accumulation

Accumulation refers to the development over time of the community's real-capital stock. Because of the intractability of the problem in full

---

[13] This has been shown here for the discrete-perpetuity model only. The extension to other paradigms of intertemporal choice would follow in the usual way, though the formulations become more complex. Somewhat more explicitly, the marginal future-product of capital equals the future *rental* on endowed capital goods—which rental, under the Crusonia-plant metaphor, is simply a percentage per unit of time and thus equivalent to a rate of interest. This traditional proposition is seemingly atemporal, like the corresponding condition stating that the wage rate is equal to the marginal product of labor. However, the role of time productivity remains fundamental: it is the formation of capital by sacrifice of consumption at earlier dates that leads to the augmented product at later dates.

generality, it is usual to concentrate on the determining conditions and the properties of two alternative classes of solutions. The first of these is the *stationary state*: a situation such that, once achieved, consumption flows and stocks of capital goods remain the same over all following time. The second is *steady growth*: a situation in which the time rates of growth of all relevant economic magnitudes so conform as to permit the same rate of expansion to continue indefinitely over time. (The stationary state may be regarded as "steady growth" at a zero rate.) In this section we will consider accumulation terminating in a stationary state, under the Crusonia-plant image of real capital. To permit stationarity, it will be assumed that the endowment of factors of production other than real capital (e.g., labor) is constant over time.

In the interests of simplicity, it is very advantageous to make an artificial assumption about repetitive choices of the accumulating individual: namely,

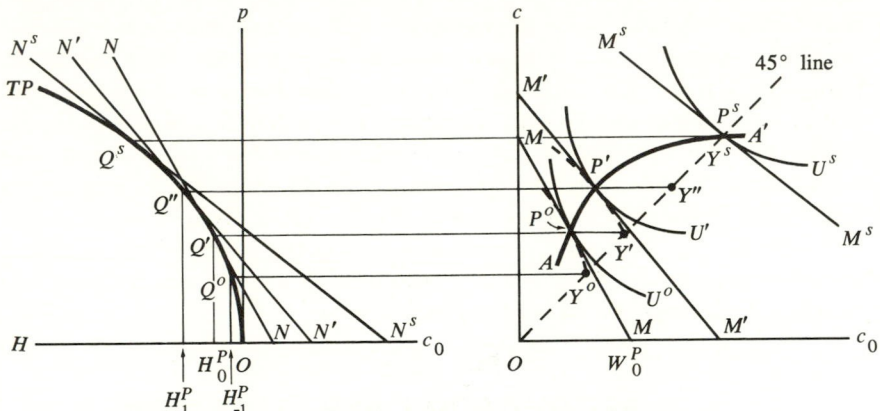

FIG. 6-3. (a) Total-product curve for Crusonia real-capital H, with successive productive optima, (b) Optimum and equilibrium conditions for representative individual, successive decisions over time, and accumulation path

that in each and every period he plans in terms of a once-and-for-all decision between then-current consumption c_0 (at *relative* time 0) and a level future flow c. Furthermore, we assume that the time-preference map as between c_0 and c remains unchanged over time.[14] This permits use of the single preference map in Fig. 6-3(b), even though the analysis portrays repeated

[14] Thus, in each period the individual is assumed to choose a future level flow as if the latter were to be immutable. But then in each succeeding period he is allowed to reconsider and choose, on the basis of the new endowment but the same preference map, between then-current consumption and provision for the remaining future. The bias imported by this assumption will be considered below. This analysis, with its artificial simplifying assumption, is based upon W. Leontief, "Theoretical Note on Time-Preference, Productivity of Capital, Stagnation and Economic Growth," *American Economic Review*, **48** (March 1958).

choices over time. We will also employ the simplifying device of a single "representative individual."

Part of the individual's productive opportunity, at time 0, is shown in Fig. 6-3(b) by the dashed curve-segment going though Y^o and P^o. [This can be regarded as part of the single-period productive opportunity PP of the earlier analysis in Fig. 6-2(b).] The productive-opportunity curve is also shown separately in the "firm diagram" of Fig. 6-3(a); as before, the curve TP associates a future perpetual sequence p with each level of real capital H (given the constant endowment of other factors). By employing a unique total-product curve to represent repeated decisions over time, we are assuming that the passage of time does not bring new opportunities into existence, nor do old ones ever expire. Thus, the productive locus remains unchanged; the individual simply moves along it over time.

The point on TP corresponding to the time-0 endowed H_0^Y $(= H_{-1}^P)$ is denoted Q^o, as in Fig. 6-2(a). The current-period optimum [symbolized by Q^* in Fig. 6-2(a)] is here denoted Q', since the current-period produced capital stock H_0^P becomes the time-1 endowed capital stock H_1^Y. The accumulation path over time is obtained by repeated application of the principles determining the single-period solution. The productive current-period optimum P^o in Fig. 6-3(b), the tangency of the productive-opportunity locus with the indifference curve U^o, is identical with P^* of Fig. 6-2(b); the market line MM with equation $W_0^P = p_0 + p/r$ is correspondingly determined.

Now, with the passage of the initial period the point P^o *becomes* Y' along the 45° line. More specifically, $P^o = (p_0, p)$ corresponds to endowing time 1 with then-current consumption claims $y_1 = p$ and also with the capital stock H_1^Y that can generate a perpetual future sequence equal to p per period thereafter.

But the individual endowed with Y' at time 1 also has productive opportunities, again represented by a dashed curve in Fig. 6-3(b). This dashed curve is nothing but the remaining portion of the over-all TP curve of Fig. 6-3(a) obtained by superimposing Q' on Y'; the assumption that the productive-opportunity curve TP of Fig. 6-3(a) remains unchanged over time means that, at time 1, the individual is in a position to make a further move along the curve. The preference map shows that such a further movement will actually be desired. The new preferred position P' represents the tangency of the dashed segment of the productive-opportunity curve with the indifference curve U'. This tangency determines the position of the new market line $M'M'$ corresponding to a higher level of attained wealth. Note that the slope of the new market line $M'M'$ is numerically less than that of the original MM, corresponding to a higher ϕ_∞ or lower r.[15] This decline

---

[15] The symbol ϕ_∞ here represents, at $t = 1$, the price of future level flow in terms of then-current consumptive claims c_1. Viewed in terms of the *relative* situation at $t = 1$, this would be thought of as ϕ_∞^0.

in the rate of interest is dictated by the declining absolute slope of the total-product or productive-opportunity curve TP, along which the individual (and the society) must move as real capital is accumulated.

NUMERICAL EXAMPLE (see Table 2)

Table 2*

		TIME 0		TIME I		TIME 2	STATION-ARITY
		Endow-ment position	Opti-mum position	Endow-ment position	Opti-mum position	Endow-ment position	Endowment and Optimum position
Capital	H	100	133.3	133.3	165.9	165.9	400
Income	y_t	100	—	115.5	—	128.8	200
Investment	i_t	—	33.3	—	32.6	—	0
Consumption	c_t	—	66.7	—	82.9	—	200
Future income flow	p	100	115.5	115.5	128.8	128.8	200
Marginal rate of time preference	$-dc/dc_0\|_U$	.25	.433	.25	.388	.25	.25
Marginal future-product of capital	p'	.5	.433	.433	.388	.388	.25
Interest rate	r	—	.433	—	.388	—	.25
Wage	w	.5	.5775	.5775	.644	.644	1.0
Rental	h	.5	.433	.433	.388	.388	.25

     * Conditions: As in Table 1.

For the utility function $U = c_0^{.2} c^{.8}$ and the productive locus $p = 10(H^P)^{1/2}$ of the earlier numerical example, the subscript zero now represents *relative* present time (absolute $t = 1$). As a result of the saving-investment decision at $t = 0$, we have seen that time 1 received an augmented real capital of 133.3, and current and future income flows of 115.5. The condition $dc/dc_0\|_U = p'$ at absolute time 1 then leads to a new real capital of 165.9—i.e., net investment at $t = 1$ of 32.6, as against consumption of 82.9. The future perpetual flow beginning at $t = 2$ is thus augmented to 128.8, while the marginal future product of capital p' and the rate of interest r fall from .433 to around .388.

Returning to the accumulation process, P' after time 1 becomes the endowment Y'', which (from the point of view of the individual reconsidering the situation in time 2) is again not an optimal position. We may now skip directly to the stationary solution $P^s = Y^s$. This is determined where the accumulation path AA of Fig. 3(b), drawn so as to pass through all the periodic productive solutions, cuts the 45° line; here, since the productive optimum is identical with the endowed position, no further change will take place. Note that the interest rate, as reflected in the slope of the market line M^sM^s, reaches a minimum (though still positive) level.

NUMERICAL EXAMPLE (see Table 2)

> With the data of the earlier example, stationarity is only possible where the marginal product of capital $p' = \frac{1}{4}$—since the marginal rate of substitution in consumption, $dc/dc_0 |_U = -\frac{1}{4}c/c_0$, equals $-\frac{1}{4}$ along the 45° line. Given the TP function $p = 10(H^P)^{1/2}$, $p' = 5/(H^P)^{1/2}$, so that the stationary real capital $H^P = 400$. The interest rate consistent with stationarity must thus be 25 per cent.

Under the conditions of this model, a *steady-growth* solution would be reflected in Fig. 6-3(b) by an accumulation path AA' in the form of a ray through the origin—with the further proviso that equal proportionate movements outward along this ray are taken in equal periods of time. Such a situation can only arise with special properties assumed for the total-product curve TP and/or the preference map. One such special case would involve a straight-line TP curve in Fig. 6-3(a) (no diminishing returns to real capital as a productive factor) and a homothetic preference map—i.e., a map whose indifference curves are such that slopes of all curves are equal along any ray drawn from the origin. The constant slope of TP would then dictate that every period's solution falls at a tangency point with this same slope, while the preference-homotheticity condition would assure that all such points lie on a ray through the origin. This ray would then become the accumulation path AA'. That equal proportionate distances would then be traversed in equal times is evident from the geometry.

Stock-Flow Analysis

The analytical elements determining the stationary state, and the rate of approach to that position, can be summarized in an alternative, interesting way by "stock-flow" diagrams like Figs. 6-4(a) and 6-4(b).[16] The stock and flow solutions are, however, ultimately constrained and determined by the standard elements of the choice-theoretic structure (preferences, productive opportunities, and so on) as illustrated in Figs. 6-3(a) and 6-3(b).

Figure 6-4(b) is the "stock diagram" that portrays the conditions determining the stationary-state equilibrium for the stock of real capital H, as related to the rate of interest r. The "consumptive-stationarity" curve CS summarizes the time-preference conditions consistent with the possibility

[16] One such treatment appears in Friedman, *Price Theory*, Chap. 13.

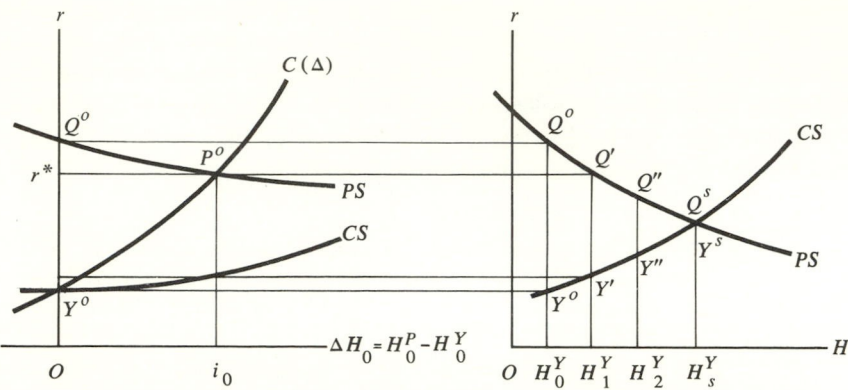

FIG. 6-4. (a) Flow diagram for augmentation of real-capital in present period (discrete), (b) Stock diagram for real-capital accumulation, with stationarity conditions

of a stationary state. For each level of H, CS shows the interest rate r at which the representative individual prefers to hold his real-capital endowment intact and not undertake any net saving. Thus, given any endowed (y_0, y), where $y_0 = y = \rho H_0^Y$ so that the endowment point is along the 45° line in Fig. 6-3(b), CS shows the interest rate at which the individual will set consumption $c_0 = y_0$—leaving produced real capital H_0^P the same as the endowed real capital H_0^Y, and consequently regenerating the same endowed future flow y for the next time period. Geometrically, in Fig. 6-3(b) the consumptive-stationary r for given H_0^Y is the absolute slope of the indifference curve cutting through the endowment-point Y^o associated with that H_0^Y. [The capital stock H generating that particular endowment point can be found, of course, by using the TP curve of Fig. 6-3(a).] Thus, the CS curve is a reflection of the indifference-curve slopes *along the 45° line*. Or, the CS curve shows the ratio between the prices of the future level flow c and current consumption c_0 necessary to make any given real-capital stock a stationary state from the point of view of time preference.

In Fig. 6-4(b) the CS curve is shown as rising, but it could in general be horizontal, rising, or falling. As H increases, so that the endowment points Y move out from the origin along the 45° line in Fig. 6-3(b), y_0 and y rise in the same proportion. Perhaps the most plausible assumption, therefore, is that CS in Fig. 6-4(b) should be horizontal (as it would be with a homothetic preference function). We show it as sloped upward (suggesting that c is *relatively* "inferior," as compared with c_0) for diagrammatic convenience only.

The "productive-stationarity" curve PS of Fig. 6-4(b) summarizes the *productive* considerations bearing on the possibility of stationarity. Specifically, for each level of H in Fig. 6-3(a) there will be a certain slope of the market line NN such that the individual (or firm) will find it productively optimal (most profitable) to employ that level of real capital without further augmentation or diminution. The negative slope of the PS curve is dictated by the diminishing-returns curvature of TP. The r represented by the absolute slope of that NN is then plotted against the corresponding H as the PS curve of Fig. 6-4(b).[17]

The intersection of PS and CS thus determines the ultimate stationary level of the capital stock and the corresponding $r = 1/\phi_\infty^0$. Only at that intersection are the marginal productive rate of substitution between c_0 and c [the slope along the TP curve in Fig. 6-3(a)] and the marginal consumptive rate of substitution [the slope along an indifference curve of Fig. 6-3(b)] equal and *also* consistent with stationarity [i.e., on the 45° line of Fig. 6-3(b)].

NUMERICAL EXAMPLE (see Table 2)

> With the marginal rate of time preference $dc/dc_0\,|_U = -\frac{1}{4}c/c_0$, the indifference-curve slopes along the 45° line all equal $-\frac{1}{4}$. The CS curve is given by the condition $dc/dc_0\,|_U = -1/\phi_\infty = -r$ along the 45° line. So CS is horizontal at the level $r = \frac{1}{4}$. Productive stationarity is achieved where $p' = 1/\phi_\infty = r$. Since $p' = 5/(H^P)^{1/2}$, the equation for PS is $r = 5/(H^P)^{1/2}$. The stationary solution is thus $H^P = 400$, confirming the result obtained earlier.

The "flow diagram," Fig. 6-4(a), displays the conditions determining the *rate* of investment i_0, or the rate of accumulation here denoted ΔH_0, in the current period. This rate can be positive or negative. Under the special Crusonia-plant assumption, net investment at time t is simply a corresponding addition to real capital: $i_t = y_t - c_t = \Delta H_t$, the increment to H in the tth period. Dealing with the discrete period-0 solution, the origin along the horizontal axis in Fig. 6-4(a) (zero net investment) corresponds to holding intact the endowed real capital H_0^Y in Fig. 6-4(b). Then the CS and PS curves, or rather the segments of those curves starting at H_0^Y, are replotted in Fig. 6-4(a). The curves are shown as relatively flat, in order to suggest that in a given brief period little change can take place in the aggregate real-capital stock.[18] Indeed, in the limiting or continuous case in which the time length of the current period approaches zero, the CS and PS curves

---

[17] Whereas the CS curve is defined specifically in terms of a zero rate of accumulation (and, in general, we could define a whole family of such curves, one for each positive or negative accumulation rate), the PS curve is independent of the accumulation rate. The reason is the special Crusonia-plant assumption, which says that each unit of c_0 saved is correspondingly added to real capital—i.e., the conversion ratio between c_0 and H_0 always remains unity, without regard to how *rapid* a pace of accumulation is being undertaken. This assumption will be modified below when we turn to consider real capital as a distinct productive commodity.

[18] Of course, the flattening of the curves must correspond to a difference of scale in the horizontal axis of Fig. 6-4(a) as compared with Fig. 6-4(b).

in the flow diagram must become horizontal. Passing over certain mathematical technicalities, let us take the liberty of interpreting the flow diagram of Fig. 6-4(a) in either a continuous or a discrete sense, as convenience dictates. The derivation of the solution in terms of the underlying productive and preference data of Figs. 6-3(a) and 6-3(b) is most direct when the discrete interpretation is employed.[19]

In order to find the current-period flow equilibrium, it is necessary to introduce a new curve—labelled $C(\Delta)$ in Fig. 6-4(a). This summarizes a different sort of time-preference data. Specifically it shows the absolute marginal rate of substitution in consumption between c_0 and c, $-dc/dc_0\,|_U$, as a function of the rate of capital augmentation $\Delta H_0 = H_0^P - H_0^Y$ or (under the Crusonia-plant construct) the rate of investment i_0. Geometrically, the consumptive-stationarity curve CS shows how marginal time preference changes as capital stock H varies, with investment i_0 held fixed at zero. The new curve $C(\Delta)$ shows how marginal time preference changes as the rate of investment varies, with H held (nearly) constant. (The shorter the unit time interval, the more nearly will H be a constant.) The $C(\Delta)$ curve is derived from the indifference-curve slopes encountered moving along the dashed productive-opportunity locus from Y^o to P^o in Fig. 6-3(b). Under the assumption that both c_0 and c are superior goods, the indifference-curve slopes thus encountered are increasingly steep. Hence [since r in equilibrium is equal to the absolute indifference-curve slope in Fig. 6-3(b)] the $C(\Delta)$ curve will be upward-sloping.

NUMERICAL EXAMPLE

Given the earlier consumptive optimality condition $\frac{1}{4}c/c_0 = r$, the equilibrium interest rate as a function of the rate of investment is found by expressing c_0 and c in terms of ΔH_0. Specifically, $c_0 = p_0 = y_0 - i_0 = 10(H_0^Y)^{1/2} - \Delta H_0$, while $c = p = 10(H_0^Y + \Delta H_0)^{1/2}$. Since $H_0^Y = 100$ at $t = 0$,

$$r = \frac{10(100 + \Delta H_0)^{1/2}}{100 - \Delta H_0}\left(\frac{1}{4}\right)$$

is the equation of $C(\Delta)$ in Fig. 6-4(a). The flow equilibrium of Fig. 6-4(a) is attained where $C(\Delta)$ intersects PS at the point P^o, which corresponds to the similarly labelled point in Fig. 6-3(b). This also corresponds to the price and quantity represented by the point Q' in Fig. 6-4(b). The equation for PS is

$$r = \frac{5}{(H_0^P)^{1/2}} = \left(\frac{5}{100 + \Delta H_0}\right)^{1/2}$$

[19] If the current period is of discrete length, then preference, exchange, or productive relationships between current income and future income raises no difficulties. But if the current period has only "infinitesimal" length, these relationships can only be interpreted in a limiting sense.

The numerical solution is then $\Delta H_0 = i_0 = 33.3$. This confirms the results obtained earlier.

In the following period a new "flow diagram" could be constructed, where the origin in Fig. 6-4(a) now represents the quantum H_1^Y in the "stock diagram." The new CS and PS curves would lie closer together vertically; $C(\Delta)$ would again coincide with CS at the vertical axis, but to the right would rise above it. Over time the periodic flow solutions will all lie along the curve PS in Fig. 6-4(b). Hence, the interest rate r falls over time—as is consistent with the results shown (declining slopes of MM, $M'M'$, and so on) in Fig. 6-3(b). In addition, the rate of investment i_t will tend to taper off as the long-term "stock solution" or stationary state is approached.

One interesting conclusion we can draw is that, in the determination of the interest rate under this model, a weightier role seems to be played by time productivity as opposed to time preference. Time preference does enter, since it helps dictate the rate of investment in each period, and therefore the *pace* of accumulation over time. But at any moment of time, r will be very close (the closer, the shorter is the length of the unit period) to the initial height along PS—the marginal product of capital for the given capital stock. If the time period is instantaneous, PS will be horizontal in the flow diagram of Fig. 6-4(a); then time productivity alone will dictate r, to which rate the marginal rate of substitution in consumption must conform.

The asymmetry between time productivity and time preference is due to the fact that the current rate of investment, under the Crusonia-plant construct, does not (greatly) affect time productivity, since it does not (substantially) change H—whereas the scale of investment does strongly affect time preference, since it radically changes the proportions between c_0 and c. The qualifying parentheses in the sentence preceding could be removed by a passage to the limit of an instantaneous current period. But at this point it is better to avoid the mathematical complications involved in the limiting process.

We may add a comment about the possible bias inherent in the distorted time view attributed to investors in the analysis. It has been assumed, to this point, that at each date the investor chose a future level sequence in the belief that the sequence would thereafter be immutable—but then at each following date we allowed and required the investor to reassess the situation and modify his choice, again under the same mistaken assumption. This astigmatic view of the future may be contrasted with a somewhat different distortion, properly called "myopia," in which the investor mistakenly believes at each moment of time that there is a horizon $T = 1$—i.e., that the two-period choice paradigm applies. Only when the future period eventuates does he visualize the next succeeding period. In the myopia case, it is clear that limited foresight will bias the decision so as to make for insufficient provision for the future. There is always "more future" than the investor realizes. The assumption here does not have so obvious a bias; the entire future is visualized, though the decision opportunities are misapprehended.[20] The bias probably works to make for insufficient provision for the *present* (if the situation dictates a positive accumulation rate). The reason is that, in the mistaken belief of the investor, he must provide for all future time through appropriate sacrifice of time-0 consumption. Then, the investor is induced to make a larger current sacrifice than he would undertake if he knew he would be permitted to accumulate gradually over a considerable span of time. The conclusion is that the true accumulation path in Fig. 6-3(b) would lie somewhat closer to the 45° line than does the curve AA'.

The true optimal path could be determined as a calculus-of-variations problem given the preference function, initial situation, and the productive-opportunity set. The path would maximize utility subject to the constraints imposed on the productive transformations between incomes of different periods. No attempt will be made here to display this solution.[21]

G. INVESTMENT, INTEREST, AND ACCUMULATION: DISTINCT CAPITAL-GOOD CONSTRUCT

In a more complete model, real capital takes the form of commodities distinct from the consumption good—as a tree is distinct from the fruit it yields, or a net is distinct from the fish it catches. For simplicity, let us assume there is only one homogeneous capital good, of perpetual life so that we need not concern ourselves with depreciation.[22] Even under this assumption, the model of production is necessarily much more complex than under the Crusonia-plant construct. It is sometimes helpful to think of two productive processes as now being involved: a capital-goods "industry" and a consumer-goods "industry." For we must now consider that capital goods are *produced*, by a process requiring some allocation of current labor as well as of previously endowed real-capital. This is to be contrasted with the Crusonia-plant construct, under which any sacrifice of current consumption simply *becomes* real capital, requiring no productive effort but only abstinence from consumption.

For consistency with the logical apparatus developed above, however, it is advantageous to treat production as a single process in any period t,

[20] See the discussions by F. M. Westfield and W. Leontief, "Time-Preference and Economic Growth," *American Economic Review*, **49** (Dec. 1959).

[21] This mathematical problem has been considered by a number of authors. See F. P. Ramsey, "A Mathematical Theory of Saving," *Economic Journal*, **38** (Dec. 1928); J. Tinbergen, "The Optimum Rate of Saving," *Economic Journal*, **66** (Dec. 1956).

[22] Under the Crusonia-plant real-capital construct, it is *never* necessary to take account of depreciation. The proportionate growth rate ρ is already defined as a *net* yield.

capable of generating differing mixes or vectors of the consumption-good and capital-good quantities—p_t and H_t^P, or p_t and the real-capital increment $\Delta H_t = H_t^P - H_t^Y$ (with the real capital formed standing as proxy, of course, for a future produced flow p). Thus, for the current period the productive opportunities are shown as PP in Fig. 6-5(b)—which looks very much like

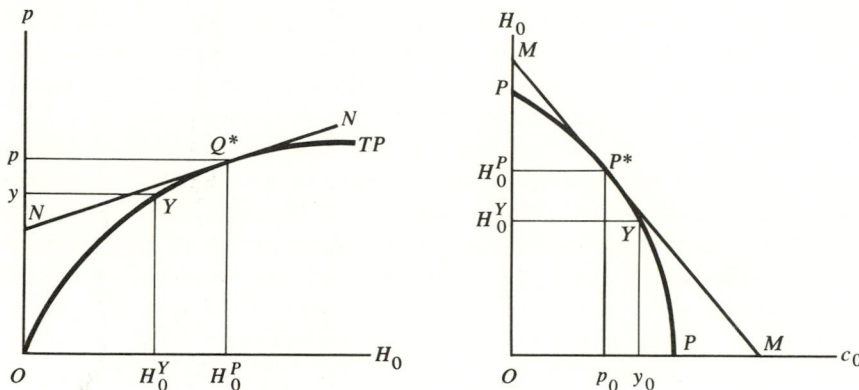

FIG. 6-5. (a) Total product curve and productive optimum, perpetuity paradigm with distinct capital-good, (b) Productive opportunity locus between current consumption and distinct capital-good, with productive optimum

Fig. 6-1(b) or 6-2(b), except that the vertical axis now shows the current-period "intermediate product" H_0 rather than the future-period "final product" of c. [Since H_0 is not an object of choice but only a productive commodity, there is no preference function in Fig. 6-5(b).] The productive-opportunity locus represents the fact that, with a given current-period factor endowment (L_0, H_0^Y), alternative output combinations of p_0 and H_0^P can be generated. The endowment point Y on the diagram represents H_0^Y and the associated current net income y_0—the quantity of c_0 that can be produced in the current period when $H_0^P = H_0^Y$—i.e., when real capital is just "maintained intact." The diagram also shows the possibility of disinvesting—converting endowed H_0^Y into c_0.

Figure 6-5(a) is equivalent to Fig. 6-2(a), except that the horizontal axis is now scaled in the normal direction. The TP curve shows the level future flow p produced by any stock of real capital and the given future flow of labor services, L. Under the perpetuity paradigm, of course, the attained real capital is expected to remain constant over all future time. Therefore, the future L and the currently generated H_0^P fix a unique future flow p of the consumptive commodity, with no options for further augmentation of H.

The determinants of the current-period productive optimum are evident, from inspection, in Figs. 6-5(a) and 6-5(b). The individual faces given market prices ϕ_0, $\phi_\infty^0 = 1/r$, and ϕ_H^0. (With current real consumptive claims c_0 as numeraire, and $\phi_0 = 1$, it is now no longer true that the price of the capital good ϕ_H necessarily equals unity.) In Fig. 6-5(b) tangency of PP with the market line MM represents the productive optimum (wealth maximum) in the formation of capital goods, the equation of MM being $W_0 = \phi_H H_0^P + p_0$. Tangency of TP with the market line NN in Fig. 6-5(a) is the productive optimum in production of future consumption goods, the equation of NN being $\phi_\infty p = \phi_H H_0^P + wL$. Of course these two optima are interdependent, since the (p_0, H_0^P) decision fixes the future p-output.

In order to have market equilibrium in the current period, the aggregate of individuals' *consumptive* optima have to be consistent with these *productive* optima. Specifically, the price ratio $\phi_0/\phi_\infty = r$—determined as the product of the absolute slopes $dc/dH_0 = \phi_H/\phi_\infty$ at Q^* and $dH_0/dc_0 = \phi_0/\phi_H$ at P^* in Figs. 6-5(a) and 6-5(b)—must be such that the desired (c_0, c) holdings as determined in time-preference diagrams like Fig. 6-1(b) represent the same time-sums as the produced (p_0, p) combinations.[23]

In return for the additional complexity of the formulation in terms of a distinct capital-good commodity, we do gain important new insights. The diminishing returns in transformations between c_0 and c, reflected in the concavity of the PP locus of Figs. 6-1(b) and 6-2(b), can now be seen to combine two logically separable elements. *First*, there is the diminishing marginal rate of substitution in production between c_0 and H_0 shown in Fig. 6-5(b). This may be described as *increasing marginal cost in investing* (or in capital-goods production), the cost being in terms of current consumption units foregone. To use a fish-net illustration: as the time rate of weaving nets increases, the marginal fish-cost per net rises, for the increased weaving rate will require the withdrawal of resources increasingly productive in alternative employments—here, in the production of consumption goods c_0 (fishing with nets, as opposed to weaving them).[24] *Second*, there is the diminishing marginal productivity, or increasing marginal cost, in the *consumer-goods industry* as represented in the shape of TP in Fig. 6-5(a). In the fish-net illustration, marginal nets will yield less heavily per annum as the stock of nets in existence increases, the reason being the limited amounts of other

---

[23] Figures 6-5(a) and 6-5(b) are intended to display the productive optimum only. To show the consumptive optimum would have required a third diagram on (c_0, c) axes, so as to permit construction of the preference map. In the interests of simplicity this development has been omitted. In effect, the relevant time-preference information is summarized in the slopes of the market lines; the price ϕ_∞ represents the marginal rate of substitution in consumption between c_0 and c in the neighborhood of the productive (p_0, p) optimum.

[24] Note that this is a strictly technological phenomenon. The changing marginal rate of substitution *in production* is quite separate from the shift in the marginal rate of substitution *in consumption* that makes additional sacrifices of c_0 for c increasingly onerous to the consumers.

resources (land, labor) available to cooperate with the increasing capital-good stock.[25]

Note the different reasons for diminishing returns in the two cases: (1) diminishing returns in investing due to the currently given amounts of *all* current resources, whose services must, therefore, be allocated between current investment and current production of consumption goods; (2) diminishing returns to capital goods due to permanently nonaugmentable stocks of the factors *other* than capital goods.

The slopes along the productivity loci of Figs. 6-5(a) and 6-5(b) may be called, respectively, the marginal future-product *of the capital good* (dp/dH_0) and the marginal product of investing $(-dH_0/dp_0$, or dH_0/di_0 since $i_0 = y_0 - p_0)$. The absolute slopes along the market lines are, respectively, ϕ_H/ϕ_∞ and $1/\phi_H$. Thus, at the productive optima $dp/dH_0 = \phi_H/\phi_\infty$ and $dH_0/di_0 = 1/\phi_H$. When the tangencies of Figs. 6-5(a) and 6-5(b) at the points Q^* and P^* hold simultaneously, we obtain

$$\left(\frac{dp}{dH_0}\right)\left(\frac{dH_0}{di_0}\right) = \frac{dp}{di_0} = \left(\frac{1}{\phi_H}\right)\left(\frac{\phi_H}{\phi_\infty}\right) = \frac{1}{\phi_\infty} = r$$

The equalities in terms of consumption flows, $dp/di_0 = 1/\phi_\infty = r$, represent the same result for the productive optimum as that obtained in the Crusonia-plant analysis—or indeed in the analysis of transformations among dated consumptions in Chapter 3 before the introduction of any real-capital concept.

So, while it is no longer true, when H is a distinct capital good, that the marginal future-product of (real) capital dp/dH_0 equals the rate of interest, we can say that *the marginal efficiency of investment dp/di_0*, the product of the marginal productivity of investing dH_0/di_0 and the marginal future-product of the capital good dp/dH_0, *equals the rate of interest*. (The term "efficiency" is intended to suggest a transformation that is a pure number except for date, numerator and denominator being measured in the same units; "product," in contrast, suggests a transformation between distinct commodities.)

An algebraic formulation of the current-period solution and the stationarity conditions under the distinct-capital-good construct will not be provided here. However, an interpretation in terms of the stock-flow representation introduced in the previous section may be instructive.

In Figs. 6-6(a) and 6-6(b), the construction is quite analogous to Figs. 6-4(a) and 6-4(b). But the horizontal axis in Fig. 6-4(a) represented both investment i_0 and accumulation $\Delta H_0 = H_0^P - H_0^Y$, identical under the Crusonia-plant construct. With a distinct capital-good commodity, however, the rate of accumulation ΔH_0 of the capital good [the horizontal axis of Fig. 6-6(a)] is not in the same units as investment i_0—the input of the consumption good into the intertemporal transformation process.

The consumptive-stationarity CS curve, as before, shows the time-preference considerations consistent with stationarity; i.e., for each H it shows the interest rate r at which the consumer will be satisfied to exactly

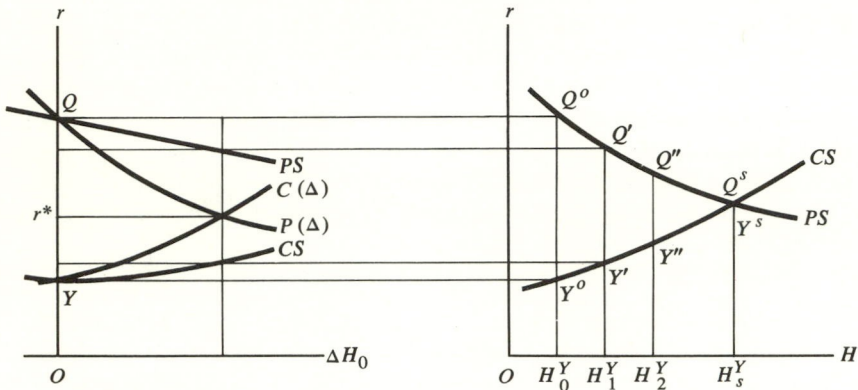

FIG. 6-6. (a) Flow diagram for accumulation rate in present period, distinct capital-good, (b) Stock diagram for real-capital accumulation, with stationarity condition, distinct capital-good

consume his endowed current income (undertake zero net saving). The CS curve is again shown as rising, although (as indicated earlier) the most plausible assumption might be horizontality. In any case, the "flow diagram" of Fig. 6-6(a) shows the CS curve as (nearly) horizontal.[26] The $C(\Delta)$ is rising as before, representing the diminishing relative preference for future consumption c as a function of the rate of formation of capital. For, as ΔH_0 and therefore also i_0 rise, current consumption becomes scarcer relative to future consumption.

We see in Figs. 6-6(a) and (b) that the curves PS and $P(\Delta)$ representing the supply (productive) considerations have shapes that are inverted analogs of CS and $C(\Delta)$ representing the demand (time-preference) considerations. [The symmetry of the productive and preference determinants here stands in contrast with Figs. 6-4(a) and (b).] The marginal rate of substitution in production is now a function of the rate of investment i_0 (and accumulation ΔH_0) as well as of the capital stock H^P, for the model now incorporates diminishing returns to investment (increasing marginal cost in producing capital goods)—whereas, under the Crusonia-plant image of real capital, the rate of conversion between c_0 and H remained necessarily 1 : 1 independently of i_0.

[26] The shorter the unit period, the more nearly horizontal.

The characteristics of the stock and flow solutions are evident in Figs. 6-6(a) and (b). Throughout the accumulation process the interest rate r remains lower than the ordinates of PS—whereas under the Crusonia-plant real-capital construct in Figs. 6-4(a) and (b) the interest rates at each moment were determined *along* the PS curve. Because of the negative slope of PS in Fig. 6-4(b), under the Crusonia-plant construct the interest rate fell with accumulation over time. But here it is not *necessarily* the case that the rate of interest declines as accumulation proceeds. However, it will be recalled that, although the consumptive-stationarity curve was shown as upward-sloping in both Figs. 6-4(b) and 6-6(b), it was suggested that the most plausible assumption is that CS is horizontal. If this is the case, since PS is in any case downward-sloping, the rate of interest will tend after all to decline over time until stationarity is reached.

NUMERICAL EXAMPLE (see Table 3)

Let us assume that the marginal rate of time preference can still be expressed as $-dc/dc_0\big|_U = \tfrac{1}{4}c/c_0$. Similarly the production function for future consumables will still be numerically taken to be $p = 10(H^P)^{1/2}$, even though H and p now refer to distinct commodities. Then the consumptive-stationary CS curve is the same as before; the equation remains $r = \tfrac{1}{4}$, at which interest rate the consumptive optimality condition $-dc/dc_0\big|_U = r$ is consistent with stationarity. The productive-stationarity PS curve is derived from the condition

$$r = \frac{dp}{di_0} = \frac{dp}{dH_0}\frac{dH_0}{di_0}$$

As before, dp/dH_0 is the marginal future-product of capital $p' = 5/(H^P)^{1/2}$. An equation has not yet been introduced for the transformation possibilities between current consumption and current capital formation. Let this equation be[27]

$$p_0^2 + 20(H_0^Y)^{1/2}\Delta H_0 = 100 H_0^Y$$

Then the marginal product of investing

$$\frac{dH_0}{di_0} = \frac{-d\Delta H_0}{dp_0} = \frac{p_0}{10(H_0^Y)^{1/2}} = \frac{p_0}{y_0}$$

Under conditions of stationarity $y_0 = p_0$, so the marginal product of investing is equal to 1—not a general condition, but a special result due to the numerical construction of this example.[28] Thus the productive-stationarity condition is

---

[27] The form $p_t^2 + 20(H_t^Y)^{1/2}\Delta H_t = 100 H_t^Y$ is the general production function. For when $\Delta H_t = 0$ so that $H_t^Y = H_t^P$, the equation $p = 10(H^P)^{1/2}$ is implied for all later dates.

[28] This cannot be a general condition, for it is not invariant with respect to a change in the unit of measurement of real capital. If the marginal product of investing were unity for real capital measured in tons, it would be 2000 for real capital measured in pounds.

$r = 5/(H^P)^{1/2}$, numerically the same as in the example of the previous section. The intersection of the CS and PS curves is given by $\frac{1}{4} = 5/(H^P)^{1/2}$, or $H^P = 400$ as before.

Consider now the current-period equilibrium under nonstationary conditions—specifically, where endowed capital $H_0^Y = 100$ so that $y_0 = y = 100$, as in the example of the preceding section. If zero investment were undertaken, the absolute marginal rate of substitution in consumption $(\frac{1}{4}c/c_0)$ would again equal $\frac{1}{4}$. But the marginal rate of substitution in production or marginal efficiency of investment

$$\frac{dp}{di_0} = p' \frac{dH_0}{di_0} = \frac{5}{(H_0^P)^{1/2}} \frac{p_0}{y_0}$$

would (with $H_0^P = H_0^Y$ and $p_0 = y_0$) equal $\frac{1}{2}$. Thus there is an incentive to invest. The optimum amount of investment is shown by the intersection of the $C(\Delta)$ and $P(\Delta)$ curves—which indicate how the marginal rates of substitution in consumption and in production, respectively, vary with the scale of augmentation of capital.

The $C(\Delta)$ curve represents the condition $r = \frac{1}{4}c/c_0$, where $c = p$ and $c_0 = p_0$ and the relations between p and p_0 are given by the future-production function $p = 10(H_0^P)^{1/2}$ and the current-period transformation equation $p_0^2 + 20(H_0^Y)^{1/2}\Delta H_0 = 100 H_0^Y$. After substitutions, this becomes

$$r = \frac{\frac{1}{4}(100 + \Delta H_0)^{1/2}}{(100 - 2\Delta H_0)^{1/2}}$$

The $P(\Delta)$ curve represents the condition that the interest rate equals the marginal efficiency of investment, $r = p' \, dH_0/di_0$. After substitutions, this becomes

$$r = \frac{\frac{1}{2}(100 - 2\Delta H_0)^{1/2}}{(100 + \Delta H_0)^{1/2}}$$

The solution is $\Delta H_0 = 20$ for the current-period augmentation of capital. This implies current-period consumption $c_0 = p_0$ of approximately 77.46, investment $i_0 = 22.54$, and the future level flow $p = 109.54$. The equilibrium for the marginal rate of substitution in consumption and in production, and therefore the rate of interest r, is approximately 35.3 per cent. The marginal product of capital $p' = 5/(H_0^P)^{1/2}$ in future production is approximately .456 and the marginal product of investing $d\Delta H_0/di_0 = .775$. The implied price for the future flow, $\phi_\infty^0 = 1/r$, is 2.83. The current price of the capital good, $\phi_H^0 = p'\phi_\infty^0$ (the value of the marginal product), is about 1.29.

In this example the rate of interest does tend to fall over time. Table 3 also suggests the courses of the wage rate and rental rate, based upon the fully explicit production function

$$p_t^2 + 2L_t^{1/2}(H_t^Y)^{1/2}\Delta H_t = L_t H_t^Y$$

Table 3*

		TIME 0		TIME I	STATION-ARITY
		Endowment Position	Optimum Position	Endowment Position	Endowment and Optimum Positions
Capital	H	100	120	120	400
Income	y_t	100	—	109.54	200
Investment	i_t	—	22.54	—	0
Consumption	c_t	—	77.46	—	200
Future income flow	p	100	109.54	109.54	200
Marginal rate of time preference	$-dc/dc_0\mid_U$	.25	.353	.25	.25
Marginal future-product of capital	p'	.5	.456	.456	.25
Marginal product of investing	dH/di_0	1	.775	1	1
Marginal efficiency of investment	$-dp/dp_0$	.5	.353	.456	.25
Interest rate	r	—	.353	—	.25
Price of future flow	ϕ_∞	—	2.83	—	4
Price of capital good	ϕ_H	—	1.29	—	1
Wage	w	.5	.548	.548	1
Rental	h	.5	.456	.456	.25

* Conditions: $U = c_0^{.2} c^{.8}$

$$p_0^2 + 20(H_0^Y)^{1/2}\Delta H_0 = 100 H_0^Y$$

$$[\text{or, with } L = 100, p_0^2 + 2L^{1/2}(H_0^Y)^{1/2}\Delta H_0 = L H_0^Y]$$

with $L_t = 100$ at all dates. When no augmentation of capital is occurring, this reduces to

$$p_t = y_t = L_t^{1/2}(H_t^Y)^{1/2}$$

Evidently, the wage rate in this example tends to rise over time, while the rental rate tends to fall.

H. CAPITAL, INTEREST, AND THE PERIOD OF PRODUCTION

As indicated in Section D above, there is a third traditional image of real capital in addition to the Crusonia-plant and distinct-capital-good constructs already analyzed. This third concept is associated with the theory of interest of Bohm-Bawerk,[29] as formalized by Wicksell.[30]

[29] E. v. Bohm-Bawerk, *The Positive Theory of Capital*, especially bk. VIII.
[30] K. Wicksell, *Value, Capital, and Rent*, tr. G. L. S. Shackle (George Allen & Unwin, Ltd., 1954), pp. 120–168.

Bohm-Bawerk's metaphor of real capital takes the form of a time-phased collection of growing consumables. Imagine, for example, a stand of growing trees distributed evenly over all ages to maturity. (We will suppose that the mature timber yielded represents a consumptive commodity.) Then the real capital of the community is a stock of *goods-in-process*. Bohm-Bawerk regards this stock as an aggregate of not-yet-matured "subsistences," whose function is to permit the adoption of "roundabout" methods of production. The subsistences scheduled to mature in the near future tide the economy over the "period of production"—the gestation interval of the individual productive units (trees) planted today. Conversely, the time-preference constraint upon the accumulation of such a stock is what prevents the period of production from being made indefinitely long.

The traditional formulation of the Bohm-Bawerk problem provides only the stationary-state solution. This avoids the mathematically awkward problem of transition from one phased time-distribution to another. The analysis here will also be limited to the stationary state. The technique followed will be to locate the position where the consumptive-stationarity and productive-stationarity conditions are mutually consistent.

Bohm-Bawerk models involve as variables the rate of production (p), the period of production (θ), the rate of interest (r), and the *value* of the capital stock (K_0). The rate of labor input (L) is exogenous, taken as constant over all time. The presentation here will diverge from traditional models in one respect. Bohm-Bawerk assumed a continuous-input process whereby the services of labor are spread evenly over the entire life of the productive unit; in effect, the function of labor is *tending* trees. In the interests of simplicity and continuity with earlier chapters, it will be more convenient to assume a point-input process here, in which the function of labor is *planting* trees. Under either productive assumption, in the aggregate there is a level flow of labor input, a level flow of productive output, and a stock of not-yet-matured subsistences. But the optimum conditions differ according as the planting of a tree does or does not involve point-input costs on the one hand, or a continuing tending requirement on the other.[31]

It is an inconvenience of Bohm-Bawerk models that, while a well-defined measure of capital *value* exists, there is no scalar measure of the time-distributed aggregate (e.g., of trees of all ages) that constitutes the *real* capital. However, the period of production θ does provide a kind of index to the volume of real capital.

The consumptive-stationarity and productive-stationarity conditions are expressed as relations between θ and the rate of interest r in the *CS* and *PS* curves of Fig. 6-7. The consumptive-stationarity condition has exactly

---

[31] An analysis of the traditional continuous-input model ("tending trees") can be found in J. Hirshleifer, "A Note on the Bohm-Bawerk/Wicksell Theory of Interest," *Review of Economic Studies*, **34** (1967). See also R. Dorfman, "A Graphical Exposition of Bohm-Bawerk's Interest Theory," *Review of Economic Studies*, **26** (1959).

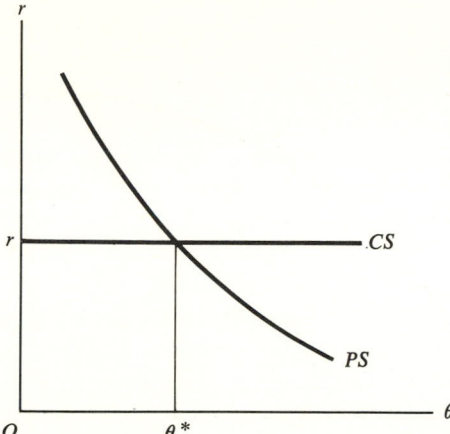

FIG. 6-7. Consumptive-stationarity and productive-stationarity conditions, Bohm-Bawerk model

the same significance as before. The productive-stationarity condition now answers the following question: Given the rate of interest r, what is the period θ associated with a productive equilibrium at which stationarity holds—i.e., at which producers find it optimal to replant the same number of trees as those currently being harvested?

For a representative producer (firm), the stationary-equilibrium production function can be shown as a relation between output per laborer and the period of production:

$$\frac{p}{L} = g(\theta) \tag{11}$$

An example of such a function is plotted in Fig. 6-8. The equation shows output p, for given θ, as proportional to the number of laborers employed. This does not deny diminishing returns with respect to labor. For, if more laborers are hired, in order to have stationary conditions with constant θ it is necessary to increase the stock of goods-in-process of all ages in the same proportion.

Next, capital value per laborer is given by [32]

$$\frac{K_0}{L} = \int_{-\theta}^{0} we^{-rt}\, dt = \frac{w}{r}\left(e^{r\theta} - 1\right)$$

$$\frac{K_0}{L} = \frac{w}{r}\left(e^{r\theta} - 1\right) \tag{12}$$

[32] This relation can be derived by compounding the value of the wage inputs dating back to time $t = -\theta$.

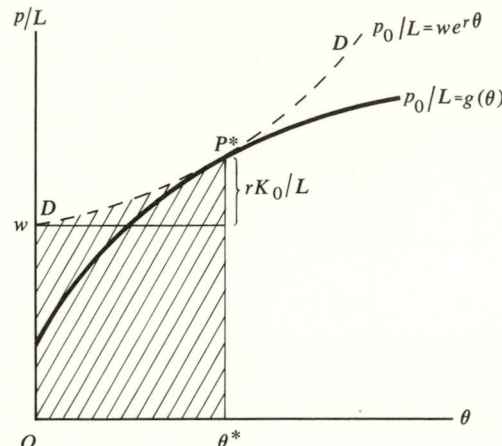

FIG. 6-8.   Determination of period of production, Bohm-Bawerk model

Entrepreneurial profit per laborer is the difference $p/L - w - rK_0/L$, the per-laborer excess of output over factor payments. Maximizing with respect to the choice of period θ leads to

$$g'(\theta) = rwe^{r\theta} \tag{13}$$

where $g'(\theta)$ is the derivative of the function in (11). But competitive pressure will enforce a zero-profit condition, in which all of output is paid out to owners of the factors:

$$p = Lw + rK_0 \tag{14}$$

The four equations (11) through (14) equal in number the variables p, w, K_0, and θ. Using these, the period θ can be expressed in terms of the interest rate r as parameter—thus obtaining the productive-stationarity curve PS of Fig. 6-7.

It is also possible to derive a direct expression for the wage w by substitutions in equations (14) and (12).

$$w = g(\theta)e^{-r\theta} \tag{15}$$

This says that the wage expended in planting is equal to the discounted value of the future output per laborer. Evidently, this is another version of the zero-profit condition. Geometrically, it corresponds to the feature of Fig. 6-8 wherein the highest discounting curve DD attainable along $g(\theta)$ is the one cutting the vertical axis at the height w.

The value-of-capital per laborer, K_0/L, is represented by the shaded area under the DD curve, representing the compounding of wage inputs for trees of all ages. And the rate of instantaneous interest yield on this capital value is the difference $p/L - w$ at time θ.

With the help of equation (15) for w, the parametric form relating θ and r can be expressed directly. By (13), $g'(\theta) = rwe^{r\theta}$. Using (15) to substitute for w, we have

$$g'(\theta) = rg(\theta) \tag{16}$$

Equation (16) has already been encountered before. It is but another version of the optimal-duration condition first expressed in equation (18) of Chapter 3. Geometrically, the equation corresponds to the tangency of $g(\theta)$ with the DD curve at the optimal duration θ^* in Fig. 6-8.

The consumptive-stationarity condition takes a very convenient form with the continuous-time utility function introduced in Chapter 3, Section E (this function was also used in the parallel discussion of Chapter 4, Section I):

$$U = \int_0^\theta v(c_t)e^{-\eta t}\, dt \tag{17}$$

where η is the "time-bias parameter" and $v(c_t)$ is the "utility-of-income function." Following the analysis of Chapter 4, Section I, the general consumptive-optimum condition is

$$\frac{v_0' e^{\eta\theta}}{v_\theta'} = e^{r\theta} \tag{18}$$

Under stationarity, $v_\theta' = v_0$, so the condition reduces to

$$r = \eta \tag{19}$$

Thus, the consumptive-stationarity curve of Fig. 6-7 will be a horizontal line with ordinate η.

NUMERICAL EXAMPLE (see Table 4)

Let $\eta = .1$, so that the interest rate at stationarity will have to be $r = 10$ per cent. Let the production function (11) have the specific form $p/L = A(1 + \ln \theta)$, with the constant $A = 10$. Then the productive-stationarity relation (16) becomes $1/\theta = r(1 + \ln \theta)$, or $10/\theta = 1 + \ln \theta$. The approximate numerical solution for the period of production θ is 4.133 years. The stationary values of the other variables are indicated in Table 4. As a check, the retrospective

Table 4

Interest rate	r	10%
Period of production	θ	4.133 years
Output per laborer	p/L	14.190
Wage	w	9.394
Capital value per laborer	$K_0/L = (w/r)(e^{r\theta} - 1)$	47.962
Earnings of capital per laborer	rK_0/L	4.796
Value of net-output stream per laborer	$K_0/L = [(p/L) - w)]/r$	47.962

valuation of capital per laborer [the accumulated value of wage inputs from equation (12)] is shown to match the capital value of the net-output stream.

I. INTEREST AND THE MARGINS OF DECISION

A compact summary of a number of the ideas of this and previous chapters can be provided by consideration of how the interest rate is related to the *margins of decision* of the economy. (Only the *real* rate of interest and the *real* decision margins will be considered in this summary.) The real margins of decision are the dimensions of barter-choice alternatives (present consumption vs. future consumption, spending vs. forming capital, and so on) that economic agents face as they adapt to the *market* data summarized by interest rates.

1. *The interest rate reflects the marginal rate of substitution between present and future consumption.*

The relations involved here are the optimum conditions $dc_1/dc_0 |_U = -(1 + r_1)$ for the two-period model, $dc/dc_0 |_U = -r$ for the discrete-perpetuity model, and so on. Geometrically, the conditions represent tangencies between market lines and indifference curves. The margin of choice involved is between dated consumptions, so that this is the time-preference margin.

2. (a) *The interest rate reflects the marginal rate of substitution between present and future production.*

Here the optimum conditions for the two-period and discrete-perpetuity paradigms, respectively, are $dp_1/dp_0 = -(1 + r_1)$ and $dp/dp_0 = -r$. Geometrically, these conditions correspond to tangencies between productive-opportunity loci and market lines. This is the productive time-widening margin.

(b) *The interest rate reflects the marginal proportionate yield of productive extension in time.*

The optimum condition envisaged here is $r = (dq_t/q_t)/dt$, where the margin of decision is whether to hold growing assets for shorter or longer durations. This is the productive time-deepening margin. And we saw in the previous section that essentially the same condition appears in the variant of the Bohm-Bawerk models there analyzed, in the form $r = g'(\theta)/g(\theta)$. This says that the interest rate equals the marginal proportionate yield of extending the period of production.

The time-preference and time-productivity margins of decision are the basic ones, according to the formulation of this work that makes dated consumptions the sole ultimate objects of choice. However, there are a number of derivative ways of expressing these same margins, as shown below.

3. *The interest rate reflects the marginal rate of return on current sacrifice, or the marginal rate of return to saving or investment.*

The optimum conditions for the two elementary paradigms can be expressed also as $dc_1/di_0 = (1 + r_1)$ and $dc/di_0 = r$. The margins of decision contemplated are how much to save (if we are thinking of consumptive choices) or invest (if we are thinking of productive choices). Since an increment of saving or investment is a decrement of current consumption $(di_0 = -dc_0)$, the consumptive or saving margin is just another way of formulating statement 1 above, while the productive or investment margin is another way of formulating statement 2(a).

4. *The interest rate reflects the marginal productivity of capital.*

In the present chapter, this relationship was shown to be an optimum condition for the Crusonia-plant construct, in which real capital H_0 is simply a stock of consumables c_0. In terms of the discrete-perpetuity paradigm employed in this chapter, the condition can be expressed as $dp/dH_0 = r$. The margin of decision envisaged concerns the amount of real capital to be attained in the current period. For a distinct capital-good commodity, it will be recalled, the corresponding optimum condition cannot be formulated this way, but instead equates the *marginal efficiency of investment* dp/di_0 to the rate of interest; this relation has already been expressed as statement 3 above.

5. *The interest rate reflects the marginal yield on capital value.*

Earlier in this chapter it was mentioned that while optimum conditions could be formulated in terms of capital values, doing so obscured somewhat the real choices involved between dated consumption claims. However, it remains true that, as an optimum condition, under the perpetuity paradigm, $r = dp/dK_0$—the rate of interest equals the marginal future-product yield calculated on the capital value of the productive process. Here the margin of decision is the amount of capital value to be held (as against the alternative of current consumption). Unlike the relation in statement 4 above, this condition is valid under all the real-capital constructs.

BIBLIOGRAPHIC NOTE

The traditional literature of capital theory—famous equally for brilliance and incomprehensibility—cannot in general be recommended to the nonspecialist. However, the following older works are still useful and most interesting:

IRVING FISHER, *The Nature of Capital and Income* (The Macmillan Company, 1912).

E. V. BOHM-BAWERK, *The Positive Theory of Capital,* tr. William Smart (G. E. Stechert & Co., 1891).

A penetrating summary of some of the older debates will be found in:

AXEL LEIJONHUFVUD, *On Keynesian Economics and the Economics of Keynes* (Oxford Univ. Press, 1968), Chap. 4.

For the Knightian viewpoint and some recent developments:

F. H. KNIGHT, "Diminishing Returns from Investment," *Journal of Political Economy,* **52** (March 1944).

M. FRIEDMAN, *Price Theory* (Aldine Publishing Co., 1962), Chap. 13.

D. DEWEY, *Modern Capital Theory* (Columbia Univ. Press, 1965).

A recent short book that takes off from the same Fisherian starting point as this study (placing the underlying *intertemporal consumptive choices* at the heart of the analysis) is:

R. M. SOLOW, *Capital Theory and the Rate of Return* (Rand McNally & Company, 1964).

This work also provides an introduction to the currently popular topic of growth theory, with some empirical applications. On growth theory, the following also make good reading:

E. S. PHELPS, "The Golden Rule of Accumulation: A Fable for Growthmen," *American Economic Review,* **51** (Sept. 1961).

A. P. LERNER, "Recent Developments in Capital Theory," *American Economic Review,* **55** (May 1965).

7 INVESTMENT DECISIONS WITH IMPERFECT FUNDS MARKETS

In Chapter 3 investment decision rules for individuals were considered in the context of perfect markets for dated consumptive claims—a situation such that a single price ratio, competitively determined, governs for exchanges between funds of any pair of dates. We considered in Chapter 3, and will again be assuming here, a one-commodity world in which the term "funds" refers to *real* consumptive claims.

Imperfect funds markets are most readily understood as restrictions or truncations of the set of financial opportunities available under perfect-market conditions. In Fig. 7-1 the familiar Fisherian two-period solution is illustrated, to bring out once more the roles of the endowment Y, the productive opportunities, here denoted PP', and the highest attainable market line, denoted MM'. The entire opportunity set is OMM' (the shaded area). The over-all optimum at C^* (attained via lending-borrowing decisions after the productive optimum P^* has been reached) is the preferred point within the range of the triangular opportunity set OMM'. The same diagram serves to portray the most extreme form of *imperfection* of funds markets: a situation such that no financial transactions at all are permitted. In that case the opportunity set would be OPP' (the crosshatched area); the best that the investor could achieve would be the "Robinson Crusoe solution" R^*.

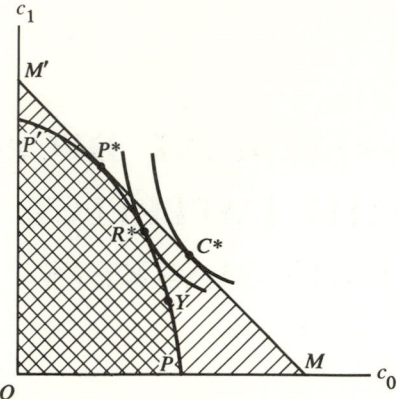

FIG. 7-1.   Opportunity sets: perfect funds markets vs. no funds markets

A. DIVERGENT BORROWING AND LENDING RATES

Constant Borrowing Cost

Evidently, there are many possible forms of imperfection intermediate between perfect funds markets (opportunity set OMM') and nonexistent funds markets (opportunity set OPP'). Considerable discussion has centered about the particular case in which there are no quantitative limits on trading, but a positive divergence exists between a constant borrowing rate r_B and a constant lending rate r_L.[1] This can be interpreted as a situation of perfect markets qualified only by a fixed per-unit cost of transacting—not an unreasonable assumption, perhaps. The implications for the opportunity set are illustrated, for the two-period model, in Fig. 7-2. There are now two kinds of market lines: the steeper "borrowing line" represents opportunities for converting funds at $t = 1$ back into funds at $t = 0$ (note the direction of the arrows); the flatter "lending line" represents opportunities for transfers forward in time. The borrowing line enlarges the opportunity set by the area PBB' to the right of the tangency at B; correspondingly, the lending line accounts for the enlargement $P'LL'$ to the left of the tangency at L.

There are three classes of solutions for the situation illustrated in Fig. 7-2, corresponding to the ranges $L'L$, LB, and BB' along the opportunity frontier. Depending on the shape of the utility function, there could be an indifference-curve tangency (a consumptive optimum C^*) in the lending

---

[1] The case in which the borrowing rate is *less* than the lending rate can be dismissed, as it implies the possibility of accumulating infinite wealth by borrowing and relending.

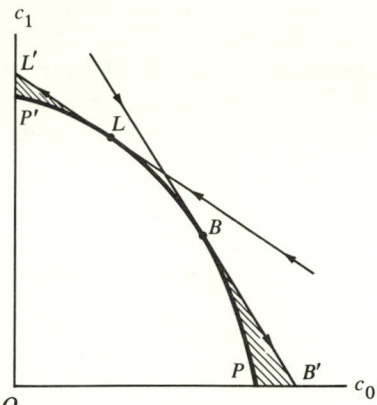

FIG. 7-2. Imperfect funds markets: divergence between borrowing and lending rates

range LL', in the borrowing range BB', or else in the middle range LB. An indifference-curve tangency in the range LL' would entail a productive optimum at L, combined with lending transactions toward the consumptive optimum northwest of L. A tangency in the range BB' entails a productive optimum at B, combined with borrowing transactions toward the consumptive optimum southeast of B. Finally, an indifference-curve tangency within the range LB excludes the possibility of benefiting by either lending or borrowing transactions; the productive optimum and the consumptive optimum coincide. In effect, the "Crusoe solution" applies within this range.

Turning now to the question of decision rules (discussed in Chapter 3 in the context of perfect funds markets), there has been some controversy as to whether the *borrowing rate* or the *lending rate* should be used, where a divergence between the two exists, in present-value calculations. From Fig. 7-2 it is evident that the correct procedure will vary according to the range in which the solution falls. If the indifference-curve tangency is northwest of L, then the productive solution is the point L of maximum present value calculated in terms of the *lending* rate. The economic logic is that since the investor will in fact be lending after having attained the productive optimum, he should adopt productive projects so long as the marginal productive yield on current sacrifice, $(-dp_1/dp_0) - 1$, exceeds the lending rate r_L in financial transactions—or, geometrically, as long as the absolute slope along PP', $-dp_1/dp_0$, exceeds the absolute slope of the lending lines $1 + r_L$. Correspondingly, if the indifference-curve tangency is southeast of B, he will be borrowing after the productive solution; hence, the productive solution is the point B of maximum present value calculated in terms of the *borrowing* rate r_B. Up to this point, the marginal productive yield is high enough to permit financing increments of productive investment by borrowing; the absolute slope of PP' is greater than that of the borrowing lines. Note that if the indifference-curve tangency falls within the "Crusoe range" LB, the optimum can only be interpreted as a present-value maximum in a formalistic sense— it does not correspond to any actual financial opportunities.

NUMERICAL EXAMPLE

Imagine an individual with productive-opportunity locus PP' expressed by the equation $p_0^2/20 + p_1 = 100$, and with preference function $U = c_0^{1/2}c_1^{1/2}$, so that the marginal rate of substitution in consumption (indifference-curve slope) is

$$\left.\frac{dc_1}{dc_0}\right|_U = \frac{-c_1}{c_0}$$

Let the lending rate $r_L = 0$ per cent and the borrowing rate $r_B = 100$ per cent.

Consider first a possible productive solution like that at L in Fig. 7-2. The condition here is $-dp_1/dp_0 = 1 + r_L$, which is numerically $p_0/10 = 1$. This determines L on PP' as the point $(10, 95)$. At this point the absolute indifference-curve slope $c_1/c_0 = 9.5$; geometrically, it is evident that the individual would now want to move *southeast* from L, by borrowing if necessary. But at L borrowing is a more costly way of obtaining c_0 than simply moving back southeast along PP'. Hence, the movement northwest along PP' to L must have been pushed too far.

Consider next the possible productive solution like that at B in Fig. 7-2. The condition here is $-dp_1/dp_0 = 1 + r_B$, or numerically $p_0/10 = 2$, which determines B as the point $(20, 80)$. At this point the absolute indifference-curve slope $c_1/c_0 = 4$, so still the individual wants to move southeast. Here. however, borrowing along BB' is more advantageous than moving southeast along $P'P$. The consumptive-optimality condition is

$$\frac{-dc_1}{dc_0} = \frac{c_1}{c_0} = 1 + r_B = 2 \quad \text{or} \quad c_1 = 2c_0$$

A second relation between c_0 and c_1 is given by the equation of the borrowing line BB'. Since this line has slope -2 and goes through the point $(20, 80)$, its equation is $c_1 = 120 - 2c_0$. The solution is $C^* = (30, 60)$.

As a check, the direct-tangency or "Crusoe-solution" R^* may also be computed. Maximizing utility subject to the productive-opportunity locus as constraint, by the usual Lagrangian technique, leads to the approximate solution $(25.8, 66.7)$. Note that this tangency is *not* between L and B. Instead, it is in the range BP along PP', and thus it is obviously inferior to the solution involving movement along BB' to $C^* = (30, 60)$. For, R^* provides less consumption at both dates than points such as $(26, 68)$ attainable along BB'.

Once we leave the sphere of perfect markets for intertemporal claims, then, the present-value rule is no longer universally correct—at least not

in the desired sense of providing an objectively calculable criterion independent of subjective preference considerations. It is only possible to state
a *utility-free rule*[2] for a limited class of cases, where one income stream (or the
set of projects leading to that income stream) clearly *dominates* another.

The usual concept of dominance (here called *simple* dominance)
refers to a situation where one income stream is never smaller, and has at
least one element greater, than another. A second class of dominance, to
be called *opportunity* dominance, may occur once financial opportunities are
taken into account. Figure 7-3 illustrates such a situation. The income

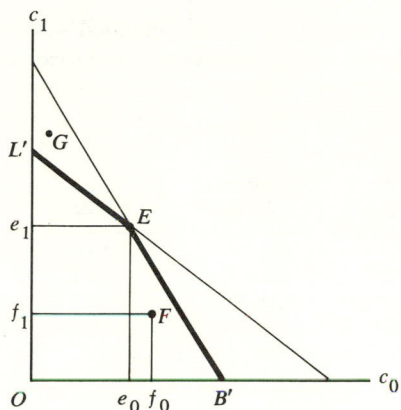

FIG. 7-3. Utility-free comparisons

stream represented by the point E is opportunity-dominant over the combination F, but not the combination G. In terms of geometry, E regarded as a
productive solution makes attainable via borrowing or lending any point
on the boundary of the opportunity $OL'EB'$; F is in the interior of this set
and so can be attained via financial transactions from the position E while
leaving something to spare. In comparing G with E, on the other hand,
indifference curves with the standard properties could be constructed showing either one or the other as preferred—so neither can be excluded by a
utility-free rule.

Algebraically, we note that in terms of actually attainable *present*
consumption (discounting future income at the borrowing rate), $e_0 +
e_1/(1 + r_B)$ is greater than $f_0 + f_1/(1 + r_B)$, while in terms of attainable *future*

[2] A concept introduced in Gordon Pye, "Present Values for Imperfect Capital
Markets," *Journal of Business*, **39** (Jan. 1966). Pye develops rules for project comparisons that
hold irrespective of preference functions *and* endowment vectors. The rules considered here
are for income-stream comparisons; hence, they are utility-free but *not* endowment-free.
They are applicable for an agent serving a client of known endowment—or for an individual's
decision process as a filtering technique (see below) before introducing subjective considerations.

consumption (compounding current income at the lending rate), $e_0(1 + r_L)$ + e_1 again exceeds $f_0(1 + r_L) + f_1$. No matter whether the investor is interested in c_0 or in c_1, E is superior to F. However, in comparing E with G, we find that this utility-free test is indeterminate.

The rule can then be formulated: If the wealth equivalent or present value of the income stream $W_0(E)$ is greater than or equal to $W_0(F)$, and the corresponding future value $W_1(E)$ is greater than or equal to $W_1(F)$, with the inequality holding in at least one of the two comparisons, then E is opportunity-dominant over F.

NUMERICAL EXAMPLE

In Table 1, the income streams and dated wealth equivalents are shown for a number of the combinations discussed in the example above. The present

Table 1*

Point	Income Stream	W_0	W_1
L	(10, 95)	57.5	105
R^*	(25.8, 66.7)	59.1	92.5
B	(20, 80)	60	100
C^*	(30, 60)	60	90

* Conditions: $r_B = 100$ per cent, $r_L = 0$ per cent.

and future values are, as before, based upon the financial opportunities $r_B = 100$ per cent, $r_L = 0$ per cent. Note that B, the best productive combination under the specific utility function of the earlier example, is here shown to be opportunity-dominant over R^* but not over L. Thus, with a different utility function, L might have been the productive optimum—but the R^* of the previous problem could never be, given the trading opportunities assumed. However, "Crusoe points" along PP' *between* L and B—such as (11.25, 88.75)—are not opportunity-dominated by either L or B.

An item of some interest is the comparison of the previous consumptive optimum, C^*, with B. It will be noted that C^* is opportunity-dominated by B, although it is obviously the case that there exist utility functions for which C^* is preferred to B. The explanation is that opportunity dominance is a concept applicable in the absence of specific preference information. Once the preference information is explicitly available in the form of a utility function, there is no contradiction in the sacrifice of opportunities that lead only to less-desired combinations.

Rising Borrowing Cost

Consider now the case, which may also be of considerable practical significance, where the borrower faces increasingly adverse rates as he expands the scale of his borrowing. (The possibility of his correspondingly driving down the loan rate as he expands his lending is seldom mentioned; presumably, this is unlikely to occur.) Taking account of rising borrowing costs requires no essential modification of principle, though it leads to an interesting new result. For simplicity, the discussion is limited to a situation in which only solutions in the borrowing range corresponding to BB' in Fig. 7-2 will be optimal.[3] Figure 7-4 shows the total opportunity set as

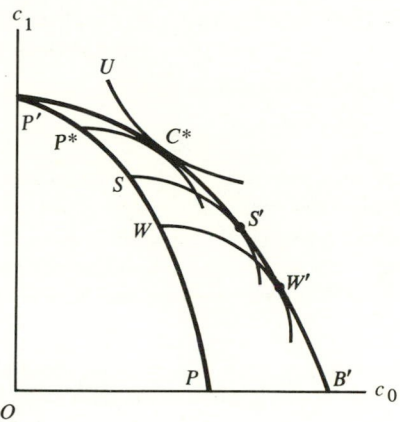

FIG. 7-4.   Imperfect funds markets: increasing borrowing rate

the area $OP'B'$, representing the original productive-opportunity set OPP' plus the area $P'PB'$ due to the borrowing opportunities now being considered. The construction is based on the assumption that marginal borrowing costs are a function only of the scale of financial transactions—so that the slopes of the possible "borrowing curves" $P*C*$, SS', WW', and so on are the same for equal horizontal distances from $P*$, S, and W, respectively.

The opportunity frontier in the borrowing range, the curve $P'B'$, is the *envelope* of these market curves. That is, $P'B'$ connects the points on the various market curves representing the maximum c_0 attainable for each given c_1. By the nature of an envelope curve, $P'B'$ is tangent to each market line at points like $C*$, S', and W'. The consumptive optimum $C*$, as illustrated in Fig. 7-4, is found where $P'B'$ is tangent to the highest indifference curve attainable. To reach $C*$, the investor must exploit his productive opportunity up to the productive optimum $P*$, and then borrow along $P*C*$ to replenish his current consumptive funds.

[3] In Fig. 7-4 the productive-opportunity frontier PP' has been drawn so steep as to make lending an uninteresting option, at least within the positive quadrant. If PP' were sufficiently flat toward the northwest, there would also be lending opportunities LL' as in Fig. 7-2.

The interesting question is: What will be the relation between the marginal borrowing cost (reflected by the absolute slope, less unity, of $P*C*$ at the consumptive optimum)[4] and the marginal productive rate (represented by the absolute slope, less unity, of PP' at $P*$)? Economic logic tells us that these two should be equal: a further increment of productive investment will be justified only so long as the marginal productive rate of return covers the marginal borrowing cost on the funds required for the investment.[5] Hence present-value calculations should employ this marginal borrowing cost as discount rate. Here again the present-value rule is not utility-free, since the marginal borrowing cost will in general depend on the preference function (location of indifference curve U).

NUMERICAL EXAMPLE

Consider an individual with the same preference function $U = c_0^{1/2}c_1^{1/2}$ as before, and also the same productive-opportunity locus $p_0^2/20 + p_1 = 100$. However, he can now borrow only at increasing marginal rates, as indicated by the equation $(c_0 - p_0)^2 = 20(p_1 - c_1)$. The marginal ratio at which he can exchange funds of the two dates, with p_0 and p_1 held constant, is $-dc_1/dc_0 = \frac{1}{10}(c_0 - p_0)$.

To obtain a solution, four relations are needed among the variables c_0, c_1, p_0, and p_1. The equation for the productive-opportunity locus has been given as well as the borrowing equation. The other two conditions are obtained by setting the marginal rate of substitution in consumption, $(dc_1/dc_0)|_U = -c_1/c_0$, equal to the slopes along the productive-opportunity locus and along the borrowing curve (or envelope of the borrowing curves). Thus,

$$\frac{c_1}{c_0} = \frac{p_0}{10} = \frac{c_0 - p_0}{10}$$

from which it follows that $2p_0 = c_0$. This confirms that borrowing does in fact take place.

The numerical solution is $P* = (18.26, 83.33)$ for the optimal productive combination, and $C* = (36.51, 66.67)$ for the consumptive combination. At $C*$ the absolute slopes c_1/c_0 of the indifference curve and $(c_0 - p_0)/10$ of the borrowing curve both equal 1.826. Thus, the marginal borrowing cost is 82.6 per cent. The marginal rate of substitution in production, $-dp_1/dp_0 = p_0/10$, also equals 1.826.

---

[4] The rising marginal borrowing cost $(-dc_1/dc_0) - 1$ should, of course, be distinguished from the rising *average* borrowing rate $(p_1 - c_1)/(c_0 - p_0) - 1$.

[5] For a proof, see J. Hirshleifer, "On the Theory of Optimal Investment Decision," *Journal of Political Economy*, **66** (Aug. 1958), p. 337.

Multiperiod Decision and Filtering Procedures

The generalization to multiperiod choice situations involves considerable operational difficulty. If between *each pair* of successive periods there are distinct though constant borrowing and lending rates, the productive solution will be associated with consequent financial transactions; in some periods lending will be called for, in other periods, borrowing, while in still others no advantageous financial transactions will be available. Then, in an over-all present-value calculation a rather complex sequence of discounting rates—the borrowing rates for some periods, the lending rates for other periods, and an intermediate subjective-preference rate for still others—will be called for. Furthermore, if the borrowing rate is nonconstant, the appropriate modification of the procedure just suggested would introduce a subjective element (as described just above) into the specification of the discount rate (the marginal borrowing costs), for periods in which borrowing is indicated.

Fortunately, some simplifications become possible in practical problems of investment decision. These often, or even typically, present themselves in the form of a limited list of discrete opportunities or projects—for productive transformation of an initially given situation (endowment vector) Y. Imagine, for example, that there are just three possible elementary projects a, b, and c. Then the practical investment problem becomes that of selecting the best time-distributed income vector among the original Y and the transformed vectors $Y + a$, $Y + b$, $Y + c$, $Y + ab$, $Y + ac$, $Y + bc$, and $Y + abc$. We will assume here for simplicity that the various projects are independent, so that the income vector $Y + ab$, for example, is simply $Y + a + b$.[6] In simple present-value problems, where a single constant rate applies for either borrowing or lending, it makes no difference whether comparisons are drawn between the *attained* wealth (W_0^P in the notation of Chapter 3) associated with the income streams Y, $Y + a$, $Y + ab$, and so on, or between present values of alternative project ensembles (W_0^Q in the notation of Chapter 3) such as a, $a + b$, and so on—since $W_0^P = W_0^Y + W_0^Q$. Where a subjective-preference element may be inserted in the productive decision, however, as may be the case whenever borrowing and lending rates diverge, it is essential to compare the over-all *income streams* associated with $Y + a$, $Y + a + b$, and so on—and not simply the payment streams for the project sets.

The first practical step is the elimination of some of the *possible* attained income streams (or the corresponding project sets)—those that are dominated by others—so as to determine the efficiency frontier. A few combinations can sometimes be eliminated on grounds of simple dominance. A number

---

[6] If projects are interdependent, specific information would have to be made available as to the returns from combinations such as ab.

of less obviously inferior options can usually also be eliminated by a generalization of the principle of opportunity dominance: an income stream such as E is opportunity-dominant over another such as F if, for *every* time period t within the range of analysis, the dated wealth equivalent $W_t(E) \geq W_t(F)$—with the inequality holding for at least one t. In the simple case in which the borrowing and lending rates are distinct but unchanged over time (and, in particular, where the marginal borrowing cost is not a rising function of borrowings), the value $W_t(E)$ is given by

$$W_t(E) = e_0(1 + r_L)^t + \cdots + e_{t-1}(1 + r_L) + e_t + \frac{e_{t+1}}{1 + r_B}$$
$$+ \cdots + \frac{e_T}{(1 + r_B)^{T-t}} \quad (1)$$

Here all prior dated income elements have been compounded forward to time t at the lending rate, while all posterior elements have been discounted back to time t at the borrowing rate. An individual who cared *only* for consumption at time t would determine the optimum by simply calculating W_t. Consequently, an income vector can be excluded as inferior on a utility-free basis only if it is dominated by another for every choice of t.[7]

When the filtering process has been carried as far as possible, the analyst is left with a set of possible income streams (and associated project ensembles), the ultimate choice among which inescapably requires subjective decision. While it may seem that it would be difficult to exclude very many possibilities by the utility-free rule, that depends on the extent of the divergence between the borrowing and lending rates. As these rates converge, the opportunity frontier becomes more and more sharply defined. In the limit the simple present-value rule is obtained, in which no ambiguity or subjective element remains as to the ranking of *productive* combinations; i.e., Fisher's Separation Theorem holds.

NUMERICAL EXAMPLE

Consider a three-period choice situation, with endowment vector $Y = (10, 0, 0)$, constant borrowing rate $r_B = 100$ per cent, and lending rate $r_L = 0$ per cent. Let the elementary projects, as defined by their payment streams, be $a = (-2, -1, 3)$, $b = (-4, 6, 2)$, and $c = (-1, 0, 2)$—plus, of course, the null project $(0, 0, 0)$. Table 2 lists all the possible project sets in terms of their payment streams, and then the corresponding attained income streams. None of the eight possibilities can be eliminated on the ground of simple dominance. The next columns show the wealth equivalents of the attained income streams, as of each of the possible dates. All but three income streams are shown to be

---

[7] It is important to recall that this filtering process applies among alternative over-all income streams or project ensembles. The filtering cannot be applied to elementary projects. As between two individual projects, one may be inferior to another and yet it might still be desirable to adopt *both*; an inferior project is not eliminated merely by the existence of a better one (unless the two are mutually exclusive).

Table 2*

FILTERING EXAMPLE, DIVERGENT LENDING-BORROWING RATES

Project Sets	Income Streams	Wealth Equivalents W_0 W_1 W_2			Undominated Income Streams
0: $(0, 0, 0)$	Y:$(10, 0, 0)$	10	10	10	$(10, 0, 0)$
a: $(-2, -1, 3)$	$Y + a$:$(8, -1, 3)$	$8\frac{1}{4}$	$8\frac{1}{2}$	10	
g $\quad b$: $(-4, 6, 2)$	$Y + b$:$(6, 6, 2)$	$9\frac{1}{2}$	13	14	$(6, 6, 2)$
g g $\quad c$: $(-1, 0, 2)$	$Y + c$:$(9, 0, 2)$	$9\frac{1}{2}$	10	11	
g $\quad a + b$: $(-6, 5, 5)$	$Y + a + b$:$(4, 5, 5)$	$7\frac{3}{4}$	$11\frac{1}{2}$	14	
g $\quad b + c$: $(-5, 6, 4)$	$Y + b + c$:$(5, 6, 4)$	9	13	15	$(5, 6, 4)$
g $\quad a + c$: $(-3, -1, 5)$	$Y + a + c$:$(7, -1, 5)$	$7\frac{3}{4}$	$8\frac{1}{2}$	11	
$a + b + c$: $(-7, 5, 7)$	$Y + a + b + c$:$(3, 5, 7)$	$7\frac{1}{4}$	$11\frac{1}{2}$	15	

*Conditions: $r_B = 100$ per cent, $r_L = 0$ per cent

opportunity-dominated, and so can be eliminated. For example, the endowment stream Y permits a consumption of 10 at $t = 0$, or 10 at $t = 1$, or 10 at $t = 2$. But $Y + a$ correspondingly permits only $8\frac{1}{4}$ at $t = 0$, or $8\frac{1}{2}$ at $t = 1$, or 10 at $t = 2$— and hence is dominated by Y. Only the surviving alternative income streams in the last column then remain for "subjective" evaluation (requiring reference to the utility function). Note the effectiveness of filtering despite the enormous gap between borrowing and lending rates.

B. CAPITAL RATIONING

The problem of optimal investment decision under the condition known as "capital rationing" (or "fixed capital budget") has been the object of extensive discussions. As so often occurs with the tricky word "capital," semantic confusions have been involved: just what is it that is supposed to be rationed or fixed? In Chapter 6 it was noted that the word "capital" has commonly been used in at least three distinguishable senses: (1) real capital (e.g., machines), (2) capital value (wealth), and (3) liquid capital (investible funds). Those analysts who have proposed various decision rules for "capital-rationing" situations generally seem to have had in mind a maximum limit or fixed quota in the third of these senses—a ration of liquid capital or investible funds.[8] This entails a truncation of the opportunity set by some kind of *quantitative* limit on investment expenditure.

[8] But the arguments offered in defense of the contention that "capital rationing" is an important (or even the normal!) situation sometimes refer to quite different meanings of "capital." Thus, it has been maintained, "capital rationing" is universal, since at any given moment each investor *owns* a fixed quantity of "capital." This vague idea seems to refer to an individual's having a given factor endowment (of real capital plus possibly other factors as well), which in turn determines his productive opportunity set—e.g., the area *OPP'* in Fig. 7-1. The "fixity" of the productive opportunity set may be true enough, but it by no means dictates a fixed quantum of investible funds. Alternatively, it has been argued that the relevant fixity is the investor's wealth. This corresponds to the individual's being constrained to make choices along a market line such as *MM'* in Fig. 7-1—a condition only true *ex post* of the productive-investment decision, and again one that does not dictate a fixed investment quota.

The "capital-rationing" problem is typically set up in linear-programming form, more or less as follows:

$$
\begin{array}{lll}
\text{Maximize} & \text{(a)} & \psi_0 q_0 + \psi_1 q_1 + \cdots + \psi_T q_T \\
\text{where} & \text{(b)} & q_t = a_{t_1} x_1 + a_{t_2} x_2 + \cdots + a_{t_j} x_J \\
\text{subject to} & \text{(c)} & q_t \geq -y_t \\
\text{and} & \text{(d)} & x_j \geq 0
\end{array}
\qquad (2)
$$

Here $(q_0, q_1, \ldots, q_T)$ is the over-all receipts-payments sequence associated with the ensemble of projects adopted; $(x_1, x_2, \ldots, x_J)$ is the list of projects available for adoption; a_{t_j} is the return (per unit of x_j) from project j at time t, returns from projects being assumed to be independent; y_t is the allowable maximum of net outlay or investment at time t (the symbolism here associates it with the corresponding element of the endowment vector in our standard analysis); finally, the $\psi_0, \psi_1, \ldots, \psi_T$ are as-yet-undetermined valuation parameters for the correspondingly dated elements q_t of the returns sequence. Each x_j must be 0 or 1, to correspond with an assumed discreteness of projects available—except that a quasi-project in the form of lending opportunities may be permitted to take on any nonnegative level. The quantitative constraint or "capital ration" at time t limits investment outlays to the endowed amount y_t, but after crediting all receipts at time t from projects adopted (including previous lending).

This formulation is, aside from the discrete form of the productive opportunities, not too different from the Fisherian productive optimization in Chapter 3. The similarity becomes clear if we think of $y_t + q_t$ as p_t, the time-t element of the productive optimum P^*.[9] But the Fisherian formulation would drop any quantitative constraint on q_t (i.e., would permit borrowing as well as lending), so that the valuation vector $(\psi_0, \psi_1, \ldots, \psi_T)$ would represent the present-value discount factors 1, $1/(1 + r_1)$, and so on. For the capital-rationing problem laid out here, it remains necessary to specify the meaning of and rationale for the constraints $q_t \geq -y_t$, and to indicate the correct valuation parameters ψ_t for use in the "payoff function" (2a).

A *quantitative limit* on the funds available for investment purposes, in a given period or periods, is considerably more difficult to rationalize than the divergence between borrowing and lending rates of the preceding section (which, as we have seen, could be attributed to the fact that transactions are not costless). The discussions in the literature have usually assumed one or the other of two related but still distinguishable conditions: (A) a ban on access to the *borrowing* side of the funds market (in effect, an *upper limit* on

---

[9] The analogy is somewhat imperfect, since here lending opportunities may be considered among the "projects." The incorporation of lending opportunities makes this a hybrid problem—not purely productive, since some financial opportunities are considered, and yet not a full optimum since *borrowing* opportunities are excluded.

investment), or (B) a postulated *fixed quota* of investment. The rationale seems applicable only for some form of multiperson decision process—involving a division of labor or of authority between distinct individuals or groups sharing in the investment decision. Thus, the assumption of capital rationing is inappropriate for a maximizing individual, but may possibly be relevant for investment decisions of complex organizations such as corporations or government agencies.

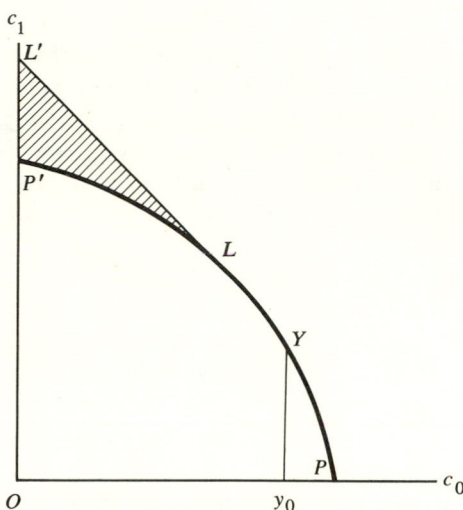

FIG. 7-5. "Capital-rationing" as a no-borrowing condition

As usual, the issues involved can be most clearly visualized in the simple two-period paradigm of choice, illustrated in Fig. 7-5. The *no-borrowing* condition (A) can be regarded as a special case of the borrowing-lending rate divergence, pictured in Fig. 7-2, in which the borrowing rate has become infinitely high. Then the total opportunity set $OPLL'$ consists of the productive opportunities OPP' augmented only by the shaded area $P'LL'$ made available by the possibility of lending. Depending upon the preference map, the consumptive optimum may be located either in the range LL' (involving a productive optimum at L and some lending) or in the range PL (a "Crusoe solution" with no financial transactions).

This could be regarded as a plausible representation of a decision-making process such as the following. Suppose that an "executive agency" has been presented with an endowment or budget Y by some higher-level "constraining authority" (such as the board of directors of a corporation, or the legislature of a government) and directed to find an optimum subject to the limited funds so made available. Presumably, the endowment combination or budget Y may itself already represent certain borrowing operations carried out as the responsibility of the constraining authority, but the executive agency is forbidden to borrow in its own right. The consequence is that at the optimum actually attainable by the executive agency in Fig. 7-5, the marginal productive rate of yield $(-dp_1/dp_0) - 1$ will exceed the lending rate whenever the solution is in the "Crusoe" range PL. This *cannot* be optimal if the borrowing rate equals the lending rate and *may* not be optimal even where r_B exceeds r_L. The deviation from optimality will be regarded here as a kind of *short-run* inefficiency. Presumably, if sufficiently attractive investment options do exist, the constraining authority will eventually see its error and itself return to the borrowing side of the funds market so as to make a larger current-funds endowment y_0 available to the executive agency. But it may be very costly to modify the constraint established for the current period (very difficult to obtain emergency action from the constraining authority). So, for some period of time, the constraint may in fact be effective.[10]

Thus, rationing of current investible funds in the *upper-limit* sense (A) expresses, perhaps, the relevant decision context for some cases of practical interest. By way of contrast, it is difficult to think of situations in which rationing of current funds in the *fixed-quota* sense (B) would ever be justified. For the latter form of rationing implies that the *current funds have no alternative uses* that need be balanced against possible commitment to investment on the part of the rationed agency.[11]

When we turn from the illustrative two-period paradigm of Fig. 7-5 to the more realistic multiperiod choice situation, the problem would seem to become more difficult in two senses: (1) we must consider the possibility of rations or constraints not only on investment at $t = 0$ but also on investment at other dates, and (2) even if only funds of $t = 0$ are rationed, the optimum for any given c_0 is no longer a simple quantum (the highest c_1 attainable) but must now somehow weigh alternative mixtures of $c_1, c_2, \ldots, c_T$.

If, however, the conclusion above is accepted that the only rationing situation worthy of attention is that of a *short-run* barrier to borrowing, one

---

[10] The implicit assumption here has been that there is no conflict of interest or divergence in objectives between the executive agency and the constraining authority—only a division of labor. More commonly, perhaps, an institutional arrangement like that described arises for a political reason: namely, because the objectives of the two groups differ. Not only may the constraining authority and the executive agency disagree as to the client's true preference function, but each may want to take into account considerations other than the *client's* preferences. Unfortunately, there is no convenient way for us to conceptualize an "optimum" when such essentially interpersonal conflicts intrude.

[11] It is common knowledge, of course, that administrators will often make wasteful commitments at the end of an accounting period rather than permit excess funds to revert to a higher-level authority. But this does not represent a fixed-quota ration, but rather problems in enforcing "correct" behavior (i.e., choices in line with higher-level preferences) under upper-limit rationing.

of the difficulties is eliminated and the other greatly simplified. First, interpreting "short-run" as referring only to $t = 0$, we can reasonably assume that as of the *present* there is no reason to postulate a constraint on borrowing in the future.[12] Thus, only the single quantitative limit on *present* funds need be considered. And second, if in fact funds can be transferred over time under essentially perfect-market conditions (except for the constraint on borrowing to acquire funds at $t = 0$), there is no problem of weighing c_1 versus c_2, and so on—an appropriate discounting or compounding process in terms of market interest rates can reduce any payments sequence to its value equivalent as of any specified future date.

The upshot of this discussion is that it does not seem necessary, after all, to express the "payoff" or criterion function in as abstract a form as equation (2a). For, a kind of adjusted present-value criterion will satisfy the requirements of the problem:

$$W_0' = q_0 + \frac{q_1}{1 + \lambda} + \frac{q_2}{(1 + \lambda)(1 + r_2)} + \cdots + \frac{q_T}{(1 + \lambda)(1 + r_2) \cdots (1 + r_T)}$$

$$(3)$$

Here the parameter ψ_0 of equation (2a) becomes unity, and ψ_1 is $1/(1 + \lambda)$. All the other ψ_t consist of ψ_1 multiplied by the market discounting factor converting funds of time t to funds of time 1. Thus, (3) can be reduced to

$$W_0' = q_0 + \frac{W_1'}{1 + \lambda} \qquad (3a)$$

Here W_1' represents the value at time 1 of all payments from $t = 1$ to the horizon $t = T$. In Fig. 7-5 we can think of the vertical axis as being changed from c_1, a simple quantum of time-1 funds, to W_1' as the time-1 valuation of all future funds associated with the project ensemble adopted.

Procedurally, one might expect the higher-level authority that issues the capital ration y_0 to simultaneously establish the level of λ for the guidance of lower-level administrators. Then if the latter do not have enough profitable productive opportunities to exhaust all their ration (i.e., if W_0' is maximized with $-q_0 < y_0$), the excess funds should be returned. But more typically, perhaps, the λ is not stated in advance. Instead, it emerges from the calculations as a "shadow price" revealing the marginal productive

---

[12] It may be too costly or too late to convene the legislature or the board of directors to enlarge the scale of this year's investment ration, but next year's quota is a variable that need not constrain current commitments. (If there is a real conflict of interest or of opinion between the executive agency and the constraining authority, this may not be correct—but we are assuming only a division of labor, and not any irreducible divergence of objectives between the two participants in the decision-making process.)

rate of return given the projects available to the executive agency. This represents an information "feed-back" to the higher-level authority, which can be used in deciding on modification of the assigned ration for this or future years.

NUMERICAL EXAMPLE

Table 3 illustrates the situation of an agency granted a current "ration" $y_0 = 2$ in a three-period decision situation, with the market interest rate $r_2 = 100$ per cent effective for discounting funds of time 2 back to time 1. There are four specific projects a, b, c, d available; they are here assumed to be

Table 3 *

Project	Payments Stream	Δq_0	$\Delta W_1'$	$\Delta W_0'$ $\lambda = 0\%$	$\lambda = 50\%$	$\lambda = 100\%$	$\lambda = 300\%$
a	$-1, 0, 2$	-1	1	0	—	—	—
b	$-1, 2, -1$	-1	1.5	.5	0	—	—
c	$-1, -1, 6$	-1	2	1	.333	0	—
d	$-1, 4, 0$	-1	4	3	1.667	1	0

* Conditions: $r_2 = 1$, $y_0 = 2$

of equal "size" so far as the drain upon the current ration is concerned. So the problem reduces to the selection of *at most* two among the four available projects. The table indicates that project a is eliminated when $\lambda = 0$ per cent, and need not be considered further.[13] Project b is eliminated at $\lambda = 50$ per cent, leaving c and d to absorb the funds available.

This is not the full answer, however, as the possibility of external lending has not yet been considered. The next two columns show that project c would be eliminated at $\lambda = 100$ per cent and project d at $\lambda = 300$ per cent. It follows that if lending opportunities were available at, say, 150 per cent, only project d should be adopted; the second dollar is then better lent at interest than invested in project c. Such a result would presumably suggest to the higher-level authority that the original ration was too large. On the other hand, if the lending rate were 10 per cent, the agency here would not lend at interest. It would adopt projects c and d, and report a λ of 50 per cent—i.e., an ability to use marginal funds profitably at any discount rate up to 50 per cent.

BIBLIOGRAPHIC NOTE

Relatively little literature exists in the area of investment choice in imperfect markets. The following may be cited:

J. HIRSHLEIFER, "On the Theory of Optimal Investment Decision," *Journal of Political Economy*, **66** (Aug. 1958).

[13] The "multiple-root" problem of Chapter 3 does not arise. The assumed availability of market exchanges among dated funds from $t = 1$ to $t = T$ reduces the calculation to a two-period rate of return—between funds of time 0 and funds of time 1.

GORDON PYE, "Present Values for Imperfect Capital Markets," *Journal of Business*, **39** (Jan. 1966).

The existence of imperfect funds markets is closely linked with the increasingly studied topic of transaction costs. On this, see:

HAROLD DEMSETZ, "The Cost of Transacting," *Quarterly Journal of Economics*, **82** (Feb. 1968).

By way of contrast, a very large body of writing exists for the topic of "capital rationing." Only two works will be cited here, an early pioneering article and a later full-scale study:

J. H. LORIE and L. J. SAVAGE, "Three Problems in Rationing Capital," *Journal of Business*, **28** (Oct. 1955).

H. M. WEINGARTNER, *Mathematical Programming and the Analysis of Capital Budgeting Problems* (Prentice-Hall, Inc., 1963).

PART II

8 PREFERENCE UNDER UNCERTAINTY

Investment is, in essence, *present* sacrifice for *future* benefit. But the present may be relatively well known, whereas the future is always an enigma. Investment thus commonly also represents *certain* sacrifice for *uncertain* benefit. The theory of intertemporal choice was developed, in Part I of this work, under the artificial assumption of a world of certainty. Despite the restrictiveness of the assumption, it was possible to derive interesting positive and normative conclusions. But some phenomena observed in the world seemingly cannot be explained without bringing in attitudes toward risk and differences of opinion—sources of behavior that come into existence only under uncertainty. Among the aspects of intertemporal choice left unexplained under the certainty assumption are the desire for "liquidity" (postulated, without attempt at justification, in Chapter 6 above), the existence of insurance, the distinction between debt and equity financing, and the bewildering variety of returns or yields on various forms of investment simultaneously ruling in the funds markets.

This chapter will first explore the meaning of preference under uncertainty where *time* is not a consideration—i.e., choices among risky[1] but contemporaneous claims. Note that in Part I the topic was intertemporal allocation without uncertainty; here we have the opposite case, allocation under uncertainty without choices over time. The latter part of the chapter

---

[1] One tradition in economic theorizing, due to Frank H. Knight, distinguishes between "risk" (supposed to be a situation in which alternative outcomes exist with *known* probabilities) and "uncertainty" (a situation with *unknown* probabilities for the outcomes). Such a distinction will not be employed in this work; for our purposes, "risk" and "uncertainty" are synonymous.

will examine the preference function where the choice options involve *both* time and uncertainty.

At this point, there will be no attempt to generate a complete choice-theoretic structure for decisions involving risk. Rather, the concern will be only to provide a foundation for *preference* under uncertainty; i.e., to develop a "theory of utility." The basis will be a version of the well-known Neumann-Morgenstern postulates of rational choice. Complete choice-theoretic structures will be formulated in several alternative ways, in the chapters that follow.

A. POSTULATES OF RATIONAL CHOICE, AND THE EXPECTED-UTILITY RULE

In a world of uncertainty, productive and exchange decisions generally deal with *assets*. An asset may be a complex entitlement to a number of commodities, at various dates, and under specified contingencies. (An asset, if tradable, will also be called a *security*.) But assets are not, in general, the objects that enter into preference functions (*goods*); rather, choice among assets will be presumed to reflect a more fundamental preference for underlying consumptive claims. Following our usual procedure, a single consumption good will be assumed throughout. And, for the time being, only contemporaneous choices are being considered, so that problems of dating can be set aside. Then assets can differ, ultimately, only in the quantities of the homogeneous consumption good (i.e., only in the incomes) they offer under the various possible contingencies. Such simplified assets will be called *prospects*—uncertain claims promising, with stated probabilities,[2] consequences specified directly or indirectly in terms of incomes in a single time period.

An *elementary* prospect is one for which the consequences are, directly, quantities of consumption incomes; a *compound* prospect may include other prospects as consequences. A standard notation for any prospect X is as follows:

$$X = (X', X'', \ldots, X^{(n)}; \ \pi', \pi'', \ldots, \pi^{(n)}) \tag{1}$$

Here the consequences X', X'', ... (which may be prospects themselves) are to be received with corresponding probabilities π', π'', ... The sum of the probabilities for any prospect, shown to the right of the semicolon, must necessarily be unity. An elementary prospect would have, to the left of the semicolon, only consumption incomes c', c'', and so on.

States of the world are particular distinct configurations of the individual's choice environment—war versus peace, for example, or sickness versus

---

[2] The concept of *probability* is taken as primitive here; no attempt will be made to justify the attachment of objective or subjective probabilities to contingencies.

health (the latter indicating that states may be defined by internal as well as external events). The individual cannot choose the states; his task is to adopt an appropriate stance (choose an action) while still uncertain as to which state will obtain. Thus, the state of the world is Nature's choice. Nature is neither benevolent nor malevolent and does not reshuffle the cards in response to the individual's selection of an action. Hence, there are definite probabilities (possibly not fully known) attached to the occurrence of each possible state. These probabilities are outside the control of the individual.[3] *Contingent consumption incomes, associated with the several different states of the world envisaged by the individual, are assumed herein to be the ultimate objects of preference entering into the utility function.*

An elementary *state-distributed prospect* will be written in the following special form, assuming S distinct states:

$$C = (c_a, c_b, \ldots, c_S; \ \pi_a, \pi_b, \ldots, \pi_S) \tag{1a}$$

Such a prospect promises a definite contingent income for each possible state of the world.

Two types of elementary prospects may be distinguished. (1) State-distributed prospects, as in equation (1a), will be denoted *hazards*—a term that suggests the "objective" quality of the risk. (2) Prospects whose outcomes are unrelated to states of the world will be called *lotteries*. Lottery prospects do not represent objective hazards associated with the uncertainty of natural events. Rather, they are "mere gambles," artificial constructs whose uncertain outcomes will not be regarded as configurations of Nature. Thus, the lottery outcome "heads on the next toss of this coin" is not, for our purposes, a state of the world.[4] An elementary lottery, then, is a prospect whose consequences are specified consumption incomes to be received with stated probabilities that are independent of which state of the world obtains. An elementary lottery with n distinct outcomes will be denoted by the form:

$$C = (c', c'', \ldots, c^{(n)}; \ \pi', \pi'', \ldots, \pi^{(n)}) \tag{1b}$$

Prospects may be compounded in a number of ways. A *lottery of hazards* offers alternative state-distributed hazards as outcomes of a gamble. A *hazard of lotteries*, on the other hand, offers lotteries as outcomes, one for

[3] It may appear that state probabilities can often be influenced by individual action. For example, the likelihood of "house damaged by lightning" can be reduced by installing lightning rods. But in any such case we assume there is a more fundamental state description available, the probabilities for which *would* be independent of human action: e.g., "stroke of lightning capable of damaging house (in absence of lightning rods)."

[4] The ultimate basis for the distinction between hazards and lotteries will appear in the discussion of the "uniqueness postulate" below.

each distinct state of the world.[5] A lottery of lotteries is merely a higher-order gamble, one whose consequences are gambles themselves.

At this point, it has been asserted that the ultimate objects of preference are the state-distributed incomes that enter into elementary hazards. What is needed now is a *rule* permitting the computation of $u(X)$, the utility of any prospect X, from the bundle of state-distributed incomes directly or indirectly contained therein (with their associated probabilities). We would not expect such a rule to be entirely objective; presumably, it would incorporate some personal parameters particular to the individual. But it would be handy if these personal parameters could be isolated from the calculable elements that would be the same for all individuals.

The *expected-utility rule* is a simple formula for calculating the utility of a prospect from the probabilities of the outcomes and a personal *preference-scaling function* for contingent incomes. For an elementary hazard (state-distributed prospect):

$$u(C) = \pi_a v_a(c_a) + \pi_b v_b(c_b) + \cdots + \pi_S v_S(c_S) = \sum_{s=1}^{S} \pi_s v_s(c_s) \tag{2}$$

The utility of the prospect C is shown as the mathematical expectation (probability-weighted average) of the $v_s(c_s)$. Here v_s is a personal "cardinal"[6] preference-scaling function for c_s—income received conditional upon occurrence of state s.

One crucial further specification, made implicitly or explicitly in almost all discussions of the expected-utility rule, is that the v function is *unique*—in the sense that $v_a(c_a) = v_b(c_b)$ whenever $c_a = c_b$, and similarly for all

---

[5] A three-element lottery of two-state hazards is represented by the form $(C', C'', C'''; \pi', \pi'', \pi''')$—where, for example, $C' = (c'_a, c'_b; \pi_a, \pi_b)$. A two-state hazard of three-element lotteries, on the other hand, is represented by $(C_a, C_b; \pi_a, \pi_b)$—where, for example, $C_a = (c'_a, c''_a, c'''_a; \pi', \pi'', \pi''')$.

[6] An "ordinal" scale merely *ranks* consequences; therefore, any positive monotonic transformation of an acceptable scale would be equally satisfactory. Suppose all we know is that more income is preferred to less. Then income itself, c, is an ordinally correct measure of preference—its logarithm, $\log c$, would serve equally well. Ordinal measures, however, do not provide a consistent scaling for differences or intervals. Thus, with the c scaling the interval from income level $c = 1$ to $c = 2$ is the same size as that from $c = 2$ to $c = 3$, but with the equally permissible log scaling the first interval is larger than the second. "Cardinal" measures provide a scale for intervals, so that we can say that one difference is larger than another. (Since marginal utilities are in the nature of differences of utility levels, a cardinal scale for utility permits us to speak of diminishing marginal utility.) A cardinally satisfactory scale may be subjected to a positive linear transformation; in comparing differences, the zero point does not matter and the unit of measurement can be multiplied by any positive constant. That is, if m is a satisfactory scaling function, then so is $m' = a + bm$, for $b > 0$. Thus, we can say that the distance from the tip of the Empire State Building to the observation tower is less than the distance between the second and 50th stories—whether we use as measure of altitude feet above ground level, meters above sea level, or miles from the center of the Earth.

states $a, b, \ldots, S$. This further condition in effect makes the state-description inessential for determination of preferences. Consequently, for *any* elementary prospect (whether hazard or lottery) with n distinct outcomes, the expected-utility rule can be applied in the "lottery form":

$$u(C) = \pi'v(c') + \pi''v(c'') + \cdots + \pi^{(n)}v(c^{(n)}) \qquad (2a)$$

Here v is the individual's preference-scaling function for income in *any* state. We can also call it the "elementary-utility function" since, evidently, $u(c) = v(c)$ for the certainty prospect of receiving income c.

We can now proceed to justify the expected-utility rule, via a theorem[7] that asserts: *Given certain "postulates of rational choice," there is a way of assigning a unique preference-scaling function v to contingent incomes such that the utility for any elementary prospect is given by the expected-utility rule (2a).* Given the utility of elementary prospects, the procedure for assigning utility values to compound prospects follows directly. That is, the same expected-utility rule is applicable, merely substituting the utilities of subprospects for the $v(c)$ as elements:

$$u(X) = \pi'u(X') + \pi''u(X'') + \cdots + \pi^{(n)}u(X^{(n)}) \qquad (2b)$$

The postulate system serving as basis for construction of the required v scale can be set forth in a number of ways. What follows is an informal treatment, concentrating upon points of economic interest rather than technical completeness, and calling upon geometrical representation as an aid to intuition. The formulation differs from a number of other presentations in bringing out explicitly the role of the concept of states of the world.

Postulates

1. *Ordering and preference direction:* As between any two alternative certain incomes, the larger is always preferred to the smaller.

This provides an *ordinal* preference scale as a starting point.

2. *Certainty equivalent:* For any elementary prospect, there is a certainty equivalent—i.e., a quantity of certain income indifferent to the prospect—such that the certainty equivalent is intermediate in size between the largest and smallest consequences of the prospect (that are received with nonzero probabilities). Conversely, for any certain income intermediate between two other consequences, a lottery involving the two other consequences can be contructed (by selection of probabilities) that is indifferent to the intermediate certainty.

---

[7] The first version of this theorem appeared in J. von Neumann and O. Morgenstern, *The Theory of Games and Economic Behavior*, 2nd ed. (Princeton Univ. Press, 1947), pp. 15–31.

The postulate asserts, in effect, that incomes in all states are quantitatively comparable, that no state is so all-important that an individual would refuse to give up contingent income in that state for *some* finite quantity of contingent income in any other state. The postulate also assures that the v function does not go to infinity within the relevant range of incomes.

3. *Independence:* Let the prospect X' be indifferent to X''. If X^* is any prospect, the prospect $(X', X^*; \pi, 1 - \pi)$ is indifferent to $(X'', X^*; \pi, 1 - \pi)$.

This postulate says that a prospect such as X' can be substituted for its preference equivalent X'' in any prospect in which the latter enters, and vice versa. "Independence" here refers to the absence of complementarity. In ordinary commodity combinations complementarity cannot be ignored: particular quantities of potatoes and butter may be indifferent, but the combination butter-and-bread is likely to be preferred to potatoes-and-bread. When we deal with prospects, however, the consequences are *alternatives* rather than combinations—e.g., bread-*or*-butter rather than bread-*and*-butter. There would seem to be no reason for preferring bread-or-butter to bread-or-potatoes—if the butter and potatoes are indifferent and the bread probabilities are the same.[8] In terms of equations (2), (2a), and (2b), the postulate justifies the "separated" form in which u is written as a sum of terms, each term being functionally associated with a single consequence.[9]

4. *Uniqueness:* The certainty equivalent for any prospect depends only upon the magnitudes of the probabilities and incomes, and *not* upon their state-labelling.

Thus, any reshuffling of incomes over states is allowable, provided that each distinct income is still received with the same probability as before. This postulate, of course, is what permits the specialization of (2) into (2a); it has been called "independence of states and rewards."

The uniqueness postulate seems to be the only one seriously vulnerable to attack. To cite a homely example, if we think of the income commodity as umbrellas, we would surely expect $v_a(c)$ to differ from $v_b(c)$ if the states a and b corresponded to "rain" and "shine." Or, if c is the ordinary income commodity, $v_a(c)$ and $v_b(c)$ might still diverge sharply if the states were "sickness" and "health" (an even more extreme example would be "life" or "death"!), for the individual would have rather different interests in and uses of income under the alternative contingencies. On the other hand, we would *not* expect the v function to shift if the incomes were contingent upon the occurrence of events such as black or red at a roulette wheel. This point

---

[8] To illustrate complementarity it has been convenient to employ a multigood illustration, though that conflicts with the single-good assumption of this chapter.

[9] The separated form means that a utility isoquant could be represented as a straight line on $v(c')$, $v(c'')$ axes in a two-consequence situation (more generally, as a hyperplane in a multiconsequence situation).

is the heart of the distinction made earlier between hazards (objective risks) and lotteries (mere gambles); the uniqueness postulate is plausible for lotteries, but really implausible for hazards—for which the external environment of choice can take on different configurations.

There are at least two lines along which a defense of the uniqueness postulate might be attempted. The first would ascribe the difficulty essentially to the inadequacy of a one-good model. It might be that sufficiently extensive listing of (possibly nonmarketable) goods can make the utility function unique. Thus, in our first example above, we might admit that $v_a(c)$ diverges from $v_b(c)$ when c represents umbrellas and a or b signify "rain or shine." But we could perhaps formulate a unique elementary-utility function of two arguments, in the form $v(c, w)$—where w is a variable representing quantities of the "fine-weather" good.[10] Or, the postulate might be defended simply as an approximation, appropriate for the bulk of investment decisions made by individuals and firms. Distinction between $v_a(c)$ and $v_b(c)$ could be reserved for those cases where choices intrinsically involve *serious* divergences in the individual's internal or external environment. Thus, we would not expect an individual's decisions with respect to life-insurance contracts to be the same as those he would make facing a quantitatively equivalent "mere lottery." (Bachelors, for example, might decline life insurance even if offered on exceptionally favorable terms.) On the other hand, the approximation might be quite satisfactory for analyzing the purchase of *property* insurance.

Accepting these "postulates of rational choice," we can show by direct construction that there does indeed exist a personal cardinal preference-scaling or v function, with which the expected-utility rule (2a) can be employed for determining the utility of any prospect. Given the uniqueness postulate, it will suffice to think in terms of lottery prospects. A geometrical illustration, for choices involving *three* distinct contingent incomes, will be employed. Figure 8-1 explains the system of "triangular coordinates" [11] used to portray all possible combinations of three increasing income levels c', c'', and c'''. The three vertices of the isosceles right triangle represent the certainty prospects for each of these incomes, or simply the incomes c', c'', and c''' themselves. The horizontal and vertical axes are scaled in terms of the probabilities π'' and π''' of receiving c'' and c''', respectively. Consequently, the sides of the triangle represent all possible two-contingency prospects. An interior point such as $D = (.3, .2)$ corresponds to $\pi'' = .3$ and $\pi''' = .2$— i.e., to the three-contingency prospect $(c', c'', c'''; .5, .3, .2)$—since

[10] Note that there is no assertion that "fine weather" is a commodity (object of trade), but only an object of preference (good). The distinction between these two will play an important role in the next chapter.

[11] This device is employed in Harry M. Markowitz, *Portfolio Selection* (John Wiley & Sons, Inc., 1959), p. 251.

$\pi' = 1 - .3 - .2$. Geometrically, for a point D, π' would be measured by the distance DB (or equivalently, DA) in Fig. 8-1.

By the ordering postulate, we know that for the individual c'' is preferred to c' but less preferred than c'''. By the certainty-equivalent postulate, we know there is a lottery involving c' and c''' that the individual will consider indifferent to the certainty of c''. The indifferent lottery will be a characteristic of the personal preference-scaling function. Suppose it is the lottery

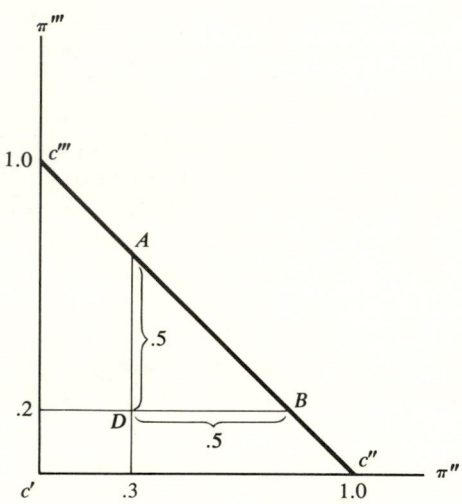

FIG. 8-1. Triangular coordinates

$E = (c''', c'; .7, .3)$, illustrated in Fig. 8-2 as the point E where $(c'', c''') = (0, .7)$ so that $c' = .3$. Let us now consider any interior point lying on the line connecting c'' and E—for example, the point $F = (.25, .525)$, which corresponds to the elementary prospect $(c', c'', c'''; .225, .25, .525)$. This point is one-fourth of the distance from E toward c'', and we can see that F is also the compound prospect $(E, c''; .75, .25)$. (Indifference between the elementary and compound formulations of F can be shown by using the independence postulate, replacing E by its elementary equivalent in terms of c' and c'''.) Now, using the independence postulate to replace E with c'' in F, we see that F is indifferent to $(c'', c''; .75, .25)$—which is simply the certainty of c''. Generalizing this example, we obtain the result: *The straight line connecting any two indifferent prospects, in this representation, is an indifference curve.* Furthermore: *The entire indifference map is a family of parallel straight lines.* For, applying the independence postulate once again, a prospect such as $G = (E, c'; .6, .4)$ in Fig. 8-2 must be indifferent to $H = (c'', c'; .6, .4)$.

We now have an indifference map—a complete ordinal preference representation for all possible probabilistic combinations or prospects involving c', c'', and c'''. To obtain a *cardinal* preference representation, it is necessary to provide a quantitative labelling of the utility levels attached to each indifference curve (and thereby, to each point in the diagram). Since

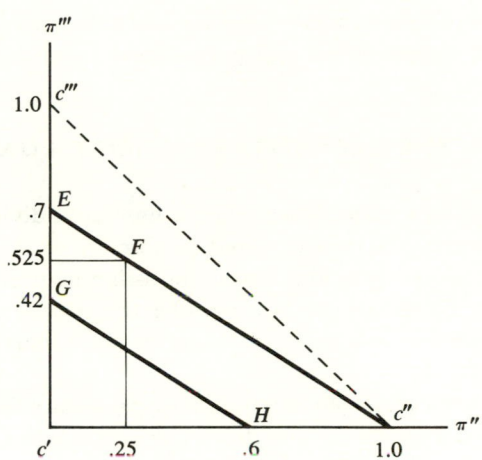

FIG. 8-2. Indifference map and cardinal utility scaling

any cardinal scale $v(c)$ is defined only up to a linear transformation, we can arbitrarily select values for any two particular c levels (thus fixing the zero and unit of measurement). A convenient choice is to fix, for the worst consequence (lowest income), c', the value $v(c') = 0$—and for the best (highest income), c''', the value $v(c''') = 1$. Then the question reduces to: What value should be assigned for $v(c'')$? So far as ordinal ranking is concerned, any number properly between 0 and 1 would suffice. *But there is just one way of assigning $v(c'')$ that makes the expected-utility rule (2a) hold true* for any prospects involving these three consequences (any point in the triangle). This number that must be assigned for $v(c'')$ is .7, the ordinate of the prospect E indifferent to the certainty of c''. More generally: *Any income level is to be assigned an elementary-utility or v value equal to the probability of success in the "reference lottery" to which that income is indifferent, where a reference lottery contains as consequences only the single best and the single worst income levels considered.*[12] Thus, since c'' was indifferent to $E = (c''', c'; .7, .3)$, we said that $v(c'') = .7$. Note that the preference scale is defined in terms of a probability.

[12] See Robert Schlaifer, *Probability and Statistics for Business Decisions* (McGraw-Hill Book Company, 1959), Chap. 2.

This scaling, together with the expected-utility rule, correctly evaluates any of the prospects of Fig. 8-2. The prospect F in the form $(c', c'', c'''$; .225, .25, .525) has $u(F) = .225v(c') + .25v(c'') + .525v(c''') = .225(0) + .25(.7) + .525(1) = .7$—thus verifying indifference with E or c''. Furthermore, it is unnecessary to carry out the reduction to elementary form, as the expected-utility rule can be used with the prospect in compound form $F = (E, c''; .75, .25)$—here $u(F) = .75u(E) + .25u(c'') = .75(.7) + .25(.7) = .7$. Similarly, any point on the indifference curve GH has the utility value .42, equal to the height of its intercept on the vertical axis—$(.6)(.7)$—the equivalent probability of success in the reference lottery involving only c' and c'''.

B. THE ELEMENTARY-UTILITY FUNCTION

In the preceding section, it was shown how an individual's given elementary-utility function $v(c)$—a cardinal preference scale for consumption incomes under certainty—provides a basis for assigning preference orderings to risky prospects. In this section we consider the reverse process; we will see how observed choices among risky prospects imply particular shapes for the $v(c)$ function.

In the section above, a convenient scaling procedure for trios of ordered certain incomes was employed. For the worst consequence (lowest income) contemplated, c', we let $v(c') = 0$. For the best consequence (highest income), c''', we let $v(c''') = 1$. Then, for any intermediate income, c'', $v(c'')$ equals the probability of success π in the "reference lottery" between c' and c''' that is indifferent to c''. Thus, if the income c'' with certainty is indifferent to the prospect $(c''', c'; \pi, 1 - \pi)$, then $v(c'') = \pi$.

Figure 8-3 shows alternative $v(c)$ scales A and B that might be constructed in terms of reference lotteries between a best income $c''' = 1000$ and a worst income $c' = 0$. To find, say, $v(250)$, one asks the following: For what reference-lottery π involving possible returns of 1000 (success) and 0 (failure) would the individual be just willing to exchange a certain income of 250? A lottery will be called *fair* if the mathematical expectation of return, here 1000π, just equals its price—here, 250—or, we can say also, if the mathematical expectation of the gamble as a whole (taking return and price together) is zero. A "favorable" gamble has positive, and an "unfavorable" gamble negative, mathematical expectation. Especially if the income commodity can be regarded as the sole basis of sustenance, one's first impression is that a reasonable individual will demand more than a merely fair lottery (one with a 25 per cent chance of success) before surrendering a certain income of 250. Curve A of Fig. 8-3 is constructed on the assumption that he would insist upon at least a 50 per cent chance of success. Then, we will say $v(250) = .5$. In demanding more than a fair lottery-equivalent before surrendering a certain income, the individual is said to display *risk-aversion*, or to be a *risk-avoider*. If the same pattern holds true all along the income scale, the $v(c)$ function will have a generally concave shape like curve A. Curve A may be said to display diminishing marginal utility of income.[13]

On the other hand, there may be individuals who show *risk-preference* (who may be called *risk-seekers*). A consistent risk-seeker would always prefer

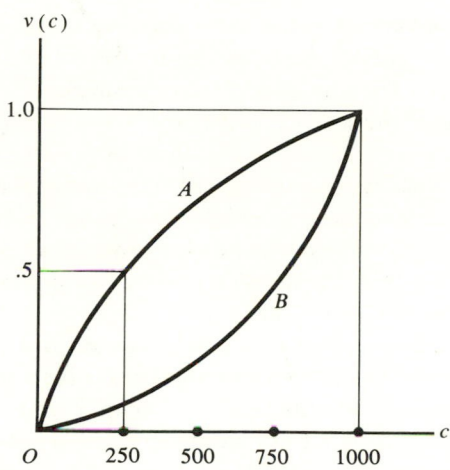

FIG. 8-3. **Risk-avoiding (A) and risk-seeking (B) elementary-utility functions**

a gamble to its expected value as a certainty; i.e., he would accept any fair gamble. In Fig. 8-3 his preference-scaling function would be of the form of the convex curve B, which shows increasing marginal utility of income.

We may now turn to aspects of observed behavior that have served as bases for inferences about the shape of the $v(c)$ function. First, as we practically never observe anyone throwing away income, we conclude that the marginal utility of income is always positive. This implies that the $v(c)$ function must have a positive slope or first derivative $v'(c)$. Second, suppose that an individual's elementary-utility function were simply linear, as in the form $v(c) = a + bc$, with $b > 0$. Then in uncertain choice situations he could maximize expected utility [the probability-weighted average of the $v(c)$] by simply maximizing expected income, for then $u = E(v) = a + bE(c)$. If one type of asset had a higher expected income per dollar invested than

[13] This holds true, of course, only for the Neumann-Morgenstern elementary-utility scaling here employed—the "success-in-equivalent-reference-lottery" measure (or linear transformation thereof).

another, the individual would then hold only the former. But this contradicts observation, for individuals typically *diversify* their asset holdings, accepting less than maximum expected returns in order to hold a variety of securities. Most analysts have been willing to infer from this behavior that individuals typically display *diminishing marginal utility of income*—the worth of a possible gain is treated as less than the worth of a corresponding equiprobable loss. Then the $v(c)$ function cannot be linear, but is concave downward like curve A in Fig. 8-3—i.e., has a negative second derivative $v''(c)$. (On the other hand, we do occasionally see people accept fair, or even unfavorable, gambles—so this inference has not been universally accepted.)

Some concave curves, however, must be ruled out as elementary-utility functions. In particular, consider the quadratic $v(c) = k_0 + k_1 c - k_2 c^2$, with $k_1, k_2 > 0$. Here the second derivative $v''(c) = -2k_2$ is always negative, but the first derivative $v'(c) = k_1 - 2k_2 c$ remains positive only over a limited region—i.e., the quadratic implies that for sufficiently large incomes, the marginal utility of income would become negative.[14] However, a number of other familiar functions have the needed properties; for example, the log function[15] $v(c) = \log(1 + c)$, the square-root function $v(c) = c^{1/2}$, and the asymptotic function $v(c) = 1 - e^{-c}$.

A more specific assertion about risk-aversion is also of interest: that individuals are *decreasingly* averse to risk as their income rises.[16] Consider the special case of an individual endowed with x units of certain income, together with a small fair gamble yielding $+z$ or $-z$ with equal probability. Thus the endowment is the prospect $(x + z, x - z; \frac{1}{2}, \frac{1}{2})$. Then there will be an "insurance premium" p which the individual would be just willing to pay to be rid of the gamble. (Equivalently, p is a "risk premium" in the following sense: an individual endowed with a sure income equal to $x - p$ would have to be awarded the premium p to make him willing to accept the gamble between $+z$ and $-z$.) Thus:

$$v(x - p) = u(x + z, x - z; \tfrac{1}{2}, \tfrac{1}{2})$$

Or, using the expected-utility rule:

$$v(x - p) = \tfrac{1}{2}v(x + z) + \tfrac{1}{2}v(x - z)$$

Then the assertion is that, for given size z of a gamble, the insurance premium p falls as x rises.

---

[14] A similar problem would arise for any function of powers of c.

[15] The simpler function $\log c$ would equal $-\infty$ at $c = 0$, which would violate the certainty-equivalent postulate.

[16] A condition suggested in J. W. Pratt, "Risk Aversion in the Small and in the Large," *Econometrica*, **32** (Jan.–April 1964).

Somewhat more generally, consider a gamble described by the random variable $\tilde{z}$, with probability distribution $f(z)$ and possibly nonzero expectation $\mu(\tilde{z})$. If the individual is endowed with certain income x together with the gamble $\tilde{z}$, the insurance premium p is defined by

$$v(x + \mu - p) = E[v(x + z)] \tag{3}$$

It can be shown mathematically that, for p to fall as x increases, the ratio of derivatives $[-v''(c)/v'(c)]$ must fall as c $(= x + z)$ increases.[17]

This specification for the shape of the $v(c)$ function may not command immediate assent. It may not be intuitively obvious that as a man gets richer, he becomes less averse to a given gamble. However, another way of formulating this point makes it much more appealing: namely, that risky assets are normal goods (sometimes called "superior" goods)—in the sense that more of them will be demanded as income or wealth rises.[18] We are considering here, of course, only risky assets that are favorable gambles (have positive expectations); for, given risk-aversion, unfavorable or even fair gambles would *never* be chosen. It does seem intuitively reasonable that, as a man grows richer, he will be inclined to balance his holdings in such a way as to increase his risky assets as well as his riskless assets. In equation (3), $\mu - p$ can be regarded as the demand price for a unit of the risky asset; i.e., an individual endowed only with sure income x will be willing to pay for the gamble $\tilde{z}$ an amount equal to its expectation μ less the insurance premium p. If the gamble is a normal good, the demand price $\mu - p$ will rise as the individual's endowment of sure income x rises—or equivalently, μ being constant for a given gamble, the risk premium p will be falling. Then, facing a given market price for each unit of this favorable gamble or asset, the individual would be inclined to buy an increased number of units as wealth rises.

Another interesting property proposed for the $v(c)$ function is that it be bounded from above—as is the function $1 - e^{-c}$, for example, but not the log function $\log (1 + c)$ or the square-root function $c^{1/2}$. A bounded function is necessary for assigning finite values to gambles of the "St. Petersburg" type. Suppose the individual's elementary-utility function were $v(c) = c^{1/2}$. Then consider a gamble constructed as follows. A coin is tossed. If it comes

---

[17] Since risk-aversion is associated with the concavity of the $v(c)$ function—its negative second derivative $v''(c)$—it might be thought that a straightening of the $v(c)$ function as c increases, reflecting diminishing $-v''(c)$, would suffice for a falling insurance premium as x increases. However, this is not the case. For example, the elementary-utility function $v(c) = 1 - e^{-c}$ has $-v''(c) = e^{-c}$, which decreases as c increases. But it may be verified that with this function, for a given gamble z there is no change in the insurance premium p as x increases.

[18] The analogous assumption, that dated consumptive claims such as c_0 and c_1 are normal (superior) goods, was used in earlier chapters.

up heads the first time, the individual wins \$1 and the game is ended; if tails, the coin is tossed again. If heads comes up on the second toss, the individual wins \$4 as a terminal payoff; if tails, the coin is tossed again. Heads on the third throw wins \$16, on the fourth throw \$64, and so on. It may be seen that the expected utility of this gamble is

$$u = E(v) = \tfrac{1}{2}v(1) + (\tfrac{1}{2})^2 v(4) + (\tfrac{1}{2})^3 v(16) + (\tfrac{1}{2})^4 v(64) + \cdots$$
$$= \tfrac{1}{2}(1) + (\tfrac{1}{2})^2(2) + (\tfrac{1}{2})^3(4) + (\tfrac{1}{2})^4(8) + \cdots$$

a series whose sum is infinite. With a bounded $v(c)$ function, however, the rapidly declining probabilities of the very high returns must eventually offset the more slowly rising $v(c)$ so as to assure that the St. Petersburg gamble will command only a finite price. The alleged observation that St. Petersburg gambles have only finite values thus is supposed to dictate a bounded function.

The weak point of the argument for imposing this specification is that no one in the actual world is in a position to *offer* a St. Petersburg gamble—to guarantee payment of possible prizes increasing without limit. If in the example above, for example, the final payoff were limited to a maximum of \$1,000,000 [approximately \$$(2)^{20}$], the gamble would be worth no more than around \$10—the approximate sure sum that a penniless individual would be willing to forego if he could receive the gamble as an alternative. We may conclude, therefore, that the evidence at hand does not suffice to require the employment of $v(c)$ functions bounded from above.

One other proposed shape for the $v(c)$ function has been the subject of considerable discussion: a doubly inflected curve like that in Fig. 8-4—with an initial concave, a middle convex, and a final concave segment.[19] This shape is designed to explain why some individuals simultaneously *insure* (pay a premium to avoid risk) and *gamble* at unfavorable odds (in effect, pay to be subjected to risk).

Consider an individual whose income will be y'' if all goes well, but is subject to a risk that with probability π' his income will be reduced to y'. Then his initial situation is the prospect $Y = (y', y''; \pi', 1 - \pi')$. The utility $u(Y) = \pi' v(y') + (1 - \pi') v(y'')$ is measured by the probability-weighted average of $v(y')$ and $v(y'')$, or geometrically by the ordinate of the point along the dashed line for which the distances to y'' and y' are in the proportions $1 - \pi'$ and π', respectively. Thus $u(Y)$ is the expected utility of the endowed prospect. It is evident from the geometry that the individual would be delighted to accept the expected income, $x = (1 - \pi') y'' + \pi' y'$, if offered as a certainty in place of the endowed prospect—i.e., he would

[19] See M. Friedman and L. J. Savage, "The Utility Analysis of Choices Involving Risk," *Journal of Political Economy*, **56** (Aug. 1948), reprinted in American Economic Association, *Readings in Price Theory* (Richard D. Irwin, Inc., 1952).

insure at fair odds. Geometrically, $u(x) = v(x) > u(Y)$. He would even be willing to pay a moderate premium p (insure at adverse odds) so as to leave him with $x - p$ as a certainty, so long as $v(x - p) > u(Y)$.

On the other hand, with the doubly inflected $v(c)$ function of Fig. 8-4 the same individual, if endowed with w as a certainty, would be delighted to

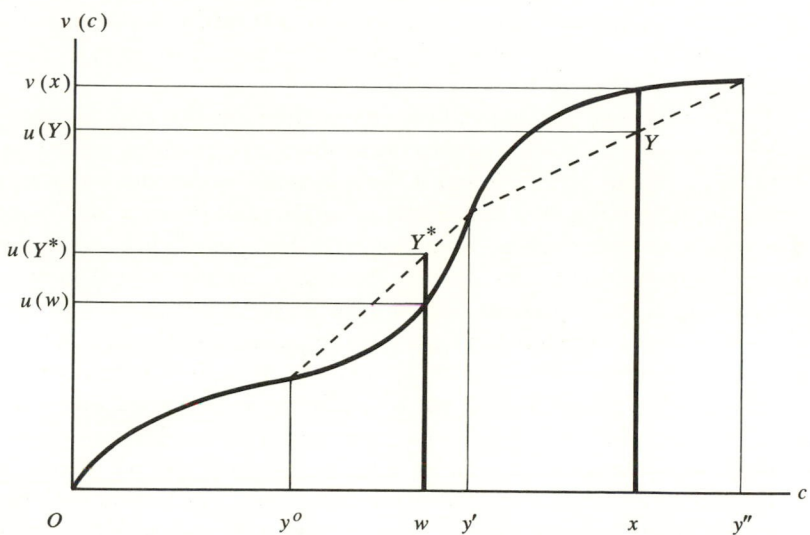

FIG. 8-4. Doubly-inflected elementary income function

exchange it for a fair lottery $Y^* = (y^o, y'; \pi^o, 1 - \pi^o)$—since $u(Y^*) > v(w)$. He would even be willing to accept a somewhat unfavorable gamble (whose expectation of return would lie to the left of w), so long as the probability-weighted average of the outcomes remains greater than $v(w)$.

With this sort of $v(c)$ function, we may note that risk-taking behavior (at fair odds) will vary depending upon wealth class. For those whose endowment falls in the first concave segment, the tendency is to insure against risk of relatively small losses but to accept fair or even unfavorable gambles so long as there is some possibility of a very large payoff. This will be particularly the case for those with incomes toward the upper end of the first concave segment—the lower middle class, we might say. The very poor, in contrast, would be much less inclined to gamble; any line drawn from the extreme left of the function in Fig. 8-4 to another point higher on the curve is likely to lie mostly below the curve itself. The upper middle class would seem to have a taste for risks of large losses; they would be inclined to make bets involving the possibility of a sharp reduction in wealth. (As for the very rich, they again would be much less likely to gamble.) The central group, finally, would be happy to accept almost any fair or near-fair bet.

The elementary-utility function of Fig. 8-4 does, then, rationalize the coexistence of gambling and insurance. But it also implies other behavior quite inconsistent with observation. It seems unlikely that the middle classes are the ones who gamble while the poor and rich are solid risk-avoiders. Indeed, if the middle classes were plungers of the type pictured, standing ready at any moment to accept gambles thrusting them into one or the other concave segment, we would expect these middle ranks to be rapidly depopulated.

If the proposed rationalization represented by the $v(c)$ function of Fig. 8-4 is rejected, there still remains the problem of explaining the existence of gambling. A clue will be found if the following is conceded to be a true observation: gambling on a scale likely to impoverish is rarely encountered in the middle or upper classes. This suggests that gambling, except among the poor, is more like a consumption good than an investment good—an activity engaged in for pleasure, rather than with the intention of changing one's wealth status. Operationally, it is quite possible to distinguish "pleasure-oriented" from "wealth-oriented" gambling. Wealth-oriented gambling, being intended to change wealth status, if efficiently conducted will take the form of once-and-for-all wagers at enormous stakes. Pleasure-oriented gambling, being designed to yield enjoyment over some period of time, will be characterized by repetitive miniscule bets practically guaranteed *not* to drastically change wealth status. What is observed at Las Vegas is very much more the small-stake than the large-stake pattern.

While some pleasure-oriented gambling is to be expected all along the income scale, it appears that a substantial amount of wealth-oriented gambling takes place *among the poor*. Indeed, in some societies, gambling has been a major social evil for that very reason. There seem to be both rational and irrational elements here. On the irrational side, apart from pathological gambling,[20] a good deal of betting is motivated by mistaken belief in "hunches" or "infallible systems."[21] Such mistaken beliefs will tend to be correlated with low income status. On the rational side, the existence of governmental or charitable relief systems rather drastically modifies the calculations in favor of risk-taking; evidently, this consideration operates at the low end of the income scale.

We may terminate this discussion, therefore, with the conclusion that

---

[20] See Dostoyevski, *The Gambler*.

[21] Note that, *given* the belief, the gambling may be quite rational. What seems irrational to the outside observer is not at all so to the one who believes himself favored by fortune or by special knowledge. Even a highly conservative risk-avoider would bet if he thought the odds were strongly enough in his favor.

for wealth-oriented decisions—essentially all we will be dealing with in this work—a concave $v(c)$ function, not necessarily bounded from above, can serve with the expected-utility rule as foundation for predicting choices among risky prospects. To this may be added (to assure that risky assets are "superior goods") the condition that $-v''(c)/v'(c)$ must fall as c increases.

C. STATE PREFERENCE: CONTINGENT CLAIMS AS DESIRED OBJECTS

From the discussion to this point, one might gain the impression that preference regarding *uncertain* choices has little in common with preference as among the commodities of standard economic theory. The familiar apparatus of convex indifference curves connecting alternative combinations of objects of choice has not made any appearance so far in this chapter. This is somewhat surprising, since in dealing with the topic of *time* preference in Part I we had no difficulty in employing the standard apparatus—once the objects of choice were specified as the dated consumption incomes $c_0, c_1, \ldots,$ c_T. One might then anticipate that there is a way of expressing choice under uncertainty as a standard economic problem, given a suitable specification of the objects of choice. We can indeed go some distance in this direction, obtaining interesting results en route.

The definition of an elementary hazard prospect $(c_a, c_b, \ldots, c_S;$ $\pi_a, \pi_b, \ldots, \pi_S)$ was based upon the concept of a set of "states of the world" $a, b, \ldots, S$ such that one and only one state will in fact occur (i.e., such that $\pi_a + \pi_b + \cdots + \pi_S = 1$). The "consequences" $c_a, c_b, \ldots, c_S$ are quantities of *contingent consumption incomes* whose actual realization will occur if and only if the corresponding state obtains; these contingent consumption claims are the fundamental objects of preference. There may or may not exist markets in which individuals can exchange contingent consumption claims against one another, before the removal of uncertainty (the assumption about the scope of market trading will be the center of attention in the next chapter).

In the simplest case, suppose that there are just two states a and b— war versus peace, for example, or prosperity versus depression. Figure 8-5 is constructed in terms of the contingent claims c_a and c_b as objects of choice. (The probability beliefs π_a and π_b are not shown explicitly; however, they enter into the shapes of the indifference curves.) Any point in the graph is a particular (c_a, c_b) prospect; note that the 45° ray from the origin, along which c_a necessarily equals c_b, is the "certainty line." Figure 8-5 differs in one crucial respect from the diagrams of similar appearance employed in previous chapters—for example, Fig. 1-1, which shows combinations of ordinary commodities A and B, or Fig. 2-1, which represents combinations of dated consumption claims c_0 and c_1. The difference is that in Fig. 8-5 the individual possesses a particular *prospect* of alternatives rather than a *combination* in the usual sense. He will ultimately be able to consume only one or the other of the elements c_a or c_b—depending upon which of the two states will actually obtain—and not both. But, making his decision prior to the removal of uncertainty, he is forced to balance his holdings so as to cover the two possibilities. Thus, although the individual cannot *consume* both, he can and will

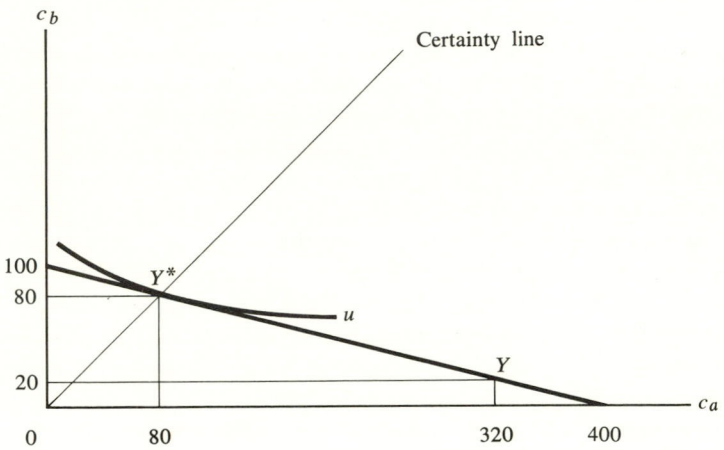

FIG. 8-5. Convex indifference curves between state-distributed claims

want to *hold* both types of claims. His actual choice will presumably depend upon his endowment, his probability beliefs as to the relative likelihoods of the two states, the market opportunities for trading claims, his productive opportunities if any, and his attitude toward risk (elementary-utility function).

Despite this divergence of interpretation, the indifference curve is shown in Fig. 8-5 with the familiar convex shape. As in the case of ordinary commodities, the justification for this shape is the principle of "nonspecialization." Common observation tells us that almost no one, offered a choice among alternative (c_a, c_b) prospects within a wealth constraint $W = \phi_a c_a + \phi_b c_b$, selects a corner solution along one axis or the other rather than an interior (tangency) optimum.[22] It should be appreciated here that a corner prospect—one for which c_a, let us say, is zero—entails more than the risk

[22] The *principle* of nonspecialization is a somewhat exaggerated or idealized version of the factual situation. Whereas individuals do typically diversify, both in ordinary consumption and contingent holdings, it is not the case that they hold positive quantities of *all* of the objects of choice.

of a possibly tolerable gambling loss. Rather, it means staking literally everything on the nonoccurrence of state a, incurring absolute impoverishment if state a should obtain.[23]

These considerations place the subject of risk-aversion in a somewhat new light. Under the Neumann-Morgenstern postulates (as expounded earlier) an individual's attitude toward risk could, without violating rationality, be either positive or negative; i.e., he might be willing to pay either a premium to acquire or a premium to disembarrass himself of, a fair gamble (see curves A and B of Fig. 8-3). But the state-preference formulation, calling on the observation of nonspecialization, dictates at least the mild degree of conservatism toward risk represented by the convex indifference curves of Fig. 8-5. Furthermore: *The convex indifference curves of Fig. 8.5 imply and are implied by a (unique) concave $v(c)$ function in Fig. 8.3, and conversely.* Thus, only curves such as A in Fig. 8-3 are acceptable preference-scaling functions. A general proof is given in a footnote.[24] If, for example, $v(c)$ has the concave shape of the function $\ln (1 + c)$, the marginal rate of substitution or slope along the indifference curve of constant $u = Ev = \pi_a \ln (1 + c_a) + \pi_b \ln (1 + c_b)$, is

$$\left. \frac{dc_b}{dc_a} \right|_u = - \frac{\pi_a(1 + c_b)}{\pi_b(1 + c_a)}$$

[23] As indicated in the previous section, a consumption floor in the form of charity or relief encourages gambling: one can then bet all one's chips on state b and still receive a certain minimum should the bet fail. Despite this, plunging on such a scale is rare enough to be considered pathological in our society.

[24] At any point (c_a, c_b) in Fig. 8-5, $u(c_a, c_b; \pi_a, \pi_b) = \pi_a v(c_a) + \pi_b v(c_b)$. In this footnote the more compressed notation $\pi_a v_a + \pi_b v_b$ will be used. (Since the uniqueness postulate is assumed, v_a and v_b are not *functionally* different—they represent the same v-function, evaluated at the points c_a and c_b.) Then, along the indifference curve:

$$\left. \frac{dc_b}{dc_a} \right|_u = - \frac{\partial u/\partial c_a}{\partial u/\partial c_b} = - \frac{\pi_a v_a'}{\pi_b v_b'}$$

$$\frac{d^2 c_b}{dc_a^2} = \frac{\partial}{\partial c_a}\left(\frac{dc_b}{dc_a}\right) + \frac{\partial}{\partial c_b}\left(\frac{dc_b}{dc_a}\right)\frac{dc_b}{dc_a}$$

$$= \frac{-\pi_a v_a''}{\pi_b v_b'} + \frac{\pi_a v_a' v_b''}{\pi_b (v_b')^2}\left(\frac{-\pi_a v_a'}{\pi_b v_b'}\right)$$

$$= \frac{-\pi_a v_a''}{\pi_b v_b'} - \frac{\pi_a^2 (v_a')^2 v_b''}{\pi_b^2 (v_b')^3}$$

A concave $v(c)$ function (negative v_a'' and v_b'') implies convex indifference curves (positive $d^2 c_b/dc_a^2$), since π_a, π_b, v_a', $v_b' > 0$. The independence postulate has been used here to let $\partial v_b'/\partial c_a = \partial v_a'/\partial c_b = 0$.

In the converse development, convexity at a given point (c_a, c_b) is not sufficient to imply that *both* v_a'' and v_b'' are negative; a positive v_a'' could be outweighed by a sufficiently negative v_b''. But in that case it will be possible to find (given the uniqueness postulate) risky combinations for which v_a'' and v_b'' are both positive, which is inconsistent with convexity. Thus, convexity *everywhere* requires that a unique $v(c)$ function be concave.

This represents convex curvature (the absolute slope rises as c_b increases and falls as c_a increases).

A fair gamble, we saw above, would never be accepted (and fair insurance would always be purchased) by an individual with a concave elementary-utility function such as curve A in Fig. 8-3. This corresponds, in the state-preference formulation, to the following proposition: *If claims to contingent incomes c_a and c_b can be purchased at prices ϕ_a and ϕ_b proportional to the state probabilities π_a and π_b, the optimum attainable point will always be on the 45° certainty line.*[25] Geometrically, the indifference curves on c_a, c_b axes as in Fig. 8-5 will have slope $-\pi_a/\pi_b$ along the 45° line.

NUMERICAL EXAMPLE

Consider an individual, with the preference function portrayed in Fig. 8-5, endowed with the certain prospect $Y^* = (80, 80; .2, .8)$. That is, in a situation where state b is regarded as four times as probable as state a, the initial position represents a holding of claims such that 80 will be received *regardless* of which state obtains. Now suppose the individual is offered instead the point Y representing the prospect $(320, 20; .2, .8)$. The transaction can be regarded in various ways, among them: (I) as an added receipt of 240 in state a in return for the sacrifice of 60 in state b; (II) as payment of 60 of certain income representing the price of a gamble, where the gamble returns the amount 300 with .2 probability (and otherwise nothing). It is evident from (II) that the movement from Y^* to Y corresponds to acceptance of a fair gamble. But the formulation in (I) is a way of saying that the prices ϕ_a and ϕ_b for the contingent state-claims are proportionate to the probabilities. We know that, offered gambles at fair odds, the individual will prefer a certainty solution. In the case considered he will prefer to stay at Y^*. This does not imply that risky prospects will never be accepted, but only that favorable odds are required.[26]

Note that in the state-preference representation a gamble is a movement away from the 45° line, while purchase of insurance is a movement toward that line. It is important to appreciate that, *depending upon the initial endowed*

---

[25] All combinations attainable by market transactions involving the risky claims c_a and c_b must lie along a constant-wealth line, so that $\phi_a \Delta c_a + \phi_b \Delta c_b = 0$. For a fair gamble or fair insurance, on the other hand, the expected gain must be zero so that $\pi_a \Delta c_a + \pi_b \Delta c_b = 0$. Hence, fair gambles or fair insurance purchases are those for which $\phi_a/\phi_b = \pi_a/\pi_b$. Maximizing $u = \pi_a v(c_a) + \pi_b v(c_b)$, subject to the wealth constraint $\phi_a c_a + \phi_b c_b = K$ (a constant), yields the condition:

$$\frac{\phi_a}{\phi_b} = \frac{\pi_a v'(c_a)}{\pi_b v'(c_b)}$$

Then the proportionality of prices and probabilities requires that $c_a = c_b$, given that $v(c)$ is unique and that $v''(c) < 0$ everywhere.

[26] Without the uniqueness postulate, the optimum would in general be off the 45° line for hazard prospects. Starting from a position of income certainty, suppose I am offered a \$100 bet at fair odds (even money, let us say) on my alma mater's next football game. If my team's losing would cause me distress reparable by financial gain, it would be conservative to bet on the other side! Here there is a divergence between $v_a(c)$ and $v_b(c)$, where the states a and b correspond to victory and defeat.

position, exactly the same contractual arrangement could represent either a gamble or insurance. A clear illustration exists in the commodity markets, where purchase of a future may represent a speculation for one individual but a hedge for another.

D. PREFERENCES INVOLVING BOTH TIME AND UNCERTAINTY

Investment, interest, and capital are all concepts that necessarily involve time. So far in this chapter, preference among uncertain contingencies has been considered in a timeless context, but only as a way of setting the stage for the topic of *intertemporal preference under uncertainty*. We can now proceed to the integration of the theories of preference under uncertainty and preference over time.

The required integration will be approached as a generalization of the theory of timeless choice under uncertainty. The key to the generalization is that each ultimate "consequence" of risky choice will no longer be a simple income c (quantum of the unique consumption good) but rather a path or sequence $\mathscr{S}$ of dated consumptions. Correspondingly, an asset is a prospect of sequences($\mathscr{S}^A, \mathscr{S}^B, \ldots, \mathscr{S}^N; \pi^A, \pi^B, \ldots, \pi^N$) instead of a prospect of timeless consumptions. Figure 8-6 represents temporal uncertainty in the form of a "tree" of five possible sequences $\mathscr{S}^A, \mathscr{S}^B, \ldots, \mathscr{S}^E$. If there are N distinct sequences, we can think of there being N states at each given date; ordinarily (as in Fig. 8-6) these states will not all be distinct, as the sequences interweave with one another. In particular, note that in Fig. 8-6 only a single state exists for c_0, i.e., that the present is not subject to uncertainty. (This assumption is convenient, but not necessary.) The entire tree of sequences represents a position that the individual may have been endowed with, or may have attained only after productive or financial transformations.

The probabilities of particular sequences, or path probabilities, are denoted $\pi^A, \ldots, \pi^N$, where of course

$$\sum_{J=1}^{N} \pi^J = 1$$

In addition, any path probability is the product of the successive conditional probabilities of the states it contains. This may be expressed as

$$\pi^J = \pi_0^J \pi_{1.0}^J \cdots \pi_{T.T-1,\ldots,1,0}^J$$

where $\pi_{t.t-1,\ldots,1,0}^J$ is the probability that the state at time t associated with the path J will obtain, conditional upon the occurrence of all the previous states associated with J. It may be noted that no constancy as to the *nature* of the several states over time is assumed; it may or may not be the case that a particular state at time t is in some sense the "same" as a state at time $t - 1$. (The repetition of notation, as in the designation "a" for the left-hand state at each date in the tree of Fig. 8-6, is purely to economize on symbolism.)

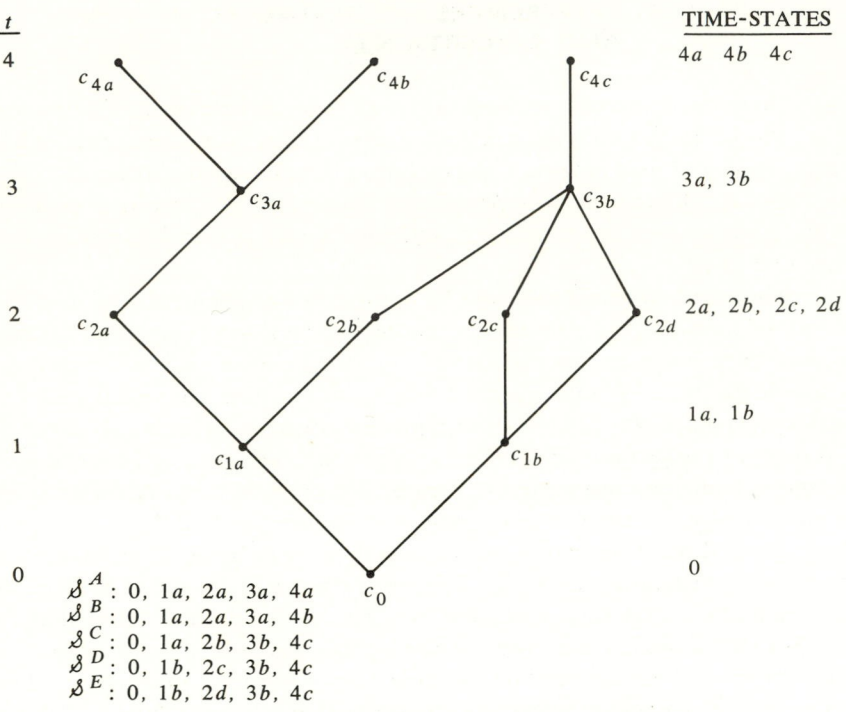

$$
\begin{aligned}
&\mathscr{S}^A : 0,\ 1a,\ 2a,\ 3a,\ 4a \\
&\mathscr{S}^B : 0,\ 1a,\ 2a,\ 3a,\ 4b \\
&\mathscr{S}^C : 0,\ 1a,\ 2b,\ 3b,\ 4c \\
&\mathscr{S}^D : 0,\ 1b,\ 2c,\ 3b,\ 4c \\
&\mathscr{S}^E : 0,\ 1b,\ 2d,\ 3b,\ 4c
\end{aligned}
$$

FIG. 8-6.   Tree of time-state sequences

A small revision of the postulates of rational choice suffices for the justification of a cardinal *intertemporal* utility function, which can be used with the expected-utility rule to evaluate the preference scaling of any time-state sequence. The main change concerns the ordering and preference-direction postulate. In place of the simple specification that more certain income is preferred to less, it is now necessary first to assume the existence of an *ordinal* preference function for all certain combinations $U(c_0, c_1, \ldots, c_T)$. Such a function is, of course, the intertemporal utility function we have worked with in previous chapters; for example, in the simple two-period paradigm, the indifference curves of such an ordinal function are portrayed in Fig. 2-1. The revised postulate might be stated as follows:

1'. *Ordering and preference direction:* As between any two certain time sequences of consumption $\mathscr{S}^A$ and $\mathscr{S}^B$, one is preferred to the other or else they are indifferent. Indifference and preference are transitive relations. The direction of preference is such that if $\mathscr{S}^A$ and $\mathscr{S}^B$ are identical sequences except that $\mathscr{S}^A$ contains one dated element larger than the correspondingly dated element for $\mathscr{S}^B$, then $\mathscr{S}^A$ is preferred to $\mathscr{S}^B$.

As before, this postulate provides an ordinal preference scale. A minor change is also required for the certainty-equivalent postulate, which might be restated as follows:

2'. *Certainty equivalent:* If sequences $\mathscr{S}^A$ and $\mathscr{S}^B$ are identical except that $\mathscr{S}^A$ contains one dated element c_t^A larger than the correspondingly dated element c_t^B of the other, then for any prospect of sequences ($\mathscr{S}^A$, $\mathscr{S}^B$; π, $1 - \pi$) there is a certainty-equivalent sequence $\mathscr{S}^*$ identical with the other two except for a c_t^* that is intermediate between c_t^A and c_t^B. Conversely, given a sequence $\mathscr{S}^*$ with an element c_t^* intermediate between two other correspondingly dated quantities c_t^A and c_t^B, a lottery of the form ($\mathscr{S}^A$, $\mathscr{S}^B$; π, $1 - \pi$) may be found (by selection of the probability π) that is indifferent to $\mathscr{S}^*$.

The independence and uniqueness postulates do not require modification. Without attempt at proof, it will be argued by analogy and example that a cardinal v function can be attached to consumption sequences such that the expected utility $u = Ev$ serves for the evaluation of any prospect of sequences.[27] As before, the construction of a suitable preference-scaling or elementary-utility v function employs the "reference-lottery" device. A worst consequence is assigned the value $v = 0$ and a best consequence the value $v = 1$, so that for any sequence $\mathscr{S}$ a cardinal utility is provided by the probability of success π in the equivalent (indifferent) lottery involving only these best and worst sequences.

NUMERICAL EXAMPLE (see Fig. 8-7)

Let us suppose a given ordinal utility function $U = c_0 c_1$. All the possible consumption sequences (c_0, c_1) are assumed to lie between one identified as best, $\mathscr{S}^Q = (8, 10)$, and one identified as worst, $\mathscr{S}^Z = (2, 4)$.[28] We note from $U = c_0 c_1$ that $\mathscr{S}^{Z*} = (8, 1)$ is indifferent to $\mathscr{S}^Z$. The sequences $\mathscr{S}^Q$ and $\mathscr{S}^{Z*}$, differing only in the dated element c_1 (i.e., lying along the vertical line $c_0 = 8$) can then be employed, via the certainty-equivalent postulate 1' and the usual reference-lottery procedure, to find a cardinal v function. This function is defined, to begin with, for combinations $(8, c_1)$ between the points $\mathscr{S}^Q$ and $\mathscr{S}^{Z*}$. Let us suppose that within this range the following specific numerical form is found by the reference-lottery technique:

$$v = \log_{10} c_1'$$

[27] The procedure used in the example below follows that of J. H. Drèze and F. Modigliani, "Epargne et consommation en avenir aléatoire," *Cahiers du séminaire d'économétrie*, **9**, 7–33 (1966).

[28] For the reference-lottery technique, the "best" and "worst" sequences need not themselves be available or possible choices; all that is required is that these limits include the available choices between them.

Here c_1' represents values of c_1 when $c_0 = 8$. Note that $v(8, 1) = 0$ and $v(8, 10) = 1$. Now, given the ordinal U function and the cardinal v function along such a vertical line intersecting the indifference curves, the cardinal utility values v for each point along the line can be transferred to the whole indifference

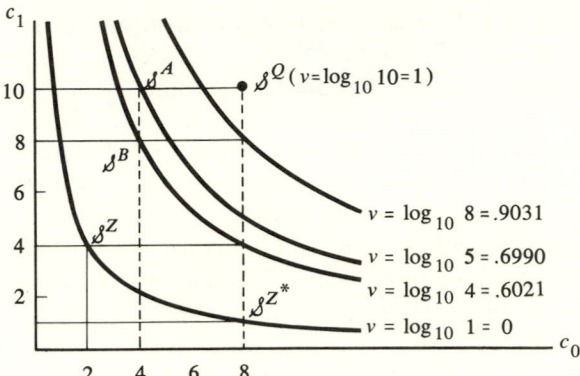

FIG. 8-7.   Intertemporal cardinal utility function

curve cutting the line at that point. Algebraically, since $8c_1' = c_0 c_1$, the cardinal function over the entire space[29] is

$$v = \log_{10}\left(\frac{c_0 c_1}{8}\right)$$

Any prospect of sequences may then be evaluated by the expected-utility rule. For example, the prospect $(\mathscr{S}^A, \mathscr{S}^B; .6, .4)$, where $\mathscr{S}^A$ is the sequence $(4, 10)$ and $\mathscr{S}^B$ is the sequence $(4, 8)$, has the expected utility

$$u = Ev = .6 \log_{10} 5 + .4 \log_{10} 4$$

$$= .6(.6990) + .4(.6021) = .66024$$

We have seen in the numerical example that a utility function u can be defined as the expectation of a generalized preference-scaling function v over alternative possible sequences of consumption. Symbolically:

$$u(\mathscr{S}^A, \ldots, \mathscr{S}^N; \pi^A, \ldots, \pi^N) = \pi^A v(c_0^A, \ldots, c_T^A)$$
$$+ \cdots + \pi^N v(c_0^N, \ldots, c_T^N) \quad \textbf{(4)}$$

There is one other formulation of the utility function that is extremely useful. Let us denote the over-all joint probability distribution of the time-states as

[29] Strictly speaking, within the limits set by $v(\mathscr{S}^Q)$ and $v(\mathscr{S}^Z)$.

Π. Evidently, for fixed Π utility can be regarded as simply a function of the $N(T + 1)$ time-state claims $c_{t,J}$. That is, there exists a function u_Π such that[30]

$$u(\mathscr{S}^A, \ldots, \mathscr{S}^N; \pi^A, \ldots, \pi^N)$$

$$= u_\Pi(c_0^A, \ldots, c_0^N; c_1^A, \ldots, c_1^N; \cdots; c_T^A, \ldots, c_T^N) \quad (5)$$

NUMERICAL EXAMPLE

Let us continue the numerical example employed above, with $\pi^A = .6$, $\pi^B = .4$, and $v = \log_{10}(c_0 c_1/8)$. Thus for any two sequences with these probabilities $u = .6 \log_{10}(c_0^A c_1^A/8) + .4 \log_{10}(c_0^B c_1^B/8)$. The particular prospect evaluated involved the sequences $\mathscr{S}^A = (4, 10)$ and $\mathscr{S}^B = (4, 8)$. In this case $c_0^A = c_0^B$, so that the present is certain. Since there are only two possibilities, c_1^A can be identified with c_{1a}—the consumption claim associated with state a at time 1—and c_1^B with c_{1b}, where $\pi^A = \pi_{1a}$ and $\pi^B = \pi_{1b}$. Then the utility function for evaluating any set of time-state claims with these probabilities can be expressed in terms of the time-state claims as

$$u_\Pi = \log_{10}\left(\frac{c_0 c_{1a}^6 c_{1b}^4}{8}\right)$$

Inserting $c_0 = 4$, $c_{1a} = 10$, and $c_{1b} = 8$, we obtain the same numerical result as above, namely $u_\Pi = .66024$.

The utility function u_Π of the numerical example above is sketched in Fig. 8-8. This type of function incorporates the probability beliefs together with the intertemporal preference-scaling of Fig. 8-7. Since all the distinct time-state claims (here c_0, c_{1a}, and c_{1b}) are axes of Fig. 8-8, no side-calculation in terms of probabilities is necessary to find expected utility. In fact, the preference map of Fig. 8-8 could in principle be obtained from observed choice behavior without ever introducing any *explicit* probability beliefs. More important, these distinct time-state claims are, at least potentially, objects that can be regarded as subject to ordinary trade—so that the construction becomes fully analogous to the utility function of ordinary consumption theory. This feature becomes the key theme of the next chapter. On the other hand it must not be forgotten that Fig. 8-7 is logically the more basic construction, and in fact some problems cannot be interpreted in terms of the function of Fig. 8-8. In particular, a change in probability estimates requires a reformulation of the entire preference function of Fig. 8-8, whereas only the side-calculation and not the preference-scaling function of Fig. 8-7 is affected.

---

[30] If the "uniqueness" postulate is not accepted, there will in general be N distinct v functions $v^A, v^B, \ldots, v^N$. Equations (4) and (5) would have to be changed correspondingly.

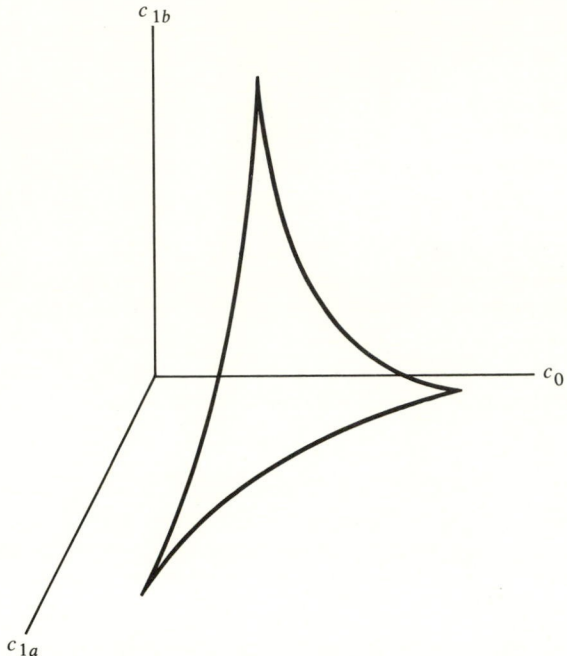

FIG. 8-8. Utility function in terms of time-state claims

BIBLIOGRAPHIC NOTE

There is an extensive literature on the "postulates of rational choice" for decision under uncertainty—limited almost entirely, however, to atemporal choices. Among the less technical presentations are:

JACOB MARSCHAK, "Decision-Making: Economic Aspects," in *International Encyclopedia of the Social Sciences* (The Macmillan Company and the Free Press of Glencoe, Inc., 1968), vol. 4.

HARRY M. MARKOWITZ, *Portfolio Selection* (John Wiley & Sons, Inc., 1959), Pt. IV.

R. DUNCAN LUCE and HOWARD RAIFFA, *Games and Decisions* (John Wiley & Sons, Inc., 1957), Chap. 2.

KARL BORCH, *The Economics of Uncertainty* (Princeton University Press, 1968), Chap. 3.

M. FRIEDMAN and L. J. SAVAGE, "The Utility Analysis of Choices Involving Risk," *Journal of Political Economy*, **56** (Aug. 1948).

Several of these references also provide discussions as to the probable shape of the elementary-utility function. This topic is also analyzed, from varying viewpoints, in:

HARRY M. MARKOWITZ, "The Utility of Wealth," *Journal of Political Economy*, **60** (April 1952).

J. W. PRATT, "Risk Aversion in the Small and in the Large," *Econometrica*, **32** (Jan.–April 1964).

J. HIRSHLEIFER, "Investment Decision Under Uncertainty: Applications of the State-Preference Approach," *Quarterly Journal of Economics*, **80** (May 1966).

On the other hand, the problem of the *intertemporal* preference function under uncertainty has not yet been widely studied. The formulation in this chapter was based upon:

J. H. DRÈZE and F. MODIGLIANI, "Epargne et consommation en avenir aléatoire," *Cahiers du séminaire d'économétrie*, **9,** 7–33 (1966).

INVESTMENT AND INTEREST UNDER UNCERTAINTY: CHOICE OVER DATES AND STATES

9

In Part I, the individual's investment decision—under the artificial assumption of a world of certainty—was viewed as the selection of a preferred pattern of *intertemporal consumption*. The aggregate of investment-consumption choices on the individual level interact so as to determine, on the market level, price ratios between pairs of dated consumption claims. Interest rates, in turn, were defined in terms of these ratios. Thus, the price ratio ϕ_1/ϕ_0 is $1/(1 + r_1)$, ϕ_2/ϕ_1 is $1/(1 + r_2)$, and so forth.

In dealing with the realm of uncertainty here, a basically similar point of view will be maintained. The individual will be assumed to choose, within his opportunity set, a preferred pattern of consumption—except that his decisions must now span the different possible *states of the world* as well as the different *dates* up to his decision horizon. Again, choices on the individual level will interact in the market so as to determine price ratios among the various commodities traded. We shall see that "riskless" and "risky" interest rates can be defined in terms of these price ratios.

The great problem of formulating the theory of investment decision under uncertainty has been to relate the commodities observably dealt with in markets (tradable assets, or *securities*) to the underlying entities entering into preference functions (goods). In the previous chapter, we saw that intertemporal preference under uncertainty could be described as attaching to alternative contingent paths or sequences $\mathscr{S}^A, \ldots, \mathscr{S}^N$ of dated consumptions. More specifically, the Neumann-Morgenstern postulates of rational choice (including, in particular, the "uniqueness" postulate)—leading to the cardinal nontemporal elementary-utility function $v(c)$—were extended so as to justify a cardinal intertemporal elementary-utility function of form $v(c_0, \ldots, c_T)$. This function could be used via the expected-utility rule and the individual's beliefs (as to the path probabilities $\pi^A, \ldots, \pi^N$) to define the utility of a prospect of sequences as

$$u(\mathscr{S}^A, \ldots, \mathscr{S}^N; \pi^A, \ldots, \pi^N)$$
$$= \pi^A v(c_0^A, \ldots, c_T^A) + \cdots + \pi^N v(c_0^N, \ldots, c_T^N) \quad \text{(1a)}$$

Furthermore, with a fixed time-state probability distribution Π, it was possible to define a more familiar-looking utility function of the time-state claims or contingent incomes c_{ts}, as elements analogous to the commodities of ordinary price theory:[1]

$$u(\mathscr{S}^A, \ldots, \mathscr{S}^N; \pi^A, \ldots, \pi^N)$$
$$= u_\Pi(c_0; c_{1A}, \ldots, c_{1N}; \ldots; c_{TA}, \ldots, c_{TN}) \quad \text{(1b)}$$

In this chapter a choice-theoretic structure will be formulated showing how individuals' preferences as to time-state contingent incomes c_{ts} interact on the market with their endowments, beliefs, and opportunities so as to establish an equilibrium vector of market prices. The extension of the Fisherian intertemporal choice-theoretic structure to a field of objects of choice incorporating both temporality and uncertainty leads to a highly idealized version of the actual process of choice over time under uncertainty. A preliminary comment on the nature of this idealization will be in order.

Two kinds of uncertainty must be clearly distinguished: *productive uncertainty* and *transactions uncertainty*. Productive uncertainty refers to ignorance as to the outcome of exogenous natural events that would be of concern even to a Robinson Crusoe isolated from all market opportunities: e.g., whether his corn crop will be a good one or not. This uncertainty, taking the specific form of individual beliefs as to the distribution of his endowment and productive opportunities over "states of the world," constitutes the subject matter of the analysis of this chapter. Transactions uncertainty, on the other hand, refers to the *exchange* opportunities. It represents the individual's ignorance as to the effective supply-demand offers of *other* individuals. With this latter kind of uncertainty, potential traders will typically incur transaction costs in the search for trading partners, the outcome of the search being a random variable. Thus, from the individual's point of view, the market is *imperfect*—in that a unique price at which all transactions may take place is not publicly known in advance. How the social contrivance of money serves to minimize the costs associated with this transactions uncertainty is the key theme of monetary theory.

---

[1] Here the *present* is assumed to be certain—there is only one state at $t = 0$. If there are N distinct sequences, we can think of there being N states at each date.

Analytically, however, transactions uncertainty is much less tractable than productive uncertainty. In this chapter, to avoid dealing with transactions uncertainty and the consequent complications of imperfect markets, it will be assumed that markets *either* are perfect or do not exist at all. Thus, intermediate degrees of imperfection, such as were discussed in the context of time-claims in Chapter 7 (see, for example, the illustration in Fig. 7-2), will not be considered here.

In the first main part of the chapter, the assumption of a world with costlessly and perfectly functioning barter markets among *all* the objects of choice—the contingent claims to income in the several states and dates— will be maintained. Here the system of markets will be said to be *complete*: every contingency corresponds to a distinct marketable commodity (security). The implications of a world where markets for some objects of choice do not exist, i.e., a world with a system of perfect but *incomplete* markets for contingent time-state claims, will be considered in the second main section of the chapter.

A. COMPLETE MARKETS FOR TIME-STATE CLAIMS

Pure Exchange

Choice-theoretic structure

As usual, let us employ the simplest possible paradigm of choice. Assume a world of pure exchange with only two time periods ($t = 0$ and $t = 1$). Let there be one present state (i.e., the present is certain) and just two distinct future states $1a$ and $1b$. We can assume that each individual attaches subjective probability estimates π^A and π^B (not necessarily the same for different individuals) to the two available time-state sequences; then the future state-probabilities π_{1a} and π_{1b} must obviously correspond exactly to the path probabilities π^A and π^B. Since complete markets exist, trading can take place among all existing classes of time-state claims c_0, c_{1a}, and c_{1b} at prices ϕ_0, ϕ_{1a}, and ϕ_{1b}. This trading occurs now (in the present); claims to current consumption c_0 may be exchanged against c_{1a} or c_{1b}, or these latter can be exchanged against each other.

There may also be trading in more complex assets (securities), consisting of packages of elementary time-state claims. A security X is defined by its contingent-claim components: $X = (x_0, x_{1a}, x_{1b})$. With complete markets, the possibility of arbitrage assures that the value of such a package is simply the *sum* of the values of its elements:

$$\phi_X = \phi_0 x_0 + \phi_{1a} x_{1a} + \phi_{1b} x_{1b} \tag{2}$$

We may also think of the elementary claims themselves as *elementary securities*, defining them in terms of time-state claims as $C_0 = (1, 0, 0)$, $C_{1a} = (0, 1, 0)$, and $C_{1b} = (0, 0, 1)$. Since any combination of claims (c_0, c_{1a}, c_{1b}) may be represented by a holding of elementary securities,[2] trading in the three elementary securities *suffices* for complete markets.

The elementary security $C_0 = (1, 0, 0)$ may be identified with "cash." It will be convenient henceforth to think of noncash securities as having the special form $X = (0, x_{1a}, x_{1b})$ with price ϕ_X. What has happened is that the (ordinarily negative) current payment associated with the security is, with reversed sign, called the security's price. This permits thinking of noncash securities as consisting of future claims only.

A choice-theoretic structure under pure exchange, where time-state claims are both the objects of choice and the objects of trade, can now be formulated in analogy with the structure set forth in Chapter 4 for dated claims under certainty. Provisionally, probability beliefs are held constant for each individual, permitting the use of the preference function $u = u_{\Pi}$ expressed in terms of time-state claims in equation (1b). In Fig. 9-1, the function sketched is analogous to that in Fig. 8-8.

$$\left.\frac{\partial c_{1a}}{\partial c_0}\right|_u = \Upsilon(c_0, c_{1a}, c_{1b})$$

$$\left.\frac{\partial c_{1b}}{\partial c_0}\right|_u = \Upsilon(c_0, c_{1a}, c_{1b})$$

Time-state preference function
($2I$ equations)   (3)

Like the equations of similar form regularly encountered before, equations (3) define the marginal rates of substitution (m.r.s.) in consumption[3] between different pairs of the objects of choice. Each m.r.s. is the partial slope of the indifference shell at a specified (c_0, c_{1a}, c_{1b}) point. The m.r.s. in terms of the third pair, $\partial c_{1b}/\partial c_{1a}$, can, of course, be derived from the other two (and so is not an independent relation). There will be a pair of independent equations of form (3) for each of the I individuals in the economy.

$$c_0 + \phi_{1a}c_{1a} + \phi_{1b}c_{1b} = y_0 + \phi_{1a}y_{1a} + \phi_{1b}y_{1b}$$

Wealth constraint
(I equations)   (4)

The wealth constraint has a familiar form, c_0 having been chosen again as numeraire, with $\phi_0 = 1$. Thus the price ϕ_{1a}, or in more complete notation ϕ_{1a}^0, can be interpreted as the ratio ϕ_{1a}/ϕ_0. This is the amount of c_0 required

---

[2] Algebraically, the set of vectors C_0, C_{1a}, C_{1b} is a basis of the space of vectors of form (c_0, c_{1a}, c_{1b}).

[3] This terminology is retained for consistency with previous chapters. Note, however, that since states $1a$ and $1b$ are alternatives, the individual cannot actually *consume* both c_{1a} and c_{1b}. However, he can and generally will want to *hold* consumptive claims covering both contingencies.

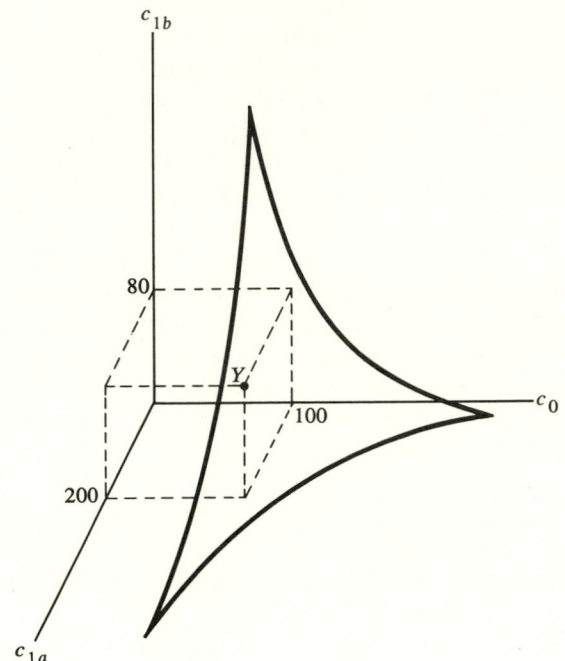

FIG. 9-1.   Utility function in terms of time-state claims

today to purchase a unit claim to consumption at $t = 1$, a claim effective if and only if state $1a$ obtains. ϕ_{1b} is interpreted similarly. Wealth is, of course, the market value of the endowment [the right-hand side of equation (4)]; it can be expressed in this form only if markets exist such that c_{1a} and c_{1b} are in fact exchangeable against c_0. In the geometrical illustration of Fig. 9-2, the constraint is the plane with intercepts 200, 666.7, and 400 on the c_0, c_{1a}, and c_{1b} axes, respectively. Wealth (in c_0-units) is, of course, the intercept of the plane on the c_0 axis.

$$
\begin{aligned}
\left.\frac{\partial c_{1a}}{\partial c_0}\right|_u &= -\frac{1}{\phi_{1a}} \\
\left.\frac{\partial c_{1b}}{\partial c_0}\right|_u &= -\frac{1}{\phi_{1b}}
\end{aligned}
\qquad
\begin{array}{l}
\text{Consumptive optimum condition} \\
\text{($2I$ equations)}
\end{array}
\qquad (5)
$$

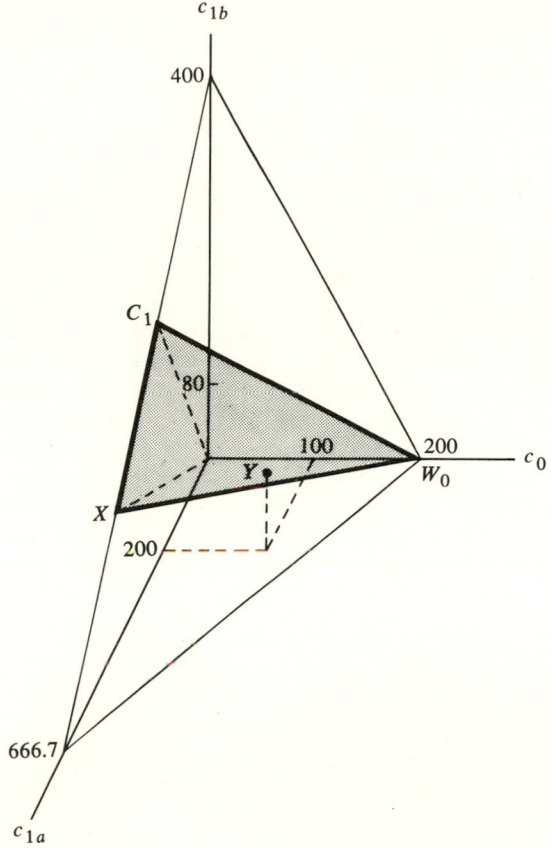

FIG. 9-2. Constraint plane in terms of claims or securities (complete markets)

The consumptive optimum conditions again have quite a familiar appearance. Finally, there are the conservation equations.

$$\begin{array}{l} \sum c_0 = \sum y_0 \\ \sum c_{1a} = \sum y_{1a} \\ \sum c_{1b} = \sum y_{1b} \end{array} \quad \text{Conservation relations (two independent equations)} \quad (6)$$

The summation is over the I individuals. The absence of productive opportunities dictates that the sum of the consumptions equals the sum of the endowments, for each time-state. As usual, one of the conservation relations can be shown to follow from the remainder of the system. Hence, there are $5I + 2$ independent relations to determine the variables c_0, c_{1a}, c_{1b}, $\partial c_{1a}/\partial c_0$, and $\partial c_{1b}/\partial c_0$ for each of the I individuals, and the two market variables ϕ_{1a} and ϕ_{1b}.

NUMERICAL EXAMPLE

Imagine a simple economy consisting of a large number I of identically situated individuals (the "representative-individual device") with one consumptive commodity (corn). Each individual has an endowment distributed as follows: 100 bushels of present corn (y_0), and contingent claims to the future crop $y_{1a} = 200$ (if the crop is bountiful—state a) and $y_{1b} = 80$ (if the crop is a meager one—state b). All individuals agree that the state probabilities are $\pi_{1a} = .6$ and $\pi_{1b} = .4$; in this example, the better-endowed future state happens also to be the more probable one. In a pure-exchange situation, it is impossible for individuals to change these endowments by planting of seed, carry-over of crop, or "consumption of capital"; individuals can modify their position only by trading. If, however, all individuals have identical beliefs and preferences (under the u_{II} formulation, their probability beliefs are incorporated within their utility functions) in addition to identical endowments and identical (null) productive opportunities, the markets must establish a set of "sustaining" prices such that each individual is satisfied to exactly hold his original endowment.

Let the utility function be, for every individual,

$$u = \ln\left(c_0 c_{1a}^{.6} c_{1b}^{.4}\right) \tag{2''}$$

In Fig. 9-1 we see an indifference shell from this function.[4] It may be noted, by taking sections of the function in planes along which c_0 is constant, that convex indifference curves between c_{1a} and c_{1b} are implied—this corresponds to risk-aversion in the sense introduced in Chapter 8, Section C. And if we consider the section in the 45° plane where $c_{1a} = c_{1b}\ (= c_1)$, we can see that normal convex (c_0, c_1) time-preference curvature is also implied for dated certain incomes.

---

[4] In the previous chapter, the numerical illustration employed the function $u = \log_{10}\left(c_0 c_{1a}^{.6} c_{1b}^{.4}/8\right)$. The formulation (2'') above represents a linear transformation of that function:

$$\log_{10}\left(\frac{c_0 c_{1a}^{.6} c_{1b}^{.4}}{8}\right) = \log_{10}\left(c_0 c_{1a}^{.6} c_{1b}^{.4}\right) - \log_{10} 8$$

$$= (\log_{10} e)\ln\left(c_0 c_{1a}^{.6} c_{1b}^{.4}\right) - \log_{10} 8$$

Since a cardinal utility function under the Neumann-Morgenstern postulates is defined only up to a linear transformation, we are really continuing to use the same function as in the previous chapter.

Since each individual's consumption pattern necessarily equals his endowment pattern, the market prices are found directly from (5)—the derivatives being taken at values of c_0, c_{1a}, and c_{1b} equal to the corresponding endowed quantities. In the numerical example employed here, the prices that sustain the endowment vector are $\phi_{1a} = .3$ and $\phi_{1b} = .5$.[5] Note that the claim to income in state b commands a higher price even though state a is more probable. The reason, of course, is that state a is relatively well endowed. The scarcity of income in state b serves to raise ϕ_{1b} over ϕ_{1a} despite the greater probability of state a.

Discount rates, risky and riskless

We can now reinterpret the prices ϕ_{1a} and ϕ_{1b} for the time-state claims in terms of *discount rates*, by analogy with the corresponding development in Chapter 4. That is, time-state discount rates r_{1a} and r_{1b} can be defined that reduce time-state claims to value equivalents in c_0-units.

$$\phi_{1a} = \frac{1}{1 + r_{1a}}$$
$$\phi_{1b} = \frac{1}{1 + r_{1b}} \tag{7}$$

In terms of these discount rates, wealth can be formulated as the *present certainty-equivalent value* of the endowment.

$$W_0 = y_0 + \frac{y_{1a}}{1 + r_{1a}} + \frac{y_{1b}}{1 + r_{1b}} \tag{8}$$

"Present certainty-equivalent value" is a generalization of the simple "present-value" concept under certainty.

These prices for time-1 states reflect an allowance for the futurity of the associated claims, as well as for their probability and scarcity. The time element may be isolated through the concept of a *riskless* discount rate in a world of uncertainty: that associated with the value of a unit riskless claim on future income. A riskless claim is a particular security (package of elementary time-state claims) of the form $C_1 = (0, 1, 1)$. The price of a future consumption unit free of uncertainty in this paradigm must be $\phi_1 = \phi_{1a} + \phi_{1b}$, for a future consumption unit can be assured, in a world of uncertainty, only by buying unit claims on each and every possible state for the given date. This leads directly to the definition of the riskless discount rate, or *pure rate of interest*, as r_1 in

$$\phi_1 = \frac{1}{1 + r_1} = \frac{1}{1 + r_{1a}} + \frac{1}{1 + r_{1b}} = \phi_{1a} + \phi_{1b} \tag{9}$$

[5] $-\dfrac{\partial c_{1a}}{\partial c_0}\bigg|_u = \dfrac{\partial u/\partial c_0}{\partial u/\partial c_{1a}} = \dfrac{c_{1a}}{.6c_0} = \dfrac{y_{1a}}{.6y_0} = \dfrac{200}{.6(100)} = \dfrac{1}{\phi_{1a}}$, whence $\phi_{1a} = .3$. The result for ϕ_{1b} is found in the same manner.

NUMERICAL EXAMPLE

In the illustration employed above, $\phi_{1a} = .3$ and $\phi_{1b} = .5$, hence $\phi_1 = .8$. The associated time-and-state discount rates are $r_{1a} = 2.33$ and $r_{1b} = 1$, while the pure rate of interest r_1 is 25 per cent.

By an extension of this idea, a general "risky" discount rate can be defined, which can be employed for discounting future income vectors that need not be identical over all states. Consider a particular risky security X with the income distribution over time-states $(0, x_{1a}, x_{1b})$. If X is traded in markets, its price, ϕ_X, must equal the value of its elementary component time-state claims:

$$\phi_X = x_{1a}\phi_{1a} + x_{1b}\phi_{1b} \tag{10}$$

Since we will want the risky discount rate to be applicable to all securities of the same *proportionate* pattern of state incomes (these are said to constitute a "risk class"), it will be convenient to normalize so as to deal with a *unit expectation* with the state-probability pattern of asset X, i.e.

$$\phi_{E\tilde{x}_1} = \frac{\phi_X}{E\tilde{x}_1} = \frac{x_{1a}\phi_{1a} + x_{1b}\phi_{1b}}{x_{1a}\pi_{1a} + x_{1b}\pi_{1b}} \tag{11}$$

where $E\tilde{x}_1$ is the expectation of future income x_1. Here $\phi_{E\tilde{x}_1}$ can be regarded as the price of the state distribution or income package $(0, x_{1a}/E\tilde{x}_1, x_{1b}/E\tilde{x}_1)$. The corresponding discount rate r_{1X} is given by

$$\frac{1}{1 + r_{1X}} = \phi_{E\tilde{x}_1} = \frac{1}{E\tilde{x}_1}\left(\frac{x_{1a}}{1 + r_{1a}} + \frac{x_{1b}}{1 + r_{1b}}\right) \tag{12}$$

The risky discount rate r_{1X} is "appropriate" for discounting the average returns of security X; i.e., applying this rate to the expectation $E\tilde{x}_1$ yields the correct market value of X:

$$\phi_X = \frac{E\tilde{x}_1}{1 + r_{1X}} \tag{13}$$

Evidently, the same r_{1X} would be applicable for all securities having the proportionate state distribution of future returns $x_{1a}:x_{1b}$. Note, however, that since individuals' probability beliefs (and thus their estimates of $E\tilde{x}_1$) may differ, the "risky" discount rate is in general a subjective calculation—not an objective market fact like the price ϕ_X, or the time-state discount rates r_{1a} and r_{1b}.[6]

[6] The riskless discount rate is also an objective market phenomenon, as is evident from equation (9). Note that this depends on the assumption that all individuals agree on the dichotomization of an uncertain future into the two states a and b.

Pursuing the illustration above, let a security X have the particular future-income vector $(x_{1a}, x_{1b}) = (10, 6)$. Since the prices of the elementary claims are $\phi_{1a} = .3$ and $\phi_{1b} = .5$, the value of the asset ϕ_X must [from equation (10)] be $3 + 3 = 6$. The state probabilities being $\pi_{1a} = .6$ and $\pi_{1b} = .4$, the expected income $E\tilde{x}_1 = 6 + 2.4 = 8.4$. Then the price of a unit expectation of income, with this proportionate state pattern, is [from equation (11)] $6/8.4$ or $.714$. From (12) or (13), we can determine the corresponding risky discount rate, appropriate for discounting expected returns of security X, to be $r_{1X} = 40$ per cent.

A risky discount rate is usually higher than the pure rate of interest. In the numerical illustration above, for example, $r_{1X} = 40$ per cent while the riskless rate, r_1, is 25 per cent. The reason is that the future-income vector $(10, 6)$ contributes proportionately more to less valuable time-state income c_{1a} than to the more valuable c_{1b}—while the riskless discount rate is associated with income vectors contributing equally to both. Thus the "package" $(10, 6)$ is less valuable than a certainty package $(8.4, 8.4)$ of the same expected return, and hence is discounted more heavily. While the language seems paradoxical, it is also quite possible for the discount rate on a "risky" package to be *lower* than the riskless or pure rate of interest—despite preference functions displaying risk-aversion. All that is required is that the risky package in question *pay off relatively heavily in the more highly valued state.*

Consider a security Z with the state vector of future returns $(6, 10)$—the reverse of the X vector of the previous example (holding the state probabilities the same, with $\pi_{1a} = .6$ and $\pi_{1b} = .4$). Since $\phi_{1a} = .3$ and $\phi_{1b} = .5$, the value ϕ_Z of this package is $1.8 + 5 = 6.8$. The expected income $E\tilde{z}_1$ of the package is $.6(6) + .4(10) = 7.6$. Then, from equation (11), $\phi_{E\tilde{z}_1} = .895$, so that the risky discount rate $r_{1Z} = 11.8$ per cent—*less* than the riskless rate of 25 per cent.

Of course there is no real puzzle. A risky (i.e., variable) package will be more desirable than a riskless (invariable) one with the same expectation of return, when the pattern of variation is such that the risky package yields higher income in the more valuable state.

Effect of changes in parameters

At this point, it would be possible to follow the path laid out in Chapter 4 so as to generate supply and demand curves for one or more of the goods c_0, c_{1a}, c_{1b}—or securities C_0, C_{1a}, C_{1b}—as functions of the various price ratios or discount rates that can be defined among the commodities. In particular, it would be possible to construct an excess-demand curve for current consumption c_0 as a function of $1/\phi_{1a}^0 = \phi_0/\phi_{1a}$, with ϕ_{1b} held constant; or as a function of $1/\phi_{1b}^0$ with ϕ_{1a} held constant; or as a function of ϕ_{1a} and ϕ_{1b} varying proportionately together; and so on. As these relationships are complex in detail while fairly obvious in principle, this development will be omitted. But it is interesting to see how the solution would be changed by modification of any of the exogenous data that determine the outcome.

For visibly displaying the analogy with the choice-theoretic structures of earlier chapters, the u_Π utility function (1b), defined in terms of the time-state claims as arguments and with probability estimates implicit rather than explicit, has been employed so far. However, when it comes to analysis of consequences of changes in exogenous data, the more explicit utility function (1a) based upon the "expected-utility rule," $u = Ev$, is more advantageous. In this form, the utility function for the paradigm of this chapter is

$$u = \pi_a v(c_0, c_{1a}) + \pi_b v(c_0, c_{1b}) \tag{1'}$$

And the key variables, the derivatives of the utility function that are equated to the reciprocals of the market prices in (5), can be expressed more explicitly (using a condensed v' notation for the derivatives of the v function) as

$$-\frac{\partial c_{1a}}{\partial c_0}\bigg|_u = \frac{\pi_a v_0'(c_0, c_{1a}) + \pi_b v_0'(c_0, c_{1b})}{\pi_a v_{1a}'(c_0, c_{1a})}$$
$$-\frac{\partial c_{1b}}{\partial c_0}\bigg|_u = \frac{\pi_a v_0'(c_0, c_{1a}) + \pi_b v_0'(c_0, c_{1b})}{\pi_b v_{1b}'(c_0, c_{1b})} \tag{14}$$

Combining (14) and (5), the sustaining prices can be expressed as

$$\phi_{1a} = \frac{\pi_a v_{1a}'(c_0, c_{1a})}{\pi_a v_0'(c_0, c_{1a}) + \pi_b v_0'(c_0, c_{1b})}$$
$$\phi_{1b} = \frac{\pi_b v_{1b}'(c_0, c_{1b})}{\pi_a v_0'(c_0, c_{1a}) + \pi_b v_0'(c_0, c_{1b})} \tag{15}$$

The utility function (1'), written in "separated" form as the expectation of values of a cardinal v function over different states, exemplifies the "independence postulate." This can also be interpreted as the assumption of zero complementarity in preference between the state incomes c_{1a} and c_{1b}:

$$\frac{\partial v_{1a}'}{\partial c_{1b}} = 0 = \frac{\partial v_{1b}'}{\partial c_{1a}}$$

That is, the marginal utility of future income in either state is independent of the amount scheduled for consumption in the other state.

It would be an equally important property, and of great analytical convenience, if zero complementarity *over dates* could also be assumed in the

v function for a given state, so that

$$\frac{\partial v_1'}{\partial c_0} = 0 = \frac{\partial v_0'}{\partial c_1}$$

This would be implied if the cardinal intertemporal elementary-utility function could also be written in "separated" form as

$$v(c_0, c_1) = v_0 + \frac{v_1}{1 + \eta}$$

Here v_0 and v_1 are dated preference-scaling functions for c_0 and c_1, respectively, while η is a constant "time-bias" parameter (it usually being assumed that $\eta > 1$). Note that η can be said to be a "discount rate for future utility." Unfortunately, there do not seem to be convincing grounds for justifying this hypothetical *time-independence* property of the intertemporal elementary-utility function.[7] However, zero time-complementarity is *consistent* with the required characteristics of the utility function; it may be thought of as an especially simple central case, illustrating particularly clearly the effects of changes in the exogenous data. Accordingly, in the discussion below both state-independence and time-independence will be assumed. Under this simplifying condition, equations (15) reduce to

$$\phi_{1a} = \frac{\pi_a v_{1a}'}{v_0'(1 + \eta)}$$

$$\phi_{1b} = \frac{\pi_b v_{1b}'}{v_0'(1 + \eta)} \tag{16}$$

---

[7] Up to now, the only restriction placed upon the time-preference function is that c_0 and c_1 are both superior goods. For superiority it is necessary that

$$\frac{\partial(dc_1/dc_0)}{\partial c_0} > 0 \qquad \text{and} \qquad \frac{\partial(dc_1/dc_0)}{\partial c_1} < 0$$

Now along the v function

$$\frac{dc_1}{dc_0} = \frac{-\partial v/\partial c_0}{\partial v/\partial c_1}$$

or in condensed notation $-v_0/v_1'$. Hence c_0 and c_1 will both be superior if $(-v_1'v_{00}'' + v_0'v_{01}'') > 0$ and $(-v_1'v_{01}'' + v_0'v_{11}'') < 0$. Since the marginal utilities v_1' and v_0' are both positive while the second derivatives v_{00}'' and v_{11}'' are ordinarily assumed to be negative, zero complementarity ($v_{01}'' = 0$) is consistent with c_0 and c_1 both being superior. However, positive cross-derivatives, or even mildly negative cross-derivatives, are also permissible if superiority is to be the only condition imposed.

NUMERICAL EXAMPLE

The utility function employed in the earlier examples, $\ln c_0 c_{1a}^{.6} c_{1b}^{.4}$, is in the u_{II} form of equation (1b). In the state-separated form of equation (1') this becomes $u = .6 \ln c_0 c_{1a} + .4 \ln c_0 c_{1b}$. And the intertemporal elementary-utility function $v(c_0, c_1) = \ln c_0 c_1$ has the time-independence property: it can be written as $v_0 + v_1/(1 + \eta)$, where $v_0 = \ln c_0$, $v_1 = \ln c_1$, and the parameter η equals unity.

The exogenous data for the pure-exchange problem are the *endowments* (distributed among individuals and, for each individual, over dates and states), the *elementary-utility functions*, and the *probability beliefs*. To facilitate

Table I

EFFECTS OF CHANGES IN EXOGENOUS DATA

	GENERAL			NUMERICAL EXAMPLE*		
	Direction of Change			Rates of Change (Elasticities)		
	ϕ_{1a}	ϕ_{1b}	ϕ_1	ϕ_{1a}	ϕ_{1b}	ϕ_1
A. *Increase in c_0-endowments*	Rise	Rise	Rise	.003 (+1)	.005 (+1)	.008 (+1)
B. 1. *Increase in c_{1a}-endowments*	Fall	0	Fall	−.0015 (−1)	0	−.0015
2. *Increase in c_{1b}-endowments*	0	Fall	Fall	0	−.00625 (−1)	−.00625
3. *Proportionate increase in c_{1a} and c_{1b} endowments*	Fall	Fall	Fall	−.0018	−.0030	−.0048 (−1)
C. *Increase in riskiness of endowments (gap between y_{1a} and y_{1b}), expectation unchanged.*	Fall[a]	Rise[a]	Rise[a,b]	−.00125	.00781	.00656
D. 1. *Reduction in time-discount rate for utility*	Rise	Rise	Rise	.3 (1)	.5 (1)	.8 (1)
2. *Increase in risk-aversion*	Fall[a]	Rise[a]	?	No numerical example		
E. *Change in beliefs (increase in probability for state a)*	Rise	Fall	Fall	+.5 (+1)	−1.25 (−1.5)	−.75 (−.562)

[a] Assuming $y_{1a} > y_{1b}$
[b] Assuming diminishing marginal risk-aversion ($v''' > 0$)
* *Conditions* Probabilities: $(\pi_a, \pi_b) = (.6, .4)$
  Utility function: $u = .6 \ln c_0 c_{1a} + .4 \ln c_0 c_{1b}$
  $= \ln c_0 + .6 \ln c_{1a} + .4 \ln c_{1b}$
  Initial endowment: $(y_0, y_{1a}, y_{1b}) = (100, 200, 80)$
  Initial prices: $\phi_{1a} = .3, \phi_{1b} = .5$

exposition, the illustration in terms of the numerical example of this chapter is integrated with the main text here. The left-hand side of Table 1 indicates generally how the sustaining prices will respond to changes in the exogenous data, while the right-hand side gives the particular numerical results. The discussion throughout employs the representative-individual device.

(A) An increase in c_0 endowments will tend to raise the prices of future claims ϕ_{1a} and ϕ_{1b} (and thus lower r_{1a} and r_{1b}, and indeed the entire structure of interest rates).[8] In the numerical example, $\partial\phi_{1a}/\partial c_0 = .003$ and $\partial\phi_{1b}/\partial c_0 = .005$.[9] Since $\phi_1 = \phi_{1a} + \phi_{1b}$, the rate of change of the price of a riskless future claim, $\partial\phi_1/\partial c_0$, is .008. Also, in this example the elasticities are unity.[10] That is, a 1 per cent rise in all c_0 endowments will increase the price of future time-state claims by 1 per cent.

Without the time-independence assumption, the expressions for $\partial\phi_{1a}/\partial c_0$ and $\partial\phi_{1b}/\partial c_0$ would involve the cross-derivative $v_{01}''(c_0, c_1)$. A negative sign for the cross-derivative (negative time-complementarity) could change the signs of the entire expressions. Thus, with sufficiently strong negative time-complementarity an increase in current endowment could actually decrease the prices of future claims. Essentially similar statements about the ambiguous direction of effect in the absence of the time-independence assumption could be made for the changes in exogenous data to be considered in the succeeding paragraphs. Henceforth, such qualifying statements will not be repeated explicitly.

(B) A proportionate combined increase of the *future* endowments would evidently tend in the opposite direction, reducing the prices of future claims. Under the simplifying assumption of time-independence, it can be seen from (16) that the increment of c_{1a} would affect only ϕ_{1a}, and the

---

[8] With state-independence and also time-independence, the general formulas [from equations (16)] are

$$\frac{\partial\phi_{1a}}{\partial c_0} = -\frac{\pi_a v_1' v_{00}''}{(1 + \eta)(v_0')^2} \quad \text{and} \quad \frac{\partial\phi_{1b}}{\partial c_0} = -\frac{\pi_b v_{1b}' v_{00}''}{(1 + \eta)(v_0')^2}$$

The probabilities and marginal utilities are all positive, while v_{00}'' is negative.

[9] For $\partial\phi_{1a}/\partial c_0$ the calculation uses the data: $\pi_a = .6$; $v_{1a}' = 1/c_{1a} = 1/y_{1a} = .005$; $v_0' = 1/c_0 = 1/y_0 = .01$; $v_{00}'' = -1/c_0^2 = -1/y_0^2 = -.0001$; and $\eta = 1$. Then

$$\frac{-.6(.005)(-.0001)}{(.01)^2} = .003$$

For $\partial\phi_{1b}/\partial c_0$, $\pi_b = .4$, and $v_{1b}' = 1/c_{1b} = 1/y_{1b} = \frac{1}{80} = .0125$. Then

$$\frac{-.4(.0125)(-.0001)}{(.01)^2} = .005.$$

[10] The elasticities are defined as

$$\frac{\partial\phi_{1a}/\partial c_0}{\phi_{1a}/c_0} \quad \text{and} \quad \frac{\partial\phi_{1b}/\partial c_0}{\phi_{1b}/c_0}$$

increment of c_{1b} would affect only ϕ_{1b}.[11] In the numerical example, $\partial\phi_{1a}/\partial c_{1a} = -.0015$, and $\partial\phi_{1b}/\partial c_{1b} = -.00625$. Using the differential expression

$$d\phi_1 = \frac{\partial\phi_{1a}}{\partial c_{1a}} dc_{1a} + \frac{\partial\phi_{1b}}{\partial c_{1b}} dc_{1b}$$

the weighted-average effect upon ϕ_1 of a proportionate change in c_{1a} and c_{1b} is about $-.0048$.[12] The elasticities are minus unity.[13] As the prices of future claims fall in consequence of the enhanced future endowments, the structure of interest rates will, of course, rise.

(C) Next, consider the effects of a change in the "riskiness" of the endowed future income distribution. The word "riskiness" may have a number of possible meanings. A shift in probabilities of the two states might be interpreted as affecting "riskiness," but this will be regarded as a change in *beliefs* (to be considered below). With given probabilities, an "increase in riskiness" may be interpreted as any modification of endowments that increases the absolute *gap* between y_{1a} and y_{1b} while leaving the expectation of future income unchanged. We can again use the differential relation $d\phi_1 = (\partial\phi_{1a}/\partial c_{1a}) dc_{1a} + (\partial\phi_{1b}/\partial c_{1b}) dc_{1b}$, but here the weighted-average effect on ϕ_1 does not have an unambiguous direction— since the changes dc_{1a} and dc_{1b} have opposite signs.[14] If, however, we can assume (in addition to the usual

---

[11] The general formulas derived from (16) are

$$\frac{\partial\phi_{1a}}{\partial c_{1a}} = \frac{\pi_a v''_{aa}}{v'_0(1 + \eta)} \quad \text{and} \quad \frac{\partial\phi_{1b}}{\partial c_{1b}} = \frac{\pi_b v''_{bb}}{v'_0(1 + \eta)}$$

Here v''_{aa} is condensed notation for the second derivative of $v_1(c_1)$ when $c_1 = c_{1a}$; v''_{bb} is defined analogously.

[12] For proportionate changes in the future endowments, $dc_{1b} = dc_{1a}(y_{1b}/y_{1a})$. And we would want to consider dc_{1a} and dc_{1b} of such sizes that their weighted average (taking y_{1a} and y_{1b} as weights) is unity. Then

$$dc_{1a} = \frac{y_{1a}(y_{1a} + y_{1b})}{y_{1a}^2 + y_{1b}^2} \quad \text{and} \quad dc_{1b} = \frac{y_{1b}(y_{1a} + y_{1b})}{y_{1a}^2 + y_{1b}^2}$$

It follows here that $dc_{1a} = \frac{70}{58}$ and $dc_{1b} = \frac{28}{58}$. Substituting in the expression for $d\phi_1$, we obtain the numerical value of approximately $-.0048$.

[13] The elasticities for separate changes in c_{1a} and c_{1b} are, respectively,

$$\frac{\partial\phi_{1a}/\partial c_{1a}}{\phi_{1a}/c_{1a}} \quad \text{and} \quad \frac{\partial\phi_{1b}/\partial c_{1b}}{\phi_{1b}/c_{1b}}$$

The elasticity for combined proportionate changes in c_{1a} and c_{1b} would naturally be defined as the same weighted average of the separate elasticities as $d\phi_1$ is of the separate derivatives. Since in the numerical example each of the separate elasticities is minus unity, their weighted average necessarily remains minus unity.

[14] By the condition that expected income remain unchanged, $\pi_a dc_{1a} + \pi_b dc_{1b} = 0$.

time-independence) that there is "diminishing marginal risk-aversion"—in the sense that the (negative) second derivative with respect to c_1 of the v function increases (becomes less negative) as c_1 rises[15]—then it can be shown that $d\phi_1 > 0$.[16] In the numerical example, $d\phi_1 = .00656$.[17] The common-sense interpretation is that an increase in the riskiness of future endowments is essentially like a decline in the effective quantity of c_1—hence it increases the price ϕ_1 (and thus lowers the pure rate of interest r_1).

(D) Turning now to *preferences* as exogenous data, there are both time preferences and risk preferences to consider. In general, these are bound up together in the shape of the $v(c_0, c_1)$ function. Under the simplifying assumption of time-independence, $v(c_0, c_1) = v_0 + v_1/(1 + \eta)$. Here η is the time-bias parameter, while risk preference is expressed by the shape of v_1 as a function of c_1.

For time preference, it is a little more convenient to think of changes in $1/(1 + \eta)$ rather than changes in η itself. Let $\beta = 1/(1 + \eta)$, where β bears the same relation to η as the price ϕ_1 bears to the discount rate r_1.

As is evident from equation (16), $\partial\phi_{1a}/\partial\beta$ and $\partial\phi_{1b}/\partial\beta$ will both be positive.[18] β, the parameter for valuing v_1 relative to v_0, will ordinarily be less than unity, and an *increase* in β is a *reduction* of utility time-discount. A reduction in the rate of discount of future utilities leads to an increase in the prices of future income claims, and thus to a fall in the entire structure of interest rates. In the numerical example, $\partial\phi_{1a}/\partial\beta = .3$ and $\partial\phi_{1b}/\partial\beta = .5$, so that $\partial\phi_1/\partial\beta = .8$. The elasticities are again unity.

Attitudes toward *risk* are indicated by the shape of the $v(c)$ function, and in particular its second derivative $v''(c)$. Risk-*aversion*, we have seen, is related to the negativity of v'' (concavity of the preference-scaling function). An increase in this concavity will then reduce the marginal utility $v'(c)$ for

---

[15] This condition, that $v_{111}''' > 0$, is implied by (but weaker than) diminishing marginal risk-aversion in Pratt's sense described in the previous chapter. Pratt's condition is $v''' > v''^2/v'$. We saw that Pratt's condition corresponded to the economic hypothesis that assets of all types are superior goods (the risk premium in the demand price of risky assets declines as income rises).

[16] Constant expectation of future income implies that $dc_{1b}/dc_{1a} = -\pi_a/\pi_b$. Fixing the order of magnitude of the differentials by the condition $\pi_a |dc_{1a}| + \pi_b |dc_{1b}| = 1$, we have $|dc_{1a}| = 1/(2\pi_a)$ and $|dc_{1b}| = 1/(2\pi_b)$. Assuming that $y_{1a} > y_{1b}$, we want $dc_{1a} > 0$ and $dc_{1b} < 0$ (to increase the "riskiness"). Substituting the differentials in the expression for $d\phi_1$:

$$d\phi_1 = \frac{\pi_a v_{aa}''}{v_0'(1 + \eta)} \frac{1}{2\pi_a} - \frac{\pi_b v_{bb}''}{v_0'(1 + \eta)} \frac{1}{2\pi_b}$$
$$= \frac{v_{aa}'' - v_{bb}''}{2v_0'(1 + \eta)}$$

Then $d\phi_1$ will be positive if v_{aa}'' exceeds (is less negative than) v_{bb}''. Since $y_{1a} < y_{1b}$ and $v_{111}''' > 0$, this condition does hold.

[17] Calculated from the differential expression for $d\phi_1$, where $dc_{1a} = \frac{5}{6}$ and $dc_{1b} = -\frac{5}{4}$. As before, $\partial\phi_1/\partial c_{1a} = -.0015$, while $\partial\phi_1/\partial c_{1b} = -.00625$.

[18] The general expressions are $\partial\phi_{1a}/\partial\beta = \pi_a v_{1a}'/v_0'$ and $\partial\phi_{1b}/\partial\beta = \pi_b v_{1b}'/v_0'$.

the better-endowed state relative to $v'(c)$ for the poorer-endowed state. If state a is better endowed, we can see from (16) that ϕ_{1a} will fall relative to ϕ_{1b}. Thus, an increase in marginal risk-aversion increases the relative premium on income in the poorer-endowed state. (No numerical example is provided for this case.)

(E) Finally, consider the consequences of a change in *beliefs*—i.e., in the probabilities π_a and π_b. As is evident from equation (16), a rise in π_a will increase ϕ_{1a} and (since $\pi_a + \pi_b = 1$) decrease ϕ_{1b}. As intuition confirms, the price of a certain future claim ϕ_1 will be reduced by a rise in the probability of the better-endowed relative to the poorer-endowed state (such a change makes future income more likely to be plentiful).[19] For the numerical example, $\partial\phi_{1a}/\partial\pi_a = .5$ and $\partial\phi_{1b}/\partial\pi_a = -1.25$, so that $\partial\phi_1/\partial\pi_a = -.75$. Here the elasticity of ϕ_{1a} with respect to π_a is again unity, but the elasticity of ϕ_{1b} with respect to π_a is -1.5; for ϕ_1, the elasticity is $-\frac{9}{16}$.

Production and Exchange

The rather full treatment provided for the pure-exchange regime above will permit a condensed discussion of the regime of exchange with production. The role of production will be assigned to the firm as in Chapter 4.

$$\left.\frac{\partial c_{1a}}{\partial c_0}\right|_u = \Upsilon_{1a}(c_0, c_{1a}, c_{1b})$$

$$\left.\frac{\partial c_{1b}}{\partial c_0}\right|_u = \Upsilon_{1b}(c_0, c_{1a}, c_{1b})$$

Time-state preference function
(*2I* equations)   (17)

$$c_0 + \phi_{1a}c_{1a} + \phi_{1b}c_{1b} = y_0 + \sum_{f=1}^{F} \epsilon_f W_0^f + \phi_{1a}y_{1a} + \phi_{1b}y_{1b}$$

Wealth constraint   (18)
(*I* equations)

$$\left.\frac{\partial c_{1a}}{\partial c_0}\right|_u = -\frac{1}{\phi_{1a}}$$

$$\left.\frac{\partial c_{1b}}{\partial c_0}\right|_u = -\frac{1}{\phi_{1b}}$$

Consumptive optimum
(*2I* equations)   (19)

The time-state preference function is unchanged from that employed for the pure-exchange analysis. The wealth constraint is modified (as in Chapter 4) to allow for augmentation of endowment by payout of present

[19] In differential form, $d\phi_1 = (\partial\phi_{1a}/\partial\pi_a)\,d\pi_a + (\partial\phi_{1b}/\partial\pi_b)\,d\pi_b$, where $d\pi_a = -d\pi_b$. From (16), taking $d\pi_a$ as positive, we see that $d\phi_1$ will be greater or less than zero according as $(v'_{1a} - v'_{1b})$ is greater or less than zero. If state a is better endowed, as assumed here, $v'_{1a} < v'_{1b}$ and $d\phi_1 < 0$.

worth of profits of the individual's ownership of firms (ϵ_f is his fractional share of the fth firm's profit as distributed over dates and states and W_0^f the present certainty-equivalent value of the firm). The equations for the individual consumptive optimum are in the usual form, as are the equations expressing the productive opportunities and the firm's productive optimum.

$$Q(q_0, q_{1a}, q_{1b}) = 0$$

$$\frac{\partial q_{1a}}{\partial q_0} = \omega_{1a}(q_0, q_{1a}, q_{1b})$$

$$\frac{\partial q_{1b}}{\partial q_0} = \omega_{1b}(q_0, q_{1a}, q_{1b})$$

Firm's productive opportunity
($3F$ equations)   (20)

$$\frac{\partial q_{1a}}{\partial q_0} = -\frac{1}{\phi_{1a}}$$

$$\frac{\partial q_{1b}}{\partial q_0} = -\frac{1}{\phi_{1b}}$$

Firm's productive optimum
($2F$ equations)   (21)

$$q_0 + q_{1a}\phi_{1a} + q_{1b}\phi_{1b} = W_0^f$$ Value of the firm
(F equations)   (22)

Equation (22) defines the net present certainty-equivalent value of the firm's productive combination, paid out as equity to owners as indicated in (18).

Finally, there are the conservation equations:

$$\sum c_0 = \sum y_0 + \sum q_0$$
$$\sum c_{1a} = \sum y_{1a} + \sum q_{1a}$$
$$\sum c_{1b} = \sum y_{1b} + \sum q_{1b}$$

Conservation relations
(two independent equations)   (23)

The consumptions (c's) and endowments (y's) are summed over the I individuals, while the firm inputs and outputs (q's) are summed over the F firms. As usual, one of the conservation relations can be derived from the rest of the system.

In all, there are $5I + 6F + 2$ independent equations to determine the individual variables $\partial c_{1a}/\partial c_0$, $\partial c_{1b}/\partial c_0$, c_0, c_{1a}, and c_{1b}; the firm variables $\partial q_{1a}/\partial q_0$, $\partial q_{1b}/\partial q_0$, q_0, q_{1a}, q_{1b}, and W_0^f; and the market prices ϕ_{1a} and ϕ_{1b}.

NUMERICAL EXAMPLE (see Table 2)

Table 2*

		Time-State Claims			Wealth
		c_0	c_{1a}	c_{1b}	W_0
Endowment	y_{ts}	100	200	80	181.0
Transformation	q_{ts}	−9.0	22.9	11.0	1.0
Optimum	$p_{ts} = c_{ts}$	91.0	222.9	91.0	182.0
Equilibrium prices	ϕ_{ts}	1	.245	.400	

* Conditions: Utility function $u = \ln c_0 c_{1a}{}^{.6} c_{1b}{}^{.4}$
Transformation opportunities: $2(100 + q_0)^2 + .2(200 + q_{1a})^2$
$+ .8(80 + q_{1b})^2 = 33{,}120$

Let the representative individual, with the same endowment $(y_0, y_{1a}, y_{1b}) =$ (200, 100, 80) and the same utility function as before, be the sole owner of a "representative firm" with productive-transformation opportunities expressed by the equation

$$2(100 + q_0)^2 + .2(200 + q_{1a})^2 + .8(80 + q_{1b})^2 = 33{,}120$$

Both the productive and the consumptive marginal rates of substitution must equal the price ratio in equilibrium:

$$\frac{\partial q_{1a}}{\partial q_0} = -\frac{1}{\phi_{1a}} = \frac{\partial c_{1a}}{\partial c_0} \quad \text{and} \quad \frac{\partial q_{1b}}{\partial q_0} = -\frac{1}{\phi_{1b}} = \frac{\partial c_{1b}}{\partial c_0}$$

But given the representative-individual and representative-firm conditions of this problem, for each time-state it must be the case that $c_{ts} = p_{ts} = y_{ts} + q_{ts}$. Then the slopes along the productive-transformation locus and along the preference map can be directly equated, leading to

$$\frac{4(100 + q_0)}{.4(200 + q_{1a})} = \frac{10 p_0}{p_{1a}} = \frac{10 c_0}{c_{1a}} = \frac{c_{1a}}{.6 c_0} = \frac{5 c_{1a}}{3 c_0}$$

or $6 c_0^2 = c_{1a}^2$, and

$$\frac{4(100 + q_0)}{1.6(80 + q_{1b})} = \frac{5 p_0}{2 p_{1b}} = \frac{5 c_0}{2 c_{1b}} = \frac{c_{1b}}{.4 c_0} = \frac{5 c_{1b}}{2 c_0}$$

or $c_0^2 = c_{1b}^2$. The numerical solution is $c_0 = 91.0$, $c_{1a} = 222.9$, and $c_{1b} = 91.0$. Thus, the individual has in effect (through the intermediary of his firm) invested 9.0 units of c_0, receiving in return an increase of 22.9 of c_{1a} and 11.0 of c_{1b}. The prices at the new equilibrium are $\phi_{1a} = .245$ and $\phi_{1b} = .400$. The reduced prices for the future claims (in comparison with the pure-exchange sustaining prices $\phi_{1a} = .3$ and $\phi_{1b} = .5$) reflect the increased quantities of those claims attained through the productive transformation. At these new prices, the wealth gain from the productive opportunity—the present certainty-equivalent value of the firm's transformation vector $(q_0, q_{1a}, q_{1b}) = (-9.0, 22.9, 11.0)$—is 1.0.

Investment and Financing Decisions

Within the paradigm of production and exchange, it will be of great interest to consider the *decision rules* to be followed in a world of uncertainty by the economic agent in: (1) choosing the scale of productive investment, and (2) determining the mode of financing (acquisition of the required c_0 input) for that investment. For the world of certainty and perfect markets, the *investment* decision was analyzed at length in Chapter 3; still in the world of certainty, the extension to imperfect markets was considered in Chapter 7. The *financing* decision received only passing reference in Part I, since in the world of certainty all methods of acquiring current claims for use in productive investment reduce to the same thing: e.g., equity shares and debt become equivalently certain claims. But under uncertainty, it is possible to acquire funds under a variety of different terms as to the partition of the riskiness and return associated with the productive investments engaged in. Hence, a significant new class of decision problems arises.

Investment decision rules

For investment decision purposes, it will be immediately evident that "present certainty-equivalent value" (*PCEV*), as used for example in equation (22), is the relevant generalization of the "present value" (*PV*) concept of the world of certainty. In either case, we are dealing with a wealth measure: the value in c_0 units, as determined in perfect (and complete) markets, of a set of present and future claims. Consequently, *PCEV* can serve as criterion for the generalization of the present-value rules discussed in Chapter 3.

In particular, the three equivalent versions of present-value rules (see Table 1 of Chapter 3) all have direct analogs here: (1) adopt that set of projects maximizing the *attained-wealth* of the economic agent (the PCEV of the time-and-state-distributed income stream attained as a result of productive investment); (2) adopt that set of projects maximizing the overall *wealth-gain* of the economic agent (the difference between the *PCEV* of the attained and of the endowed income streams); (3) adopt any project as an increment if and only if its separately calculated *PCEV* is positive. Note that the project can be considered as a kind of asset; its *PCEV* is then (under perfect and complete markets) simply the sum of the values of the associated claims, as in equation (2). As was the case for the *PV* measure, the *PCEV* valuations can be expressed by weighting the future claims by their respective prices (in the paradigm here considered, these would be ϕ_{1a} and ϕ_{1b} for state-a and state-b claims respectively) or by the associated discount factors [here, $1/(1 + r_{1a})$ and $1/(1 + r_{1b})$, respectively].

In practical discussions of investment decision rules in business or public-policy contexts, the usual approach has been to seek for each date t some *single* payments estimate and associated discounting factor for use in calculation of *PCEV*. Such a reduction to a "point estimate" at each date would not be at all necessary if the actual market prices ϕ_{ts} for the time-state claims were known. For there would then be no difficulty in maximizing *PCEV* in formulas like equation (22). But the heart of the problem is that *the time-state prices are not readily visible*, mainly because of the enormous number of different states of the world conceivable at any given date. So in practice some kind of simplified decision rule is indeed necessary.

There have been two main lines of attack on the problem: (a) the state-distribution of the possible payments s_t at time t could somehow be reduced to a certainty-equivalent as of that date, permitting the use of the riskless discount factor $1/(1 + r_t)$ in determination of the *PCEV*; or, (b) the mathematical expectation of the payment, Es_t, could be used with a discount rate appropriate to the "risk-class" of the investment. In the simple paradigm of choice among time-state claims (c_0, c_{1a}, c_{1b}) examined here, the relations between the prices of securities and the associated discount rates were shown above in equation (9) for the riskless case, and equation (13) for the risky discount rate.

While either line of attack can lead in principle to the same correct result, the informational gaps that are the source of the difficulty require in practice the employment of method (b) above. The basic idea can be expressed in the following prescription: If the *PCEV* for a project cannot be computed directly because the prices (and associated discount factors) for the time-state claims are unknown, it will suffice to use for each date the mathematical expectation of returns discounted by the "risky discount rate" associated with the risk-class in which the investment falls. Thus, the practical requirements are that an estimate of the mathematical expectation of return is available, that the project can be classified with others of the same proportionate time-state distribution of returns (the "risk-class"), and that the discount rate associated with that risk-class is known. While there may be errors committed on any of these scores, the third is the only one presenting *conceptual* difficulties. The idea here is that decision-makers evaluating a government power project, for instance, might reasonably consider it to fall in the same risk-class as all or some private power projects. The historical results of past power investments provide a basis for estimating the mathematical expectation of returns from current investment in comparable private projects, while the security markets that quote prices for bonds and equities provide information that can be used via equation (13) to infer how the market discounts these future expectations.

A government agency is considering a project requiring an input of 5 units of c_0 and yielding the returns distribution $(s_{1a}, s_{1b}) = (10, 6)$, where the state-probabilities are $\pi_{1a} = .6$ and $\pi_{1b} = .4$. The state-prices ϕ_{1a} and ϕ_{1b} are unknown. However, it is observed that a unit expectation of future return with the same proportionate distribution—i.e., a hypothetical security X' with $x'_{1a} = \frac{25}{21}$ and $x'_{1b} = \frac{15}{21}$—has value $\phi_{X'} = \frac{5}{7}$. In effect, then, from equation (13), $1 + r_{1X} = 1/(\frac{5}{7}) = \frac{7}{5}$—so that the risky discount rate for returns of this risk-class is 40 per cent. Hence the *PCEV* of the project in question is $-5 + \dfrac{.6(10) + .4(6)}{1.4} =$ $+1$, so that the project should be adopted.

Indeterminacy of debt-equity mix

In the paradigm of this chapter, trading among the claims c_0, c_{1a}, c_{1b} (or elementary securities C_0, C_{1a}, C_{1b}) suffices to provide "complete" markets—markets permitting exchanges among all the objects of choice entering into individuals' preference functions. There could also, it was recognized, be trading in complex securities (packages of the elementary time-state claims), constrained by the consideration that the value of any such package must equal the sum of the values of its elements. In analysis of the firm under uncertainty, it is usual to recognize the existence of at least two classes of complex securities: debt and equity. It will be of some interest to reinterpret the choice-theoretic structure to allow for these.

Let the aggregate time-state distribution associated with the debt securities issued by a particular firm be (d_0, d_{1a}, d_{1b}) and for the equity securities (e_0, e_{1a}, e_{1b}). It is not actually necessary here to detail the properties of these securities, but we can interpret the debt claims as "senior" (though not necessarily riskless) and the equity claims as "junior" claimants to the firm's prospective receipts (q_{1a}, q_{1b}). The firm obtains its aggregate current input q_0 by a mixture of debt and equity contributions:

$$q_0 = d_0 + e_0 \qquad \text{Firm's input balance}$$
$$\text{(F equations)} \qquad (24)$$

The contingent firm outputs are distributed as debt and equity payments:

$$q_{1a} = d_{1a} + e_{1a} \qquad \text{Firm's output balance}$$
$$q_{1b} = d_{1b} + e_{1b} \qquad \text{($2F$ equations)} \qquad (25)$$

Let us define the aggregate present certainty-equivalent values of the debt and equity securities in the usual way:

$$D_0 = d_0 + \phi_{1a}d_{1a} + \phi_{1b}d_{1b}$$
$$E_0 = e_0 + \phi_{1a}e_{1a} + \phi_{1b}e_{1b} \qquad \text{Values of debt and equity} \qquad (26)$$

Then it follows immediately, given the definition of W_0^f in (22), that

$$W_0^f = D_0 + E_0 \qquad \text{Modigliani-Miller equation[20]} \qquad (27)$$

The Modigliani-Miller equation asserts that the value of the firm, determined by its prospective payments stream [equation (22)], is a constant to which the sum of the values of its debt and equity claims must adapt. Note that the assumption of complete markets is crucial to this result, as is the absence of transaction costs and other external drains in the form of corporate or personal taxes, bankruptcy penalties, and so on. Only under this idealizing assumption do the individuals and firms together comprise a *closed system*, with no losses to the outside.[21]

In modifying the choice-theoretic system to incorporate debt and equity claims, one would need to add the $4F$ firm variables d_{1a}, d_{1b}, e_{1a}, e_{1b}. But there are just $3F$ new equations, (24) and (25). Thus the augmented system is *underdetermined*: no basis is provided for the determination of the proportions of debt as against equity claims that will be issued by firms. The question of debt-equity indeterminacy has been hotly debated by corporate-finance specialists as well as by theorists. Like equation (27), the conclusion of indeterminacy is dependent upon the special conditions of the model, in particular the "closed-system" assumption. Even within the model of complete markets, allowing for considerations such as taxes and bankruptcy penalties would presumably permit the determination of an optimal debt-equity mix for the firm, and a market equilibrium of debt and equity issues for all firms together. The conditions determining such an equilibrium will not be stated here. As will be seen below, however, the model of incomplete markets leads to a rather different conclusion as to debt-equity indeterminacy.

B. INCOMPLETE MARKETS FOR TIME-STATE CLAIMS

Securities in Complete and Incomplete Markets

The number of distinguishable contingencies even at a single date may be almost unimaginably great. Uncertainty will not normally take the form of a simple dichotomy like "good crop" versus "bad crop." It would quite commonly be better represented by a continuum of outcomes—an infinite number of possibilities—even with respect to one state-defining variable,

---

[20] F. Modigliani and M. H. Miller, "The Cost of Capital, Corporation Finance and the Theory of Investment," *American Economic Review*, **48** (June 1958), 268.

[21] A fuller treatment appears in J. Hirshleifer, "Investment Decision Under Uncertainty: Applications of the State-Preference Approach," *Quarterly Journal of Economics*, **80** (May 1966), 264–268.

and there may be an enormous number of such variables. With positive costs of establishing markets, we cannot suppose that claims to income under each distinguishable contingency will in actuality be separately traded. Rather, there will in general be trading only in a limited number of the instruments we call *securities*. The assumption in this section will be that a finite list of securities A, B, ..., Z exists, where any security X represents a defined quantum of income under each and every time-state contingency. This is still an idealization, in that uncertainty is supposed *not* to attach to the contingent return of a security, given the time-state that obtains. In the real world, even the knowledge that the crop is exactly K million tons may not entirely relieve uncertainty as to the payoff of a particular security—e.g., whether a particular agricultural firm will meet the payments due on its bonded debt. But our assumption here is that all individuals agree on the distribution of incomes over the various time-state contingencies represented by any given security.

In the analysis of the choice paradigm of the previous section (one state at $t = 0$, and only two at $t = 1$), it was assumed that trading could costlessly take place in any of the time-state claims c_0, c_{1a}, c_{1b}—or, equivalently, in the corresponding elementary securities C_0, C_{1a}, and C_{1b}. For complete markets within the paradigm of choice considered here, *any three* securities X, A, B whose associated payments vectors are linearly independent will suffice. That is, it must not be possible to find constants k_1 and k_2 such that $X = k_1 A + k_2 B$ (for any of the three securities considered as X).

NUMERICAL EXAMPLE

Figure 9-2 serves to illustrate complete market opportunities for trading among the following three securities: the elementary present claim or the "cash" security $C_0 = (1, 0, 0)$, with $\phi_0 = 1$ as usual; the future certainty security $C_1 = (0, 1, 1)$, with $\phi_1 = .8$; and another compound future security $X = (0, 3, 1)$, with $\phi_X = 1.4$. (These prices are consistent with the pure-exchange numerical illustration earlier, where the market prices of the elementary future time-state claims were $\phi_{1a} = .3$ and $\phi_{1b} = .5$.) Holdings n_0 of C_0 are represented by distances along the c_0 axis, and holdings n_1 and n_X of C_1 and X by distances along the indicated rays in the c_{1a}, c_{1b} plane. The numerical endowment of time-state claims $Y = (100, 200, 80)$, with an endowed wealth $W_0^Y = 100 + 200(.3) + 80(.5) = 200$, corresponds here to endowed *security holdings* $n_0^Y = 100$, $n_1^Y = 20$, $n_X^Y = 60$—with the same W_0 value (200) when calculated in terms of the prices $\phi_1 = .8$ and $\phi_X = 1.4$.

In Fig. 9-2 the shaded region shows the portion of the plane $W_0 = 200$ attainable by nonnegative holdings of C_0, C_1, and X. The individual need not be restricted, however, to nonnegative security holdings in seeking a preferred consumptive combination. Suppose, for example, that at the ruling prices his preferred consumptive vector $(c_0^*, c_{1a}^*, c_{1b}^*)$ in terms of time-state claims is $(100, 300, 20)$. This can be attained from the security endowment $n_0^Y = 100$, $n_1^Y = 20$, $n_X^Y = 60$ by trading 140 units of C_1 for 80 units of X, so as to end up with holdings $n_0 = 100, n_1 = -120, n_X = 140$. The negative holding may be regarded as "selling short," but not in the sense of selling something the individual does not possess. Rather, we can think of the individual as in a position to generate or "issue" units of the security C_1. In this example, his endowment of time-state claims provides him with the wherewithal to satisfy the purchasers of the "short" 120 units of C_1. Suppose state a obtains at time 1. Then the 140 units of X held provide $c_{1a} = 420$, of which only 120 need be deducted to satisfy the claims of the purchasers of C_1. If state b obtains, there are 140 units of c_{1b} with which to satisfy claims aggregating to 120.[22] It may be noted that in the simple (c_0, c_1) choice paradigm under certainty, "borrowing" (the exchange of future claims c_1 for current claims c_0) could similarly have been regarded as the "issuance" of a security or bond C_1—a title to future consumption. In either case, the only required limitation is that the issuing individual be in a position to fulfill the claims of the purchasers of securities—i.e., that the issuer's over-all position consist of nonnegative quantities of all the underlying objects of choice.

The existence of the three tradable securities C_0, C_1, and X in Fig. 9-2 thus suffices for completeness of markets with respect to the choice-objects c_0, c_{1a}, c_{1b}. With the natural restrictions that C_0 ("cash") will always be one of the securities, and that the other two yield returns in *future* time-states only (since any time-0 return could simply be deducted from the security price), the linear-independence condition reduces to a still simpler form. For then *any* two securities A and B in addition to C_0 would suffice for completeness, provided only that the future claims associated with A and B are not strictly proportional.[23]

Under complete markets, the endowment could always be expressed as an exact holding of securities—whether of C_0, C_{1a}, C_{1b} in the earlier discussion, or of C_0, C_1, X in the example above. Under incomplete markets, however, the endowment will not in general consist of an exact holding of securities. The individual's endowment may stem at least in part from his ownership of productive yet not necessarily marketable *assets*. His endowed time-state distribution may then be any nonnegative combination of c_0, c_{1a}, and c_{1b}—that is, any point in the positive octant of Fig. 9-2 (including the axes).[24]

NUMERICAL EXAMPLE

Suppose there is a single tradable security other than cash, specifically $C_{1a} = (0, 1, 0)$—that is, the elementary claim to income in time-state $1a$. Then,

---

[22] This could be regarded as "selling short" in the sense of "short hedging" on the commodity exchanges (where an individual is in a position to make physical delivery against his short position).

[23] Geometrically, with strict proportionality A and B would lie along the same ray from the origin, so any combinations of A and B must also be limited to that ray. Hence, not all combinations of choice-objects would be attainable.

[24] The assumption that the endowment must be expressible as an exact holding in terms of tradable securities has been commonly made in the portfolio-selection and capital-budgeting literatures; such an assumption may be quite inappropriate.

if $\phi_{1a} = .3$ as before, Fig. 9-3 indicates that the set of combinations attainable from the endowment by market trading between C_0 and C_{1a} is limited to the nonnegative portion of a line rather than of a plane in (c_0, c_{1a}, c_{1b}) space.[25]

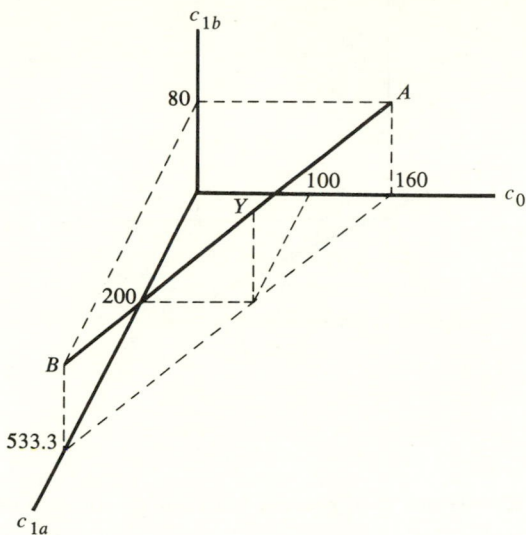

FIG. 9-3. Constraint line, trading between C_0 and C_{1a} only

Similarly, Fig. 9-4 indicates the line attainable when the single noncash tradable security is $C_1 = (0, 1, 1)$—that is, when only future certainties can be traded against present income—if $\phi_1 = .8$, as before.[26]

Incompleteness of markets, like the imperfection of markets studied in Chapter 7, prevents an unambiguous determination of *wealth* W_0 as a present certainty-equivalent value of discounted future payments. There will still in general be a "realizable wealth" or "liquidation value"—the net market value in C_0 units of the marketable securities owned, less those issued by, the individual. But this realizable wealth does not summarize all the time-state income claims over which the individual has command. Inability to convert all contingent incomes into a common unit of measure means that a general utility-free criterion for investment decisions, such as the present-value rule of Chapter 3, is not available. The consequences for investment choice are more or less analogous to those investigated in Chapter

[25] The geometrical construction is based upon an endowment vector $Y = (100, 200, 80)$. With $\phi_{1a} = .3$, the attainable line connects the points $A = (160, 0, 80)$ and $B = (0, 533.3, 80)$.

[26] The geometrical construction is again based upon the endowment vector $Y = (100, 200, 80)$. With $\phi_1 = .8$, the attainable line connects the points $A' = (164, 120, 0)$ and $B' = (0, 325, 205)$.

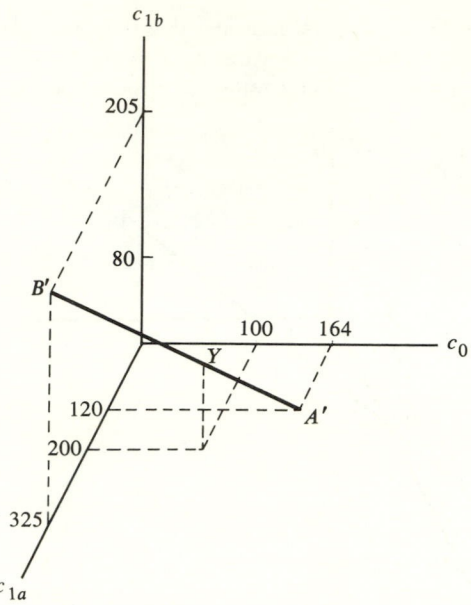

FIG. 9-4. Constraint line, trading between C_0 and C_1 only

7. In addition, of course, incompleteness of the system of markets will affect the equilibrium prices of those securities that are traded.

Equilibrium and Social Loss in Incomplete Markets

The choice-theoretic structure determining market equilibrium under pure exchange—when some single specified security X is the only tradable instrument aside from the "cash" security C_0—will now be set down.

$$\left.\frac{\partial c_{1a}}{\partial c_0}\right|_u = \Upsilon_{1a}(c_0, c_{1a}, c_{1b})$$

$$\left.\frac{\partial c_{1b}}{\partial c_0}\right|_u = \Upsilon_{1b}(c_0, c_{1a}, c_{1b})$$

Time-state preference function
($2I$ equations)   (28)

$$c_0 + n_X \phi_X = y_0$$

$$c_{1a} - n_X x_{1a} = y_{1a}$$

$$c_{1b} - n_X x_{1b} = y_{1b}$$

Market constraints
($3I$ equations)   (29)

The time-state preference functions are unchanged. But under in-complete markets the market opportunities are not bound by a single-equa-tion wealth constraint, it being no longer possible to unambiguously deter-mine "wealth." In (29), n_X represents the number of units held of the security $X = (0, x_{1a}, x_{1b})$—where, as we have seen, n_X can take on positive or negative values (so long as the attained combination of time-state claims remains within the positive octant).

The consumptive optimum condition is that an appropriately *weighted* *sum* of the inverted marginal rates of substitution equal the price of the security X.[27]

$$\left.\frac{-\partial c_0}{\partial c_{1a}}\right|_u x_{1a} + \left.\frac{-\partial c_0}{\partial c_{1b}}\right|_u x_{1b} = \phi_X \qquad \begin{array}{l}\text{Consumptive optimum}\\ (I \text{ equations})\end{array} \qquad (30)$$

Finally, the conservation equations may be expressed in terms of hold-ings of current claims c_0 and securities n_X. For the latter, the net sum must be zero—i.e., the number of units "issued" must equal the number purchased. (This form of the conservation condition results from having the endowments expressed only as state-claim totals c_0, c_{1a}, c_{1b}, and not as holdings of securities; any securities sold then have to be generated or "issued" out of the endowed state claims.) As usual, one of the conservation equations is redundant.

$$\begin{array}{l}\sum c_0 = \sum y_0 \qquad \text{Conservation relations}\\ \sum n_X = 0 \qquad \text{(one independent equation)}\end{array} \qquad (31)$$

[27] This equation follows from the usual Lagrangian procedure for maximizing utility subject to all three of the constraints (29).

$$\mathscr{L} = u(c_0, c_{1a}, c_{1b}) - \lambda_1(y_0 - c_0 - n_X\phi_X) - \lambda_2(y_{1a} - c_{1a} + n_X x_{1a})$$
$$- \lambda_3(y_{1b} - c_{1b} + n_X x_{1b})$$

$$\frac{\partial \mathscr{L}}{\partial c_0} = \frac{\partial u}{\partial c_0} + \lambda_1 = 0$$

$$\frac{\partial \mathscr{L}}{\partial n_X} = \frac{\partial u}{\partial c_{1a}}\frac{dc_{1a}}{dn_X} + \frac{\partial u}{\partial c_{1b}}\frac{dc_{1b}}{dn_X} + \lambda_1\phi_X + \lambda_2\left(\frac{dc_{1a}}{dn_X} - x_{1a}\right) + \lambda_3\left(\frac{dc_{1b}}{dn_X} - x_{1b}\right)$$

$$= \frac{\partial u}{\partial c_{1a}}x_{1a} + \frac{\partial u}{\partial c_{1b}}x_{1b} + \lambda_1\phi_X = 0$$

Then

$$\lambda_1 = -\frac{\partial u}{\partial c_0}$$

$$\phi_X\frac{\partial u}{\partial c_0} = \frac{\partial u}{\partial c_{1a}}x_{1a} + \frac{\partial u}{\partial c_{1b}}x_{1b}$$

$$\phi_X = \frac{-\partial c_0}{\partial c_{1a}}x_{1a} + \frac{-\partial c_0}{\partial c_{1b}}x_{1b}$$

In all there are $6I + 1$ independent equations to determine the individual variables $\partial c_{1a}/\partial c_0$, $\partial c_{1b}/\partial c_0$, c_0, c_{1a}, c_{1b}, and n_X, and the single market variable ϕ_X.

NUMERICAL EXAMPLE

Under pure exchange, consider the case where the single noncash security X is $C_1 = (0, 1, 1)$—i.e., only future certainty claims can be traded against cash. We cannot see the effect of the resultant impairment of trading while employing the simplifying representative-individual assumption used above, with $(y_0, y_{1a}, y_{1b}) = (100, 200, 80)$. In such a situation no actual trading takes place, prices always adjusting to sustain the endowment vector.[28] Let us assume instead that there are equally numerous individuals of types j and k. The j-individuals have endowments $(y_0^j, y_{1a}^j, y_{1b}^j) = (200, 0, 0)$, while for the k-individuals $(y_0^k, y_{1a}^k, y_{1b}^k) = (0, 400, 160)$. Thus, the aggregate social totals remain unchanged from the earlier example. Given that the utility functions all remain the same, with $u = \ln c_0 c_{1a}^{.6} c_{1b}^{.4}$, under complete markets it is evident that the equilibrium prices would remain $\phi_{1a} = .3$ and $\phi_{1b} = .5$ as before. Both classes of individuals would then have wealth of 200 and would thus both attain the former optimum at $(100, 200, 80)$. But now the markets are incomplete. To meet their desires for future consumption, the j-individuals must buy equal amounts of c_{1a} and c_{1b}—while the k-individuals in acquiring c_0 can only sell their future state-holdings in this same $1:1$ proportion.

The numerical result may be obtained as follows. Note that $x_{1a} = x_{1b} = 1$ in equation (30), if certainty claims only may be traded. At any given price ϕ_X, the j-individuals (who must buy X to provide for their future consumption) will purchase just enough to make the equality in (30) hold. And at each price ϕ_X, the k-individuals (who must "issue" X to obtain funds for current consumption) will sell just enough so that the equality in (30) holds for them as well. The conservation relations (31) are satisfied at the price $\phi_X \doteq .9439$. Supply-demand balance occurs when, at this price, the k-individuals issue some 105.94 units of X while the j-individuals are just willing to purchase the same quantity. The payment made, in exchange, is just 100 units of c_0. Note that .9439 rather higher than the price .8 determined under complete markets.[29] The implied "pure rate of interest" defined in the relation $\phi_1 = 1/(1 + r_1)$ is about 5.94 per cent as compared with 25 per cent under complete markets. The optimal consumptive position for the j-individuals is $(100, 105.94, 105.94)$ and for the k-individuals is $(100, 294.06, 54.06)$. In utility terms, the k-individuals (holders of future claims) have benefited from the restrictions on trading, but the j-individuals (holders of current claims) have lost an even greater amount.[30]

---

[28] Under these circumstances ϕ_1 would necessarily remain .8, the price of a future certainty claim under complete markets.

[29] If the price were the same $\phi_1 = .8$ as under complete markets, j-individuals could sell 100 units of c_0 for 125 each of c_{1a} and c_{1b}. But this would leave the k-individuals with only 35 units of c_{1b}; the utility function is such that they would demand a much higher price for C_1 before letting c_{1b} fall to such a level. At higher prices, however, the k-class individuals become relatively wealthier, so that the final outcome favors them.

[30] That the loss to the j-individuals is "objectively" greater than the gain to the others can be shown in terms of the increments and decrements of c_0 (or of either of the other objects of choice) necessary to restore the two classes to the previous utility levels.

The new equilibrium is obviously not Pareto-optimal; opportunities for mutually advantageous trade remain. However, this conclusion neglects the cost of establishing and operating markets. When these costs are considered as well, we cannot be sure that the incomplete-markets equilibrium is socially inefficient.

Reconsideration of the "Optimal-Finance" Problem

Under complete markets, and making the usual "closed-system" assumption, we saw in the first part of this chapter that there was no unique optimum mode of financing an investment or a firm. No matter how invest-ment funds are obtained on the securities markets (i.e., no matter what mixtures of securities are issued as titles to the contingent income streams associated with the returns from investment), arbitrage assures that under complete markets the sum of the market values of the securities must equal the present certainty-equivalent value of the income stream.[31]

Under incomplete markets, however, it will not in general be the case that marginal rates of substitution of the different contingent claims are equated among individuals. Compare equations (19)—which indicate that under complete markets

$$\left.\frac{-\partial c_0}{\partial c_{1a}}\right|_u = \phi_{1a} \quad \text{and} \quad \left.\frac{-\partial c_0}{\partial c_{1b}}\right|_u = \phi_{1b}$$

for every individual—with equation (30), which states a weaker condition for incomplete markets (with cash C_0 and X the only securities traded):

$$x_{1a} \left.\frac{-\partial c_0}{\partial c_{1a}}\right|_u + x_{1b} \left.\frac{-\partial c_0}{\partial c_{1b}}\right|_u = \phi_X$$

NUMERICAL EXAMPLE

In the example under a system of complete markets, the absolute (inverted) marginal rates of substitution $-\partial c_0/\partial c_1$ and $-\partial c_0/\partial c_{1b}$ for every individual were equal to the respective prices $\phi_{1a} = .3$ and $\phi_{1b} = .5$. But under incomplete markets, while the weighted sum is equal to $\phi_X = .9439$ for each individual, the separate marginal rates of substitution differ. In particular, $-\partial c_0/\partial c_{1a}$ is equal to .5664 for the j-individuals but .2040 for the k-individuals, while $-\partial c_0/\partial c_{1b}$ equals .3776 and .7399 for the two classes, respectively.

Under incomplete markets it will be possible to "tailor" the set of securities issued so as to meet the needs of distinct classes of investors—to take advantage of the divergences in marginal rates of substitution brought

---

[31] The statement above is a generalized version of equation (27), which concerned the special case of just two securities ("debt" and "equity").

about by the constraints on trading. In the absence of any costs associated with the issuance of securities, it will always be optimal to issue a complete set of elementary securities (e.g., C_{1a} and C_{1b} in the example above).[32] But this will require as many securities as there are distinct elementary time-state claims. In practice, therefore, it would be necessary for any firm to compromise on a relatively small number of securities (in comparison with the enormous number of distinguishable "states of the world"). The aggregate effect of such compromises by all firms will in general still leave open possibilities on the margin for profitable "financing" decisions—security combinations issued to provide funds for investment. Hence we must conclude that the Modigliani-Miller proposition about the absence of a financing optimum is valid only for the idealized case of complete markets.

NUMERICAL EXAMPLE

Suppose that a firm, having access to a single discrete productive opportunity, enters our previous pure-exchange economy. Let its productive opportunity be such that 1.1 units of c_1 could be obtained, with certainty, for a sacrifice of one unit of c_0. In our numerical example under complete markets, where $\phi_1 = .8$ (the riskless interest rate $r_1 = 25$ per cent), this would not have been profitable. But in the same example with incomplete markets the opportunity is a profitable one. If, to begin with, only cash C_0 and certainty claims C_1 were being traded, the firm could finance the investment by selling the 1.1 units of C_1 at the previous equilibrium price $\phi_1 = .9439$,[33] thus reaping a profit of $1.0383 - 1 = .0383$.

Let us now suppose instead that this firm contemplates generating one or more *new types* of securities. Evidently, the firm would reap maximal gain if it were to issue 1.1 of C_{1a} and 1.1 of C_{1b}. The C_{1a} would be sold to the j-individuals (for whom $-\partial c_0/\partial c_{1a}|_u = .5664$), the C_{1b} to the k-individuals (for whom $-\partial c_0/\partial c_{1b}|_u = .7399$). The aggregate profit would then be $1.1(.5664 + .7399) - 1 = .4369$.

C. GENERALIZATIONS AND CONCLUSIONS

The theory of decision under uncertainty developed in this chapter has perhaps been surprising in one respect: it entirely excludes the "vagueness" we usually associate with uncertainty. Uncertainty here has not taken the form of vague ignorance, but rather of quite precise beliefs. The contrast with models of choice under certainty is simply that the beliefs dealt with assign nonzero probability to more than one conceivable state of the world.

[32] Or, *any* set of securities whose returns vectors span the entire space of time-state incomes.

[33] It is assumed that the opportunity is of such a limited scale that prices are not substantially affected.

We may call this a model of "precise uncertainty"; as such, it lacks psychological verisimilitude to the ignorance, confusion, and doubt that represent our feeling of "vague uncertainty" about the nature of the world and our knowledge of it.

In order to analyze, we must simplify and idealize. What is the nature of the idealization represented by a model of "precise uncertainty"? Individuals need not have identical beliefs as to the probabilities of occurrence of the various states. But each individual must know in advance the nature of his own entitlement—i.e., his state-distributed endowment. Also, he must know the state-distributed consumption vectors attainable through his productive and market opportunities. This implies, among other things, that he knows the state-distributions of claims associated with any security in which he might trade—a strong assumption![34]

Employing the model of precise uncertainty, a crucial distinction was made in the chapter between a system in which markets are *complete*—i.e., where every recognized object of choice (time-state claim) can be exchanged in markets—and one in which markets are *incomplete*. The assumption of complete markets leads to a natural generalization of Fisher's analytical structure—including, in particular, the Separation Theorem leading to wealth as an objective investment-decision criterion. But once it is realized how unimaginably numerous is the set of all distinguishable states of the world, and that markets cannot be provided without cost, we are forced to the realization that in the real world markets will necessarily be incomplete. Then, time-state claims will be tradable only through a limited number of the contingent-income combinations we call *securities*.

The key conclusions can be set down as generalizations of equations (19) and (30) above. With S states at each future date and T future periods, the optimum condition under pure exchange with complete markets becomes

$$\left. \frac{-\partial c_0}{\partial c_{ts}} \right|_u = \phi_{ts} \qquad (t = 1, \ldots, T; \; s = a, \ldots, S) \qquad (32)$$

Thus, the individual will choose (within his wealth constraint) a vector of time-state claims $(c_0; c_{1a}, \ldots, c_{1S}; \ldots; c_{Ta}, \ldots, c_{TS})$ such that for every c_{ts} the inverted marginal rate of substitution in consumption between c_0 and c_{ts} equals in absolute value the price of c_{ts} in c_0 units.[35] And of course the market-clearing or conservation conditions $\sum c_0 = \sum y_0$ and $\sum c_{ts} = \sum y_{ts}$ assure that the prices must be such that the individuals are willing in the aggregate to hold the endowed totals of all claims.

[34] Analogous, however, to the assumption in standard price theory that the individual is aware of the cost and utility associated with all attainable combinations of commodities.

[35] If we were to allow the possibility of a corner solution (zero holdings) for one or more of the claims, the condition $-\partial c_0/\partial c_{ts} < \phi_{ts}$ would hold when $c_{ts} = 0$.

The introduction of production (modification of endowments via physical transformations) would dictate the alteration of this system in familiar ways; there would be for each individual a productive as well as a consumptive optimum, the former being governed by a wealth-maximization criterion. If firms are the productive agents, the firm's objective under complete markets remains wealth maximization—where wealth is the aggregate market value (a discounted present certainty-equivalent value) of the produced income stream. Finally, under complete markets and in the absence of external drains such as taxes, all modes of financing investments are equivalent. All possible sets of claims to the firm's income streams have the same wealth value, so there is no "financing optimum."

In the more realistic case of incomplete markets, the ultimate objects of choice (the time-state claims) are tradable only via a limited set of securities. Then, generalizing the condition (30), which applied for the simplified case of just one noncash security X, to the situation in which a list of noncash securities $A, B, \ldots, Z$ are traded, we have

$$\left.\frac{-\partial c_0}{\partial c_{1a}}\right|_u x_{1a}^A + \cdots + \left.\frac{-\partial c_0}{\partial c_{1S}}\right|_u x_{1S}^A + \cdots + \left.\frac{-\partial c_0}{\partial c_{Ta}}\right|_u x_{Ta}^A + \cdots$$

$$+ \left.\frac{-\partial c_0}{\partial c_{TS}}\right|_u x_{TS}^A = \phi_A$$

$$\left.\frac{-\partial c_0}{\partial c_{1a}}\right|_u x_{1a}^Z + \cdots + \left.\frac{-\partial c_0}{\partial c_{1S}}\right|_u x_{1S}^Z + \cdots + \left.\frac{-\partial c_0}{\partial c_{Ta}}\right|_u x_{Ta}^Z + \cdots$$

$$+ \left.\frac{-\partial c_0}{\partial c_{TS}}\right|_u x_{TS}^Z = \phi_Z$$

(33)

As in (32), the derivatives are inverted marginal rates of substitution in consumption between c_0 and c_{ts}, each being a function as before of the entire consumptive vector $(c_0; c_{1a}, \ldots, c_{1S}; \ldots; c_{Ta}, \ldots, c_{TS})$. The individual chooses, among all the vectors attainable via his limited trading opportunities, so as to have the weighted sum of these marginal rates of substitution equal the market price of any security he holds.[36] And, of course, the conservation conditions assure that the security prices adjust to permit the quantities issued to equal the quantities held of each.

It may be noted that, for a given list of tradable securities, this system shows the determination of both the quantities of securities traded (issued) and their market prices. However, the consumptive optimum depends not merely upon the holdings of tradable combinations in the form of securities, but rather upon the over-all time-state entitlement vector—including, in general, both tradable and nontradable time-state claims, and allowing for

[36] Again, for a security X not held at all, the corresponding equality in (33) is replaced by an inequality whereby the weighted sum on the left is less than the market price ϕ_X.

the fulfillment of all "short" positions in contingent trades. It thus follows also that wealth maximization is not in general the appropriate productive optimum condition for the firm or the individual—if by wealth we mean the *market* value in numeraire (c_0) units of the time-state entitlement. The individual (or the firm that he owns) may be in a position to generate time-state vectors that are highly desired even though not completely tradable. Thus, for incomplete markets it is the case (as it was in general for imperfect markets) that the productive optimum solution cannot be entirely segregated from the consumptive optimum. We might expect to see firms with particular types of productive opportunities owned by individuals whose tastes and endowments were suited to the types of contingent returns generated (i.e., there will be a "clientele effect"). It follows also that there will be in general a "financing optimum": given the firm's produced vector of time-state incomes, there will be some particular set of securities issuable by the firm that will optimize the position of the original owners.

Finally, even this more general choice-theoretic structure involving incomplete markets fails to provide any explanation of *how many* security markets will be set up, and *just which* possible time-state income combinations will constitute members of the set of tradable securities. The solution to this problem would require us to face squarely the problem of transaction costs, a task not attempted in this study. For in the absence of such costs there would be no barrier to having complete markets. Nor would there be any reason for markets to be imperfect. Thus we see that incompleteness of markets—the existence of nontradable time-state claims—and imperfection of markets—divergences between buying and selling prices—are both responses to the fact that exchange is not the costless process assumed in standard theoretical presentations.

BIBLIOGRAPHIC NOTE

The original formulation of the state-preference approach, in an atemporal context, appeared in an article in French by Kenneth J. Arrow. A later English translation will be cited here:

K. J. ARROW, "The Role of Securities in the Optimal Allocation of Risk-Bearing," *Review of Economic Studies*, **31** (April 1964).

The extension of this model of uncertainty to choices over time is due to Gerard Debreu:

G. DEBREU, *Theory of Value* (John Wiley & Sons, Inc., 1959), Chap. 7.

The significance of the problem of incomplete markets for time-state claims was recognized and emphasized by Karl Borch, for whom a more recent work will be cited:

K. BORCH, *The Economics of Uncertainty* (Princeton Univ. Press, 1968), Chap. 8.

Expositions and applications of the time-state formulation are provided in:

J. HIRSHLEIFER, "Investment Decision Under Uncertainty: Choice-Theoretic Approaches," *Quarterly Journal of Economics*, **79** (Nov. 1965), and "Investment Decision Under Uncertainty: Applications of the State-Preference Approach," *Quarterly Journal of Economics*, **80** (May 1966).

Recent work has emphasized further the significance of the problem of incomplete markets:

STEWART C. MYERS, "A Time-State-Preference Model of Security Valuation," *Journal of Financial and Quantitative Analysis*, **3** (March 1968).

PETER A. DIAMOND, "The Role of a Stock Market in a General Equilibrium Model with Technological Uncertainty," *American Economic Review*, **57** (Sept. 1967).

10 INVESTMENT AND INTEREST UNDER UNCERTAINTY: MEAN AND STANDARD-DEVIATION AS OBJECTS OF CHOICE

In the previous chapter, claims to income (consumption) sequences under alternative contingent time-state configurations were taken to be the objects of choice. As we have seen, this specification is a natural extension into the domain of uncertainty of Fisher's formulation of the objects of choice as alternative *certain* sequences of income over time. Despite its analytical attractiveness, this "time-state-preference" formulation has not as yet been successfully applied in empirical research. The central empirical question in this field is to explain the relationships that exist among the prices (or, equivalently, among the yields) of the various types of securities found on the capital markets: e.g., the relationship between the prices of more and less "risky" securities. It is premature to rule out the possibility of fruitful empirical researches founded upon time-state preference. But the absence of a natural, agreed-upon, and *manageably small* set of state definitions puts severe obstacles in the way of interpreting data about observable security behavior in terms of underlying choices for sequences of time-state claims.

In this chapter an alternative line of approach to the problem of risky choice over time will be considered. As in the time-state formulation, the underlying objects of choice will represent a *reduction* of the observed com-modities traded in markets—securities—to more fundamental entities that (it is hypothesized) enter into individuals' preference functions. The more fundamental entities here are taken to be the statistical parameters (in particular, the mean and standard-deviation) of the probability distributions of income that might be obtained by holding alternative combinations (portfolios) of securities. Under the time-state formulation, each security

277

was regarded as a package of elementary time-state claims. Here a security will be regarded as a title to uncertain income with particular statistical properties. In either formulation, it is not the characteristics of securities in isolation that are relevant, but rather the contributions of securities to over-all portfolio parameters and, ultimately, to over-all income (consumption).

Why is it necessary to reduce securities to more fundamental objects of choice? Why not treat securities themselves as objects of choice akin to the commodities of ordinary price theory? It would indeed be just as possible to construct utility functions for security packages—from the underlying Neumann-Morgenstern preference-scaling or elementary-utility function $v(c)$ or, in intertemporal form, $v(c_0, c_1, \ldots, c_T)$, introduced in Chapter 8—as it is to construct utility functions for packages of time-state claims, or for packages of income with particular statistical properties. The objection to such a "security-preference" approach is that we do not want to take the list of securities in existence at a moment of time as a fixed framework (at least on the social level of analysis). A given physical aggregate of time-state claims, for example, may be divided and marketed ("financed") in various security forms—as can a probability distribution of physical income with particular statistical parameters. The reductionist approach here and in the previous chapter in effect asserts that the current list of securities marketed is merely accidental, that the more fundamental objects of choice could equally well be packaged into many alternative security combinations. This is not really a satisfactory assumption, but it does seem closer to the mark than taking the existing list of securities as a rigid pattern into which individual preferences for various types of incomes under uncertainty must be forced. Ultimately, of course, the list of securities in existence should be treated as neither an arbitrarily fixed framework nor as a merely accidental partitioning of more fundamental income claims—but rather as itself the result of optimizing choice. But, as we have seen in Chapter 9, this problem cannot be solved without directly facing the difficult issue of transaction costs—which presumably determine the numbers and types of securities for which it pays to create markets.

As in the previous chapter, the initial discussion here will develop the analytical structure for risky but *timeless* choices. After a review of usual current formulations that run in terms of pure exchange and fixed scale of investment (the "portfolio-analysis" approach), the analysis will be extended to the regime of production and exchange. And finally, the result will be generalized to the decision problem involving time as well as risk.

A. THE PREFERENCE FUNCTION

If the statistical properties of uncertain income are the objects of choice for investors' decisions, so that particular assets or securities are valued only insofar as they contribute to these statistical measures, which parameters specifically are to be the governing ones? The obvious choices are the *mean* μ, a measure of the central tendency of income, and the *variance* σ^2 or its square root, the *standard-deviation* σ—either serving as a measure of the variability or riskiness of the uncertain income. Since σ is measured in the same units as μ, while σ^2 is not, it will be more convenient here to formulate the problem as one of choice between combinations of mean and standard-deviation. In a diagram such as Fig. 10-1, the investor's endowment of

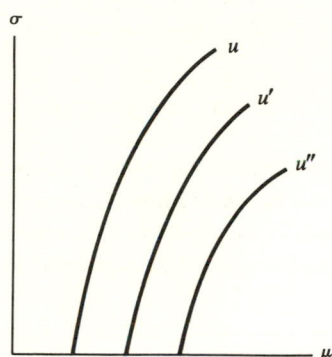

FIG. 10-1. Preference function.

assets (endowed portfolio) could be represented as a point on μ, σ axes, while the opportunity set would be the entire range of μ, σ combinations attainable by exchanging the endowed portfolio for other ones—via market or productive transformations. The first question is whether the preference function can indeed be satisfactorily reduced to an indifference map on these axes. Assuming the answer is favorable, the second question concerns the restrictions that must be placed upon the allowable shape of the indifference curves. These are the issues to be explored in this section.

Mean and standard-deviation of what? As the problem has usually been posed, the individual has a fixed "capital" (i.e., capital value)—the market value of his endowed portfolio of assets. He is supposed to be interested only in the *terminal value* that the portfolio will attain at the end of the decision period, terminal value being subject to uncertainty. Since the opportunity to augment or diminish "capital" by decreasing or increasing current consumption is excluded, the optimization involved is timeless.[1]

---

[1] Intertemporal choice will be considered in Section F below.

Then in this simplified problem the individual can equally well be said to be interested in the statistical parameters of the probability distribution of his future wealth (either absolute wealth or its proportion to his original "capital") or of his future income (either the absolute or proportionate yield generated by his chosen portfolio).

Let the given initial "capital" (capital value) be symbolized as K_0, and the terminal value of the portfolio (future wealth) as $\tilde{W}$.[2] The terminal date may be considered to be one time period from the present.[3] The following related random variables can be defined:

$$\tilde{\rho}: \quad \text{the proportionate portfolio yield}$$
$$K_0\tilde{\rho}: \quad \text{the absolute portfolio yield}$$
$$1 + \tilde{\rho}: \quad \text{the proportionate portfolio return}$$
$$K_0(1 + \tilde{\rho}): \quad \text{the absolute portfolio return.}$$

Evidently

$$\tilde{W} = K_0(1 + \tilde{\rho}) \tag{1}$$

While any of the above random variables suffices to describe the uncertainty involved, the nontemporal Neumann-Morgenstern elementary-utility function $v(c)$ is most naturally applied to W (representing potential consumption in the future period). Thus the expected-utility rule can be written

$$\max u = Ev(\tilde{W}) \tag{2}$$

To convert u into a function of the statistical parameters of $\tilde{W}$, $v(W)$ can be expanded in a Taylor's series about its expected value $E\tilde{W} = \mu$:

$$v(W) = v(\mu) + \frac{v'(\mu)}{1!}(W - \mu) + \frac{v''(\mu)}{2!}(W - \mu)^2$$

$$+ \frac{v'''(\mu)}{3!}(W - \mu)^3 + \cdots \tag{3}$$

Taking expectations, noticing that the expectation of $(W - \mu)$ is zero and that the expectation of $(W - \mu)^2$ is variance σ^2:

$$u = Ev(W) = v(\mu) + \frac{v''(\mu)}{2!}\sigma^2 + \frac{v'''(\mu)}{3!}E(W - \mu)^3 + \cdots \tag{4}$$

---

[2] A tilde indicates that the symbol below stands for a random variable. The tilde will be omitted except when it is desired to emphasize this feature.

[3] In previous chapters the symbol K_0 (capital value in the current period) was defined by $W_0 - c_0 = K_0$. Thus, capital value is what is left of original wealth after subtracting current-period consumption. The usage is the same here. The *future* wealth W here can be regarded as standing for W_1—wealth one time period from now, prior to the consumption decision at that future date.

The terms suggested by the dots are functions of the fourth or higher powers of $(\tilde{W} - \mu)$—higher moments about the mean, in statistical terminology.

The key question is: Under what circumstances, if ever, are we justified in saying that u is simply a function of μ and σ? Possible justifications may be found in the properties we are willing to assume for the preference-scaling function $v(W)$ or in the properties of the probability distribution of $\tilde{W}$.

First, if the elementary-utility function is *quadratic*—if it takes the form

$$v(W) = a + bW + cW^2$$

where a, b, c are positive or negative constants—then the third derivative $v'''(W)$ is necessarily zero together with all higher derivatives. Thus, u becomes a function of μ and σ only in (4):

$$u = v(\mu) + \tfrac{1}{2}v''(\mu)\sigma^2 = a + b\mu + c(\mu^2 + \sigma^2)$$

With u as parameter, this equation represents a family of indifference curves on μ, σ axes, as in Fig. 10-1. By completing the square, it may be verified that the curves are a set of concentric circles, centered at $\mu = -b/2c$, $\sigma = 0$.

In studying the elementary-utility function in Chapter 8, we saw that $v(W)$ could not take on quadratic form without ultimately violating one or other of the properties: (1) nonnegative marginal utility, $v'(W) \geq 0$, or (2) diminishing marginal utility, $v''(W) < 0$.[4] For the quadratic above, these conditions become $b + 2cW \geq 0$ and $c < 0$. Only if all the values of W considered as possible fall within a restricted range may the quadratic approximation for $v(W)$ be more or less satisfactory. Specifically, the conditions above hold only for $W \leq -b/2c$. We see, therefore, that the allowable range thus derived for W corresponds to the northwest quadrant of the circular indifference curves.[5] Only in this quadrant will the indifference curves be positively sloped (i.e., μ is a "good" while σ is a "bad") and concave downward (representing decreasing willingness to tolerate larger σ in exchange for larger μ). A quadratic elementary-utility function thus leads to a highly special indifference map, with acceptable properties only over a limited range.

Turning now to possible restrictions on the probability distribution of $\tilde{W}$, the *central limit theorem* leads to results of interest. A full discussion of this

---

[4] The desirability of requiring *nonnegative* marginal utility of income is obvious; *diminishing* marginal utility is required to explain why all of wealth is not held solely in the security promising highest expected proportionate yield—i.e., to explain diversification.

[5] The circular shape of indifference curves derivable from a quadratic $v(W)$ was pointed out in Karl Borch, "Indifference Curves and Uncertainty," *Swedish Journal of Economics*, **70** (1968).

theorem would be too technical here. Essentially, however, it says that the distribution of the sum of a large number N of random variables tends toward the normal probability distribution as N increases. Now portfolio income $\tilde{W}$ can be regarded as a random variable which is the sum of the individual random variables represented by returns on the component securities. Since the normal is a two-parameter distribution, the mean μ and standard-deviation σ of the distribution summarize all the relevant information. Thus, if $\tilde{W}$ is normal, indifference curves can be drawn on μ, σ axes. Furthermore, it can also be shown that if the preference-scaling function $v(W)$ has the properties (1) and (2) above, the indifference curves willll be positively sloped and concave downward.[6]

The tendency to normality is stronger, the closer to normal are the individual random variables, and the more independently distributed they are one from another; however, normality is approached, though it may be only slowly, even when the individual random variables are far from normally distributed and even when their separate distributions are (less than perfectly) correlated. In the case of portfolios of securities, the individual securities will typically not have normal probability distributions of income, and there may be considerable correlation among their distributions. Thus the assumption of normality for the portfolio probability distribution is a somewhat restrictive one, holding only for what may be called "well-diversified" portfolios. Unfortunately, there is no general rule about how large N must be for a portfolio to be well diversified.

It will be of interest to consider the effect upon expected utility of the size and sign of the third moment—entering into the leading term in (4) dropped if normality were to be assumed. The third moment is said to be a measure of *skewness*: in Fig. 10-2, we see three otherwise similar distributions with negative (long-tail to left), zero (symmetrical tails), and positive (long-tail to right) skewness. With equal means and standard-deviations, which type of distribution is the investor likely to prefer? Suppose he were offered his choice of two gambles: X offers .999 probability of losing $1 and .001 probability of gaining $999, while Y offers .999 probability of gaining $1 and .001 probability of losing $999. X and Y have the same mean and variance, but X is positively skewed and Y negatively skewed. Almost all commercial lotteries and games of chance are of form X, thus suggesting that individuals tend to have a preference for positive skewness. Then the

---

[6] These results were proved for the normal distribution in James Tobin, "Liquidity Preference as Behavior Towards Risk," *Review of Economic Studies*, **25** (Feb., 1958), pp. 74–76. Tobin originally believed that the results held for *any* two-parameter probability distribution. However, it was later discovered that *only* the normal distribution met the required conditions. The normal is the only two-parameter distribution (of finite variance) that is "stable"; i.e., a sum or other linear combination of normal variables remains normal. See M. S. Feldstein, "Mean-Variance Analysis in the Theory of Liquidity Preference" and James Tobin, "Comment on Borch and Feldstein," *ibid.*, **36** (Jan., 1969).

coefficient of $E(W - \mu)^3$ in equation (4) should be positive, requiring a positive $v'''(\mu)$.[7]

Diversification, whose primary purpose is to reduce the variance of income, also tends to eliminate skewness—whether positive or negative (since the normal distribution approached has zero skewness). We

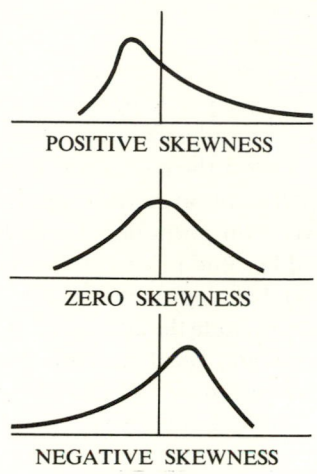

POSITIVE SKEWNESS

ZERO SKEWNESS

NEGATIVE SKEWNESS

FIG. 10-2. Skewness.

should expect to see, therefore, lesser desire to diversify where skewness of the portfolio held is positive, greater desire to diversify where skewness is negative.

One other aspect of portfolio return has been considered in the literature: the *sequential* nature of the risks. Suppose that at each successive time period up to a terminal date T, the proportionate yield $\tilde{\rho}_t$ on any fixed portfolio is a random drawing from a probability distribution such that $\tilde{\rho}_t = \rho_{ts}$ with probability π_{ts}—there being S distinct values of ρ_{ts}. (We may think of these as S distinct states at each date.) Note, in particular, the assumption that this probability distribution is identical for all t, so that we can write $\rho_{ts} = \rho_s$ and $\pi_{ts} = \pi_s$. Then *terminal wealth*, $\tilde{W}_T$, equals

$$\tilde{W}_T = K_0(1 + \tilde{\rho}_1)(1 + \tilde{\rho}_2) \cdots (1 + \tilde{\rho}_T) \tag{5}$$

[7] This is the diminishing marginal risk-aversion condition discussed in Chapter 9, and derived from the Pratt condition on the elementary-utility function discussed in Chapter 8. The Pratt condition, based upon the observation that richer people require a smaller risk-premium to hold risky assets, was that the ratio $-v''(W)/v'(W)$, or in condensed notation $-v''/v'$, decreases as wealth rises. This implies that $v''' > v''^2/v'$. But since the ratio on the right is necessarily positive, $v''' > 0$ is implied by the Pratt condition.

It is intuitively evident (the proof will not be given here) that for large T the value of W_T will approach the product of K_0 and the compounded *geometric average* of the probability distribution of $(1 + \rho_t)$ at each single date:

$$W_T \doteq K_0 G^T \tag{6}$$

where

$$G = (1 + \rho_1)^{\pi_1}(1 + \rho_2)^{\pi_2} \cdots (1 + \rho_S)^{\pi_S} \tag{7}$$

This suggests that the arithmetic mean μ and the standard-deviation σ of the probability distribution of portfolio returns perhaps are not the relevant statistical parameters to be considered in the selection of portfolios subject to repeated risks, and that instead the geometric average G should serve as the choice criterion.[8] The following argument can be adduced in favor of the geometric average: Given two portfolios A and B such that $G_A > G_B$, for sufficiently large T it will become practically certain that $W_A^T > W_B^T$—as is evident from the fact that W^T approaches $K_0 G^T$.

However, it seems reasonable that the investor ought still to be influenced by the consideration that one portfolio may have a much more highly dispersed probability distribution for W^T than the other. The issue ought not to be posed really as a conflict between the use of the geometric average G of the distribution of $(1 + \rho)$ on the one hand, and the use of the mean and variance of the *same* distribution on the other hand. For, under the conditions of the problem as posed—with repeated risks, and with the assumption that W_T, potential consumption at $t = T$, is the only source of utility—the investor following the μ, σ approach would be interested in the probability distribution not of $K_0(1 + \rho)$ but of $W_T = K_0 g^T$. Here $g^T = (1 + \rho_1) \cdots (1 + \rho_T)$, so that g is the *sample* geometric average after T trials. Thus the mean and standard-deviation of concern here are parameters of the sampling distribution of the sample geometric average to the Tth power, or simply of the product of T random variables $(1 + \rho)$. These parameters are in fact functions of the simple mean and standard-deviation of the distribution of $(1 + \rho)$ for a single period.[9]

The development that follows will employ the μ, σ preference function as sketched in Fig. 10-1. As we have seen, the justification for such a function is less than fully convincing. But the approach is an eminently manageable approximation, leading to simple and convenient results about the equilibrium prices of even quite complex securities and portfolios. The ultimate test, of course, is not convenience but predictive reliability—an issue that remains to be determined.

[8] As proposed, in particular, by H. A. Latané, "Criteria for Choice among Risky Ventures," *Journal of Political Economy*, **67** (April 1959).

[9] Denoting the mean and variance of the distribution of $(1 + \rho)$ as M and V, it can be shown that the expectation Eg^T of the compounded geometric mean is M^T, while its variance $E(g^T - Eg^T)^2$ equals $(V + M^2)^T - M^{2T}$.

B. THE OPPORTUNITY SET

At any moment of time there exist, in the capital markets, a considerable number of securities $X = A, \ldots, Z$ among which the individual may distribute his "capital" K_0 (i.e., the value of his endowment).[10] Letting n_X^+ be the number of endowed units of security X,[11] n_X the number he chooses to hold, and ϕ_X the price of a unit holding of security X (e.g., of a share, bond, or other entitlement), the investor has a budget constraint in the form of

$$\sum_{X=A}^{Z} n_X \phi_X = \sum_{X=A}^{Z} n_X^+ \phi_X = K_0 \tag{8}$$

The information as to the prices of the various securities is public. In addition, each individual will have his own private beliefs as to the returns on holdings of individual securities. Letting $\tilde{R}_X$ be the random variable of absolute return per unit of security X, we can denote by m_X and s_X the mean and standard-deviation of the distribution of $\tilde{R}_X$, and as r_{XY} and C_{XY} the correlation coefficient and covariance of the distributions of $\tilde{R}_X$ and $\tilde{R}_Y$. Following the usual statistical definitions of these parameters:

$$m_X = E(\tilde{R}_X) \tag{9}$$

$$s_X = \sqrt{E(\tilde{R}_X - m_X)^2} \tag{10}$$

$$r_{XY} = \frac{E[(\tilde{R}_X - m_X)(\tilde{R}_Y - m_Y)]}{s_X s_Y} = \frac{C_{XY}}{s_X s_Y} \tag{11}$$

The investor's opportunity set is portrayed as the shaded region in Fig. 10-3 on μ, σ axes—where μ and σ represent the mean and standard-deviation of wealth $\tilde{W}$ (absolute return on over-all portfolio) attainable through alternative security holdings. Thus $\tilde{W} = \sum_{X} n_X \tilde{R}_X$. The portfolio parameters are related to the security parameters by

$$\mu = \sum_{X} n_X m_X \tag{12}$$

$$\sigma = \sqrt{\sum_{X} \sum_{Y} n_X n_Y s_X s_Y r_{XY}} = \sqrt{\sum_{X} \sum_{Y} n_X n_Y C_{XY}} \tag{13}$$

---

[10] There is an implicit assumption here that all the assets of interest to the individual are completely and perfectly marketable.

[11] In this chapter the superscript ($^+$) replaces the familiar superscript (^{r}) for signifying endowment values of the variables.

The shaded region of Fig. 10-3 represents all the μ, σ combinations attainable for an individual with a given capital K_0. The points labelled A, B, C, ... show what can be attained by portfolios limited to the single correspondingly labelled security (i.e., one-security portfolios). Denoting by μ_X the mean and by σ_X the standard-deviation of such a one-security portfolio, $\mu_X = K_0 m_X/\phi_X$ and $\sigma_X = K_0 s_X/\phi_X$ (since for a one-security portfolio $n_X = K_0/\phi_X$). Of particular interest are *efficient* portfolios, represented by the southeast boundary of the opportunity set (combinations with

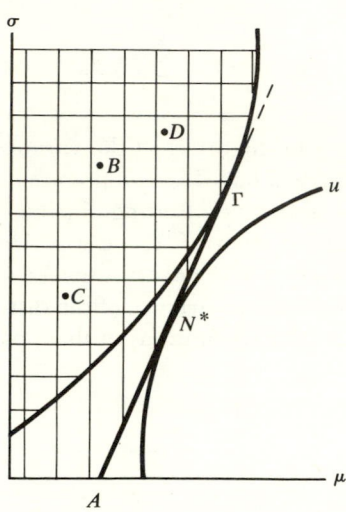

FIG. 10-3. Opportunity set and optimum portfolio.

minimum σ for given μ, or maximum μ for given σ). The fact that few of the single-security portfolios are on the efficient frontier is no mere happenstance, but reflects the power of diversification in reducing σ.

The bearing of the coefficient of correlation upon the effectiveness of diversification is illustrated in Fig. 10-4, which indicates the μ, σ combinations attainable by holding mixtures of two securities D and E (in proportions $\delta = n_D\phi_D/K_0$ and $\varepsilon = n_E\phi_E/K_0$, so that $\delta + \varepsilon = 1$). If $r_{DE} = 1$ (perfect positive correlation), all mixtures of D and E yield portfolio μ and σ lying along the straight line connecting points D and E, at distances from the end-points corresponding inversely to the proportionate holdings δ and ε.[12] If the returns on D and E are uncorrelated ($r_{DE} = 0$), the portfolio μ, σ

[12] It will always be the case that $\mu = \delta\mu_D + \varepsilon\mu_E$ (since $n_D m_D = \delta\mu_D$ and $n_E m_E = \varepsilon\mu_E$). Also, since $n_D = \delta K_0/\phi_D$ and $s_D = \sigma_D\phi_D/K_0$, then $n_D^2 s_D^2 = \delta^2\sigma_D^2$ (and an analogous relation holds for E). And if $r_{DE} = 1$, then

$$\sigma = \sqrt{n_D^2 s_D^2 + 2n_D n_E s_D s_E r_{DE} + n_E^2 s_E^2} = \sqrt{\delta^2\sigma_D^2 + 2\delta\varepsilon\sigma_D\sigma_E r_{DE} + \varepsilon^2\sigma_E^2}$$
$$= \delta\sigma_D + \varepsilon\sigma_E$$

combinations will lie along the middle curve of Fig. 10-4 (the proportionate holdings being measured by the relative distances along the μ axis). The effect of diversification in reducing σ is so great that, with $r_{DE} = 0$, the point E (representing the one-security portfolio held in E) is no longer efficient; it will always be dominated by some mixture of D and E.[13] Thus, with zero correlation, one-security portfolios tend to be driven out of the efficient set. With perfect negative correlation ($r_{DE} = -1$), the effect is still more extreme: it will then always be possible to find a mixed portfolio

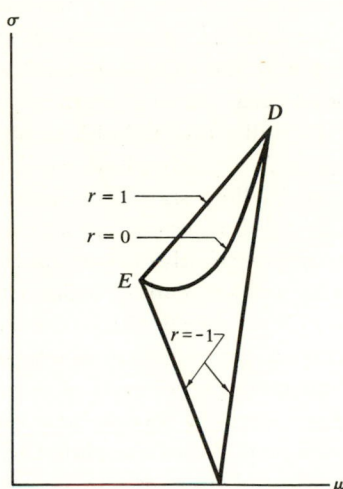

FIG. 10-4. Effect of diversification.

with zero standard-deviation,[14] and the curve for portfolio mixtures breaks into two lines connecting each of D and E with the zero-σ combination.[15]

With nonnegative holdings of any number of securities, it is evident that the efficient frontier of the opportunity set will have the generally convex-downward shape shown in Fig. 10-3. There may be a linear segment

[13] This is shown in Fig. 10-4 by the negative slope of the curve for $r_{DE} = 0$ in the neighborhood of point E. Now

$$\frac{d\sigma}{d\mu} = \frac{d\sigma/d\delta}{d\mu/d\delta}$$

where $d\mu/d\delta = \mu_D - \mu_E$ and

$$d\sigma/d\delta = [\delta\sigma_D^2 - \varepsilon\sigma_E^2 + (\varepsilon - \delta)r_{DE}\sigma_D\sigma_E]/\sigma$$

With $r_{DE} = 0$, and since the denominator $\mu_D - \mu_E$ is positive, the slope $d\sigma/d\mu$ will be negative at point E (when $\delta = 0$).

[14] With $r_{DE} = -1$, $\sigma = \delta\sigma_D - \varepsilon\sigma_E$. For $\delta^* = \sigma_E/(\sigma_D + \sigma_E)$, $\sigma = 0$.

[15] Since σ must be nonnegative, we choose one or the other root according as δ is greater or lesser than δ^*. For $\delta > \delta^*$, $d\sigma/d\mu = (\sigma_D + \sigma_E)/(\mu_D - \mu_E)$; for $\delta < \delta^*$, the negative of this. In either case, the slope is constant.

extending from the μ axis, tangent at a point such as Γ to the curved boundary.[16] There will be such a linear segment if: (1) there exist one or more "riskless" securities (securities for which $\sigma = 0$), or (2) there are two securities with perfect negative correlation. If either (or both) these conditions hold, one or more portfolios will exist for which $\sigma = 0$. It will henceforth be assumed that there does indeed exist a *single riskless security*, A. The opportunity set in the absence of such a riskless opportunity is shown as the heavily shaded region in Fig. 10-3; the riskless opportunity makes attainable the additional range of possibilities indicated by the lightly shaded region.

In the usual formulation of the portfolio-selection problem, it is generally assumed that the line $A\Gamma$, representing mixtures of the riskless single-security portfolio A and the tangency combination of securities Γ, can be extended northeastward (dashed segment) beyond the point Γ. In the dashed segment the individual is holding negative quantities of A. In less paradoxical language, the individual would borrow on a riskless basis—this might be called "selling short" or, better, *issuing* a number of units of the riskless security A—thus permitting a greater holding of the risky combination Γ.[17] (This corresponds also to purchasing "on margin," except that in the real world such purchases cannot ordinarily be financed on a riskless basis, as the transaction is not free of risk to the lender.)

We saw in the previous chapter that it was perfectly reasonable to assume that an individual could issue units of a security, provided only that his attained state distribution of income was such that he could with certainty meet all the contingent claims associated with such issuance. The corresponding principle, as applied to issuance of a riskless security in a μ, σ model, is that units of such a security can be generated only insofar as the attained portfolio contributes a level of *certain* return capable of paying off the certain claims issued. But the attained portfolio, if $\alpha < 0$, will consist of a holding of risky securities only. It is reasonable to assume, however, that securities are the sources of zero or positive, but never negative incomes[18]—this corresponds to giving securities a "limited-liability" property, under which the worst possible outcome is that the security becomes entirely valueless. Then in general a risky portfolio will be associated under all contingencies with *some* positive amount of certain income. Unfortunately,

---

[16] There may also be a linear segment elsewhere along the efficient frontier, a result that would follow if within that segment all the efficient portfolios were perfectly positively correlated.

[17] The portfolios along $A\Gamma$ satisfy the conditions $\mu = \alpha\mu_A + \gamma\mu_\Gamma$ and $\sigma = \alpha\sigma_A + \gamma\sigma_\Gamma = \gamma\sigma_\Gamma$ with the proportions $\alpha + \gamma = 1$. The extension through Γ corresponds to permitting α to become negative. The line cannot be meaningfully extended southwest through A, since σ cannot be less than zero.

[18] This eminently reasonable assumption conflicts with the normality condition needed to justify the specification of the preference function in terms of μ and σ. If the variance of the normal distribution is relatively small, however, there may be essentially no probability weight in the negative-income region. A well-diversified portfolio will, of course, tend to have relatively small variance.

it is not possible to tell from knowledge of only μ and σ just how much certain income the portfolio will generate. Thus, the line $A\Gamma$ can be extended a limited but undetermined distance beyond Γ.

The individual's opportunity set will change in response to shifts in his command over resources, due either to changes in his personal endowment or to changes in the terms upon which securities may be disposed of or acquired. First, suppose that an individual's capital K_0 is increased without changes in security prices (e.g., he is presented with a gift augmenting his initial endowed holdings). This enables him to buy proportionately more of *every* security. Thus, if a point (μ^*, σ^*) was previously on the efficient boundary of his opportunity set, and if capital is increased in the proportion k, the corresponding attainable point would now be $[(1 + k)\mu^*, (1 + k)\sigma^*]$.

Suppose instead that the individual's security endowment is fixed but that the price of a particular security X, not held in his initial endowment, falls by the factor k. Then the point $X = (\mu_X, \sigma_X)$ corresponding to the one-security portfolio X would shift proportionately outward along the ray out of the origin to $[\mu_X/(1 - k), \sigma_X/(1 - k)]$. This point would not in general be on the efficient frontier, but evidently all combinations in which X enters would also tend to shift in the same general direction.

To make further progress, simplifying assumptions are necessary. A very fruitful assumption is *homogeneity of beliefs*: every investor attaches the same values for the mean m_X and standard-deviation s_X of the distribution of returns of every security, and for the correlations r_{XY} among the returns. It follows from this that the opportunity sets of all individuals have the *same* proportionate shape, differing from one another only by the scale factor of individual endowed capital K_0. In particular, the slope $d\sigma/d\mu$ of the linear portion of the efficient frontier (of the line $A\Gamma$ in Fig. 10-3) will then be *the same for every individual*, though corresponding points on the line will be displaced nearer or further from the origin in proportion to the investor's K_0.[19]

C. CHOICE-THEORETIC SYSTEM

The choice-theoretic system for the simplified portfolio-balance problem[20] here being considered can now be set down in more or less familiar

[19] Suppose that K_0 for one individual is such that the point A has μ, σ coordinates $(a, 0)$ and the point Γ has coordinates (f, g). Then the equation for $A\Gamma$ is $\sigma = g(\mu - a)/(f - a)$, so that the slope $d\sigma/d\mu = g/(f - a)$. An individual with K_0 larger by the proportionate amount k has coordinates $(ka, 0)$ and (kf, kg) for the points corresponding to A and Γ, so that the equation becomes $\sigma = g(\mu - ka)/(f - a)$, with the slope remaining the same.

[20] Simplified because the scale of investment (as against the alternative of current consumption) is held fixed, because only a pure-exchange paradigm is being considered, and because a fixed list of securities is assumed (thus ruling out the problem of optimal "financing" of investment). The discussion here of the simplified portfolio-balance problem is based upon: (1) W. F. Sharpe, "Capital Asset Prices: A Theory of Market Equilibrium Under Conditions of Risk," *Journal of Finance*, **19** (Sept. 1964), and (2) Jan Mossin, "Equilibrium in a Capital Asset Market," *Econometrica*, **34** (Oct. 1966).

form. Let there be I individuals $(i = 1, \ldots, I)$ and a fixed list of Z securities $(X = A, \ldots, Z)$. Securities provide utility for an individual only through their effect on his portfolio μ^i and σ^i, via equations (12) and (13) repeated here:

$$\mu^i = \sum_X n^i_X m^i_X \qquad \begin{array}{l} \text{Definition of portfolio } \mu^i \\ (I \text{ equations}) \end{array} \qquad (12)$$

$$\sigma^i = \left(\sum_X \sum_Y n^i_X n^i_Y C^i_{XY} \right)^{1/2} \qquad \begin{array}{l} \text{Definition of portfolio } \sigma^i \\ (I \text{ equations}) \end{array} \qquad (13)$$

The superscript "i" is applied to designate the individual *holdings* n^i_X, individual *beliefs* as to the statistical parameters (m^i_X, s^i_X, C^i_{XY}), and individual *portfolio variables* (μ^i, σ^i). (To simplify notation, the superscript will be omitted except for emphasis or to avoid possible confusion.)

As in the usual choice paradigm, there are equations representing (for each individual) the marginal rate of substitution along the utility isoquant:

$$\left. \frac{d\sigma}{d\mu} \right|_u = \Upsilon(\mu, \sigma) \qquad \begin{array}{l} \text{Preference function} \\ (I \text{ equations}) \end{array} \qquad (14)$$

The individual optimization is subject to a budget constraint, which in this case fixes the market value of the attained portfolio as equal to that of the endowed portfolio (the "capital value" K_0):

$$\sum_X n_X \phi_X = \sum_X n^+_X \phi_X \qquad \begin{array}{l} \text{"Capital" constraint} \\ (I \text{ equations}) \end{array} \qquad (15)$$

A single riskless security, A, is assumed to exist; it will be convenient to provisionally select A as numeraire, so that ϕ_A takes on a constant value.[21]

The optimality condition equates the slope $d\sigma/d\mu \big|_u$ of the utility isoquant to that of the efficient boundary of the market opportunity set. The latter slope, in the simpler choice paradigms considered earlier, has been simply equal to the price ratio; here, it takes on a more complex form:

$$\left. \frac{d\sigma}{d\mu} \right|_u = \frac{(1/\sigma) \sum_Y n_Y C_{XY}}{m_X - m_A \phi_X / \phi_A}, \quad \text{for} \quad X = B, \ldots, Z \qquad \begin{array}{l} \text{Optimality condition} \\ [I(Z-1) \text{ equations}] \end{array}$$

$$(16)$$

[21] Since ultimately we will want current income c_0 to serve as numeraire, ϕ_A will later become a variable.

The development of the optimality equations is relegated to a footnote,[22] but the result is not difficult to interpret. For each individual, it must be the case that for every risky security held (permitting either positive or negative holdings), the marginal rate of substitution between μ and σ is the same. The denominator on the right represents the marginal contribution to portfolio μ, as dollars are reallocated from the riskless security A to the security X. For such a reallocation,

$$\frac{d\mu}{dn_X} = \frac{\partial\mu}{\partial n_X} + \frac{\partial\mu}{\partial n_A}\frac{dn_A}{dn_X} = m_X - \frac{m_A\phi_X}{\phi_A}$$

where the partial derivatives are taken from the definition of portfolio μ in (12). That is, the marginal contribution (within the budget constraint) to μ of adding one unit of X equals (the mean return m_X on X) − (the mean return m_A on A times the number of units of A given up in purchasing a unit

[22] To maximize utility subject to the wealth constraint, the usual Lagrangian is formed:

$$\mathscr{L} = u - \left(\sum_X n_X\phi_X - K_0\right)$$

Maximizing with respect to n_X:

$$\frac{\partial\mathscr{L}}{\partial n_X} = \frac{\partial u}{\partial\mu}\frac{\partial\mu}{\partial n_X} + \frac{\partial u}{\partial\sigma}\frac{\partial\sigma}{\partial n_X} - \lambda\phi_X = 0$$

or

$$\lambda = \frac{\dfrac{\partial u}{\partial\mu}\dfrac{\partial\mu}{\partial n_X} + \dfrac{\partial u}{\partial\sigma}\dfrac{\partial\sigma}{\partial n_X}}{\phi_X}$$

where

$$\frac{\partial\mu}{\partial n_X} = m_X \quad\text{and}\quad \frac{\partial\sigma}{\partial n_X} = \frac{\sum_Y n_Y C_{XY}}{\sigma}$$

Thus, for every security the marginal utility per dollar is equal to the common value λ.

Now for the riskless numeraire security A, ϕ_A is a constant, while $s_A = 0$ and $r_{AX} = 0$ for all X. Substituting A for X in the expression for λ, we see that

$$\lambda = \frac{\dfrac{\partial u}{\partial\mu}m_A}{\phi_A}$$

Hence:

$$\frac{\partial u}{\partial\mu}m_X + \frac{\partial u}{\partial\sigma}\frac{\partial\sigma}{\partial n_X} - \frac{\partial u}{\partial\mu}\frac{m_A\phi_X}{\phi_A} = 0$$

And since

$$\frac{d\sigma}{d\mu} = -\frac{\partial u/\partial\mu}{\partial u/\partial\sigma} \quad\text{we have}\quad \frac{d\sigma}{d\mu} = \frac{\partial\sigma/\partial n_X}{m_X - m_A\phi_X/\phi_A}$$

which is the result in the text (writing out the expression for $\partial\sigma/\partial n_X$).

of X). Similarly, the numerator on the right represents the marginal contribution to portfolio σ as dollars are reallocated from A to X. Since $s_A = 0$,

$$\frac{d\sigma}{dn_X} = \frac{\partial\sigma}{\partial n_X} = \frac{1}{\sigma} \sum_{Y=A}^{Z} n_Y C_{XY}$$

where the partial derivative is taken from the definition of portfolio σ in (13). So the condition states that, for every security, the marginal contribution to μ per unit marginal contribution to σ must be the same—for reallocations within the budget constraint.

Finally, there are the conservation equations, one of which can be shown to follow in the usual way from the remainder of the system.

$$\sum_{i=1}^{I} n_X = \sum_{i=1}^{I} n_X^+ \qquad \begin{array}{l}\text{Conservation relations} \\ (Z-1 \text{ independent equations})\end{array} \qquad (17)$$

There are thus $3I + IZ + Z - 1$ equations. There are $3I$ variables in the form of the μ, σ, and $d\sigma/d\mu$ for each individual; IZ variables in the form of the security holdings n_X; and finally $Z - 1$ variable prices ϕ_X. Thus the counts of variables and equations match; as usual, consideration of the second-order conditions needed to guarantee the existence of a unique solution will be omitted.

The incorporation into this system of the special assumption of homogeneity of beliefs leads to an interesting interpretation. Under homogeneity of beliefs all individuals' opportunity sets are, as already indicated, of the same shape, with magnitudes proportional to individuals' endowed capital values K_0^i—and, in particular, the slope of the budget constraint line $A\Gamma$ is the same for every person. Thus, if all individual solutions N^* consist of tangencies to $A\Gamma$ (including the possibility that the tangency is on the extension beyond Γ corresponding to negative holdings of the *riskless* security A), it follows that $d\sigma/d\mu$ at equilibrium is the same for all individuals. The reciprocal of this slope may be regarded as the "price of risk" (in terms of mean return) ϕ_σ/ϕ_μ—or rather, σ being a "bad" rather than a good, its negative can be so regarded. The price of mean return, in terms of the riskless security A as numeraire, is evidently $\phi_\mu/\phi_A = \partial n_A/\partial\mu = 1/m_A$. Since $-d\mu/d\sigma$ is the price of σ in terms of μ, the price of σ in terms of *numeraire A* or ϕ_σ/ϕ_A is $-(d\mu/d\sigma)/m_A$. Thus, the capital constraint (specifically, the efficient linear border of the opportunity set) can be written in terms of μ and σ and their "prices" as

$$\mu\phi_\mu + \sigma\phi_\sigma = K_0 = \phi_A\left(\frac{\mu}{m_A} - \frac{d\mu}{d\sigma}\frac{\sigma}{m_A}\right) \qquad (18a)$$

This is, of course, the equation of the line through the points A and Γ in Fig. 10-3. This "capital budget line" can also be written in the very useful form:

$$\frac{d\sigma}{d\mu} = \frac{\sigma}{\mu - m_A K_0/\phi_A} \tag{18b}$$

Equation (18b) says that the *excess mean portfolio return* (excess over what could have been obtained by holding only the riskless security) is proportional to the portfolio standard-deviation that the individual is willing to accept.[23]

Results of interest can also be obtained about optimum portfolios and about security prices in equilibrium. From the optimality condition (16), it must be the case that the following holds, for each individual, as between any pair of risky securities X and Y:

$$\frac{\sum_J n^i_J C_{XJ}}{m_X - m_A \phi_X/\phi_A} = \frac{\sum_J n^i_J C_{YJ}}{m_Y - m_A \phi_Y/\phi_A} \tag{19}$$

Summing over the I individuals, and writing $\sum_{i=1}^{I} n^i_Y$ as $\bar{n}_Y$ (a constant, since the total of holdings is conserved):

$$\frac{\sum_J \bar{n}_J C_{XJ}}{m_X - m_A \phi_X/\phi_A} = \frac{\sum_J \bar{n}_J C_{YJ}}{m_Y - m_A \phi_Y/\phi_A} \tag{20}$$

Note that this is a relation among the security prices determined entirely by "public" parameters (the given social totals $\bar{n}_J$ of securities and the homogeneous beliefs about the security means and covariances).

[23] The formal justification can be shown as follows. Writing out the optimality condition (16) for the risky securities:

$$\frac{(1/\sigma) \sum_X n_X C_{BX}}{m_B - m_A \phi_B/\phi_A} = \cdots = \frac{(1/\sigma) \sum_X n_X C_{ZX}}{m_Z - m_A \phi_Z/\phi_A}$$

Multiplying the numerator and denominator of the first ratio by n_B, the second by n_C, and so on, and then using the principle of "corresponding addition" [i.e., the rule that if a variable $x = a/b = c/d$, then $x = (a + c)/(b + d)$] leads to

$$\frac{d\sigma}{d\mu} = \frac{(1/\sigma)\left(n_B \sum_X n_X C_{BX} + \cdots + n_Z \sum_X n_X C_{ZX}\right)}{n_B m_B + \cdots + n_Z m_Z - m_A(n_B \phi_B + \cdots + n_Z \phi_Z)/\phi_A}$$

$$= \frac{(1/\sigma)(\sigma^2)}{\mu - n_A m_A - m_A(K_0 - n_A \phi_A)/\phi_A}$$

$$= \frac{\sigma}{\mu - m_A K_0/\phi_A}$$

From inspection, it is evident that equations (19) and (20) above will be satisfied if $n^i_X/\bar{n}_X = k^i$, for every risky security—that is, if each individual i holds at his optimum N^* a "characteristic fraction" k^i of *every* risky security $B, \ldots, Z$. This result corresponds to the geometric consideration that all the individual solutions are tangencies along the line $A\Gamma$ (and its extension); i.e., *every individual will hold the "all-risk" combination Γ together with some positive or negative quantity of the riskless security A.* We may write $N^* = \gamma\Gamma + \alpha A$, where $\alpha + \gamma = 1$ and γ must be positive. Since the Γ^i for each individual will lie along the same ray through the origin, the distance from the origin being proportional to his endowed capital K^i_0, and since the social totals of all the risky securities must be held, it follows that an individual's Γ^i will consist of a holding of the fraction $K^i_0/\left(\sum_i K^i_0 - \bar{n}_A\phi_A\right)$ of *every* risky security.[24] Since he will desire to hold the fraction γ of his K_0 in the form of Γ, we obtain the result that for every risky security X

$$k^i = \frac{n^i_X}{\bar{n}_X} = \frac{\gamma^i K^i_0}{\sum K^i_0 - \bar{n}_A\phi_A} \tag{21}$$

This relation reveals how the individual's holdings of the risky securities $B, \ldots, Z$ are a function of his endowed capital K^i_0 and what might be called his "risk-preference parameter" γ^i. Finally, it is evident that while holdings of the riskless security A may be positive or negative, the characteristic fraction k^i held of all the *risky* securities cannot be negative (since a negative k^i would imply a negative γ—i.e., a tangency along $A\Gamma$ in the impossible region below the horizontal axis).

It will now be possible to relate the prices ϕ_X of the individual securities to their statistical properties. For portfolios as a whole, the mean return attainable by the investor increases linearly with the standard-deviation he is willing to accept, as shown by equation (18b)—$d\sigma/d\mu = \sigma/(\mu - m_A K_0/\phi_A)$—where under homogeneity of beliefs $d\sigma/d\mu$ represents the exchange rate between σ and μ determined by the market. And we saw that (16) could be interpreted as

$$\frac{d\sigma}{d\mu} = \frac{d\sigma/dn_X}{d\mu/dn_X}$$

so that each risky security's marginal contribution to μ is proportional to its marginal contribution to σ, for every individual, in reallocations between X and the riskless security A.

[24] The individual choosing to hold none of A can devote to Γ all of his total endowed capital K^i_0, while the aggregate value of all the risky securities in the market must equal the aggregate of endowed capital values $\sum K^i_0$ less the aggregate market value of the numeraire commodity, $\sum n_A\phi_A = \bar{n}_A\phi_A$.

Now $d\mu/dn_X = m_X - m_A\phi_X/\phi_A$, and thus is a "public" parameter involving only the homogeneous beliefs and not the private holding variables n^i_X or portfolio properties μ^i and σ^i. Since $d\sigma/d\mu$ is also public (given homogeneous beliefs), it must be the case that $d\sigma/dn_X = \partial\sigma/\partial n_X$ is so as well. Thus the numerator on the right of (16), $\sum n_Y C_{XY}/\sigma$, while seemingly involving the private variables n^i_Y and σ^i, must be expressible in terms of public statistical properties. It is shown in the footnote that $\partial\sigma/\partial n_X$, the marginal contribution of X to portfolio σ^i (for any individual i) is equal in equilibrium to the *correlated* standard-deviation of security X:

$$\frac{\partial\sigma}{\partial n_X} = r_{XN*}s_X \tag{22}$$

Here r_{XN*}, the correlation coefficient of returns on security X with returns on the individual's optimal portfolio $N*$,[25] must be the same for all individuals[26] and is thus a "public" parameter. Consequently we have the important result:

$$\frac{d\sigma}{d\mu} = \frac{r_{XN*}s_X}{m_X - m_A\phi_X/\phi_A} \qquad \text{Security-valuation equation} \tag{23}$$

[25] The covariance of X and $N*$ is given by

$$C_{XN*} = E\left\{(R_X - m_X)\left[\sum_Y n^*_Y(R_Y - m_Y)\right]\right\}$$
$$= \sum_Y n^*_Y E(R_X - m_X)(R_Y - m_Y) = \sum_Y n^*_Y C_{XY}$$

By definition, $r_{XN*} = C_{XN*}/s_X\sigma$ (the σ_{N*} associated with the optimal holding is simply σ in our notation). Thus

$$\frac{\partial\sigma}{\partial n_X} = \frac{C_{XN*}}{\sigma} = r_{XN*}s_X$$

[26] To show that r_{XN*} is the same for all individuals, we first show that $r_{XN*} = r_{X\Gamma}$, where $r_{X\Gamma}$ is the correlation between the returns on X and the returns on the individual's "all-risk" portfolio Γ.

$$C_{X\Gamma} = E\left\{(R_X - m_X)\left[\sum_Y n^\Gamma_Y(R_Y - m_Y)\right]\right\} = \sum_Y n^\Gamma_Y C_{XY}$$

$$r_{X\Gamma} = \frac{C_{X\Gamma}}{s_X\sigma_\Gamma}$$

Since $N* = \gamma\Gamma + \alpha A$, $n_Y = \gamma n^\Gamma_Y$ (for $Y = B, \ldots, Z$). Then $C_{X\Gamma} = C_{XN*}/\gamma$. Similarly, $\sigma = \gamma\sigma_\Gamma$. Thus

$$r_{X\Gamma} = \frac{C_{XN*}/\gamma}{s_X\sigma/\gamma} = r_{XN*}$$

Now, all Γ^i portfolios are identical except for an individual scale factor proportional to K^i_0. Hence the $C^i_{X\Gamma}$ and the σ^i_Γ will both vary among individuals only in response to this scale factor, which will cancel out in the determination of $r_{X\Gamma}$.

This tells us that any security price ϕ_X must so adjust that a proportionality relationship holds between the unfavorable feature of *correlated standard-deviation* $r_{XN^*}s_X$ and the favorable feature of *excess mean return* $m_X - m_A\phi_X/\phi_A$ associated with a unit holding of X (excess over what could have been obtained by holding the same number of dollars in the riskless security A). The factor of proportionality is $d\sigma/d\mu$—the market rate of exchange between mean and standard-deviation of portfolio return. The analogy with the earlier equation (18b) will be immediately apparent. The ratio $\sigma/(\mu - m_A K_0/\phi_A)$ on the portfolio level corresponds to the ratio $r_{XN^*}s_X/(m_X - m_A\phi_X/\phi_A)$ on the level of the individual security: the security excess mean return corresponds directly to the portfolio excess mean return in the denominator, while in the numerator it is the security's *correlated standard-deviation* that is relevant and enters into portfolio standard-deviation. By rearranging (23), an explicit solution for the security price variable is obtained:

$$\phi_X = \phi_A\left(m_X - \frac{d\mu}{d\sigma} r_{XN^*}s_X\right)/m_A \tag{23'}$$

The relation (23) is plotted in Fig. 10-5, and again in Fig. 10-6 after converting from a per-share to a per-dollar basis [by dividing numerator and denominator of (23) by the security price ϕ_X]. In the former diagram there exists a family of parallel *isoprice* lines, each line showing the combinations of correlated standard-deviation and excess mean return per share consistent with a given ϕ_X. All the lines have slope $d\sigma/d\mu$. The intercept with the horizontal axis is, of course, where $m_X = m_A\phi_X/\phi_A$: here, the correlated

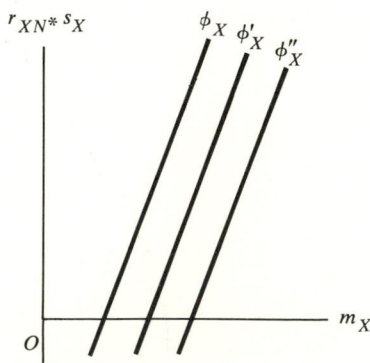

FIG. 10-5. Iso-price lines.

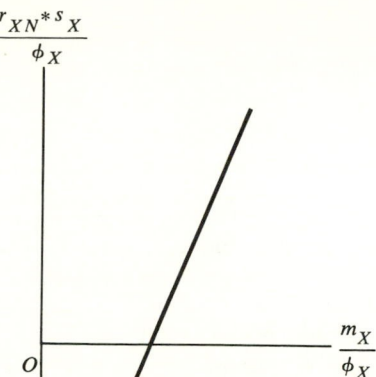

FIG. 10-6. Security-valuation line.

standard-deviation being zero, the price ϕ_X adjusts to make the excess mean return zero.

After dividing through by ϕ_A, we obtain in Fig. 10-6 a single "security-valuation line," showing the market relationship between correlated standard-deviation per dollar and excess mean return per dollar. We see from the diagrams that a risky security *negatively* correlated with optimal portfolios must have an excess mean return that is negative—i.e., a mean return less than that of the riskless security. It should be observed, however, that a risky security will normally be positively correlated with optimal portfolios—since under homogeneity of beliefs every such security must itself enter as a positive component of each individual's optimal portfolio.

NUMERICAL EXAMPLE

A competitive economy with a large number I of "representative individuals" will be assumed, all having the identical utility function $u = \mu^{10}e^{-\sigma}$. (It can be verified that this function is consistent with the properties of the illustrated function in Fig. 10-1.)[27] Each individual is endowed with exactly one unit each

[27]

$$\frac{\partial u}{\partial \mu} = 10\mu^9 e^{-\sigma} = \frac{10u}{\mu} > 0$$

$$\frac{\partial u}{\partial \sigma} = -\mu^{10}e^{-\sigma} = -u < 0$$

$$\frac{d\sigma}{d\mu} = -\frac{\partial u/\partial \mu}{\partial u/\partial \sigma} = \frac{10}{\mu} > 0$$

$$\frac{d^2\sigma}{d\mu^2} = -\frac{10}{\mu^2} < 0$$

Table I

Security	m	s	ϕ
A	1	0	1
B	1	3	.46
C	1	4	.04

All $r_{XY} = 0$.

of securities A, B, and C. The statistical parameters of the securities are summarized in the m and s columns of Table 1. The returns distributions for all pairs of securities are assumed to be uncorrelated.

In the last column, A as numeraire is assigned the price 1. The prices $\phi_B = .46$ and $\phi_C = .04$ (though fixed by the market from the point of view of each individual) are not exogenous parameters but represent the solution of the supply-demand relationships implicit in the equation system. The solution process is based upon the consideration in the "representative-individual" model that the prices must be such as to sustain the endowment $n_A^+ = n_B^+ = n_C^+ = 1$ for all individuals. This tells us immediately that $\mu = \sum_X n_X^+ m_X = 3$, and

$$\sigma = \left(\sum_X \sum_Y n_X^+ n_Y^+ r_{XY} s_X s_Y \right)^{1/2} = \left(\sum_X n_X^+ s_X^2 \right) = \sqrt{0 + 9 + 16} = 5.$$

The slope of the utility isoquant is then $10/\mu = 10/3 = d\sigma/d\mu$. The optimality condition (16) can next be solved separately for B and C, leading to the prices $\phi = .46$ and $\phi = .04$. With these prices, finally, the individuals' endowed capital K_0 is found to be

$$n_A^+ \phi_A + n_B^+ \phi_B + n_C^+ \phi_C = 1 + .46 + .04 = 1.50$$

The equation of the budget constraint in terms of μ and σ can be obtained by substituting in (18b) to get $10/3 = \sigma/(\mu - 1.50)$ or $\sigma = (10/3)\mu - 5$. In Table 2 are shown the characteristics of the three portfolios of interest along the budget constraint: the certainty portfolio A, the optimal portfolio N^*, and the all-risk portfolio Γ.

Table 2

Portfolio	n_A	n_B	n_C	μ	σ
A	1.50	0	0	1.50	0
N^*	1	1	1	3	5
Γ	0	3	3	6	15

Table 3

Security	r_{XN}^*	$r_{XN}^* s_X$	$m_X - m_A \phi_X / \phi_A$
A	0	0	0
B	.6	1.8	.54
C	.8	3.2	.96

Security	$\dfrac{r_{XN}^* s_X}{\phi_X}$	$\dfrac{m_X}{\phi_X} - \dfrac{m_A}{\phi_A}$
A	0	0
B	$\frac{90}{23}$	$\frac{27}{23}$
C	80	24

In Table 3 the correlated standard-deviations and the excess mean returns are shown, on a per-share basis above and on a per-dollar basis below. It may be verified that the results obtained by direct computation are consistent with the security-valuation equation (23).[28]

D. NATURE OF THE SOLUTION

In this section we shall briefly consider the economic significance of some aspects of the solution obtained above for the simplified portfolio-selection problem, before turning to generalizations in the following section.

The possibility of nonuniqueness of the solution for the optimal portfolio has received some attention. In Fig. 10-3, nonuniqueness would entail two or more tangency points Γ and Γ' between the opportunity set and the budget line. It is evident from the geometry that if two points are so tangent, the entire border of the opportunity set between Γ and Γ' must coincide with the budget line. Then an individual's optimal portfolio $N^* = \gamma\Gamma + \alpha A$ could equally well be achieved by a mixture of Γ' and A, and possibly in other ways as well. This need not cause the analyst great concern. There are no market forces favoring multiple solutions as against a unique solution; such a state of affairs would be the merely accidental result of particular

---

[28] The direct computation of r_{BN}^* is obtained via

$$C_{BN^*} = \sum_Y n_Y C_{BY} = n_B s_B^2 = 9$$

so that

$$r_{BN^*} = \frac{C_{BN^*}}{s_B \sigma} = \frac{9}{3 \cdot 5} = \frac{3}{5}$$

Similarly, r_{CN}^* can be computed as $\frac{4}{5}$. The other elements of the table can then be computed directly.

combinations of numerical security parameters happening to represent a kind of "perfect substitutiveness" in generating efficient μ, σ vectors.

More significant is the consideration that the solution may entail *negative holdings* (i.e., issuance) of the riskless security A (by some, but not all individuals). Note that the necessarily positive social total $\bar{n}_A$ of the riskless security is fixed in this analysis (presumably determined by underlying productive considerations—see below), so the negative holdings of one individual must be balanced by increased positive holdings of others.

Of course, there are limits on the extent to which riskless bonds A can be issued to purchase a riskless security "on margin." As indicated above, these limits cannot be expressed in terms of the mean and variance, since they depend upon the precise character of the "unfavorable" tail of the distribution of outcomes. The inequality (24) expresses the limit by

$$|n_A m_A| \leq \min \sum_{X=B}^{Z} n_X \tilde{R}_X \quad \text{Margin limit inequality} \atop (n_A < 0) \tag{24}$$

The condition is that the worst (minimal) portfolio outcome must be such as to cover the principal and interest on the riskless securities sold to other individuals.

Another point of considerable interest is the possibility that one or more of the *security prices* might turn out to be negative in the solution of the equation system. This should not be entirely surprising, since every security is an indissoluble package of a "good" (excess mean return) and a "bad" (correlated standard-deviation). The mathematics of the problem dictate that, regardless, the aggregate of all the security endowments must be held— and a negative price may be necessary to induce the holding of one or more such securities.

NUMERICAL EXAMPLE

With the same utility function $u = \mu^{10} e^{-\sigma}$, consider a riskless security A for which, as before, $m_A = 1$, $s_A = 0$, and $\phi_A = 1$. Let there be a single risky security B, with $m_B = 1$ and $s_B = 6$. Under the representative-individual model, $\mu = \sum_X n_X^+ m_X = 2$, $\sigma = \left(\sum_X \sum_Y n_X^+ n_Y^+ C_{XY} \right)^{1/2} = \sqrt{36} = 6$, and $d\sigma/d\mu = 10/\mu = 5$. Solving from equation (16), we have $\phi_B = -\frac{1}{5}$.

If the utility function is validly stated in terms of μ and σ, it would appear that the community is worse off for having such a security in existence. One might then be inclined to say that no such security would come into existence; the productive solution underlying the assumed security endowment could not be such as to require the issuance of a negative-priced security. All this, however, does not get to the heart of the difficulty. It is reasonable to assume, as indicated above, that all securities are of a "limited-liability" nature—that ownership of a security is associated with a nonnegative probability distribution of income. So, no security *ought* to have a negative price; anyone should be delighted to receive a security as a gift, since it augments his income under some contingencies and reduces it under none. The possibility of negative prices for desirable securities is thus a somewhat unexpected symptom of the unsatisfactory formulation of utility in terms of mean and standard-deviation.

E. PRODUCTIVE AND FINANCING DECISIONS

In the simplified portfolio-balance choice paradigm so far considered, the investors merely distribute their holdings over a fixed list of securities assumed to pre-exist in the economy. In this section the *generation* of the numbers and types of securities in the economy will be examined in terms of the productive and financing decisions of firms.

Consider now the optimizing problem for the productive firm in the μ, σ paradigm. The *intertemporal* aspect of the problem is still set aside, so that we will be dealing with ways of transforming a fixed sacrifice of current consumption into alternative probability distributions of future income. The entrepreneur will be interested in attaining the productive combination of maximum market value—since doing so would provide the maximal capital value K_0 for the portfolio-balance decisions of the firm's owners.

In the first instance, the productive optimum can be isolated from decisions involving financing by assuming the latter to be on a simple all-equity basis; that is, each firm will issue only one type of security, representing a simple proportionate share in the firm's net income under all contingencies. Then the productive decision of firm f can be regarded as the selection of the characteristics of a single security f to be offered on the capital market. Nothing essential will be lost if we assume that the *number* of shares $\bar{n}_f$ of the firm's security (stock) is arbitrarily fixed, so that the goal of the productive firm can then be regarded as the maximization of share value ϕ_f. The value of the firm, $W_0^f = \bar{n}_f \phi_f$, will, of course, then also be a maximum.

We know from (23), however, that the price ϕ_X for any security is a function of the mean return per share m_X and the correlated standard-deviation per share $r_{XN} \cdot s_X$. Figure 10-7 shows a normal tangency optimum at Q^*; the firm has moved along its productive-opportunity locus to find the highest isoprice line attainable for its shares. The tangency condition is simply that the rate of productive transformation $d\,(r_{fN} \cdot s_f)/dm_f$ between correlated standard-deviation of return and mean return equals the rate of exchange $d\sigma/d\mu$ (slope of the isoprice lines) ruling in the market between

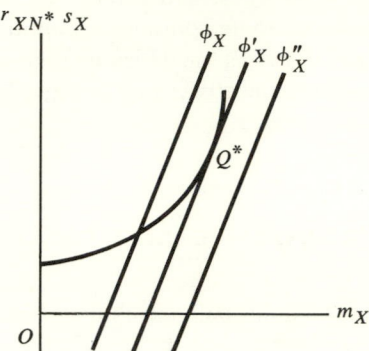

FIG. 10-7. Productive optimum of firm

portfolio μ and σ.[29] Note that the factors r_{fN*} and s_f appear always multiplied together; it is an increase in the product of these two—in the *correlated standard-deviation*—that represents the cost incurred in attempting to increase the mean return m_f by productive transformations. Since

$$r_{fN*}s_f = (1/\sigma)C_{fN*} = (1/\sigma) \sum_Y n_Y C_{fY}$$

the correlated standard-deviation is a function not only of the firm's own standard-deviation s_f but of all the covariances C_{fY} as well. This means that in maximizing its security price ϕ_f, the firm has many dimensions of choice: not only its own security parameters m_f and s_f, but the security covariances C_{fY} too. (In equilibrium, of course, the value of C_{fY} also has to be satisfactory to the firm issuing security Y.)

Having obtained the optimal solution under the assumption of simple equity financing, we can now consider explicitly the *problem of optimal finance*: is it possible for the firm to do any better by issuing a mixture of securities?

---

[29] Formally, the firm seeks to maximize $\phi_f = \phi_A[m_f - (d\mu/d\sigma)r_{fN*}s_f]/m_A$ subject to the productive-opportunity constraint $Q(m_f, r_{fN*}s_f) = 0$. After forming the usual Lagrangian, the partial derivatives are

$$\frac{\partial \mathcal{L}}{\partial m_f} = \frac{\phi_A}{m_A} - \lambda \frac{\partial Q}{\partial m_f} = 0$$

$$\frac{\partial \mathcal{L}}{\partial (r_{fN*}s_f)} = - \phi_A \left(\frac{d\mu/d\sigma}{m_A}\right) - \lambda \frac{\partial Q}{\partial (r_{fN*}s_f)} = 0$$

Then

$$- \frac{\partial Q/\partial m_f}{\partial Q/\partial (r_{fN*}s_f)} = \frac{d(r_{fN*}s_f)}{dm_f}\bigg|_Q = \frac{d\sigma}{d\mu}$$

Under the state-preference closed-system model with complete markets, we have seen that no unique financial optimum exists. In that model, alternative combinations of securities constituting an exhaustive set of claims to the over-all productive vector of future state-incomes attained by the firm have, necessarily, in sum a value just equal to that of the productive vector itself. Thus, looking at the problem as the choice of an optimal proportion of debt and equity securities, we saw that the "debt-equity mix" is indeterminate. A similar result will be demonstrated here for the mean vs. standard-deviation model.

For simplicity, assume that the firm f issues just two classes of securities: debt D^f and equity E^f. (As usual, the superscipt will be dropped where there is no danger of confusion.) And nothing essential will be lost in assuming that to each share of f that would have been issued under simple equity financing there will now correspond *one unit each* of D and E.

Then the problem reduces to showing that the sum of the prices of the debt and equity shares equals the share price under simple equity financing: $\phi_f = \phi_D + \phi_E$. Since the debt and equity together represent an exhaustive set of claims to the income generated, it must be the case that $\tilde{R}_f = \tilde{R}_D + \tilde{R}_E$. Then, necessarily, $m_f = m_D + m_E$. And it is shown in the footnote that $r_{fN^*} s_f = r_{DN^*} s_D + r_{EN^*} s_E$.[30] Using the security-price relation (23'), it follows that $\phi_f = \phi_D + \phi_E$. Multiplying by the common number of the two types of claims leads to an equation that can be written:

$$W_0^f = D_0^f + E_0^f \qquad \text{Indeterminacy of debt-equity mix} \qquad (25)$$

That is, the value of the productive combination (equal to the aggregate security value under all-equity financing) is equal to the sum of the values of the aggregate of debt and equity shares in mixed financing.

Some light will be shed upon the indeterminacy question if we set down the choice-theoretic system for the mean, standard-deviation paradigm of choice, under a regime of production and exchange. In the interests of simplicity, all the covariances C_{XY} (for $X \neq Y$) will be taken to be constants —although, in general, they are variables subject to optimizing choice by the firms issuing the corresponding securities. It will be assumed, in addition, that a single riskless security A exists that is *not* issued by firms (government bonds, perhaps) and that serves as numeraire with $\phi_A = 1, m_A = 1, s_A = 0$, and fixed total number of units $\bar{n}_A$.

---

[30] By definition, $r_{XN^*} = C_{XN^*}/s_X \sigma$. Since $\tilde{R}_f = \tilde{R}_D + \tilde{R}_E$,

$$C_{fN^*} = C_{DN^*} + C_{EN^*}$$

Then

$$s_f r_{fN^*} = \frac{C_{DN^*}}{s_D \sigma} s_D + \frac{C_{EN^*}}{s_E \sigma} s_E = s_D r_{DN^*} + s_E r_{EN^*}$$

$$\mu = \sum_X n_X m_X$$

Definition of portfolio μ
(I equations) $\qquad$ (12)

$$\sigma = \left(\sum_X \sum_Y n_X n_Y C_{XY} \right)^{1/2}$$

Definition of portfolio σ
(I equations) $\qquad$ (13)

$$\left. \frac{d\sigma}{d\mu} \right|_u = \Upsilon(\mu, \sigma)$$

Preference function
(I equations) $\qquad$ (14)

$$\frac{d\sigma}{d\mu} = \frac{(1/\sigma) \sum_Y n_Y C_{XY}}{m_X - m_A \phi_X / \phi_A}$$

Optimality condition
$[I(Z-1)$ equations] $\qquad$ (16)

$$\sum_X n_X \phi_X = \sum_X n_X^+ \phi_X$$

"Capital" constraint
(I equations) $\qquad$ (26)

The equations governing the individual security-holding decisions are unchanged.

Under simple equity financing, there would be F distinct securities associated with the F firms. The total number of distinct securities is then $Z = F + 1$. For each firm security, the total number of units issued, $\bar{n}_f$, is an arbitrary constant.[31]

There is also the definitional relation:

$$r_{XN^*S_X} = \frac{\sum_Y n_Y C_{XY}}{\sigma}$$

Definition of correlated standard-deviation
$[(Z-1)$ equations] $\qquad$ (27)

Turning now to the productive equations:

$$Q(m_f, r_{fN^*S_f}) = 0$$
$$\frac{d(r_{fN^*S_f})}{dm_f} = Q'(m_f, r_{fN^*S_f})$$

Firm's productive opportunity
($2F$ equations) $\qquad$ (28)

$$\frac{d(r_{fN^*S_f})}{dm_f} = \frac{d\sigma}{d\mu}$$

Firm's productive optimum
(F equations) $\qquad$ (29)

Finally, we have the conservation relations, one of which is redundant:

$$\sum_I n_X = \sum_I n_X^+$$

Conservation relations
($Z-1$ independent equations) $\qquad$ (30)

---

[31] Note that the arbitrariness of having, say, 100 shares at $1 rather than 20 shares at $5 is *not* considered disturbing here. This rests upon a judgment to the effect that the choice, on the firm's part, as to whether to have a larger number of cheaper or a smaller number of dearer shares does not pose a serious analytical problem. A more complete analysis would provide instead an optimizing explanation for the firm's choice in this dimension as well.

There are then $4I + I(Z - 1) + 2(Z - 1) + 3F = 3I + IZ + 2(Z - 1) + 3F$ equations, corresponding to the $3I + IZ$ individual variables (I each of μ^i, σ^i, and $d\sigma/d\mu$, and IZ of n^i_X), the $3F$ firm variables (F each of m_f, s_f, and $d(r_{fN^*}s_f)/dm_f$), and the $2(Z - 1)$ security variables ϕ_X and r_{XN^*}.

Returning to the first numerical example above, we continue to assume a large number I of "representative individuals" with utility functions $u = \mu^{10}e^{-\sigma}$. Let each individual be endowed with one unit each of three securities A, B, and C. As indicated in the text, A has given characteristics $m_A = 1$, $s_A = 0$, and serves as numeraire with $\phi_A = 1$. In addition, all the covariances between pairs of distinct securities, C_{XY} for $X \neq Y$, are assumed to equal zero—so that the firms in effect have productive opportunities whose uncertain returns are distributed independently of one another.

Securities B and C correspond to the two firms assumed to exist, each being limited to simple equity financing. The firms are each attempting to maximize $\phi_f = \phi_A[m_f - (d\mu/d\sigma)r_{fN^*}s_f]/m_A$, which in this problem reduces to $\phi_f = m_f - (3/10)s_f^2/5$ (since for the optimal portfolio N^* held by the representative individual, $\sigma - 5$). Let the constraint for firm B be $.72s_B = 1.16 + m_B^2$ and for firm C be $.96s_C = 2.84 + m_C^2$. It may then be verified that firm B will choose the characteristics $m_B = 1$, $s_B = 3$ and firm C the characteristics $m_C = 1$, $s_C = 4$. With simple equity financing, these will generate securities which investors are willing to hold at the equilibrium prices $\phi_B = .46$ and $\phi_C = .04$ of the earlier example.

Allowing for mixed financing, continuing to assume a fixed number of shares of each type, we would have

$$\phi_f = \phi_D + \phi_E \tag{31}$$

In place of the previous single variable ϕ_f, we now have ϕ_D and ϕ_E—the values of debt and equity shares, respectively, of firm f. But since we do not have enough equations to correspond to the increased number of variables, the system as a whole is underdetermined.

The indeterminacy of the debt-equity mix, here as in the time-state model, is an unsatisfying result. For, the choice of an optimal mode of "financing" a firm's productive investments is universally considered to be an essential portion of the behavior of capital markets that economic theory should explain. In the time-state model, the key to the idealization that swept the problem out of existence lay in the assumptions of "complete markets for time-state claims" and "no external drains." The same applies to the mean, standard-deviation model of this chapter. Here "complete markets" will exist more easily in that only portfolio μ and σ enter into preference functions. Equation (18a) shows that the equilibrium is such as to generate an implicit price for μ and for σ in terms of alternative security holdings. And the absence of taxes, transaction costs, and so on, again assures "no external drains." Thus, the problem of optimal financing remains a challenge for a more general model.

F. INTERTEMPORAL CHOICE

The traditional formulation of the mean vs. standard-deviation portfolio problem has held constant the investor's "capital" K_0—an aggregate market value available for purchase of securities. It is not at all difficult, however, to let the investor balance current consumption c_0 against the "capital" K_0. Limiting ourselves to the two-period problem (the horizon $T = 1$), there would then be three variables serving as arguments of the utility function: current consumption c_0 (assumed certain), and the mean μ and standard-deviation σ of consumption at $t = 1$. For consistency with previous chapters, c_0 can now take over the function of numeraire ($\phi_0 = 1$), so that ϕ_A can become a variable. Having discussed the productive and financing optima in a timeless context above, we can minimize difficulties by returning to a pure-exchange model in considering the choice-theoretic system in the context of intertemporal decision.

$$\left.\frac{\partial \mu}{\partial c_0}\right|_u = \Upsilon_\mu(c_0, \mu, \sigma)$$

Preference function

$$\left.\frac{\partial \sigma}{\partial \mu}\right|_u = \Upsilon_\sigma(c_0, \mu, \sigma)$$

($2I$ equations)   (32)

$$\mu = \sum_X n_X m_X$$

Definition of portfolio μ (I equations)   (12)

$$\sigma = \left(\sum_X \sum_Y n_X n_Y C_{XY}\right)^{1/2}$$

Definition of portfolio σ (I equations)   (13)

$$c_0 + \sum_X n_X \phi_X = c_0^+ + \sum_X n_X^+ \phi_X$$

Budget constraint   (33)

The budget constraint now shows $K_0 = \sum n_X \phi_X$ as a variable to be balanced against current consumption c_0, within the limit set by the endowed sum $c_0^+ + K_0^+$.

For the preference function, three marginal rates of substitution can be defined among the choice-variables c_0, μ, and σ, but of course any two determine the third. The optimality conditions equate these marginal rates of substitution to functions of the price variables:

$$\left.\frac{\partial \mu}{\partial c_0}\right|_u = \frac{m_A}{\phi_A}$$

$$\left.\frac{\partial \sigma}{\partial \mu}\right|_u = \frac{(1/\sigma) \sum_Y n_Y C_{XY}}{m_X - m_A \phi_X/\phi_A} \quad \text{for } X = B, \ldots, Z$$

Optimality conditions[32]
(IZ equations) (34)

Note that the condition for the marginal rate of substitution between μ and σ is unchanged from the nontemporal equation (16).

Finally, there are the usual conservation relations:

$$\sum_I c_0 = \sum_I c_0^+$$

$$\sum_I n_X = \sum_I n_X^+ \quad \text{for } X = A, \ldots, Z$$

Conservation relations
(Z independent equations) (35)

Evidently, since A is the riskless security, the riskless rate of interest r_1 may be defined as the discount rate r_1 in $\phi_A = 1/(1 + r_1)$. Risky rates of interest may be similarly defined in terms of the risky security prices ϕ_X.

The consideration of productive opportunities would permit the community as a whole to transform current consumption opportunities c_0 into future consumption opportunities with associated μ and σ—whereas, of course, under pure exchange the individuals can adjust via the market but the community totals remain fixed. Since no essentially new problems are involved, however, the choice-theoretic system for this paradigm will not be explicitly presented here.

[32] Maximizing the Lagrangian $\mathscr{L} = u - \lambda \left(c_0 + \sum_X n_X \phi_X - c_0^+ - \sum_X n_X^+ \phi_X \right)$ yields

$$\frac{\partial \mathscr{L}}{\partial c_0} = \frac{\partial u}{\partial c_0} - \lambda = 0$$

$$\frac{\partial \mathscr{L}}{\partial n_X} = \frac{\partial u}{\partial \mu} \frac{\partial \mu}{\partial n_X} + \frac{\partial u}{\partial \sigma} \frac{\partial \sigma}{\partial n_X} - \lambda \phi_X = 0$$

Making use of the properties of the riskless security A,

$$\lambda = \frac{\partial u}{\partial c_0} = \frac{m_A \partial u/\partial \mu}{\phi_A} \quad \text{or} \quad \frac{\partial \mu}{\partial c_0} = -\frac{\partial u/\partial c_0}{\partial u/\partial \mu} = -\frac{m_A}{\phi_A}$$

giving us the first condition. Substituting for λ in the second Lagrangian condition yields

$$\frac{\partial u}{\partial \mu} m_X + \frac{\partial u}{\partial \sigma} \frac{\partial \sigma}{\partial n_X} - \frac{m_A}{\phi_A} \frac{\partial u}{\partial \mu} \phi_X \quad \text{or} \quad \frac{\partial u}{\partial \mu} \left(m_X - \frac{m_A \phi_X}{\phi_A} \right) + \frac{\partial u}{\partial \sigma} \frac{\partial \sigma}{\partial n_X} = 0$$

Then,

$$\frac{\partial \sigma}{\partial \mu} = -\frac{\partial u/\partial \mu}{\partial u/\partial \sigma} = \frac{\partial \sigma/\partial n_X}{m_X - m_A \phi_X/\phi_A}$$

One further generalization is to the multiperiod problem. Here the utility function would have to have as arguments the means and standard-deviations of consumption at a number of future dates. If such a specification of the utility function is accepted for a single future date, there would seem to be no objection to be made to the generalization to multiple dates. The result would then determine prices for securities as packages of the dated μ's and σ's representing the objects of choice.

G. THE μ, σ FORMULATION AS AN APPROXIMATION: COMPLETE AND INCOMPLETE MARKETS

In dealing with intertemporal decision under uncertainty, the formulation in terms of mean and standard-deviation of future income (consumption) as objects of choice can be regarded as a special case of the more general formulation in terms of time-state claims as objects of choice. There are two distinct respects in which the μ, σ approach is a special case.

First, for any such statistical formulation, "a dollar is a dollar"—whereas, at least in principle, the time-state formulation can allow the preference-scaling function $v(c)$ to vary as a function of the state. Thus, a dollar in state a need not carry as much weight as a dollar in state b, even when the probabilities π_a and π_b are equal and when $c_a = c_b$.[33] Second, even given a unique $v(c)$ function, expected utility can be expressed exactly in terms of mean and standard-deviation of income (consumption) as arguments only if, as we have seen earlier in this chapter, either: (a) the elementary-utility function is quadratic, *or* (b) if all the opportunities available have approximately normal probability distributions. But, we know, neither condition can be really defended, at least on a priori grounds.

However, all analytical and empirical work in economics requires the use of more or less radical simplifying assumptions, the justification for which can only be determined by the results obtained. It is a great advantage of the μ, σ formulation that a rather direct connection exists between theoretical and potentially observable variables. For example, the analyst might identify present beliefs on the part of investors as to the mean and standard-deviation of return on a particular security with the corresponding measures calculated from the past ten years (let us say) of recorded experience with the same security. Such an identification is, of course, arguable. On the other hand, it seems far more difficult to find any observable correlate for beliefs taking the form of the probabilities associated with a set of alternative future states.

---

[33] It was indicated earlier that variation of the $v(c)$ function with state is essential in understanding decisions like those involved in the purchase of life insurance. The mere statistical properties of the payoff on the insurance contract do not show the full picture, when we are comparing dollars under the state "Dead" with dollars under the state "Alive."

Finally, the distinction between regimes of complete and of incomplete markets—a distinction central to the discussion of the time-state model in the previous chapter—has not yet been alluded to here. From one point of view the problem of providing complete markets might seem to be much less serious in the mean, standard-deviation model. For, a horizon date of T and S distinct states per future time period imply $TS + 1$ objects of choice (if there is only a single present state) in the time-state model—with S being in principle a very large number. But if only μ_t and σ_t at each future date enter into preference functions, there are but $2T + 1$ objects of choice. Even a relatively modest number of securities Z would seem to permit the generation of implicit prices for every object of choice.

However, matters are not so nearly ideal on the practical level. Consider the situation of a typical individual, for whom a very large proportion of his income stems from personal effort (labor services). In effect, his "portfolio" is heavily dominated by the probability distribution of returns on the asset represented by claims to his own labor.[34] Now it is reasonable to assume that the typical individual would want to diversify, reducing his disproportionate holding of rights to his own labor services (which are subject to risks as to personal health, technological obsolescence, and so on). To some extent this can be done. It is possible to "buy a piece of" the risky earnings of members of a few professions—such as boxers and actors. Or, long-term contracts can be written shifting a larger or smaller share of health and obsolescence risks to the purchaser of the labor services. Still another possibility is for the individual to buy insurance protection against particular hazards (especially ill-health). However, it is evident that by and large individuals do remain disproportionately "locked in" to the single asset of earnings on their own personal services.

What is the source of the difficulty here? It would seem that we are dealing with a kind of market imperfection. The problem is not, however, in the mechanism of the market itself but in the nature of the claim to be transferred. Setting aside possible legal limitations on contracts for personal services,[35] there is still the question of incentives. A man is unlikely to work quite so hard if he only "owns 10 per cent of himself"—i.e., if he has sold off in advance claims to 90 per cent of his own earnings. Ultimately, the difficulty comes back to the uniqueness of labor as a commodity—the fact that the laborer is tied to his work. If effort is an important consideration, the individual will commonly find that his labor services are worth more to himself than to others. We may say that the asset in question is "personalized."

[34] Such a disproportionate holding of a single asset also raises the question of whether portfolios are ever "well diversified." This point will not be pursued here, however.

[35] Some types of personal-service contracts may be illegal, or at any rate not legally enforceable. A somewhat comparable situation may exist in the case of land, which in certain societies has been nonalienable. In such a case a "land-poor" class may develop, of individuals unwillingly holding portfolios dominated by land ownership.

In terms of the categories of this chapter, the mean-return parameter m_L (and possibly also the s_L and r_{XL}) of the "labor" security of a particular individual is not constant but is modified under exchange. Since the change is generally adverse to the purchaser, the effect is to restrict the market opportunity set. Thus, trades of personalized assets are hindered in somewhat the same way that transaction costs hinder trade in general. Indeed, the personalization problem can be subsumed under the heading of transaction costs—by assuming that delivery of the personalized commodity *can* be made effective, but only at the expense of strict policing, which naturally cannot be costless. As in the previous chapter, we find that the idealization of complete and perfect markets—which follows from the assumed absence of transaction costs—is not adequate to provide a fully satisfactory explanation of intertemporal choice under uncertainty.

BIBLIOGRAPHIC NOTE

Pioneering formulations of the μ, σ approach to risky choice include:

J. R. HICKS, "A Suggestion for Simplifying the Theory of Money," *Economica*, N.S., **2** (Feb. 1935).

J. MARSCHAK, "Money and the Theory of Assets," *Econometrica*, **6** (Oct. 1938).

JAMES TOBIN, "Liquidity Preference as Behavior Towards Risk," *Review of Economic Studies*, **25** (Feb. 1958).

The fullest development, on the level of individual portfolio choice, is:

HARRY M. MARKOWITZ, *Portfolio Selection* (John Wiley & Sons, Inc., 1959).

The extension to the determinants of market equilibrium appeared in two important articles, which (though limited to the pure-exchange paradigm with fixed lists of securities) have nevertheless provided the basis for the development in this chapter:

WILLIAM F. SHARPE, "Capital Asset Prices: A Theory of Market Equilibrium Under Conditions of Risk," *Journal of Finance*, **19** (Sept. 1964).

JAN MOSSIN, "Equilibrium in a Capital Asset Market," *Econometrica*, **34** (Oct. 1966).

Another significant related contribution is:

JOHN LINTNER, "Security Prices, Risk, and Maximal Gains from Diversification," *Journal of Finance*, **20** (Dec. 1965).

Interesting empirical results are to be found in:

WILLIAM F. SHARPE, "Risk Aversion in the Stock Market: Some Empirical Evidence," *Journal of Finance*, **20** (Sept. 1965).

WILLIAM F. SHARPE, "Mutual Fund Performance," *Journal of Business*, **39** (Jan. 1966).

11 A CONCLUDING NOTE

Economic theory is and will remain an unfinished story. Starting with a basic structure of concepts and relationships, it will always be possible to specialize the analysis in the interests of simplicity and concreteness, and to generalize it in the interest of wider applicability; to make new distinctions, and then to reunify ideas on a higher level; and to modify one principle or assumption after another—as called for in the effort to improve the prediction and exploration of behavior.

The basic structure of economic theory, and the unifying theme of this volume, has been the choice-theoretic system—whose elements are the agents of choice and objects of choice, preference functions and opportunity sets, optimization under constraint, and market equilibrium. Arising first in the context of timeless decision (ordinary price theory) as explained in Chapter 1, the choice-theoretic system was generalized to cover decisions over time under certainty (Chapters 2–7) and then extended further to cope with the problem of uncertainty as well (Chapters 8–10). By making an appropriate specialization, we have been enabled to use the simplified model of a world of pure exchange wherever convenient. By adding in Chapter 5 an artificial choice-object, "liquidity" (defined as the real value of money holdings), we established a connection with current theories of money.

A host of further generalizations and applications await development. In a world of uncertainty, to give one illustration, *information* becomes a useful commodity—acquisition of information to eliminate uncertainty should then be considered as an alternative to productive investment subject to uncertainty. (This conception would evidently tie in with Bayesian analysis in probability theory.) Such a formulation would permit the incorporation of technological progress as an endogenous variable (a probabilistic function of research investments), rather than as an exogenous source of disturbance for economic models.

The line of advance most forcefully demanded by results in previous chapters is improvement of the theory of exchange. The standard assumption has been that markets are both complete and perfect, so that equilibrium is instantaneously and costlessly attained. This assumption leads to the beautiful Fisherian result that productive optimization of the firm can be entirely *separated* from consumptive optimization of the individual (the "present-value rule" of Chapter 3). This result has served us well, up to a point. But we know that markets do not operate costlessly; there is a technology of exchange as well as a technology of production. It is therefore not surprising to find phenomena that are inexplicable under costless exchange. We have seen that, under the time-state model of Chapter 9, markets cannot really be complete—while under the mean, standard-deviation model of Chapter 10, they cannot be perfect. In either case, we have been forced to leave open the question of the number and nature of markets that do exist. The assumption of costless exchange prevents a satisfactory treatment of the debt-equity mix in corporate finance (telling us that it makes no difference!), and leaves no real basis for the existence of money. Finally, a more satisfactory model of the exchange process would perhaps enable a treatment of the consequences of transactions executed at nonclearing prices, thus making possible a better connection between the theory of choice and models of business fluctuation ("macroeconomics").

INDEX

INDEX OF NAMES

INDEX OF TOPICS